DRAWING
THE NATURAL WORLD

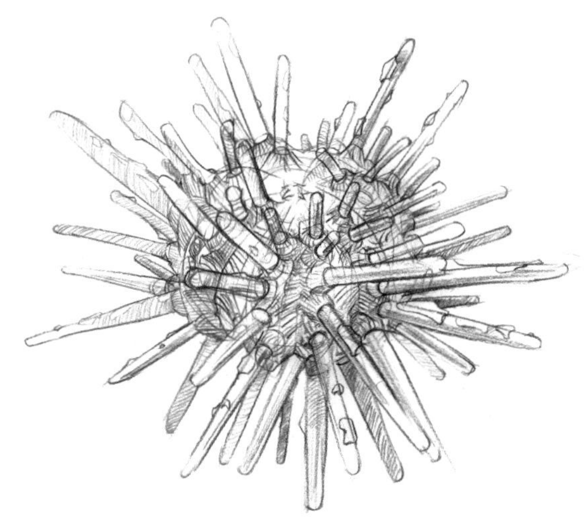

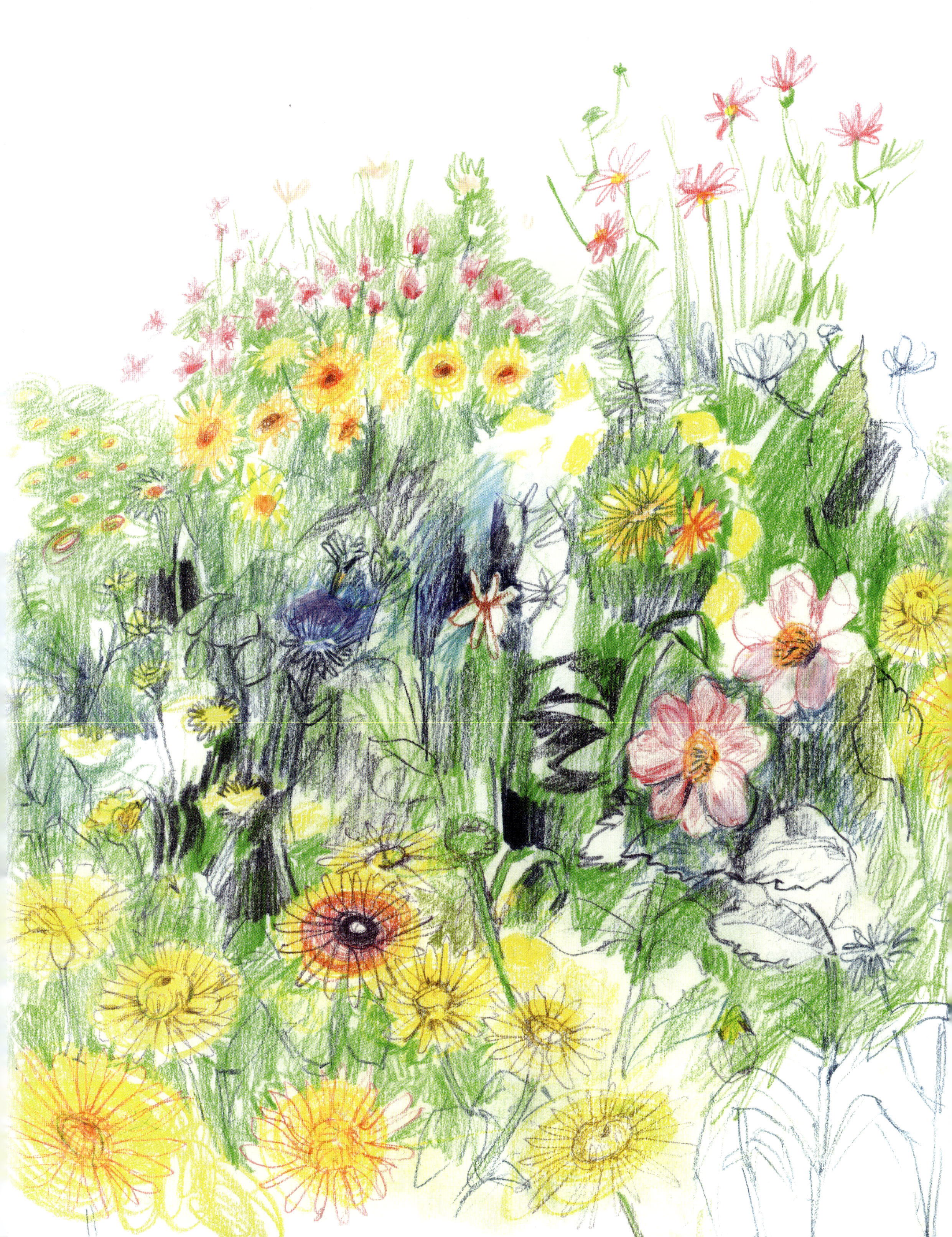

DRAWING
THE NATURAL WORLD

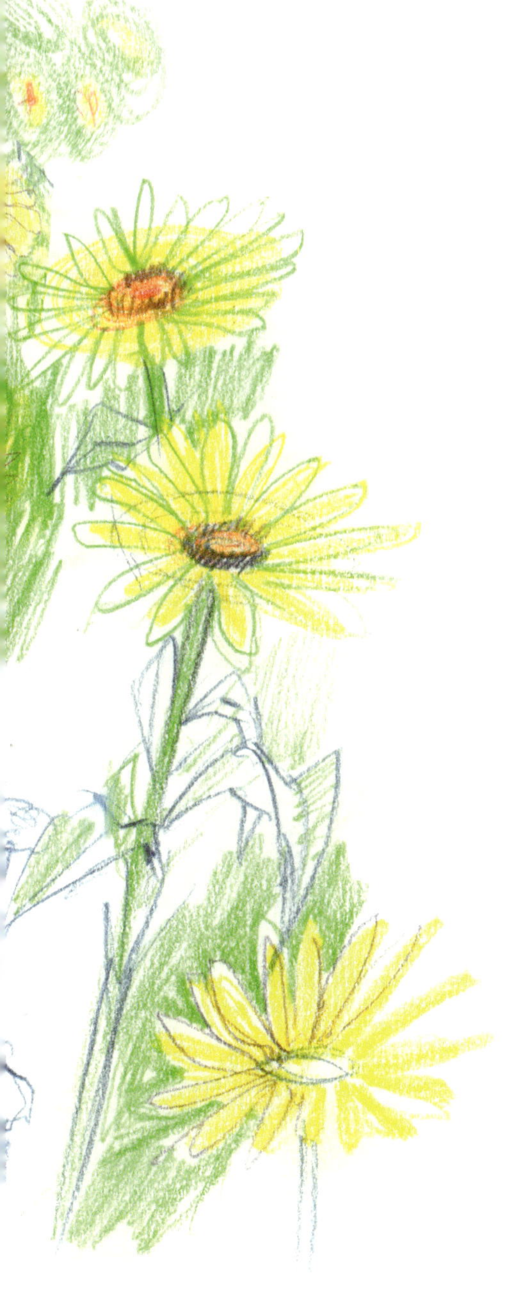

TIM POND

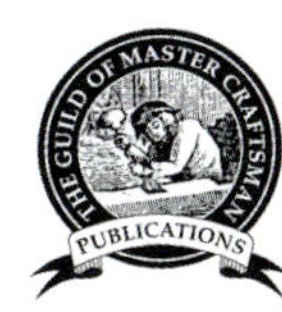

Contents

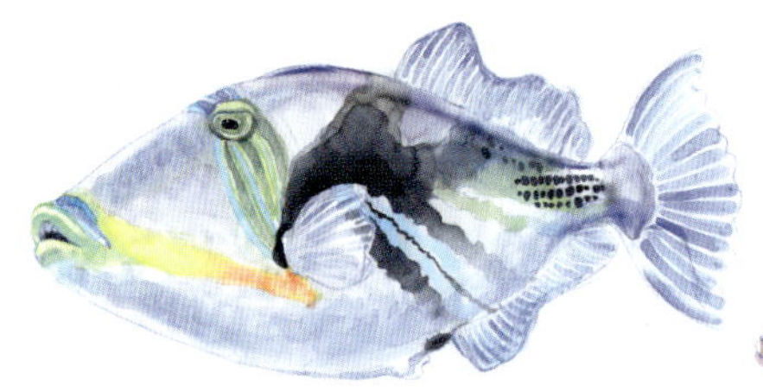
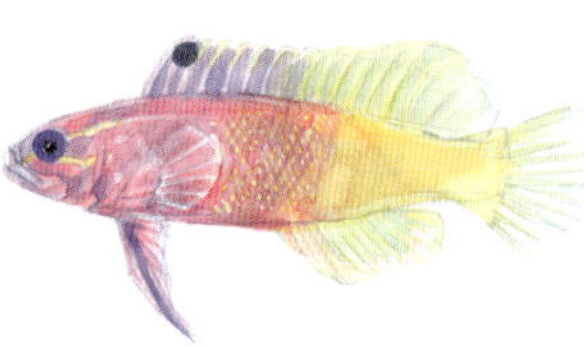

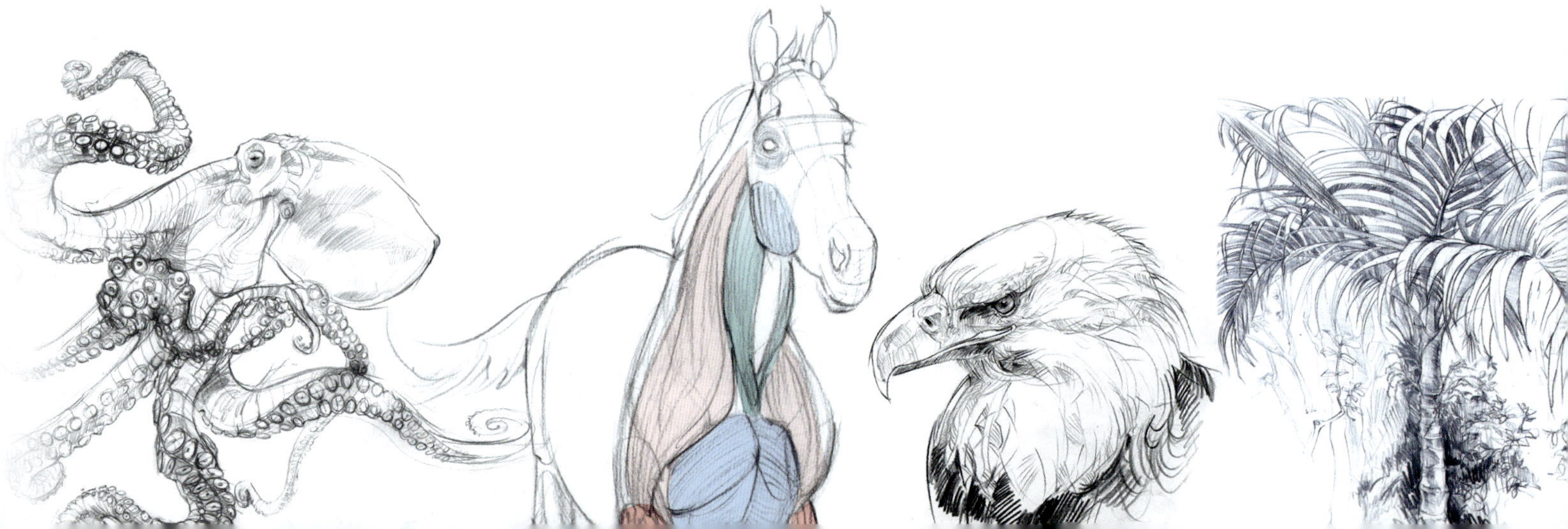

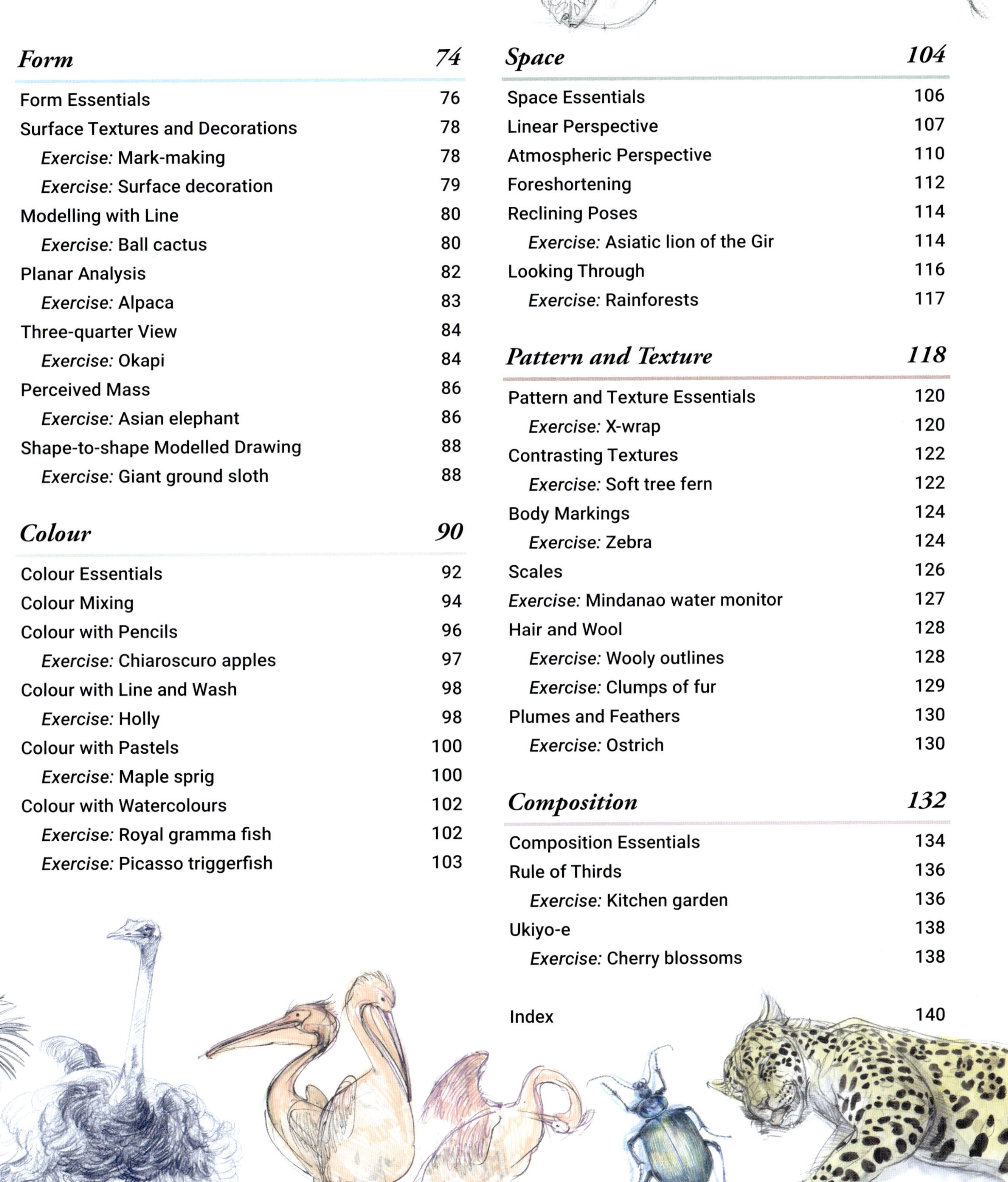

Introduction

Nature and drawing are subjects I have loved since before I could talk, and in this book I share my passion for both and explore what connects them. Using a host of drawing ideas and techniques suitable for beginners and experienced artists, my aim is to help you look at the natural world with fresh eyes and to encourage you to have fun drawing it. You will find a complete course on drawing that is designed to help you get outdoors with a sketchbook and make drawing a part of your life.

Drawing is a crucial component of a creative person's development and underpins all the visual art disciplines. The exercises in this book are designed to equip you with an armoury of skills. I have structured the chapters accordingly, so you will be ready to take on any landscape, still life or moving animal challenge. Each chapter aims to instil the importance of observing, analysing and drawing. We look at the familiar in new and unfamiliar ways to bring a fresh pair of eyes to accessible subjects. Each project spotlights different aspects of the elements in art, whether line, shape, space, form and tone, texture and pattern, colour or composition. Step-by-step instructions break the process down for anyone to easily follow.

However, this book is not just about the finished result: it also looks at the dynamic relationship between the viewer and the natural subject. It will increase your awareness of the world around you as you make your observations, which stimulates creative thinking and the ability to make connections. The simple act of observing and translating what we see onto paper can bring us closer to the natural world and engender a greater sympathy for the subject. Moreover, drawing can reveal not only the subject but also the creator's personality. People who look at your drawings will be able to connect with your thoughts and feelings.

▲ **Australian green tree frog**
(*Ranoidea caerulea*)
A long pelvis creates the triangular sacral hump on the back of a frog to aid jumping. Most arboreal species are tiny because they rely on slender branches to hold their weight. However, the plump green tree frog can grow up to 4½in (11.5cm) in length.

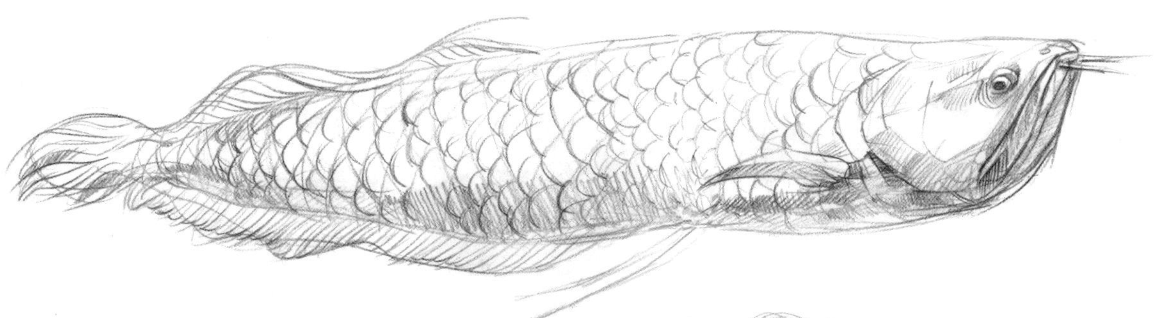

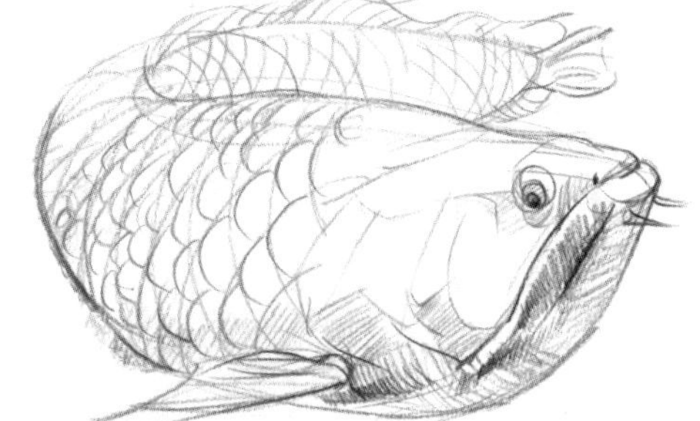

◀ Silver arowana
(*Osteoglossum bicirrhosum*)
Arowanas are a group of
ancient freshwater bony fish,
also known as 'bony tongues',
so called as they have a bone
on the floor of the mouth.

*'If I have made any valuable
discoveries, it has been owing
more to patient observation
than any other reason.'*

Isaac Newton

Developing your own approach

My own approach to drawing is to first concentrate on the fundamental concepts, such as proportion, contour, gesture, weight and structure, then I move on to the surface to explore colour, detail, pattern and texture. I also focus on feeling and expression to make my sketches of animals and plants come alive. My drawings emphasize what I call 'natural realism', primarily made in front of a live model, whether animal or plant.

Nevertheless, instead of imposing 'my way' of sketching, I want you to use the projects as a starting point. Drawing is as individual as handwriting, and everyone following these tutorials will have a unique result. Pick and choose projects that focus on what you wish to achieve, from representational accuracy to dynamic expressionism. You will find a solid background in formal concepts and sketching techniques, but I encourage you to be playful and experiment with them. I see the artist as the sternest critic of their own work, but with the ability to learn from their mistakes and adapt. I want you to find joy in the 'Hey, that's not bad!' feeling on finishing a sketch.

Don't worry if your drawings look nothing like the examples, as long as you spend time trying. The more effort you put in, the more you will get out of drawing. Don't be afraid of making mistakes. Heads typically will be too large at the beginning of your drawing journey, and this is something that all of us need to check on at all stages of proficiency. I have included a wide variety of materials and techniques to cater to various tastes. At the beginning of each exercise, there will be a list of materials required for the activity. Please do not use it as gospel. Mix and match with what you have without going out and buying new materials.

What makes a good drawing?

Drawing refers to the act of creating marks on a surface, often a pictorial representation of an object or place. It can also depict something that does not exist, such as an abstract expression. Representational drawing is, at its heart, a culmination of a set of abstract marks that, when brought together, create the impression of a subject. Everyone can draw, and while many will measure an artist's skill based on the technical accuracy of the depiction of the subject, there are other qualities to consider. Drawings that lack photographic accuracy may stand out and be an artistic success for many other reasons, such as their sense of movement, an economy of marks, or their weight or spatial or expressive qualities.

Be enthusiastic about the subjects you decide to draw. When the subject is close to the artist's heart — for example, if the artist loves birds — there can be a degree of integrity in the work. Emphasis on what makes a drawing appealing changes over time, but we can draw valuable lessons from art history. Rembrandt, one of the greatest draughtsmen, was fascinated with observing and journalling his daily life between grand oil portrait commissions. Nothing was too simple, not even a dog in the street. My favourite drawings tend to be full of life, where the artist's marks are clearly visible, regardless of the period.

Drawing the natural world is a way of learning about its structures and seeing it with greater clarity, a way to feel more connected and bound to it. I want drawing to be a process that brings you closer to nature through patient observation and calmness. Drawing is a fantastic activity for feeling part of the natural world and discovering. So let's learn to draw together!

Explore the Natural World Through Drawing

Through drawing the natural world, I want you to discover connections between the evolution of species and symbiotic relationships. All the plants and animals have evolved together, creating a web of life of incredible complexity and breathtaking diversity. Engaging with the varieties of life that inhabit the earth will bring delight. Just as an author writes about what they know, I encourage you to experience and learn about the raw materials of nature, and the best way to do this is to use all of your senses.

Immersive discoveries

As pictures are seen with the eyes, it is easy to forget that being in a location or observing an object is an accumulated experience of all five senses. We do not simply observe with our eyes. We also smell with our noses, listen with our ears, taste with our tongue and touch with our skin. All five senses play an important role in making sense of an animal, plant, rock or place. Before you begin any study, take time to soak up the atmosphere or touch the object you are about to sketch. Is it a rough pine cone or a smooth pebble? Feel the weight of a heavy, warty cooking apple, touch the tip of your finger on the sharp thorn of a rose or taste the sour flavour of a lemon.

I strongly suggest you immerse yourself in nature and go wandering with your sketchbook. Go into the middle of an autumnal wood, for example, with golden leaves tumbling around you, then close your eyes, breathe deeply and focus on the smells of the damp moss, the wet tree trunks and even the earth itself. Concentrate on your individual senses, such as sound, and listen to the wind rustling the leaves and the birds twittering. Pick a blackberry from a bush and taste its dark plummy flavour. Touch the rough texture of bark or the soft spring of a bed of moss.

Experiential learning

The process whereby you 'learn by doing' and reflect on the experience is referred to as experiential learning. Learning to draw is a highly personal journey similar to learning to ride a bicycle, falling off and then modifying your actions so you don't fall off again. Drawing starts with a hands-on concrete experience, reflection and the formation of abstract concepts and active experimentation of those concepts. This book provides a foundation of drawing skills that will give you the confidence to go forward by yourself, like taking the stabilizers off a bicycle. Nevertheless, just like learning a musical instrument or learning to walk, the first steps of drawing are also the hardest.

As with any discipline, practising drawing will improve coordination between your eye, muscle movement and hand. It is not years of practice that improves skill but the amount of pencil miles one puts in. For this reason, I suggest you have fun with activities that can be carried out at museums, wildlife parks and botanical gardens, whether as an individual or part of a group activity. In this way, you will gain drawing experience directly from nature, whether plant or animal, that will help you get to know it more intimately.

Extended thinking

Drawing can also allow us to make associations we otherwise might not have thought of in a non-linear way. It is a fantastic tool that can be applied to any career, perhaps explaining how to put something together, planning a bathroom or creating a map. Charles Darwin (1809–1882) even doodled an evolutionary tree of life to develop his theory of natural selection and Thomas Edison (1847–1931) filled his journals with sketches that led the way to the invention of the light bulb. Virtually all children draw as a tool for learning, but far too often this is replaced for many by the written word as we grow up. Practical considerations aside, drawing can be a wonderful tool for self-expression and be practised as a pleasurable and meditative activity.

Modes of drawing

Various techniques and approaches will create different results on paper. The approaches to drawing can be seen a little like music. For example, a new piece of music can be created by combining a set of pre-existing patterns, which lead to a composition that creates the desired outcome. Likewise, the marks for a drawing might be a highly structured approach, such as a jazz-like interpretation of gestural lines that capture the dance of a flamingo or that shatter the world into pieces to reimagine it in a Cubist fashion. Find those approaches that you feel have integrity and that drive in you a genuine curiosity for your subject.

Drawing or sketching?

The words 'drawing' and 'sketching' are interchangeable in most contexts, although the following definitions could be loosely applied. Drawing is a more careful and accurate process than sketching, resulting in highly detailed works of art. Drawings can be created from life when the subject holds the pose for an extended period or is static. Sketching is a quick process that focuses on general shapes and proportions. Sketches can be imprecise and fleeting, with just a few lines to capture the essence of the pose.

Finding your own style

Each artist will create a drawing of the same subject with a different style of mark-making that is as individual as handwriting. This will be obvious if you happen to attend a drawing class. Don't worry about intentionally creating your own style, as this can lead to overly mannered and stylized drawings. It will develop naturally with practice and experimentation. Regardless, it is always useful to look at the drawings created by other artists, which can help you to learn about the different abstract qualities of other approaches and inspire you to experiment with other techniques.

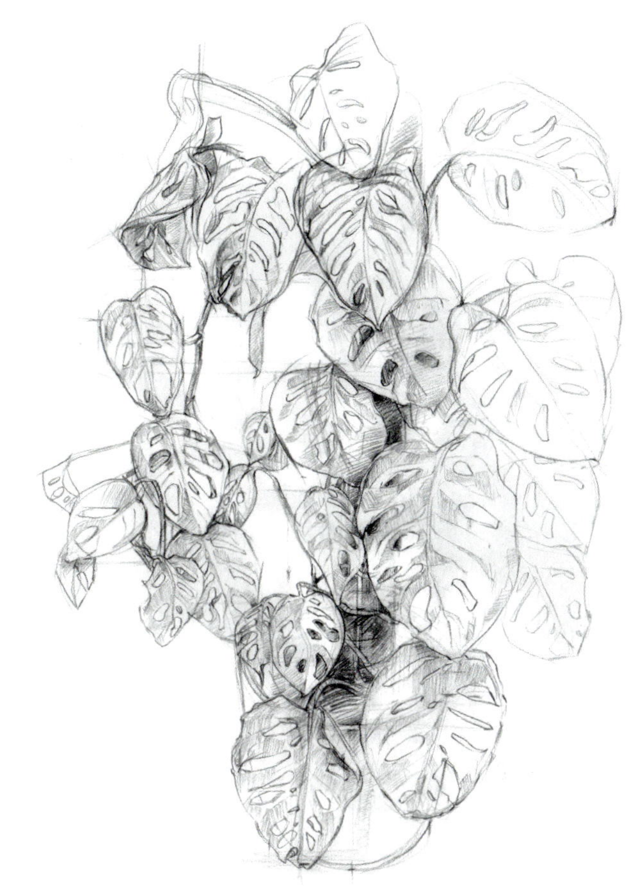

▲ Extended drawing

Stationary subjects, such as this monstera monkey leaf plant (*Monstera adansonii*), will allow for more polished renders. These will enable you to use your entire repertoire of skills to realize a drawing with detailed shading.

▼ Mixed media drawings

It is important to play and experiment to find your own style. Mix different media to create expressive and colourful drawings, such as in this Japanese soldierfish (*Ostichthys japonicus*).

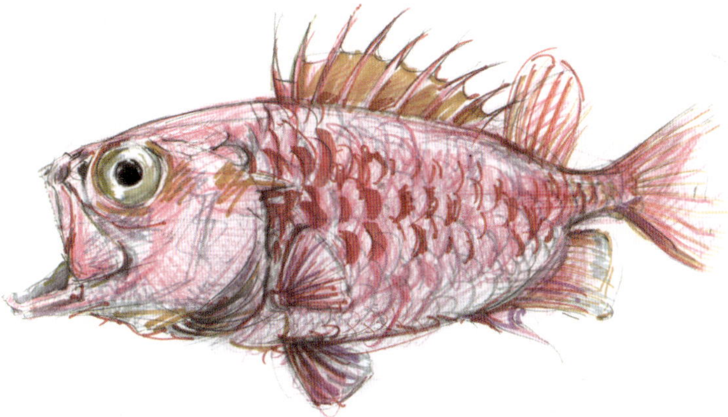

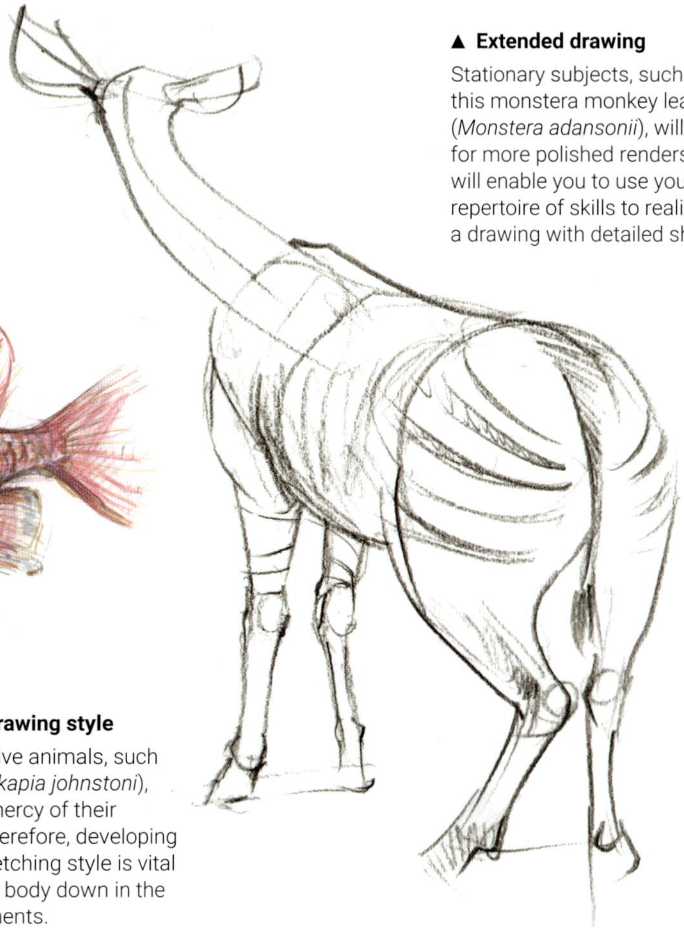

► Shorthand drawing style

When drawing live animals, such as this okapi (*Okapia johnstoni*), you are at the mercy of their movements. Therefore, developing a shorthand sketching style is vital to get the entire body down in the briefest of moments.

Materials

A drawn image is the result of applying media to a surface. The earliest drawings appeared on cave walls drawn by Palaeolithic humans in a dim flickering firelight. A crude mixture of charcoal and ferric-rich umbers and ochres were mixed with spit and animal fat before being applied to the walls, which stained the porous rock surface in the same way as an Italian fresco. In the Lascaux cave in France, socket holes have been found in the walls, suggesting a scaffold system similar to the one Michelangelo used to paint the Sistine chapel. Since then, a dazzling array of media has become available to the artist.

Here are some of the materials that I use on a daily basis. These have been selected for their exceptional qualities and speed of use in a busy schedule. However, it is essential to remember that even investing in the most expensive equipment will not outstrip the quality of intention giving to the act of drawing.

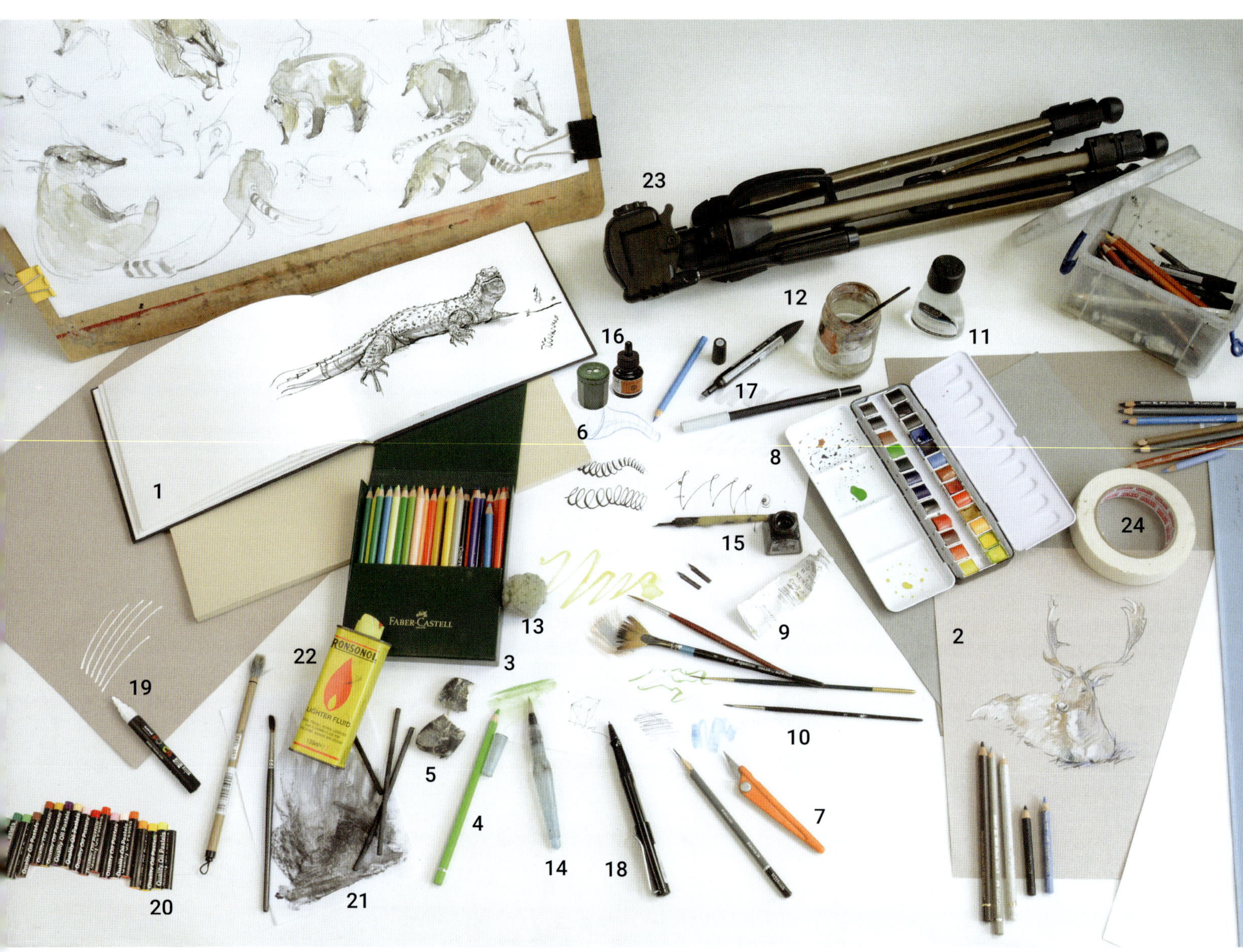

1. Sketchbooks and paper

The sketchbook is at the heart of the artist's work. It is a mobile art studio as well as a highly personal document, where you can experiment with new techniques, record ideas and make notes about the subject you draw. Everyone's sketchbook is different, and there is joy in looking through another artist's book – a visual journal is like a window to the soul of the artist. A sketchbook is often considered to be a playground for the artist, a place to develop sketches to aid larger studio paintings. However, in the approach for this book, the sketchbook is the final gallery piece, a work of art in itself. I avoid spiral-bound books, as the pages rub together and smudge the artwork. I prefer the paper of my sketchbook to have a bit of a 'tooth', or roughness, rather than being smooth. My favourite sketchbook, whether watercolour or cartridge (drawing) paper, is A3 size (11¾ x 16½in), which can open to A2 size (16½ x 23⅜in) and create plenty of working space.

I draw on good quality drawing cartridge paper. It typically comes in weights between 150gsm (72lb) and 300gsm (140lb), the heavier stocks being closer to card than paper. It is versatile and relatively tough with a slight tooth that can support a high level of detail. I have a preference for 200gsm (90lb).

2. Mid-tone paper

I also use a mid-tone pastel paper. Mid-tone paper is great to experiment with and an excellent option for painting animals that have a mottled coat, such as an African hunting dog. You can plunge into the darker values of the pelt with transparent watercolour, then add white gouache to create the lighter colours. It can also help enhance the white plumage of a duck by creating contrast with the background. I've had good results using a high quality pastel paper. Choose one that comes in a wide range of hues and responds like 190gsm (90lb) cold-pressed watercolour paper. To prevent the paper from buckling,

use less water than when working on watercolour paper. The paper has two surfaces: one side has a fine grain, which I prefer; the other side has a honeycomb texture. For quick sketches, you can use less costly sugar (or construction) paper, but this paper doesn't last as long.

3. Graphite and colouring pencils

Most people primarily draw in pencil because of its erasability and range of tonal abilities. I use a B pencil or softer in graphite. These pencils have a thin rod of grey toning material of graphite or carbon, which is the substance that remains behind on a piece of paper. Graphite pencils are measured in the HB range, H meaning hard (pencils in this range are suitable for technical drawings) and B meaning black (pencils in this range are more suitable for artistic and expressive drawings).

When it comes to colouring pencils, I highly recommend using artist's quality oil-based pencils, which can be sharpened to a fine point. Note that colouring pencils do not erase as well as graphite, but they leave an attractive sketchy colourful line. Using high quality pigments will guarantee vibrant colours and a strong impact on the paper.

4. Watercolour pencils

Otherwise known as water-soluble pencils, watercolour pencils are a versatile art medium. They can be used dry like standard colouring pencils or with water. In wet application, the artist first lays down the dry pigment, then follows up with a water-loaded paintbrush to disperse the colour into a wash. This technique can also blend colours together. I like to work with them alongside brush watercolour.

5. Putty eraser

A knead-able putty eraser can remove graphite pencil marks by absorbing the particles rather than wearing them away. They are soft and less abrasive than standard erasers, so they won't damage the surface of the paper.

6. Pencil sharpener

When sketching at any public venue it is obviously better to leave no trace, which is why I use a quality sharpener with a receptacle for catching the shavings.

7. Scalpel

In the studio, a scalpel can be used to whittle the tip of a pencil into a long shaft, which creates a greater variety of loose marks and works well using an underhand grip.

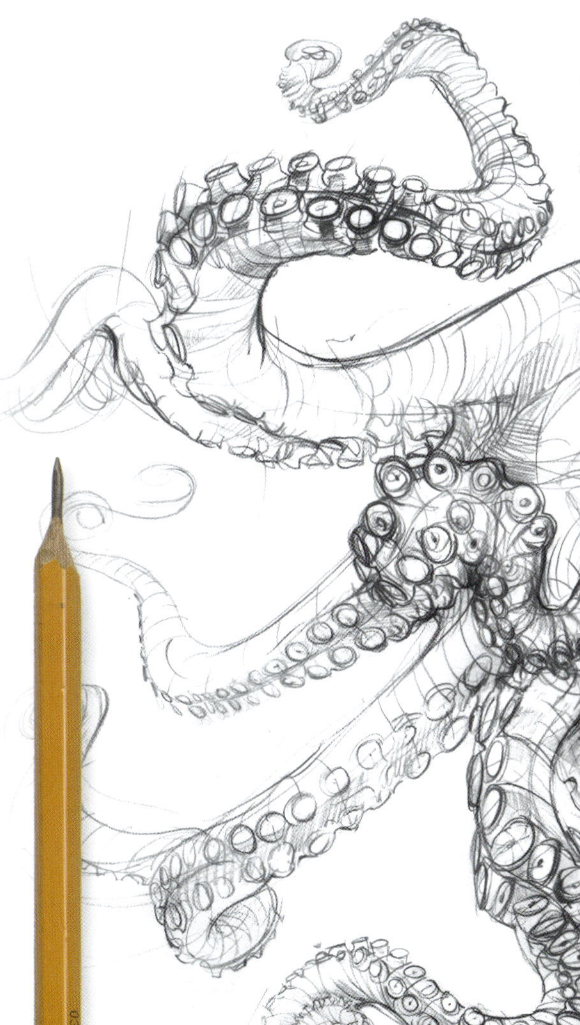

▼ **Capturing line quality**
Be flexible about how you approach the physical qualities of a subject. The swirling roller-coaster arms of a gelatinous octopus can be evoked with a scrawling pencil line.

8. Watercolour paints

There are two grades of watercolour paints: student and professional. Professional, or artist's quality, watercolour paint is typically made with better quality pigment with a longer permanence. It gives the artist a greater range and brilliance of colour. I use a 24 half-pan travel set in a metal tin for durability and versatility.

9. White gouache

If you use white as I do, I recommend swapping the Chinese white for a tube of permanent white gouache. It has far better coverage and is much more effective.

10. Watercolour brushes

As well as being capable of holding a lot of water, watercolour brushes need to lay down watercolour paint gently and smoothly. They are specially made to allow the artist to control the flow of the colour from the brush to the paper. There are several types of watercolour brush and it's worth experimenting with them. A mop brush can hold a lot of water and allows for easy coverage. A fan brush is good for creating fur textures. Rigger brushes are the longest and thinnest round watercolour brush, with a long, tapering point that is made for drawing and excellent for continuous fine lines. It is one of my favourite brushes. Chisel brushes have shortened hairs and a square shape. They can be used dynamically at an angle to create sharp lines (which is particularly good for branches, twigs and grasses) or they can be used flat to make a stubby mark or fill in a shape. As they are so versatile, the brushes I use most are round brushes. With pressure, they apply medium coverage and they return to their shape by lifting off, allowing the tip to create detail. They are ideal for drawing with the brush rather than filling in, creating exciting, dynamic, fluid brushwork.

The size of a brush is denoted by a number. Larger brushes have larger numbers and vice versa. I recommend the following for starting out in round brushes: small (around size 3), medium (5–6) and large (12). Mix and match, collect over time and find your own personal favourites.

11. Granulation medium

The particles of some pigments, such as the ultramarines and cadmiums, naturally clump together to form what are called granulations. The same effect can be achieved for pigments that would normally form smooth washes, such as alizarin crimson and Winsor violet, by using a granulation medium. It can also be used to enhance the effect for pigments that granulate naturally. When I use a granulating medium, I can never be too sure what will happen, but if I want speckles, I'll mix some granulation medium with the paint on my palette. I pump the water with the granulation medium to help break up the particles and try to capture the nitty-gritty appearance of the subject by pushing the brush around fairly vigorously to create a peppery texture.

12. Jar of water

I use an old jam jar for water in my studio. When sketching in the field, I take an old plastic soup pot to fill with water, so as to avoid the risk of breakages.

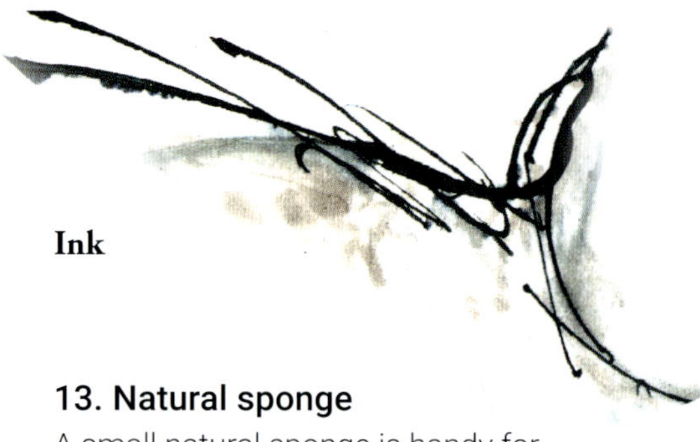

13. Natural sponge

A small natural sponge is handy for lifting out and clearing up puddles.

14. Brush pens

You can fill the barrel of these versatile, nylon-tipped brush pens with watercolours or water-soluble inks for line work or colour washes.

15. Dip pens

A dip pen used with ink can create lively line work full of expression (see page 98). I recommend using a pen with a medium elastic drawing nib. These nibs can produce hair-like to medium-thick lines, depending on the pressure placed upon them.

16. Colouring inks

Applied with dip pens, colouring inks work in a similar fashion to watercolour but they are already in liquid form. They are often made of dyes rather than pigments, so most of them will have a powerful staining effect. These inks can be used to create expressive drawings.

▼ Diversity
A range of artist's quality brushes will enable you to create a diverse set of brush marks.

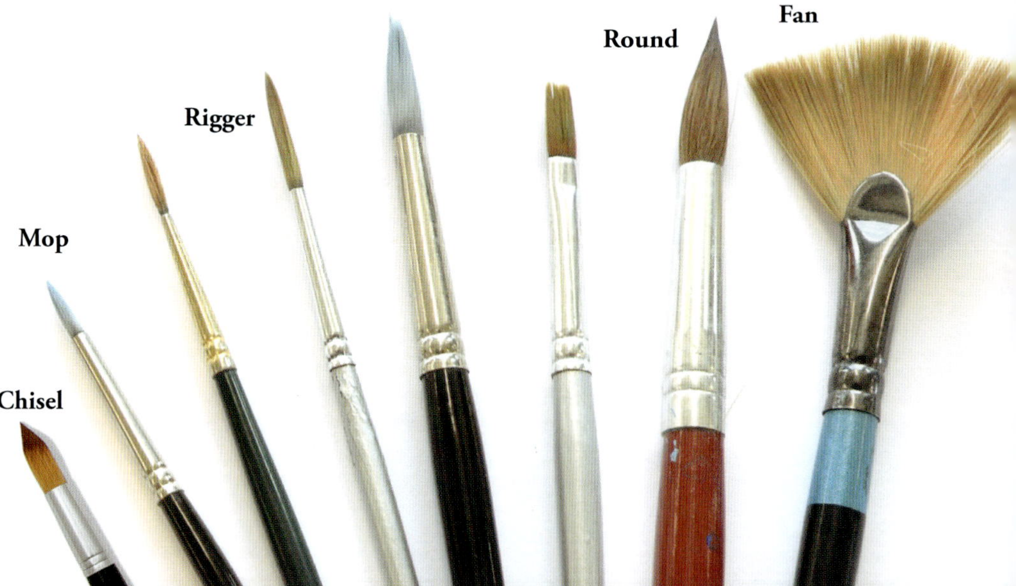

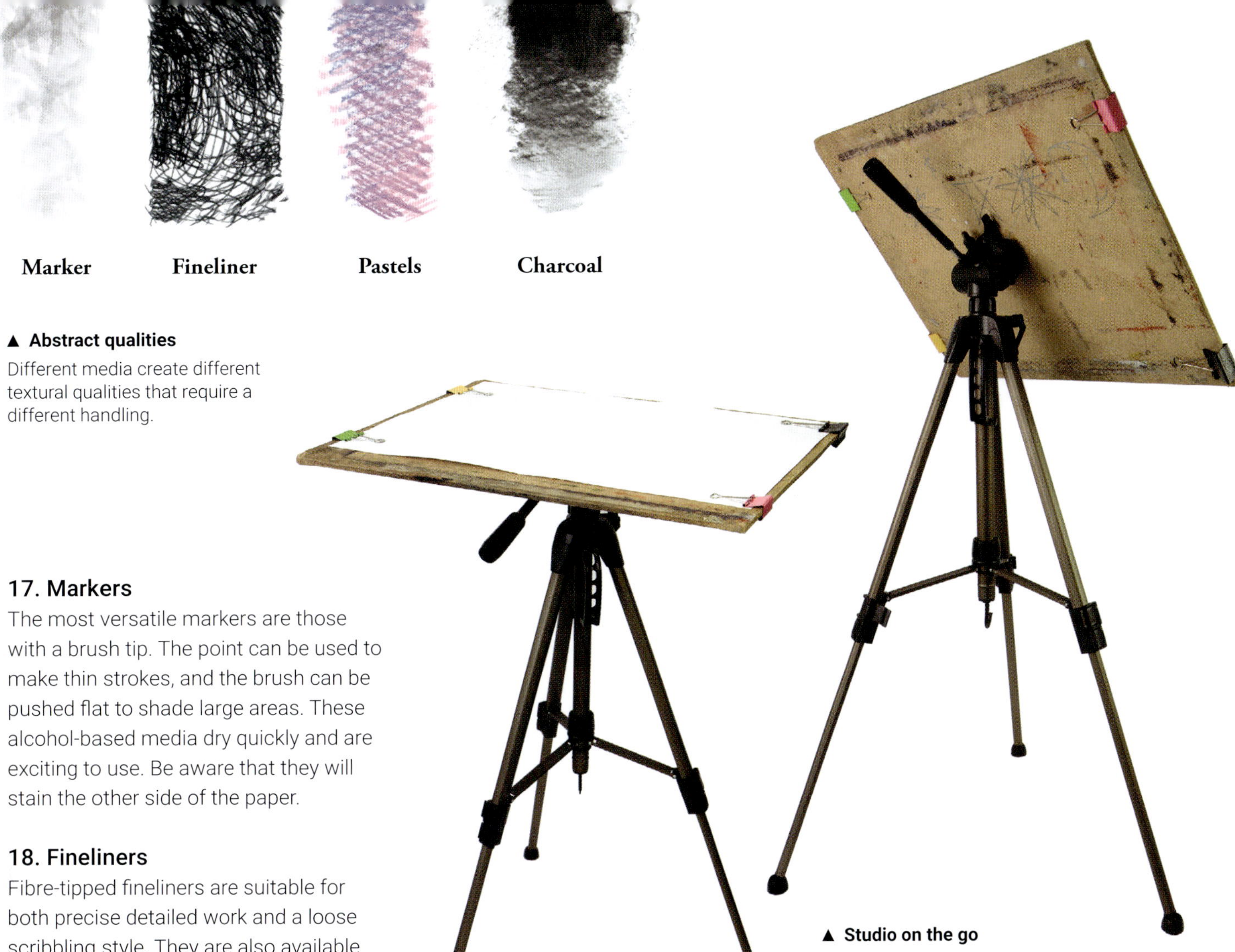

▲ Abstract qualities
Different media create different
textural qualities that require a
different handling.

▲ Studio on the go
Try to ensure that what you pack
with you for sketching is light and
as convenient to use as possible.

17. Markers
The most versatile markers are those
with a brush tip. The point can be used to
make thin strokes, and the brush can be
pushed flat to shade large areas. These
alcohol-based media dry quickly and are
exciting to use. Be aware that they will
stain the other side of the paper.

18. Fineliners
Fibre-tipped fineliners are suitable for
both precise detailed work and a loose
scribbling style. They are also available
with waterproof ink, which means that
they won't bleed when watercolour is
laid over the top.

19. White paint pens
Opaque white paint pens are water-
soluble when wet and water-resistant
when fully dry to a consistent matte
finish. The felt tips lay down the paint
with ease, but they usually have to be
shaken before use. They are suitable
for adding highlights on mid-tone or
dark paper in a similar fashion to chalk
on a blackboard.

20. Pastels
You can apply pigment directly to a
surface without using a brush by using
pastels. Whether you use oil- or chalk-
based pastels, use your fingers to
smudge or blend them on the paper
to bring out their vibrant colours and
create dynamic effects, such as scraping
through layers.

21. Charcoal
Black, crumbly charcoal sticks, pencils
and even powder leave microscopic
particles in the paper, resulting in a
dense, powdery line. The overall result is
less precise than hard graphite pencils,
so charcoal is better reserved for making
looser studies (see page 72).

22. Lighter fluid
Besides being an excellent stainless
cleaner, lighter fluid is extremely useful.
It can be combined with charcoal to
liquefy the carbon particles and create
painterly marks with a brush.

23. Tripod easel
One of my favourite pieces of equipment
is a tripod easel. To create my own,
I drilled a partial hole in a lightweight A2
(16½ x 23⅜in) drawing board, and then
glued the plate of a camera tripod to the
centre of the bottom of the board. One of
its significant advantages is that you can
sketch at an angle and then lay it flat for
watercolour. Also, when using a tripod
easel, both hands are free rather than
one holding the sketchbook.

24. Masking tape
For a non-marking tape, use masking
tape, a paper tape with a low adhesive
strength and low tack, which makes
it easy to remove without leaving any
residue or traces behind.

First Steps

Before you start capturing the natural world in your sketchbook, you need to know how to hold your chosen media, develop your eye to hand coordination skills and learn how to break down any subject into simplistic components.

Getting to grips with your drawing media

Be flexible about the different ways you hold your drawing media. Different grips will allow you to make different types of marks, from the suggestive to precise detail. Experiment with your grips to discover the effects they have on your mark-making.

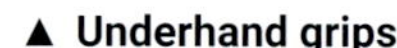

▲ **Writing grip**
This familiar firm grip is the one I primarily use. Holding the media close to the tip is good for detailed work.

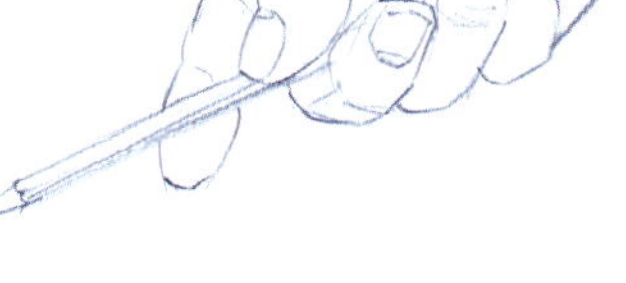

▲ **Distant hold**
A loose distant hold is good for creating gestural marks.

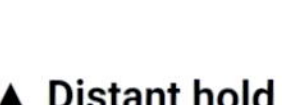

▲ **Underhand grips**
A loose underhand grip allows for a lot of movement from the wrist to create sweeping arcs. I tend to use this grip for roughing out and creating gesture drawings.

Warming up

Pen mileage and repetition can build confidence that can help with the anxiety of creating marks on a blank page. In this tutorial, we are not drawing anything from observation but playing with drawing games. Start with the straight line exercise, then move on to creating curved lines. The final stage is to draw freehand ellipses, which can be challenging, but they are a fundamental element of drawing.

Go through the motions first and 'air draw' before your pencil touches the paper, so that you will be confident with the smoothness and symmetry of the mark. You can sketch the first line lightly and then refine the ellipse. Make sure that the shapes have round corners and are not spiky.

Learn to use your body's natural geometry by locking your arm to create straight lines and by using the arc of a wrist or ball-and-socket joint of the shoulder to create smooth arcs and ellipses. Doing this will help to stop you developing bad drawing habits, such as sketching feathery lines where a single clear straight line will do.

▶ **Straight**
Create seven straight lines that progressively get darker. Push away from your body. Try locking your arm at your elbow. Explore long and short lines.

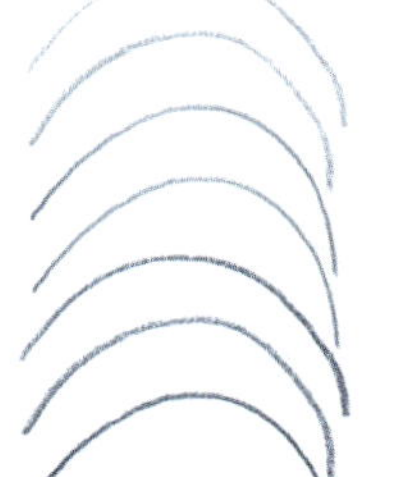

◀ **Curves**
Create seven straight lines that progressively get darker. Try to memorize the motion of your arm so that you can control the shape of your curves.

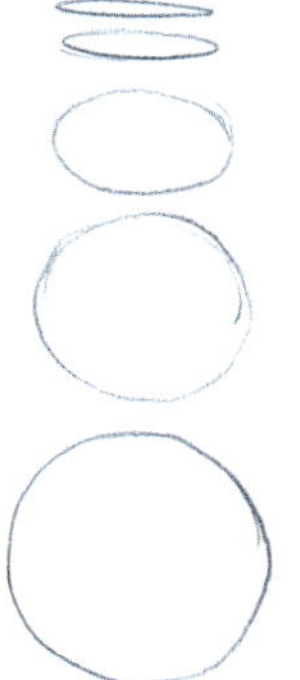

◀ **Ellipses**
Start with the narrowest angle near the horizon and then open the mouth of the ellipse incrementally.

Constructed drawings: combining primary forms

Creating drawings using the principles of construction will make your subjects appear solid. Construction is about conceiving the subject in the most basic geometric shapes, such as a barrel for the chest of a goat and tubes for the arms and legs.

The initial steps are playing with the primary forms to break your subject down into its main body parts, then to see these in their most elemental forms. To help do this, I have developed devices that I call widgets and gizmos.

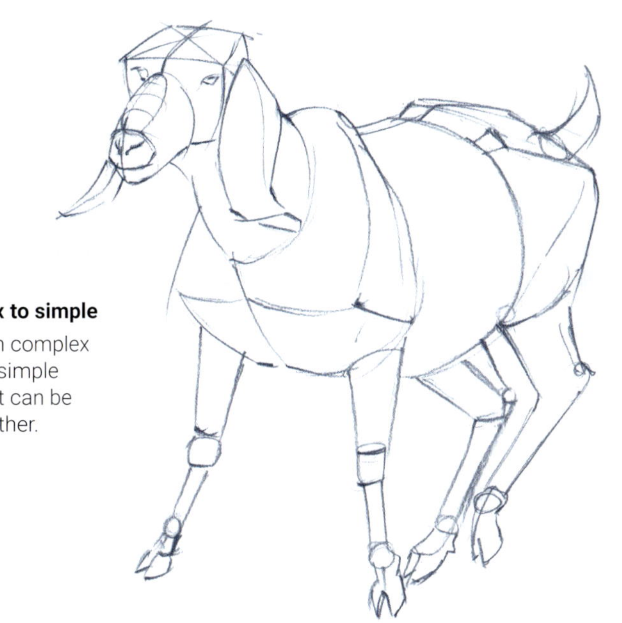

► Complex to simple
Break down complex forms into simple shapes that can be joined together.

Widgets

The simple, three-dimensional forms that I call widgets can be combined to make a larger form. While they can help draw a stationary subject, they are particularly useful when an animal is in motion. If you break it down into widgets before you start, you can then quickly place the basic forms at the appropriate angles.

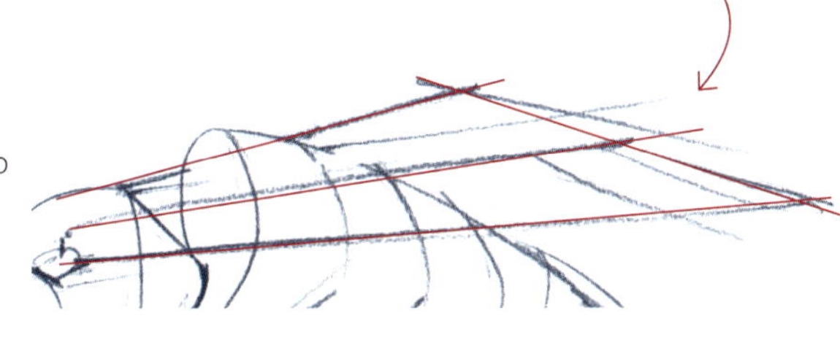

◄ Sum of parts
Develop an eye for breaking any subject down into its most basic components.

Gizmos

A gizmo is essentially a flat, abstract version of a widget. These little devices are an aid that provide an understanding of the form, such as breaking this wasp head down into simple abstract shapes. Once understood, this simple geometrical device can be rotated.

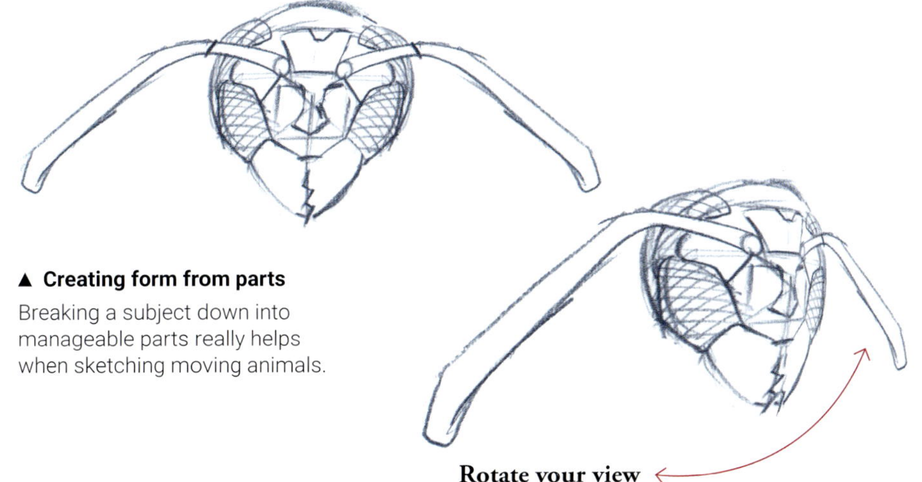

▲ Creating form from parts
Breaking a subject down into manageable parts really helps when sketching moving animals.

Study Sheets

One of the best approaches to improving observational abilities and hand-eye coordination is to make study sheets. A study sheet can be about anything you find interesting and you wish to understand better. You can blend brief gestural studies with more detailed work. Investigations into individual parts of the subject can be included, such as a paw study or a close-up of a leaf. You can include anything you like, from written notes to colour swatches. I usually work with a large sheet of paper attached to a light drawing board with a bulldog clip or an open double page of an A3 (11¾ x 16½in) sketchbook to allow for plenty of space to fit the subject on the paper.

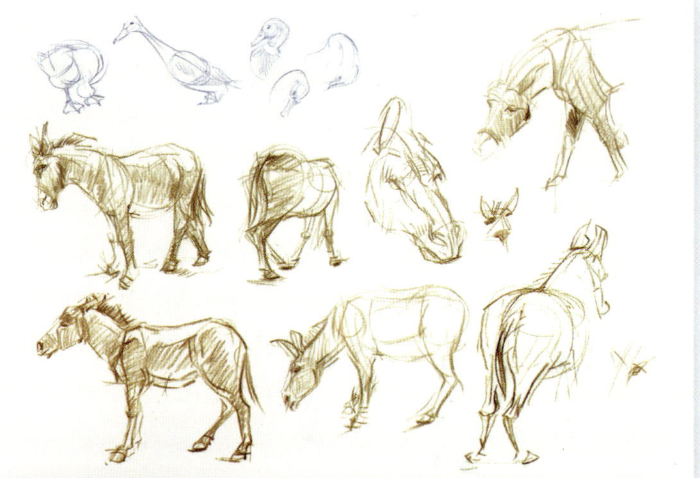

▼ **Farmyard sketches on sugar paper**
Deen City Farm, UK

Animals in motion

Trying to capture moving or dozing animals helps to bring your drawings to life, making the animals appear alive on paper. Rather than make a formal portrait, you can observe life in its widest pursuits on a study sheet by capturing life in many informal positions. As wild animals are not likely to sit for a portrait, the study sheet will result in a combination of many different views. Each pose will allow you to get to know your animal's character a little closer. You can use a study sheet to record the animal's physical traits and behaviours, which will be often repeated. Even the best reference material cannot replace the experience of putting in time with live animals.

A gestural study sheet is one of the most incredible ways to get started when drawing a live animal. There is a thrill in getting acquainted with sketching a new species. I think of these like any new introduction. Ask questions, such as 'Where do you live? What do you like to do? What do you like to eat?', and so on, as you would in an ordinary conversation. Focus on capturing the essence of the animal's pose and character.

Gestural sketching takes a keen eye, quick hand movements and a sense of understanding the subject, which will grow over the drawing session with repeated observation and sketching. If I'm drawing an animal that is moving around, I aim to create a sequence of rapid, flowing, undetailed studies. Animals will normally hold a pose for less time than it takes to draw them, but this isn't a problem because the unfinished sketches help you to build a visual memory of the subject through the different arrangements of the primary forms (see page 15). I usually write little thoughts in the corner of the page of the sights and sounds of what I am witnessing as I draw.

I often draw on top of sketches to refine them or have another go without any real thoughts on technique. This is because the focus of the entirety of my attention is in capturing the shape of the head, body, arms and legs as they flow along a line of action. I try not to worry about the page's appearance as it

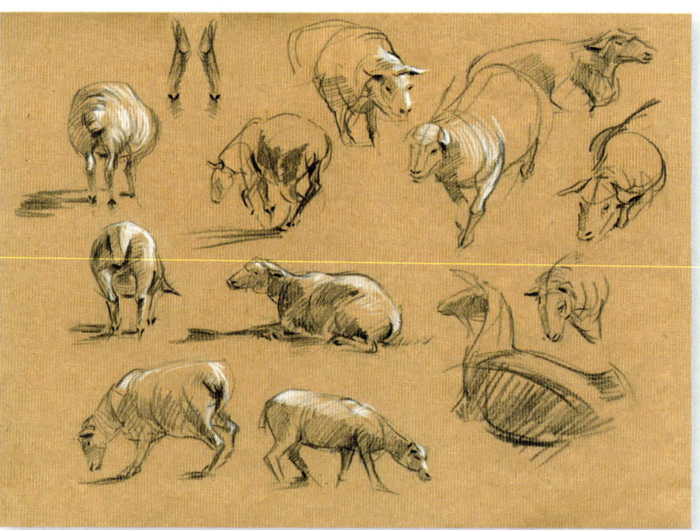

▲ **Sheep sketches on brown wrapping paper**
Deen City Farm, UK

evolves with serendipity. This type of drawing is a by-product of an investigation. What is important is that your hand has been activated following the instructions from your eyes. Try to feel like you are almost touching the animal, stroking it, feeling the bones and muscles. Rather than being about creating a polished result, study sheets increase our understanding.

Starting with the first sketch

Before you begin any drawing, decide what you want to achieve in your mind. Various factors might set parameters of your approach, such as length of pose and choice of media. I always observe for a while before making any mark on the page. I tend to start with a side pose to familiarize myself with the body parts, from nose to tail. Begin by just throwing out a line – the curve of the back, for example, or a series of light loops. Then try to become more ambitious, capturing more athletic postures. I use swift, loose lines while barely looking at the page. I do not bother with an eraser but will rework the sketch to get the right line – the idea is to keep sketching without distraction.

Early on, check the proportions of the size of the head in relation to the body, as there is a tendency to sketch the head too big. As frustrating as it is, your model will likely be constantly on the move, but this will give your marks vigour and energy, bringing your drawings to life. Always work quickly. Even though your animal might be momentarily standing still, they will soon move, even if dozing. I quickly switch from one sketch to another one as it changes position. I start and stop every time the animal moves, then return to a sketch as the animal returns to a similar position, resulting in a dynamic page of finished and unfinished sketches strewn across the paper. You will be surprised by what you see and get to know your subject a little closer!

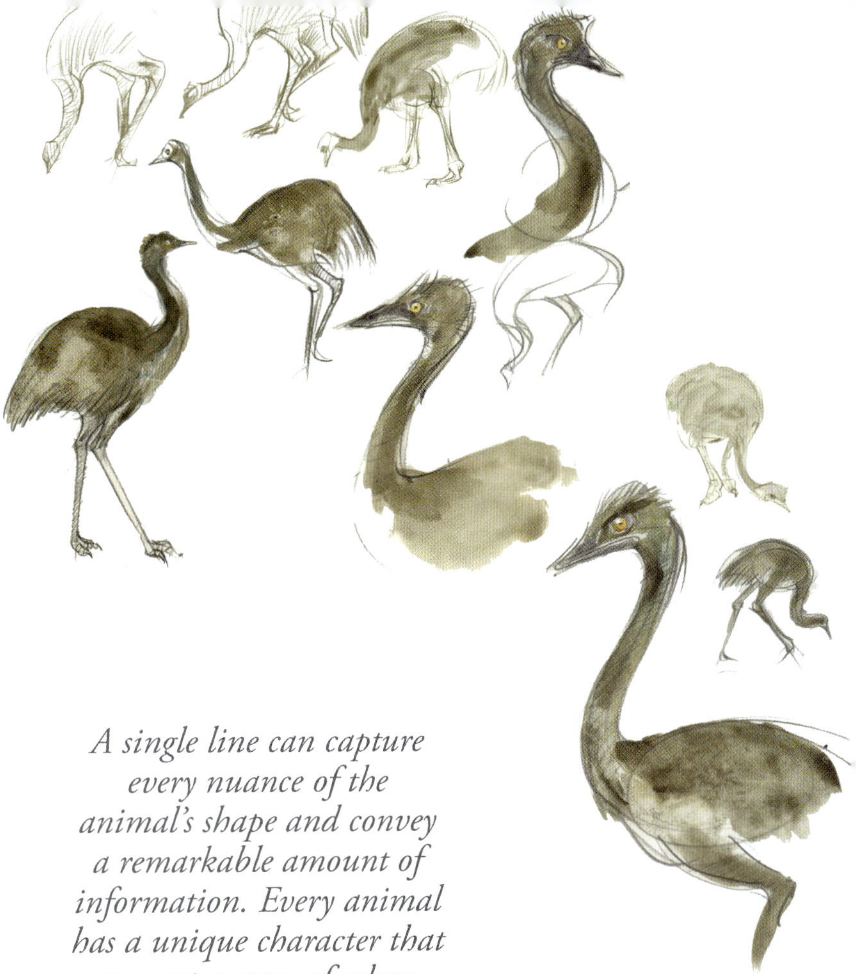

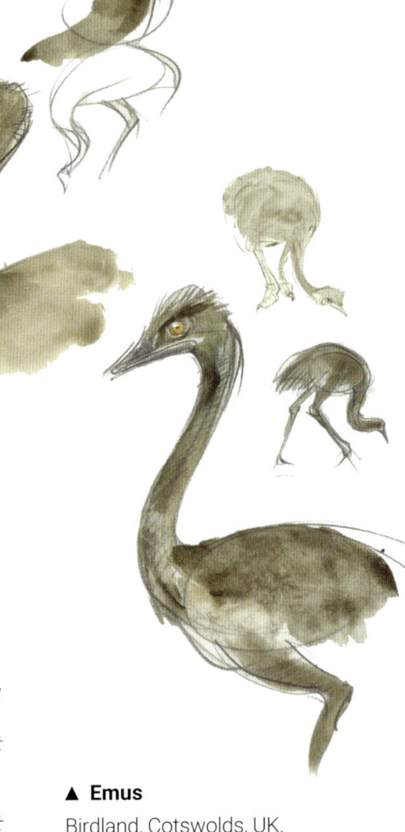

▲ **Emus**
Birdland, Cotswolds, UK.

A single line can capture every nuance of the animal's shape and convey a remarkable amount of information. Every animal has a unique character that you get a sense of when working from life that can't be achieved from sketching from a photograph.

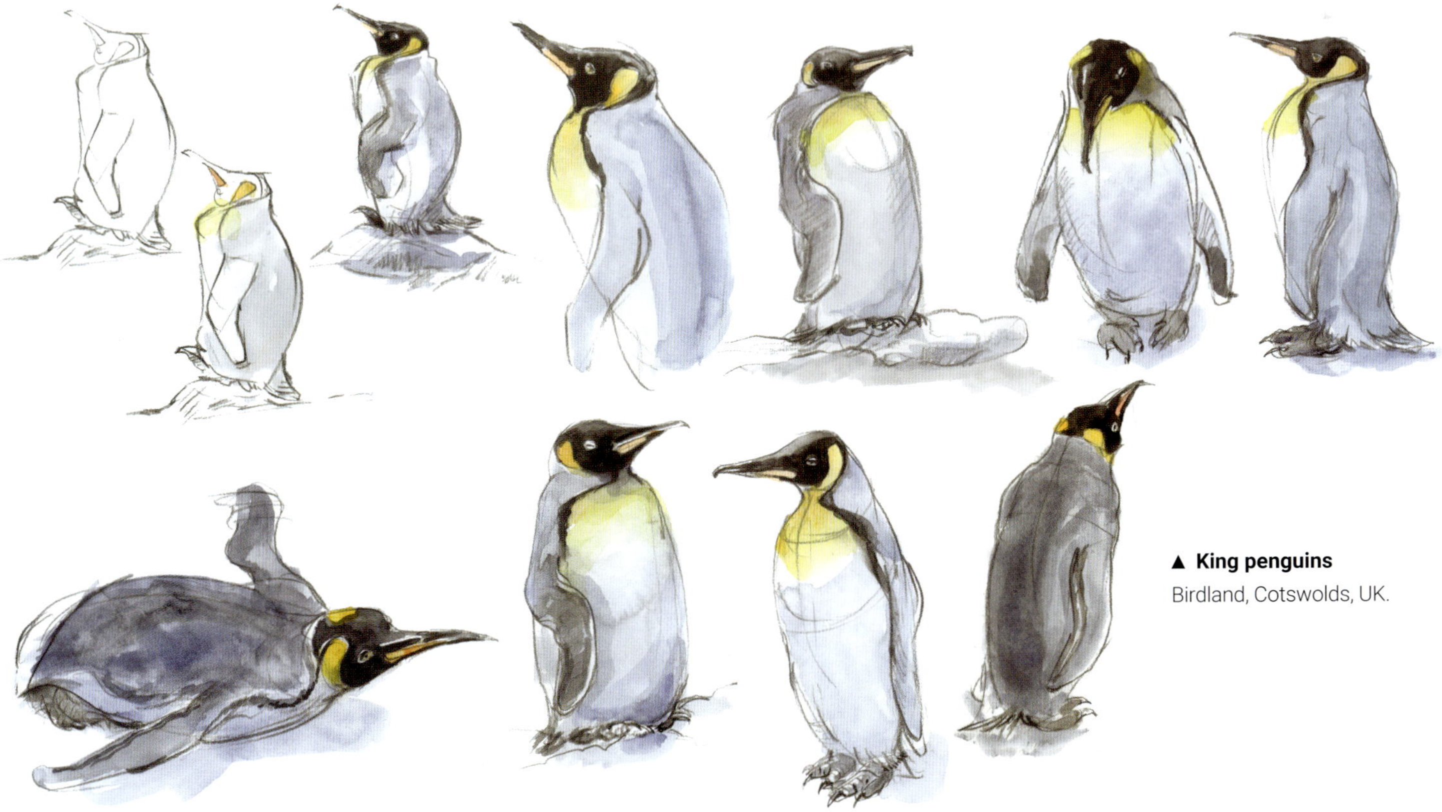

▲ **King penguins**
Birdland, Cotswolds, UK.

Anatomy

For artists who are drawing animals and want their drawings to come alive and be full of structure and tension, it is crucial that they understand anatomy. I find it particularly beneficial when sketching animals in motion as they walk, swim, hop, gallop, flutter, slide or fly. At the same time, anatomy should be applied with sensitivity to what is actually seen in real life – not like the caricatured muscle definitions of a bodybuilder.

With an understanding of an animal's bone structure, you can articulate its skeleton at crucial pivot points and ensure it doesn't feel like a stuffed toy. And a basic knowledge of the varying muscle shapes is useful for bulking out many creatures. Indicating these malleable forms can help bring a sense of tension and elasticity to your animal drawings. Knowing where to place the occasional groove or mass will make your short-haired animals appear to have life-like muscles beneath the skin.

Rather than having the skeleton on the inside, insects and arachnids have theirs on the outside. This exoskeleton is created from a strong substance called chitin. The exoskeleton is a suit of armour and is shared with their ancestors, the sea arthropods. To be able to grow, they need to shed this armour. All insects follow the same body plan, and one of the best ways to draw insects is to break their body down into segments.

When drawing birds, it's very useful to have an understanding of feathers. They are one of the miracles of evolution – they are made of keratin and evolved from reptile scales in the days of the dinosaurs. Feathers obscure the body beneath by tiling it; however, we can still get a sense of the large pectorals beneath that are adapted for flight. Feathers are distributed in feather tracts. Understanding these tracts, particularly on the wing, is vital to sketching birds.

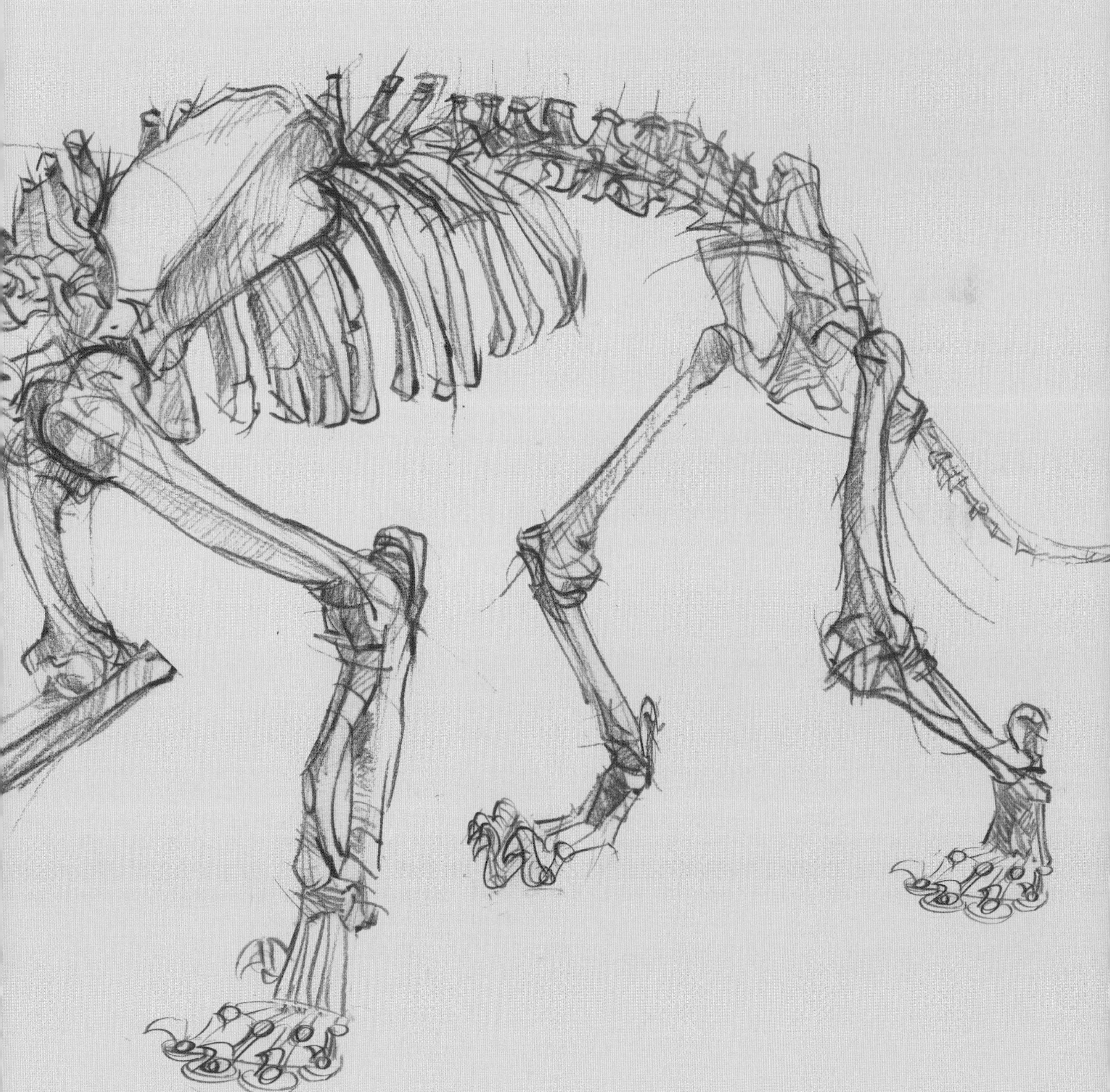

▼ **Sabre-toothed cat in pencil**
Sabre-toothed cats roamed North America
and Europe some 23 million to 2.6 million
years ago. The enlarged canines of the
sabre-toothed cat tell us that it was a
formidable carnivore capable of stabbing
attacks on large prey.

Bones

Bones create an internal armature that on some animals, such as an elephant or cow, appear quite stiff and rigid, but on others, such as the cheetah, they are gracile, loose and flexible, allowing for an incredible dexterity of movement. We will look closely at all tetrapods, a superclass of animals that includes all limbed vertebrates (backboned animals) that constitutes amphibians, reptiles, birds and mammals. All these types of animals evolved from a common ancestor some 400 million years ago from a species of lobe-finned fish that came out of the sea, looking a bit like a salamander (except that it wasn't a true salamander, at least not yet). Now hundreds of millions of years later, its descendants, including us, have taken over the land. These include snakes and whales, which lack four limbs but are still considered tetrapods because they evolved from animals with four limbs. Look for similar bones in these animals, whether they are adapted to hopping, walking and running, digging, flying, climbing or swimming. To draw convincing tetrapods, it is essential to see beneath the skin to the armature on which hangs suspended muscles, fat and skin.

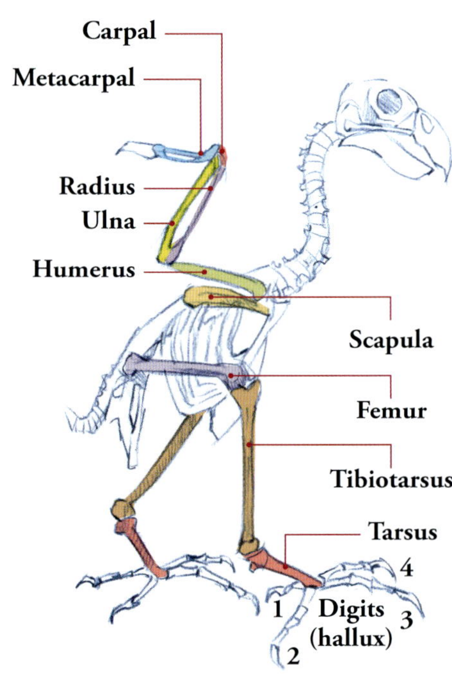

▲ **Kākāpō, or owl parrot**
(*Strigops habroptilus*)

Construction and structure

Understanding where the bones are beneath the skin will help to give your sketches a feeling of structure and prevent the subjects from looking like soft toys. It will also provide you with an understanding of the pivot points, which are the points of articulation, such as the shoulder and hip (ball and socket), elbow and knee (hinge), wrist (radial) and ankle (hinge). There are additional pivot points in your fingers and thumb, toes and neck. Some animals have highly mobile tails for balance and communication – howler monkeys even have a prehensile tail that can act like an additional limb.

Comparative limbs

Richard Owen published *On the Nature of Limbs* in 1849. In it he graphically demonstrated that all vertebrate species were built on the same skeletal plan and devised the vertebrate archetype. Richard Owen noted that they were all the same bones in the same order, although some of these body plans had become specialized. A komodo's front feet have become powerful claws for digging burrows. The skin between the fingers of a bat's hand has become webbed for flight, in a similar fashion to a duck's foot for swimming. So while the outside appearance of all tetrapods is incredibly diverse, from the rear fluke of a swimming dugong (a sea cow) to the high viewpoint of a giraffe's long neck (which still has seven cervical vertebrae like humans) overseeing the African savannahs, they all share this remarkably similar body plan. At times they can be hard to comprehend, whether the breathtaking repeating vertebrae and ribs or the lost limbs of a snake.

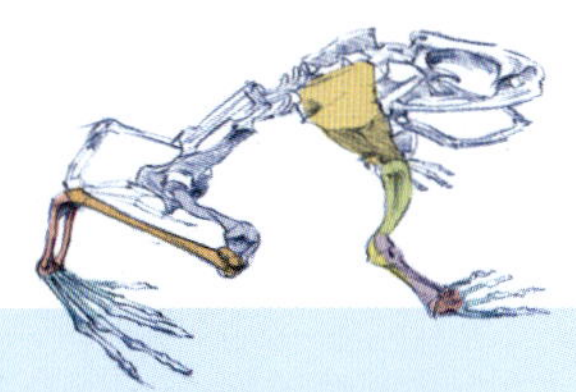

Common frog
(*Rana temporaria*)

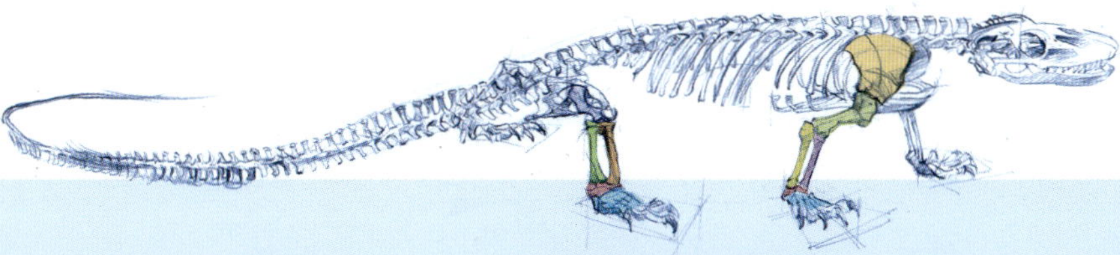

Komodo dragon
(*Varanus komodoensis*)

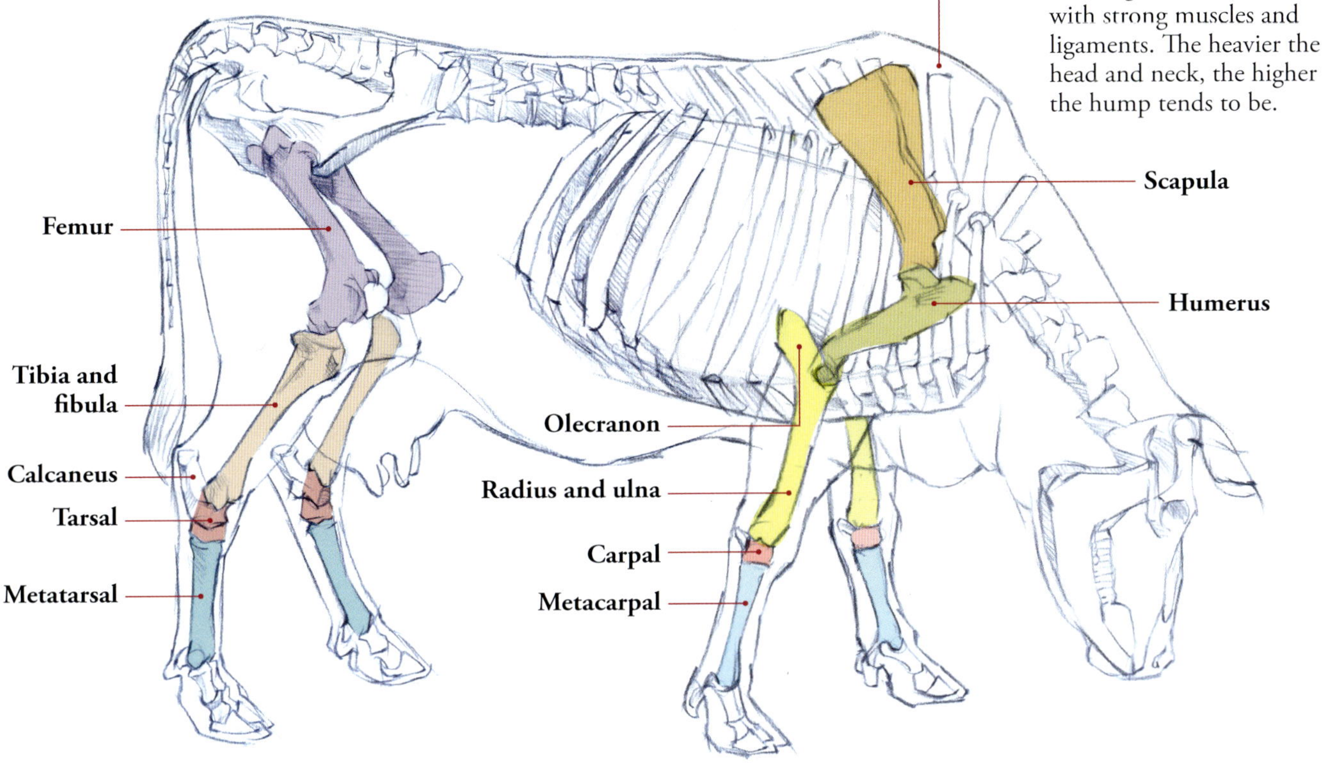

Arm/forelimb

- Scapula
- Humerus
- Radius
- Ulna
- Carpal
- Metacarpal

Leg/hindlimb

- Femur
- Tibia
- Fibula
- Tarsal
- Metatarsal

▼ **Same bones, but different skeletons**

Divergent evolution has led to homologous limbs, which means they have the same relative position, value or structure. The limbs of humans, apes, cats, lizards and frogs are examples of homologous structures. All of these structures – the arm, leg, flipper and wing – are supported by the same arrangement of bones beneath.

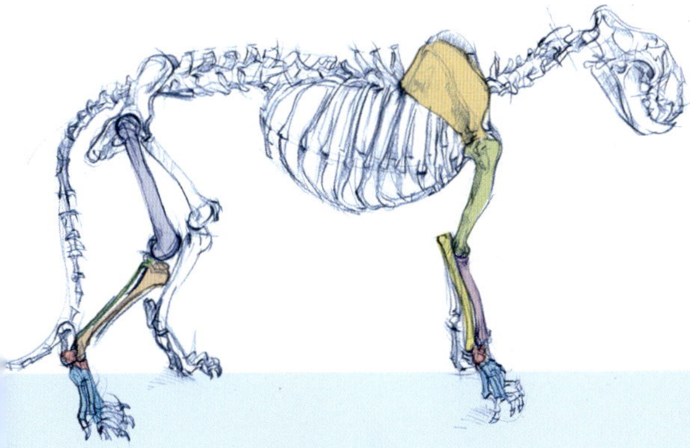

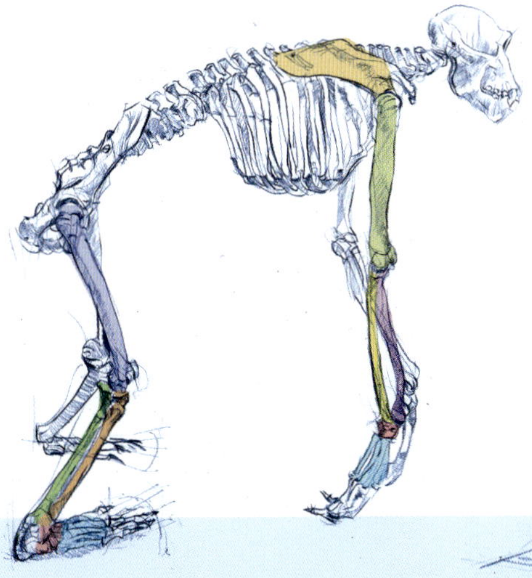

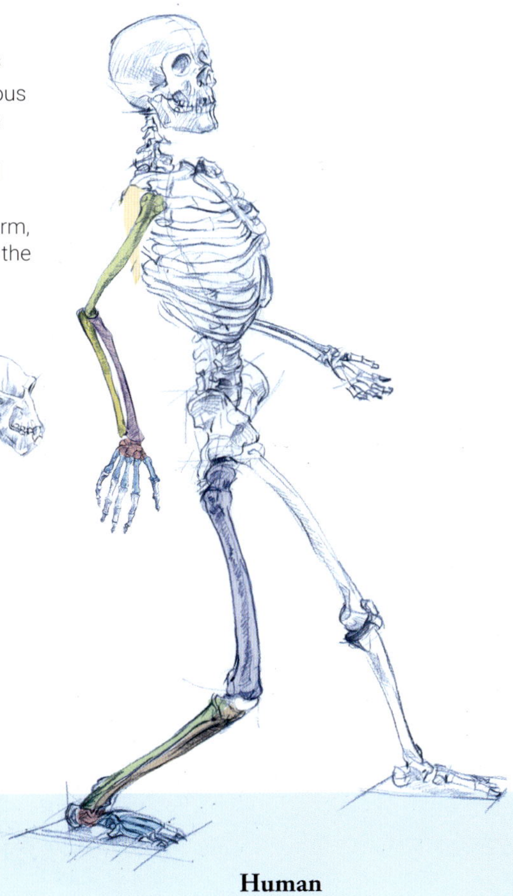

Posture and Gait

Understanding what we are seeing is equivalent to decoding the mysterious world of nature that surrounds us. Knowing about the three hand and foot archetypes that apply to the large group of tetrapods can help us to draw them more accurately. Understanding where the heel bone or wrist are located, for example, will help us understand the points of articulation and weight distribution and enable us to more convincingly draw the way the body is being supported in all sorts of poses.

Manners of walking

There are three primary arrangements of the limbs of the tetrapods that move over solid ground. Knowing what is going on beneath the skin is beneficial to create a feeling of structure.

Plantigrade

In terrestrial animals, plantigrade locomotion means walking with the toes and metatarsal bones and heels planted flat on the ground. The primary advantages of a plantigrade foot are stability and weight-bearing ability because plantigrade feet have the largest surface area. The primary disadvantage of a plantigrade foot is the lack of speed. To remember this stance, think of the foot being planted on the floor.

Wolverines are powerful predators and scavengers with plantigrade feet that have five toes on each foot. Its padded feet help it walk in the snow.

Digitigrade

In terrestrial vertebrates, digitigrade locomotion is created by walking or running on the toes. A digitigrade animal stands or walks with its toes touching the ground, but the rest of its foot, particularly the heel, is raised. Digitigrades generally move more quickly and quietly than other animals, making them excellent predators. I think of a digitigrade stance primarily as tiptoeing to make a quiet ambush. Most birds are classified as digitigrade animals, meaning they walk on their toes rather than the entire foot.

Not all digitigrades are predators. A rabbit's survival depends upon how fast it moves and so has digitigrade feet. Their hind legs are longer than their front legs, which allows them to accelerate quickly from a still position. Wild rabbits can reach an incredible speed of up to 45 mph (70 km/h), whereas domestic rabbits tend to be slower at 30 mph (50 km/h).

Unguligrade

The group of large mammals that are distinguished from other animals by the presence of hooves are known as ungulates. These include odd-toed ungulates, such as horses and rhinoceroses, and even-toed ungulates, such as deer and hippopotamuses. Equids – the horse, zebra and donkey – are the only species with a single hoof.

It helps to know about how many toes an animal has when sketching in the field. Most terrestrial ungulates use the hoofed tips of their toes to support their body weight while standing or moving. In addition, the pay off for lengthening their fore and hind legs for a quick spring of escape is that both the radius and ulna in the arms and the tibia and fibula in the legs have become fused, causing the loss of rotation and dexterity that humans and other animals have in these limbs.

▼ Pentadactyl limb

A limb with five digits, which is known as being pentadactyl, is the basic template found in all amphibians, reptiles, birds and animals, including a human hand or foot – and this suggests that all these animals are derived from one common ancestor. Sometimes these digits have evolved and are reduced from the original five to a lower number, but there are never more than five fingers. Hippos have four toes on each hoof, making them even-toed. Tapirs have four toes on their front feet, but their hind feet have evolved down to three, making them an odd-toed ungulate.

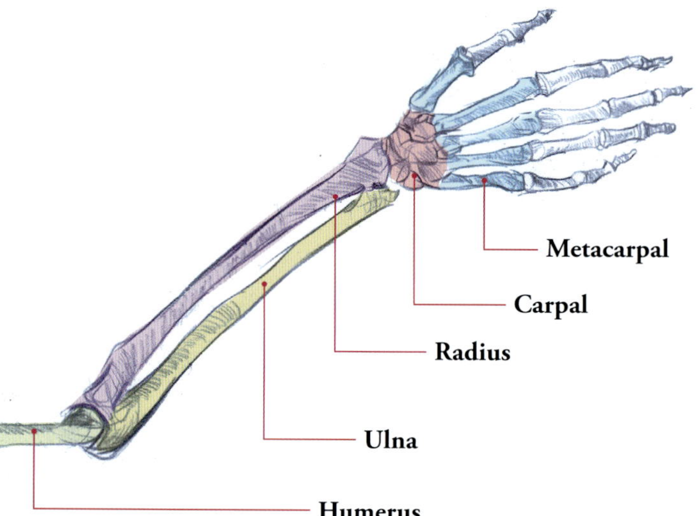

▶ Front hand, paw and hoof positions

Place your hand in the following three positions. Notice how your thumb doesn't touch the ground, just like a cat or dog in the digitigrade position.

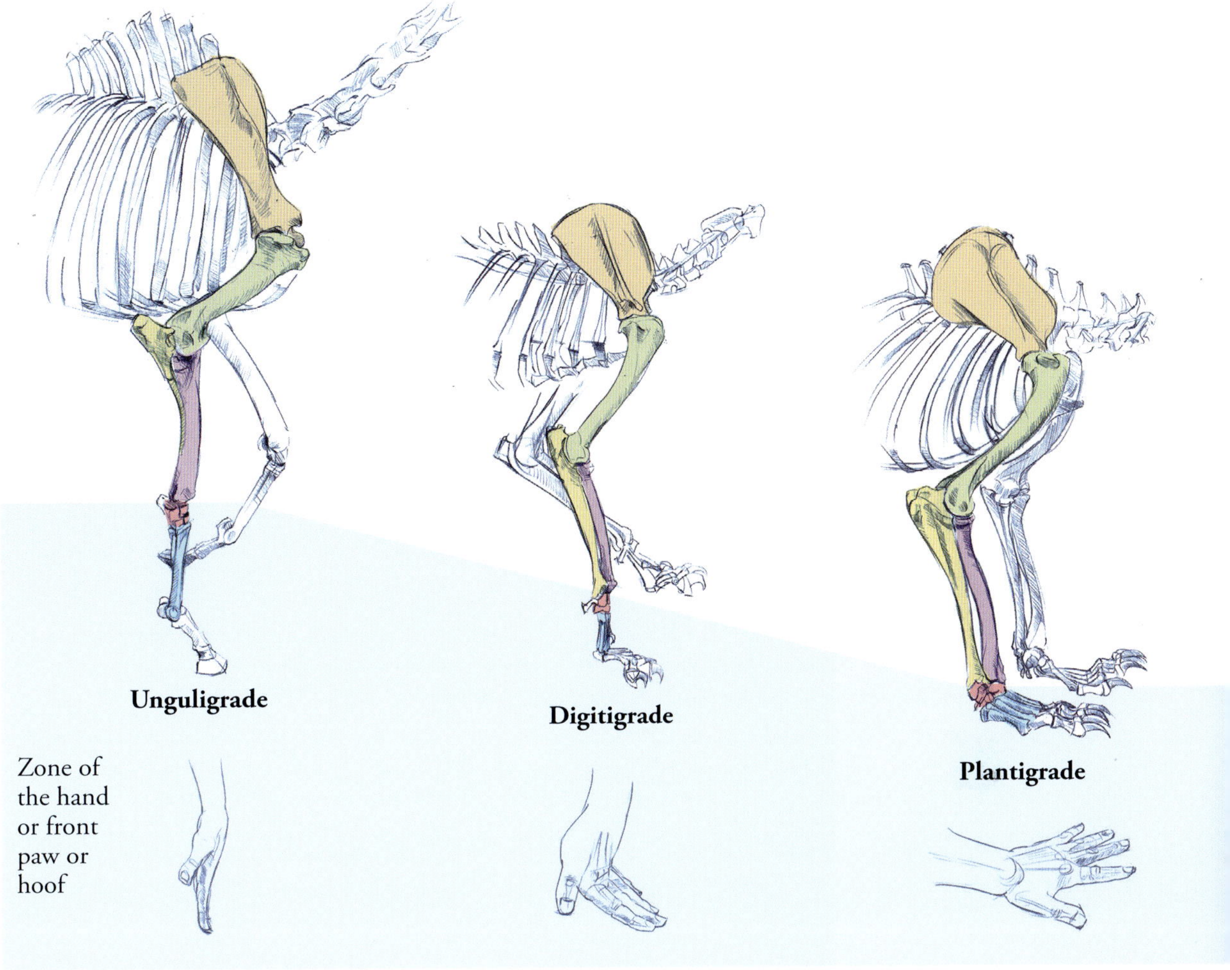

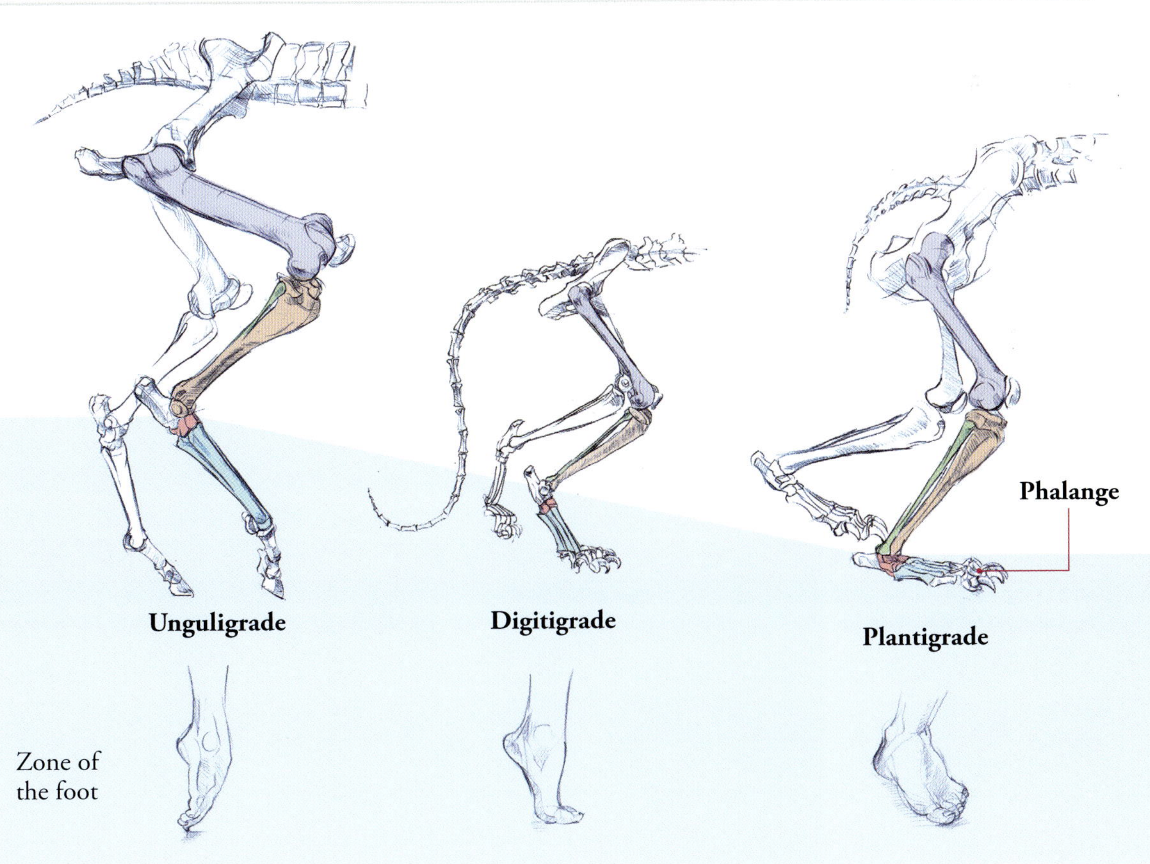

▶ Foot and hind leg positions

Imagine that you are each class of animal by placing your foot in the following three positions.

Muscles

The skin and fur of some mammals are thin enough to allow us to catch a glimpse of the muscles that lie beneath. It is not just thick fur that obscures their shapes. A layer of fat softens their appearance, which on some arctic-adapted animals takes the form of thick insulating blubber that hides them completely. However, a basic knowledge of the varying muscle shapes is useful for bulking out many creatures and can help with the surface expression of skin on the many animals in which they are visible. Indicating these malleable forms can help bring a sense of tension and elasticity to your animal drawings.

Many Renaissance artists, including Leonardo da Vinci, were also skilled anatomists. These artists examined how the bones and muscles worked in order to create more life-like depictions of human and animal bodies. Understanding the major surface muscles is tremendously helpful for modelling. It is also a satisfying feeling to be able to put a name to the lumps and bumps you see. In humans, muscles are more or less apparent depending on a range of factors such as body fat, athleticism, youthful skin compared to the sagging skin, and the wrinkles of old age.

Antagonistic muscles

The muscles' primary function is to create movement through contraction. Muscles are attached to the skeletal scaffolding of the body via elastic tendons. They are typically arranged into groups to create complex movements and counter-movements. When a muscle contracts or bunches up, it shrinks and pulls on the bone to which the tendon is attached. When a muscle relaxes, its size returns to normal. However, muscles can only pull and do not have the ability to push, so muscles work against each other in antagonistic pairs; these muscle pairs create movement when one contracts (flexor) and the other relaxes (extensor).

► Look for similar muscles

The biceps muscle that we use for lifting is very small on quadrupedal animals and appears as a slight impression on the inside of the upper arm (see the front of the dog on page 28). However, a lot of other muscles on our upper torso are easy to identify on other animals.

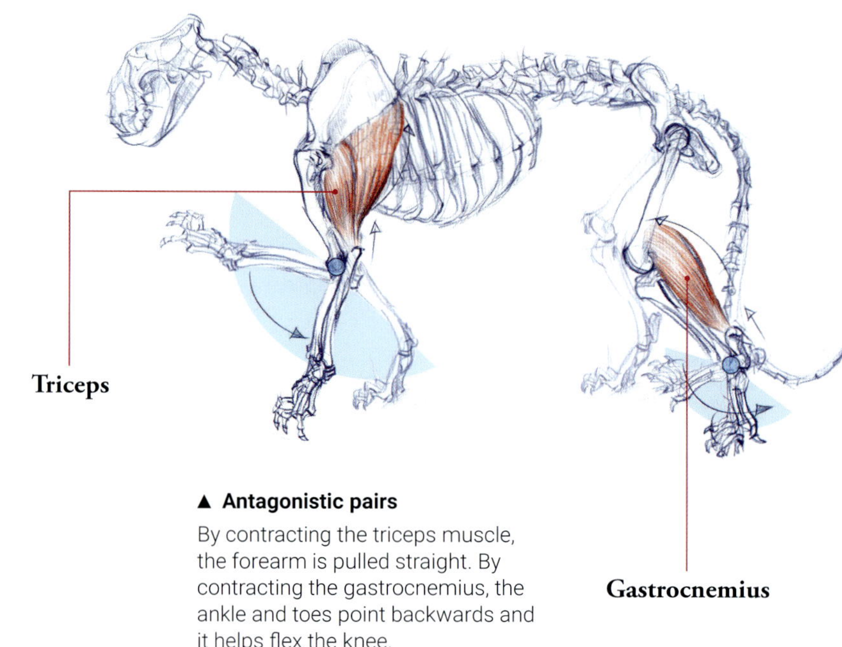

▲ Antagonistic pairs
By contracting the triceps muscle, the forearm is pulled straight. By contracting the gastrocnemius, the ankle and toes point backwards and it helps flex the knee.

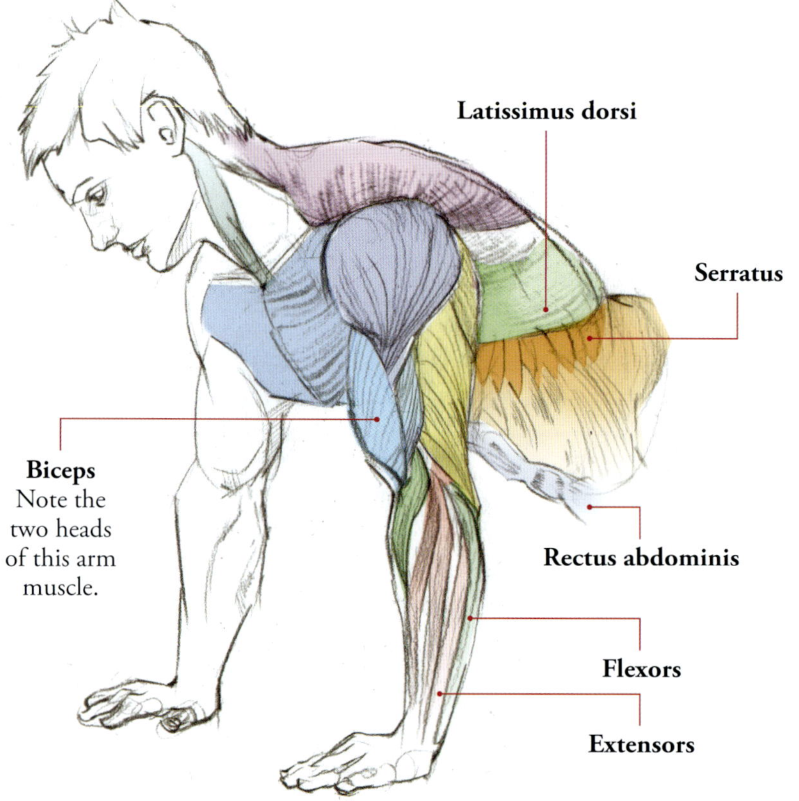

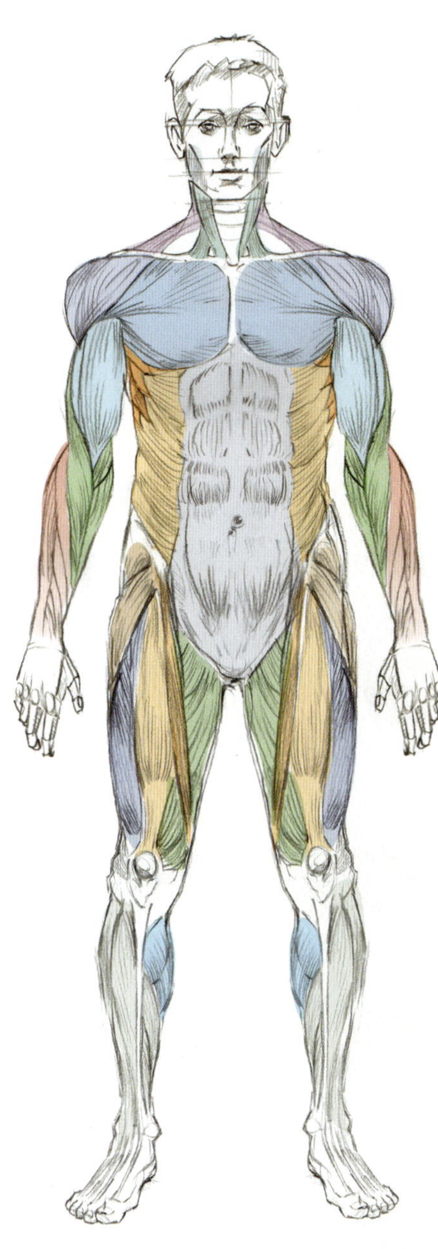

Shoulders and arms

Sternocleidomastoid
A pair of muscles that turn and nod the head.

Deltoid
A rounded triangular shoulder muscle.

Pectorals
A combination of four muscles that exert a force on the upper limb.

Biceps
Two-headed muscle of the arm which enables us to lift objects.

Brachioradialis
Primarily flexes the forearm at the elbow.

Extensors
Aid wrist movement.

Torso and upper legs

Serratus
Pulls the shoulder forward.

External oblique
Wraps around the side of the torso.

Rectus abdominis
Commonly called the abs.

Sartorius
Along with the rectus femoris, it flexes the thigh and extends the leg.

Rectus femoris

Vastus lateralis
The largest of the quadriceps.

Vastus medialis
Another part of the quadriceps.

◀ **Front view of muscles**

Movement is created by muscles when they contract in response to an electrical current. There are hundreds of muscles in the majority of animals, but as artists we only need to learn a handful of them to help transform our drawings.

▶ **Back view of muscles**

Notice how the muscles are mirrored, divided by the spinal chord that runs down our back, with the trapezius extending across the upper back.

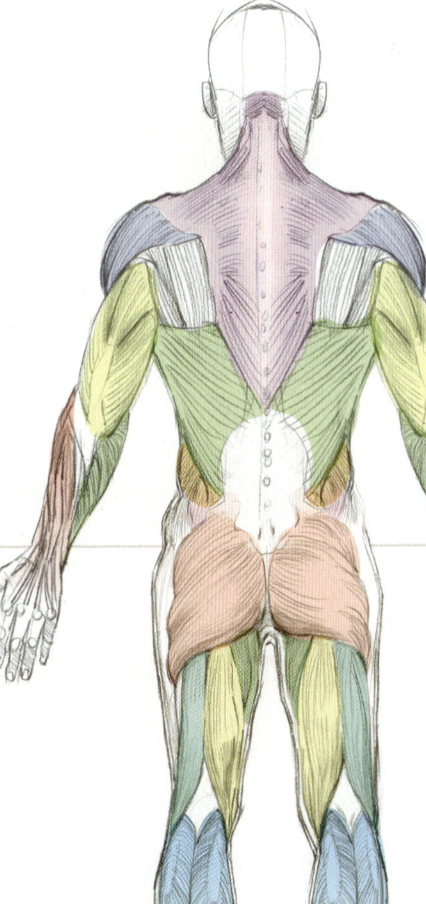

Shoulders and arms

Triceps
This three-headed arm muscle is responsible for extending the elbow joint and straightening the arm.

Trapezius
A broad diamond-shaped muscle, it covers the upper shoulders and neck.

Back and legs

Latissimus dorsi
Large, flat back muscle.

Gluteus medius
A hip muscle.

Gluteus maximus
Largest of the three hip muscles.

Adductor magnus
Largest hip adductor

Semitendinosus
One of the three hamstring muscles in the thigh.

Biceps femoris
A long thigh muscle.

Gastrocnemius
The calf muscle, connected to the heel bone by the Achilles tendon, the strongest of the tendons.

Transform what you already know to other animals

You don't have to learn the muscles of every animal. Instead, use your knowledge of your own muscles to understand which are the most significant. Animal forelimbs share a similar arrangement of muscles, although not all, to our own arms. You only need to learn a few to bring a sense of heightened realism and dynamism to the expressive surface of the skin. The muscles of your shoulders and hips are more pronounced than those that wrap around your torso, and the same is true of most animals. I always group flexors and extensors together to simplify.

Anatomy helps use make sense of what we are seeing. You can us simple coloured charts to create frameworks that can be turned around in your imagination to understand how the muscles and bones appear at different angles and poses.

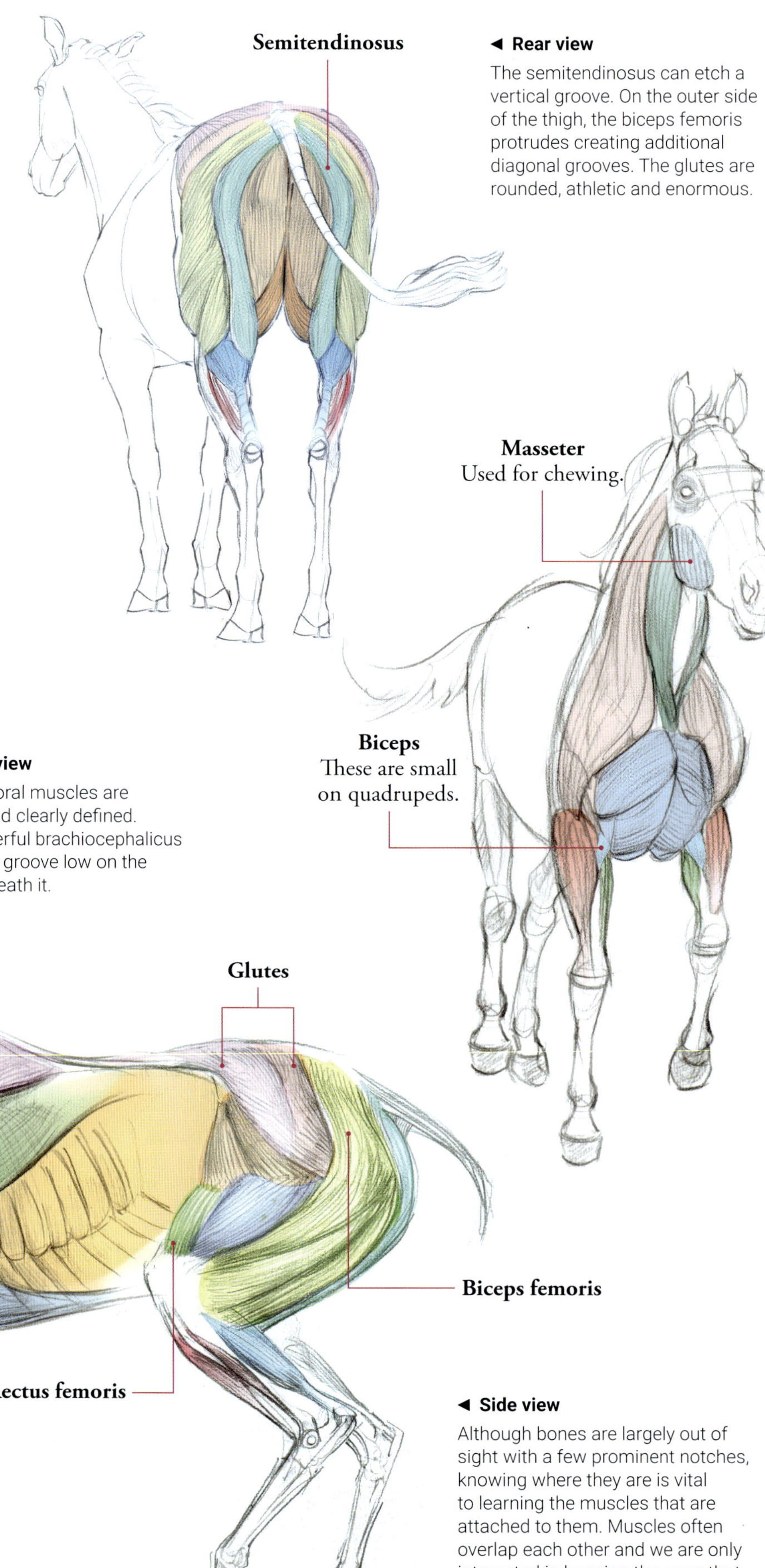

Semitendinosus

◄ Rear view
The semitendinosus can etch a vertical groove. On the outer side of the thigh, the biceps femoris protrudes creating additional diagonal grooves. The glutes are rounded, athletic and enormous.

Masseter
Used for chewing.

Biceps
These are small on quadrupeds.

► Front view
The pectoral muscles are strong and clearly defined. The powerful brachiocephalicus creates a groove low on the neck beneath it.

Glutes

Biceps femoris

Brachiocephalicus
Humans do not have this muscle, which has a range of functions in moving the horse's neck, head and shoulder.

Rectus femoris

◄ Side view
Although bones are largely out of sight with a few prominent notches, knowing where they are is vital to learning the muscles that are attached to them. Muscles often overlap each other and we are only interested in learning the ones that affect the outer form of the body.

Shading muscles

Lumps of muscles push beneath the skin to create bumps and ripples that can be formed by laying in shading. Getting these marks in the right place can make your drawing feel sophisticated. Every animal is different (even of the same breed – think about the huge variation in dogs): some are rounder where a thick layer of fat hides the muscle's shapes, or in an athletic animal where the muscles are more pronounced. Muscles are just one factor. As animals age, just like humans, their skin sags and wrinkles. Try to rely more on what you see than copying a muscle chart, as you rarely see every muscle on any animal. Learning the muscles can seem overwhelming, but you don't need to carry a map around in your head; a photocopy of a skeleton and muscle chart can be slipped between the pages of your sketchbook.

Although the arrangement of muscles is similar on mammals, the outside appearance can have different emphasis – for example, sometimes there are bones poking through. A cow is an interesting sedentary subject to sketch, where the noteworthy protrusions are as much bones as muscles that seem to hang off a stiff skeleton. The rear of a horse is more rounded with athletic muscles bursting beneath the surface.

▶ Bony cow

Although cows do have muscle, their bones are prominent. Notice how the head of the humerus pokes through at the shoulder and the blade of the scapula can create a surface impression. On the hips the iliac blade and pubic bone are clear landmarks but so are the bowl-like mound of the vastus lateralis muscle. The ribcage creates a large barrel, but the torso muscles are thin and don't make much of an impression on the surface. On lean animals, you will be able to see ribs poking through.

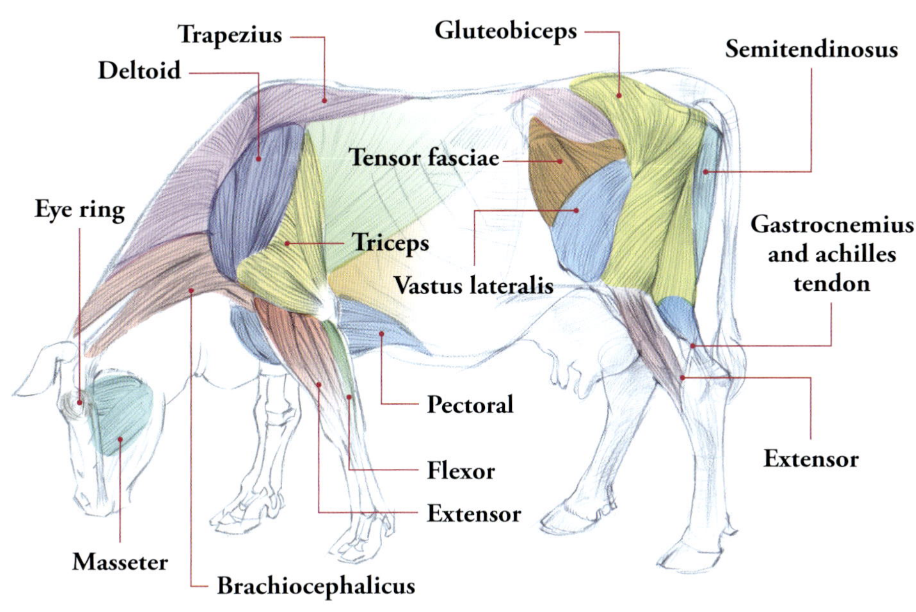

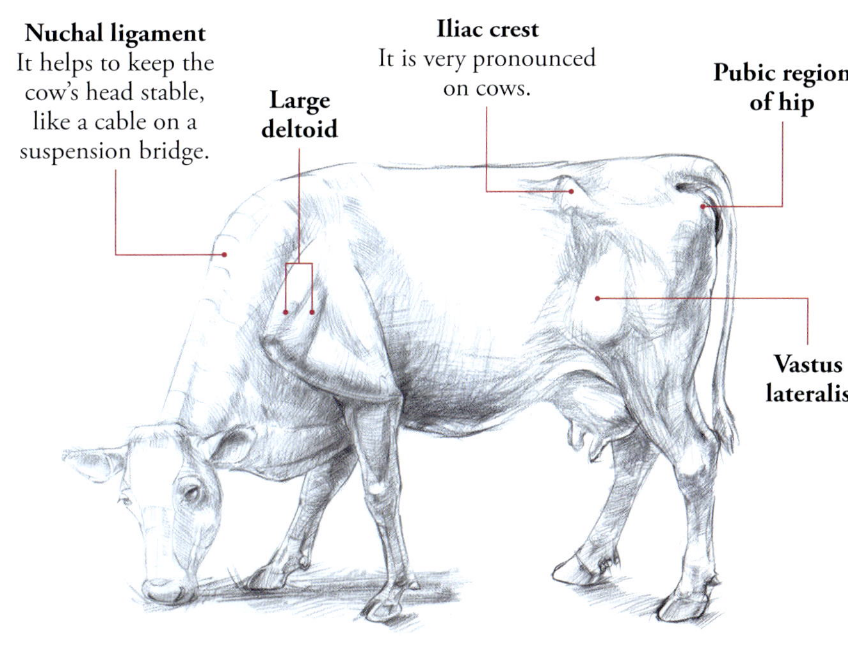

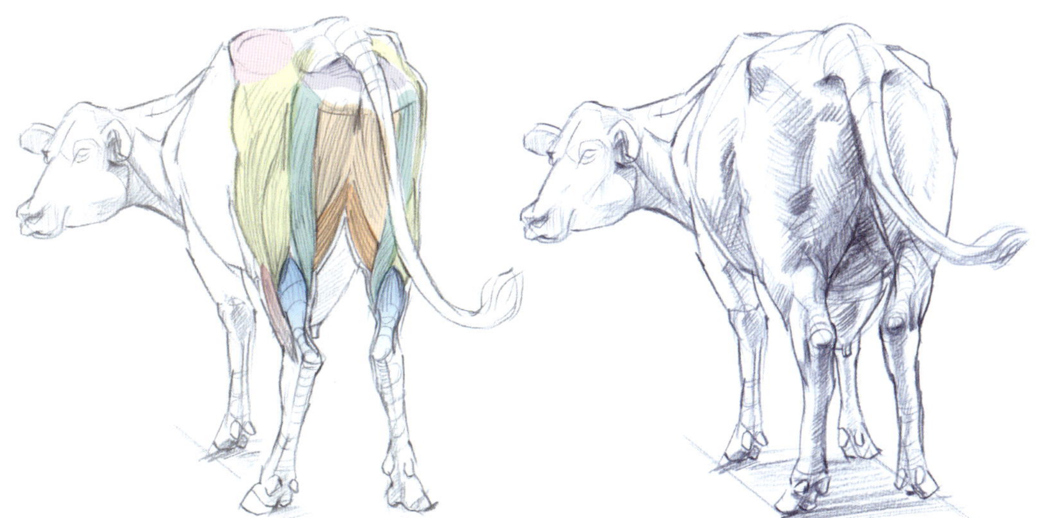

◀ Hindquarters

The hips' prominent bony iliac crest and pubic area protrude on cows, whose body seems to hang off a rigid skeleton. The gluteobiceps are made up of the biceps femoris fused to the back of the gluteus superficialis. It is not found in horses, dogs or cats, which have separate gluteus superficialis and biceps femoris muscles. Both these muscles create some mounded angled definitions, and in terms of drawing, they can be thought of in the same way.

The muscles of a dog

Dogs and cats were born to run. Both are extremely agile and can achieve high speeds in an elegant demonstration of coordination between bones, tendons and muscles. Between both the fore and hind legs is the bridge of a springy spine. Because of the spine's flexibility, dogs can move their legs far forward and backwards when running, giving them substantial power and speed.

When drawing a dog, focus on the few major muscles that are visible on the surface of the body. From nose to tail, the main observable muscles include the brachiocephalicus, which often creates what is called the jugular groove on the neck. The deltoid creates two descending ridges attaching to the spine of the scapula. The latissimus dorsi creates a ridge on the side of the body as it wraps from the upper humerus and splays out in a triangular shape to the spine.

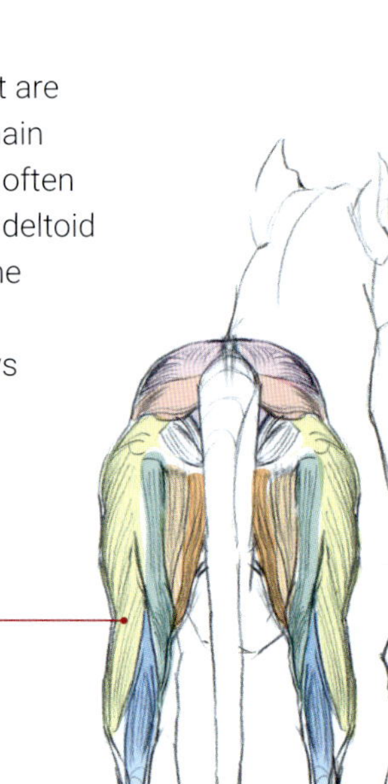

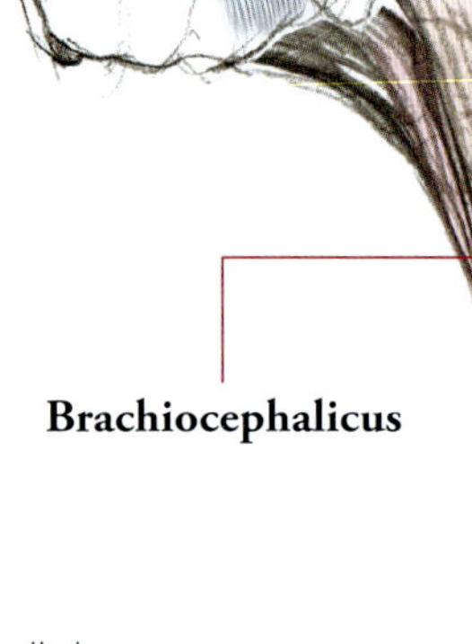

▶ Rear view

The biceps femoris bulges on the outside of the thigh. The semitendinosus can create a vertical groove. The glutes are small, rounded and solid; the iliac blade of hips can push from beneath on top and at the ischium below the tail.

▲ Front view

The pectoral muscles that attach the limbs to the thorax are strong and clearly defined on athletic animals. The sternocephilcus muscles create two ribbons from the sternum to the head.

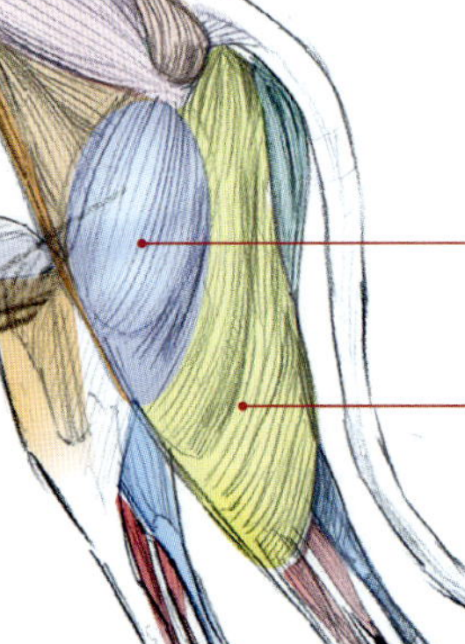

▶ Side view

Dogs traditionally have an elongated snout and paws with non-retractable claws. The brachiocephalicus covers much of the neck and there is definition in the powerful back leg. The vastus lateralis muscle creates a bulge above the knee.

Pads

A dog walks on pads beneath its toes and the ball of its foot in a digitigrade stance.

Whippet

Dogs are excellent anatomical models for an artist. For example, the athletic whippet below – a subject famously drawn by the German Renaissance artist Albrecht Dürer – offers a sinewy, springy display of coordinated movement.

Dogs (*Canis familiaris*)
A species is a group of organisms capable of interbreeding and producing fertile offspring and does not normally breed with other groups. Dogs show incredible variation but can all interbreed and produce fertile offspring. Dogs are therefore one species with numerous breeds. All these dog shapes have evolved unnaturally by humans through crossbreeding animals with similar characteristics.

1 *Create a light structural sketch. Having an understanding of the underlying bone structure helps articulate the limbs.*

2 *Start lightly coaxing the form from the paper. Note the location of the light source, which tends to fall from above and places the bottom of the animal in shade.*

Olecranon
It creates a prominent notch.

Calcaneus
It creates a nobble.

3 *Nurture your shading to create darker values so the muscles are sculpted on the page.*

Ribcage

Deltoid

Glutes

Jugular groove

Semitendinosus
It creates narrow definition.

Triceps
It creates a mound-like pack.

Vastus lateralis
It creates a mound above the knee.

Biceps femoris

Extensors

Latissimus dorsi
A large, thin flat muscle wrapping the width of the middle and lower back can create a lower lip.

Achilles tendon
Shading an indentation beneath the Achilles tendon creates tension.

Birds

You should study a flying bird's skeletal system before trying to construct the body on its delicate air-filled bones. You will need to be able to sense the bird's energy, intention and vitality to visualize this skeleton in suitable poses. And you will need to know how feathers develop, tuck and insert on top of the body to conceal it to be able to sketch them in their correct groups and get them aligned. It's important to note that the appearance of the feather groups can change, for example the feathers can be fluffed up when the bird is cold to trap warm air or moved together when flying.

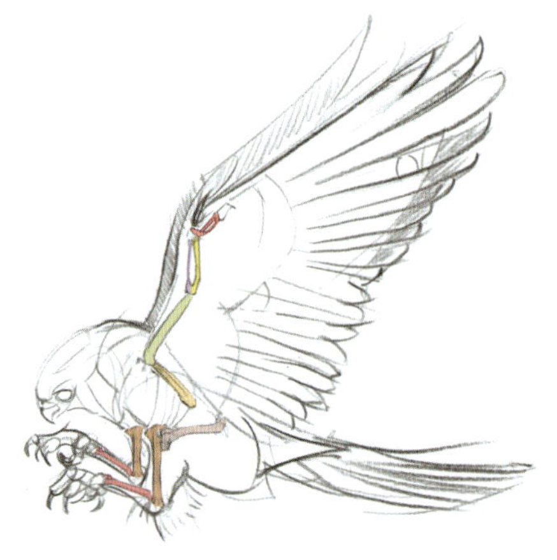

Over millions of years, the wing has allowed birds to live everywhere, from tundras to tropics, high up in the mountains and even in the ocean. The freedom their domain offers – the sky – has enabled birds to circumnavigate the globe and occupy a vast number of niches. Over time, some also evolved to become flightless, such as the ostrich and kakapo, while penguins took to 'flying' underwater.

The discovery in the nineteenth century of a fossil of *Archaeopteryx*, which translates as 'ancient feather or wing', has given us a transitional species between dinosaurs and modern birds and helped solve the mystery of where birds came from. *Archaeopteryx* lived about 150 million years ago and possessed characteristics shared by both reptiles and birds, including feathers attached to its body and anatomy indicating that it walked and perched on tree branches like a bird. It possessed a reptile-like bony tail with feathers attached and reptilian teeth with bony jaws and a snout rather than a beak.

There are more than 10,000, at times highly diverse, bird species. They range in size from the Cuban Bee hummingbird, which at just 2¼in (6cm) is often mistaken for a bee, to the ostrich – males of which can grow up to 9ft (2.70m) in height. Over time, birds have evolved to adapt to their lifestyle. For example, a stork has long legs to keep its feathers dry above the water while it hunts for fish with its spear-like beak. The shoebill stork has a beak that resembles a clog, which it uses

to snatch and swallow various prey animals. A penguin uses an oily secretion to preen its feathers, making it waterproof so it can fish for food. To climb trees and grub for food, the woodpecker has two toes pointed forward, and two toes pointed backwards. Yet, among this incredible visual diversity, all birds follow the same skeletal body plan with a wide variety of proportions and bone density.

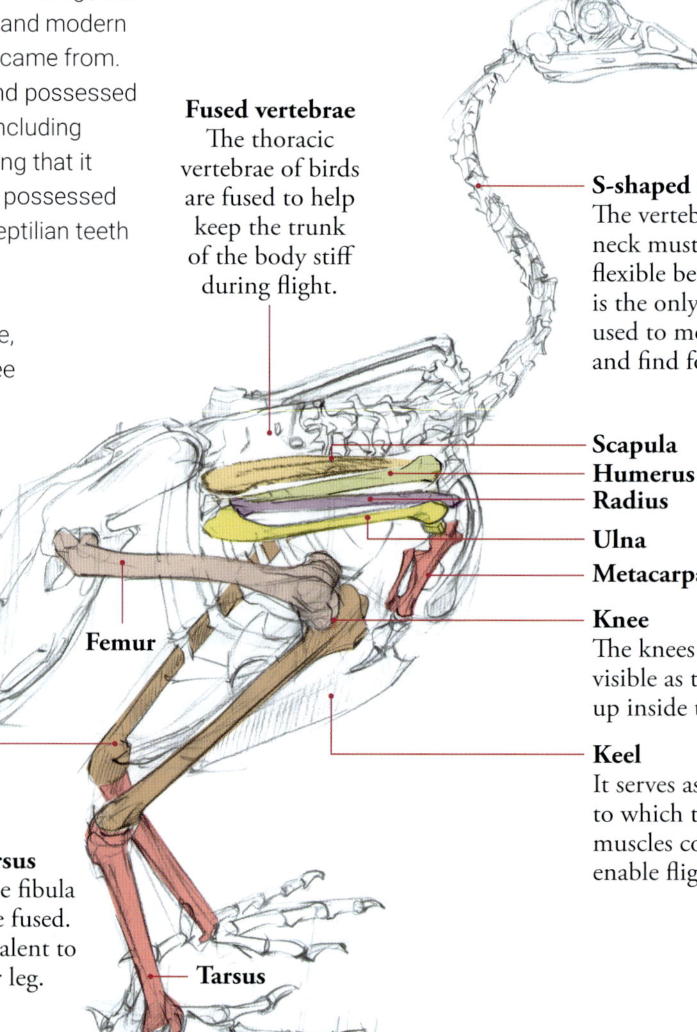

Fused vertebrae
The thoracic vertebrae of birds are fused to help keep the trunk of the body stiff during flight.

S-shaped neck
The vertebrae in the neck must be extremely flexible because the bill is the only body part used to move objects and find food.

Scapula
Humerus
Radius

Ulna
Metacarpal

Knee
The knees are not visible as they are high up inside the body.

Keel
It serves as an anchor to which the pectoral muscles connect to enable flight.

Femur

Tibiotarsus
On birds, the fibula and tibia are fused. This is equivalent to our lower leg.

Tarsus

Wings

Fused thoracic vertebrae
The thoracic vertebrae and other neck vertebrae are fused to keep the bird's trunk stiff.

◄ **Into the air**
The wing tip supplies most of the propelling force while the basal area provides aerial support.

Neck vertebrae
The repeating vertebrae of the neck provide a great deal of movement for the head. It can be drawn as an S shape.

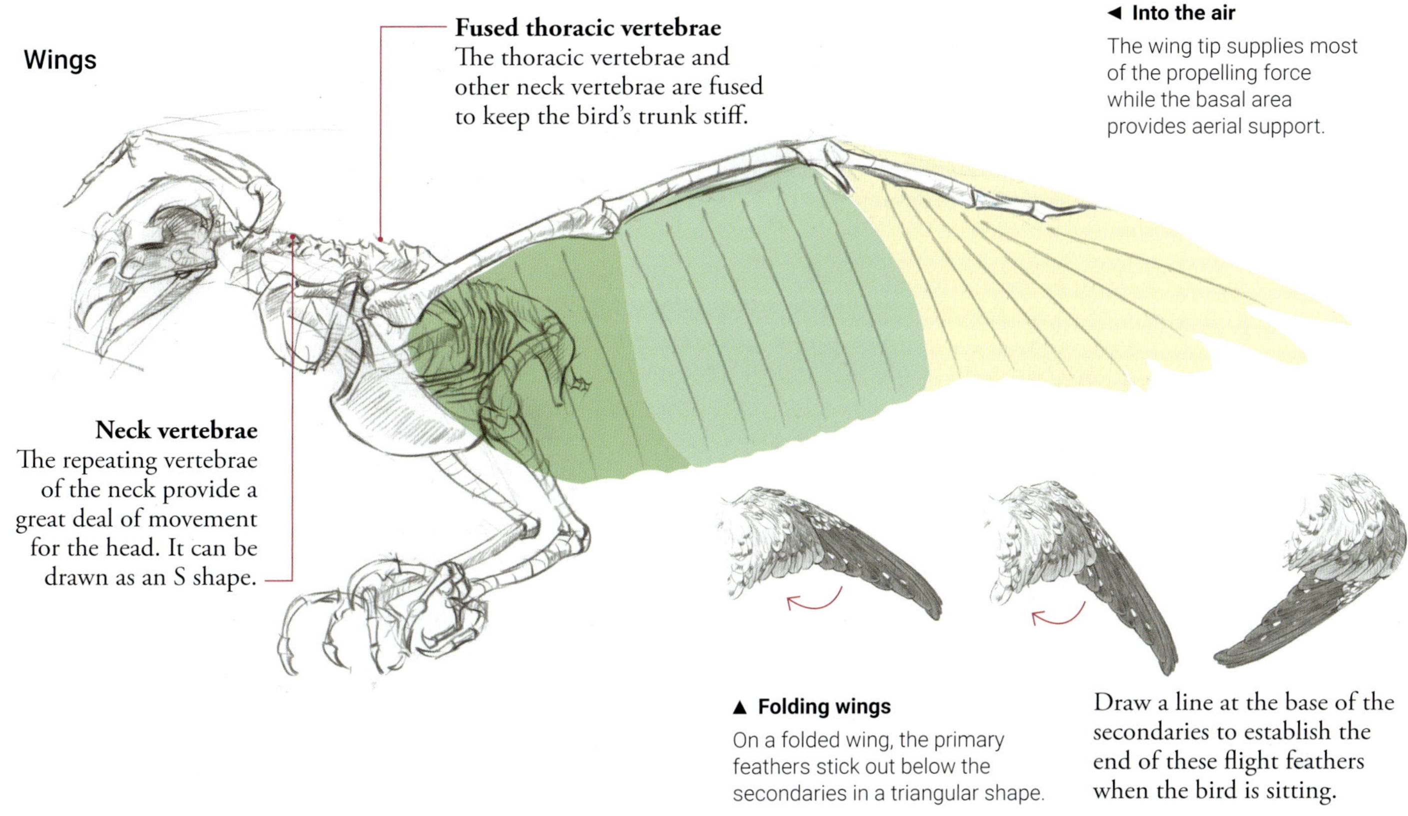

▲ **Folding wings**
On a folded wing, the primary feathers stick out below the secondaries in a triangular shape.

Draw a line at the base of the secondaries to establish the end of these flight feathers when the bird is sitting.

Eyes, beaks and feet

▼ **Beak**
Capturing the bird's character begins with capturing the essence of the beak. A beak is a fantastic tool for eating various foods without adapting different teeth types. In the Galápagos, Charles Darwin famously observed how different finch beaks adapted to eating different food sources.

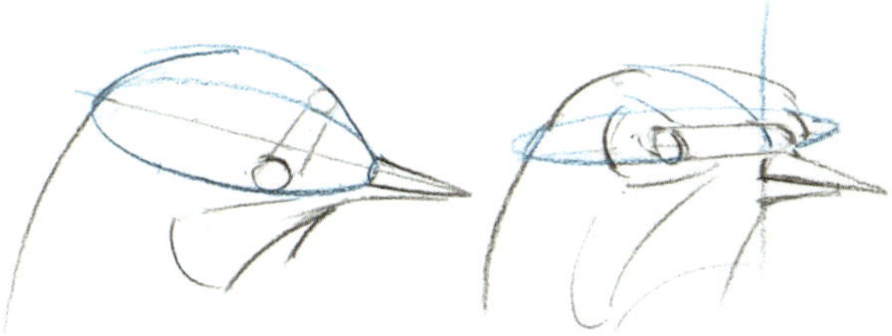

◄ **Bird's eye gizmo**
There is a tendency to draw the eyes too high up. On most birds, the eyes are on the same level as the beak and look down it. This cross line gizmo comes in handy. The eye is looking down the beak to catch its food with precision.

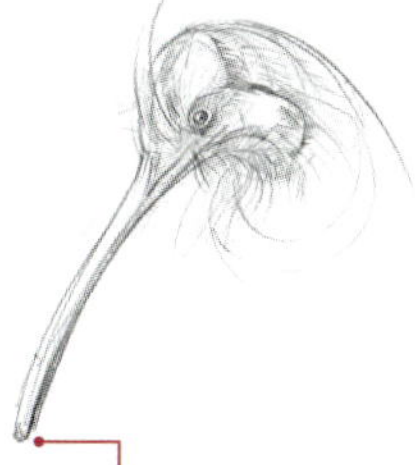

Nostril

Nostril

Nostril
The Kiwi is the only bird to have its nostrils at the end of its beak, which it uses to probe the soil.

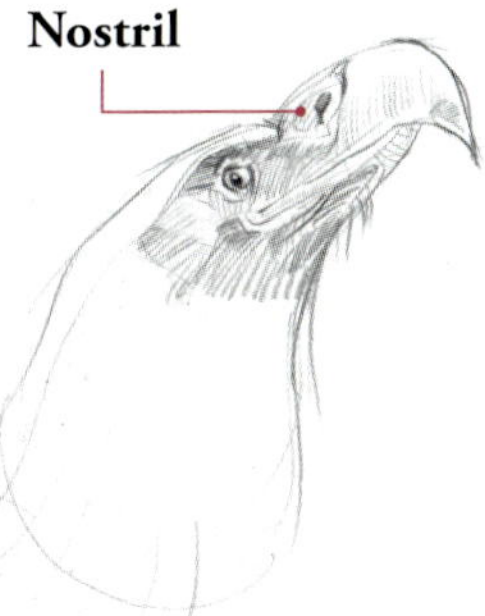

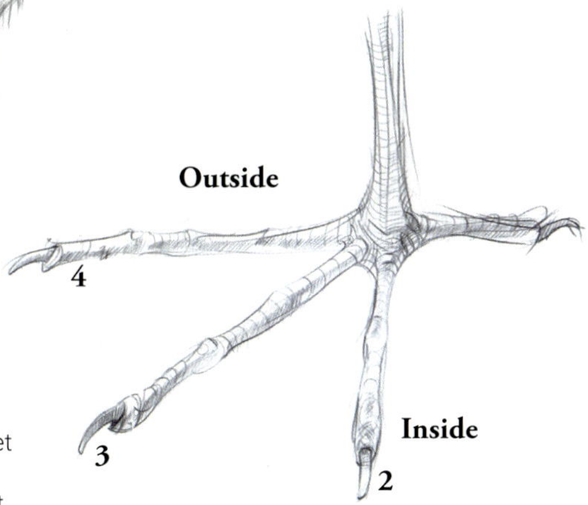

► **Feet**
Most birds have four toes, three facing forward and one facing back. The toes of some birds are adapted to meet different needs. Ducks have webbed feet for swimming, and talons are the feet of raptors and owls for killing. The exact number of toes and their arrangement varies – ostriches have only two toes.

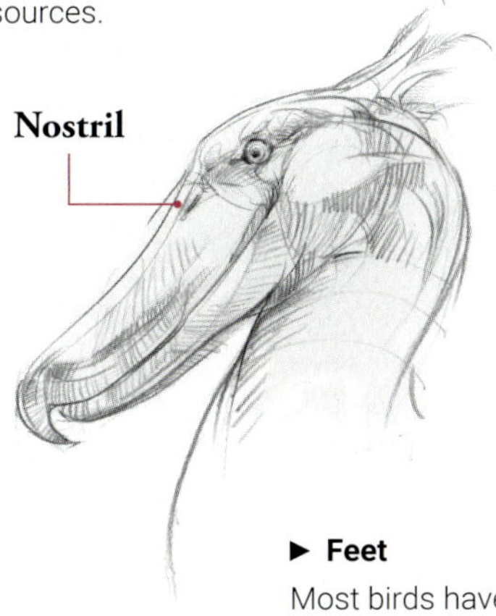

Outside

4

3

Inside

2

Feathers

Feathers are one of the miracles of evolution and have a history that goes back more than 150 million years. They are made of keratin, like birds' scales on their legs and those of reptiles. It is from scales that feathers have evolved. The leading theory suggests that feathers first evolved on dinosaurs for their insulation properties; later, small dinosaur species with longer feathers may have found them helpful in gliding.

Feathers grow from specific regions on the bird's body in six different types, though not all birds have all six, particularly the flightless birds. Unlike other bird feathers, flight feathers attach directly to the bird's bones and must be rigid and flexible simultaneously. The central rachis of flight feathers are lined on either side with vanes that have barbs to form flat, aerodynamic vanes. Contour feathers contribute to creating an aerodynamic shape and can be colourful. Down feathers are soft and fluffy and provide insulation to the bird. In appearance, semiplume feathers look like a combination of contour and down feathers, providing the bird with extra insulation. Filoplumes are very small and provide sensory information for birds to fly efficiently. Bristle feathers are short and stiff and located around the eyes and at the base of a bird's beak.

These feather groups define the shape and contours of a bird, and the patterns on the feathers relate directly to the underlying feather group. The stiffness or softness of the feathers will influence how you go about depicting them with either a sharper or softer, more impressionistic mark. Knowing which group of feathers is on top of each other helps with flying birds. This order rapidly breaks down on flightless birds, such as ostriches, or swimming birds, such as penguins, as the flight feathers have evolved towards other functions, with their purpose changed towards warmth and waterproofing.

► **Feathers for flight**

The primary function of the flight feathers, also known as remiges, from the Latin for 'oarsman', is to aid in the generation of both thrust and lift, enabling flight. Flight feathers are stiff, so you can use a sharper line in your mark-making. Don't give all your feathers the same delineation – down feathers can be sketched with a softer, more impressionistic mark.

Secondary feathers

These are attached to the ulna bone in the bird's forearm. Depending on the species, the number of secondaries ranges from nine to 25. They appear straight in both flying and seated positions. These feathers provide lift and are thus abundant in soaring birds.

Tertial feathers

Tertials are the three or four feathers on a bird's 'upper arm'. They are the short, innermost feathers on the back edge of a wing, close to the bird's body. They cover the gap between the body and the wing and are not as crucial for flight as the primary and secondary feathers.

Rectrices

The rectrices, or tail flight feathers, are mainly concerned with stability and control. They are used like a rudder, helping to steer and balance the bird and allowing the bird to twist and turn in flight. These feathers also act as a brake for landing. They can fan outwards for braking in flight and inwards in a seated stance.

Primary feathers

The primary feathers on a bird's wing are the longest, attached to and radiating out from the 'hand and finger' region like a fan. They are in charge of thrust in flight, which propels the bird forward. Most birds have nine to 11 primaries, but some have as many as 16. Primary feathers are asymmetrical with shorter filaments on their leading edge, which allows birds to cut, twist and turn through the air with ease, much like an aircraft wing.

▶ Coverts

Coverts are small feathers that sit on top of the wing's primary feathers (remiges) and help the wing's aerofoil to be smoother, streamlined and aerodynamic. The primary coverts are positioned on top of the primaries, and the secondary coverts are positioned on top of the secondary feathers.

▶ Alula

Also called the bastard wing, alula is Latin and means 'winglet'. It is the freely moving first digit – a bird's 'thumb'. It typically bears three to five small flight feathers, which 'ping out' for acrobatics.

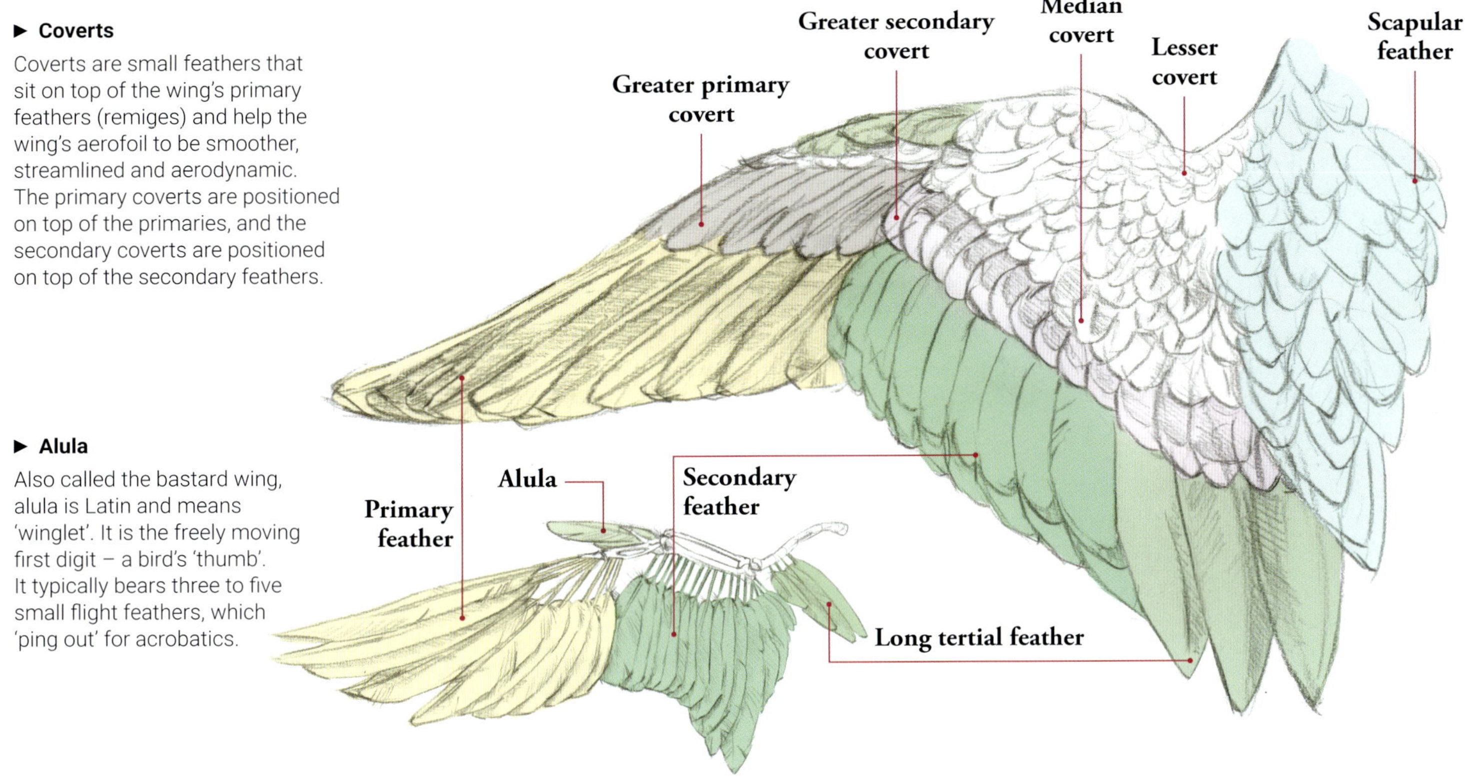

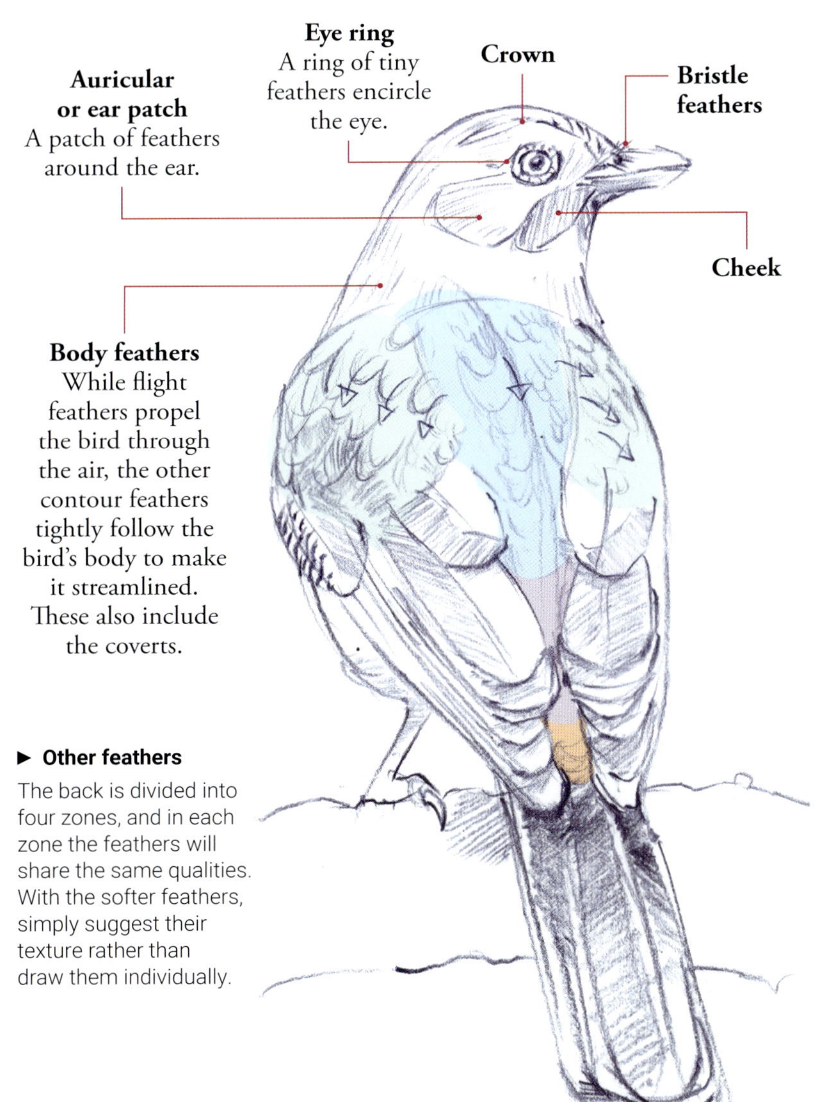

Auricular or ear patch
A patch of feathers around the ear.

Body feathers
While flight feathers propel the bird through the air, the other contour feathers tightly follow the bird's body to make it streamlined. These also include the coverts.

▶ Other feathers

The back is divided into four zones, and in each zone the feathers will share the same qualities. With the softer feathers, simply suggest their texture rather than draw them individually.

Mantle
The upper part of the back, which can stick out on some species, such as owls, is covered by feathers that run in a straight direction. These feathers are often streaked.

Scapula feathers
The Latin word for 'shoulder' is scapula. On birds, the scapulas are body feathers covering the wing's top. They can fan out in an outward direction or straight along back as in waterfowl and raptors. On some species, such as flamingos, these can be very long for insulation and appear highly decorative.

Rump feathers
When birds fold their wings, they normally completely cover their rump feathers. When birds droop their wings, such as when they are hot, these become visible. These feathers point downwards.

Upper tail coverts
The uppertail coverts have more definition than the softer rump feathers. Usually hidden in a seated stance, these stiffer feathers are often streaked or dark-tipped in most species. The peacock train consists not of tail quill feathers, but highly elongated upper tail coverts.

Insects

Just as Richard Owen illustrated how all vertebrate animals shared the same skeletal structure (see page 20), we can find a comparable example in the world of insects or entomology. All insects have the same basic body structure made up of simple interconnected components, and one of the most effective methods for drawing insects is to think of each of the body parts separately.

The head, thorax and abdomen are the three main components of an insect's body. The antennae, eyes and mouth parts are located on the head. The legs and wings are joined to the thorax, which is the central portion of the body. The abdomen houses digestive and reproductive organs. A small aperture known as spiracles line the sides of both the thorax and the abdomen to allow insects to breathe.

An insect's body is surrounded by an exoskeleton created from chitin. This is a tough substance akin to human fingernails. The exoskeleton provides an insect with a frame to which muscles can be attached, and these muscles are used to move the insect through contraction. Additionally, the exoskeleton shields the insect from physical harm, and it is also the source of the wide range of hues, forms and sizes that make insects so colourful, fascinating and diverse.

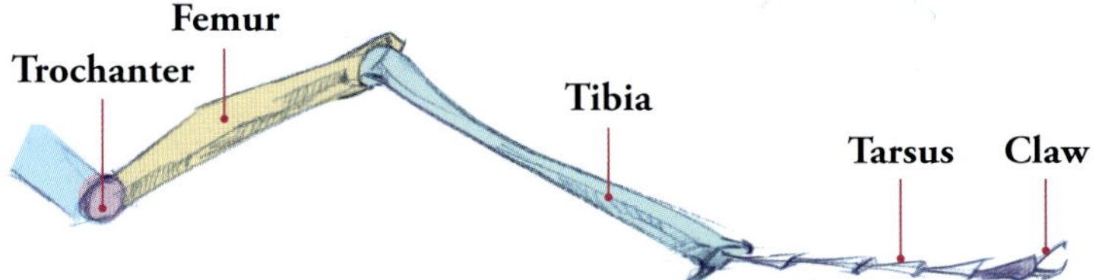

▶ Long thorax underneath
In some species, from above it may look like the back legs are attached to the abdomen. This is incorrect as the thorax is longer on the underside of the bug.

▲ Insect leg
One of the hardest things about drawing insects is getting the legs right. The front legs tend to point forwards while the other two pairs tend to point backwards. We can think of the leg of an insect in a similar manner to our own as a way of remembering them: the femur is our thigh, the tibia is our lower leg, the tarsus is our foot and the claw is our toe.

▶ The three main body parts
While a top-down view is useful for identification, a three-quarter view is a more exciting and dynamic angle to draw. I initially identify the three main body segments of head, thorax and abdomen and the central bilateral line of symmetry. Light construction lines are used to align both the legs and horns.

Tip
Some beetles have a very smooth and shiny exoskeleton. I try to capture this by shading in puddles of liquid shapes in three tones, using highlight, mid-tone and dark.

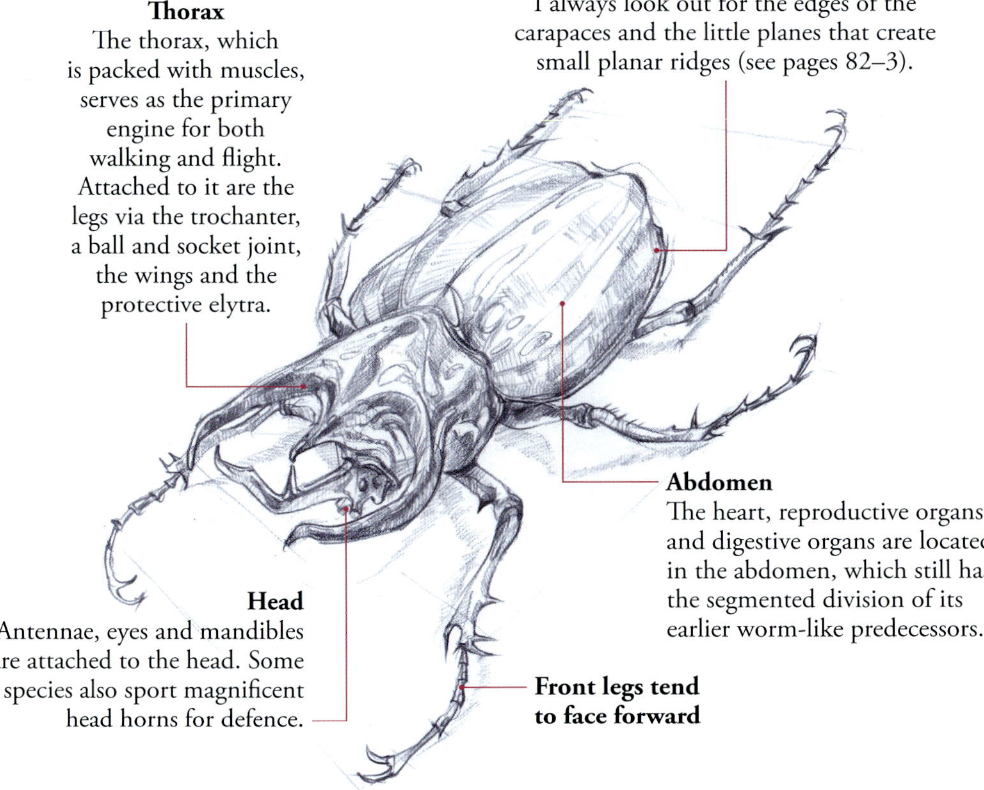

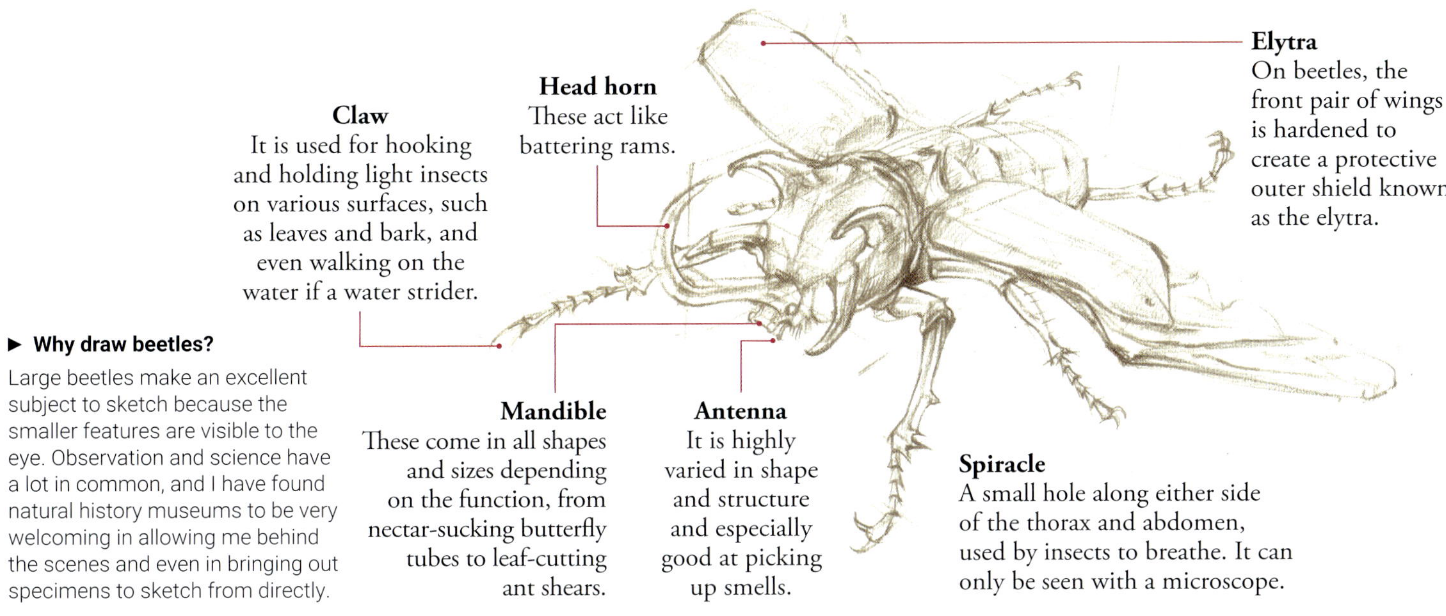

▶ **Why draw beetles?**

Large beetles make an excellent subject to sketch because the smaller features are visible to the eye. Observation and science have a lot in common, and I have found natural history museums to be very welcoming in allowing me behind the scenes and even in bringing out specimens to sketch from directly.

Forest caterpillar hunter

Many insects have nanoscale structures on their bodies that refract and reflect, creating iridescent light that changes as you observe them from different angles. Artist's quality colouring pencils are a good medium for capturing this vivid luminescence.

Materials
- Artist's quality colouring pencils
- Cartridge (drawing) paper or sketchbook
- Sharpener
- Putty eraser

Forest caterpillar hunter
(*Calosoma sycophanta*)

As its names implies, this beetle is a predator, and it was introduced to New England from its native Europe in the early twentieth century to control gypsy moths.

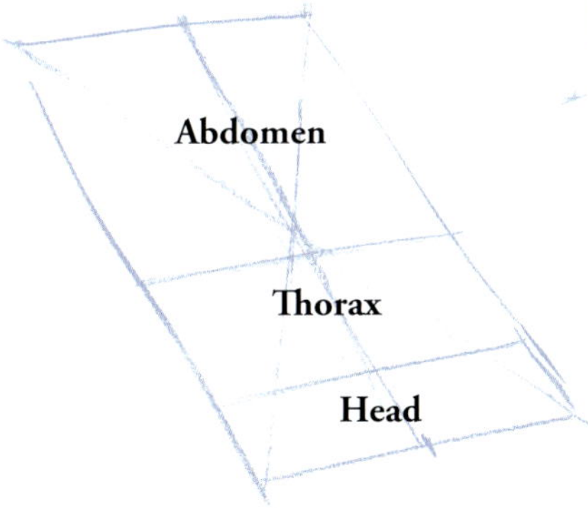

Abdomen

Thorax

Head

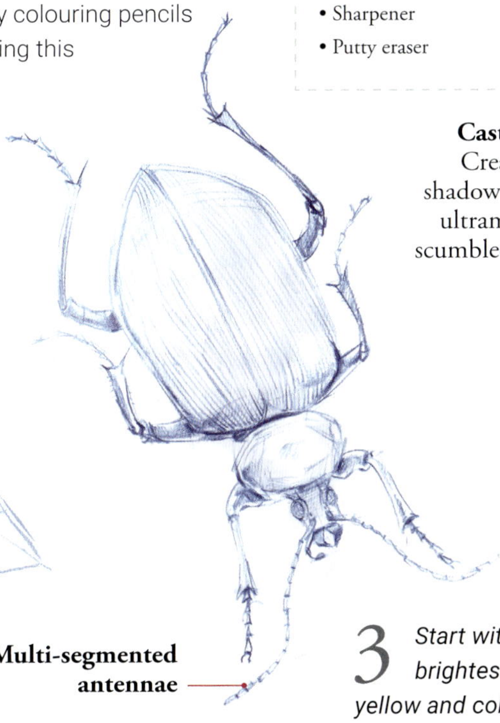

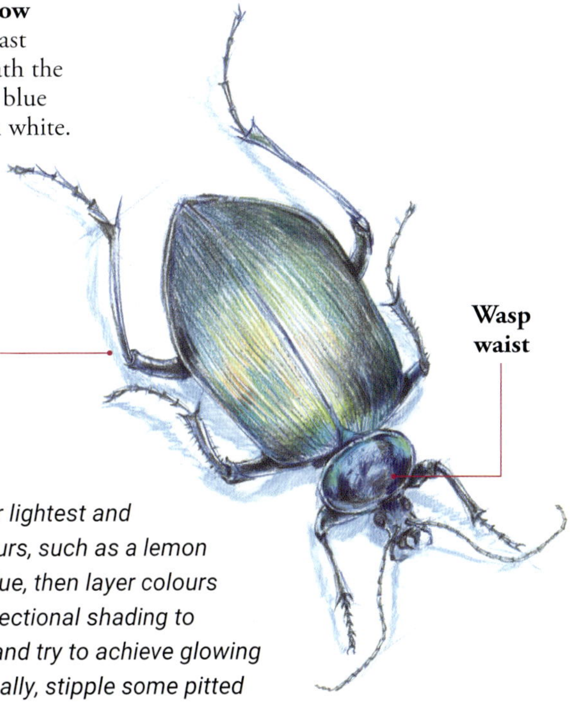

Cast shadow
Create a cast shadow beneath the ultramarine blue scumbled with white.

Wasp waist

Multi-segmented antennae

1 *To sketch an insect in perspective, draw or imagine an underlying frame into which the three main body parts fit.*

2 *Create a tonal under drawing in an ultramarine blue, keeping the tip really sharp to capture the lined texture on the elytra.*

3 *Start with your lightest and brightest colours, such as a lemon yellow and cobalt blue, then layer colours over the top with directional shading to blend on the paper and try to achieve glowing metallic shades. Finally, stipple some pitted dots to capture miniscule divots of texture. With colouring pencils, there is a need to be flexible and approximate the colour depending on the range of colours available. Progress from the broader colours to the detail.*

Black	Blue violet	Ultramarine blue	Phtalo blue	Cobalt blue	Cobalt turquoise	Cobalt green	Emerald green	Light green	Lemon yellow	Cadmium orange

Line

When it comes to observing nature for your drawing, you will discover that there are no limits to the variety of lines that exist. From the layers of sediment in geological strata to the swirling gelatinous lines of a jellyfish's tentacles, the finest filigree of veins in a leaf skeleton and the sharpest spines of a cactus, lines are found in abundance. Thick, thin, straight, curved or wavy, smudged or sharp. An exciting drawing, like nature, is built around this variety.

The line plays a crucial role in drawing, and it is possible to convey a vast amount of information with just a few strokes. There are many types of line: they can be thick or thin; straight or curved; carefully drawn descriptive details or bold expressionistic marks. Lines can be sharp and expressive, broken, whimsical, impressionistic and even playful.

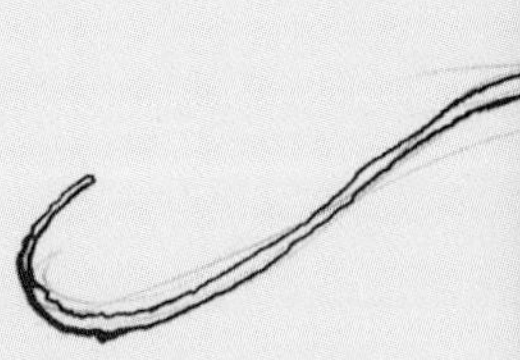

There are a variety of visual conventions that mark-making can imply. Artists create lines for many different reasons, from delineating an edge to creating a pattern or texture and modelling a form. A mastery of the line is also essential for the other disciplines in drawing – for example, line is used to create tone by cross-hatching (see page 64) or space by foreshortening (see pages 112–13).

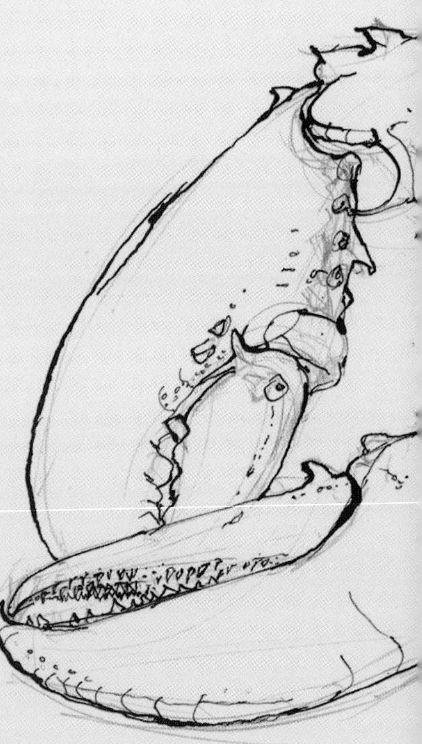

The type of media you use can have an impact on the line you draw. For this reason, it is essential to become familiar with the various materials and explore their linear possibilities. After you have selected a subject, ask yourself what media would be best. A soft, waxy pencil might suit sketching a moving animal where ease of use is vital to get the beast down on paper; however, a graphite pencil sharpened to a fine tip would be better when drawing fine locks of hair.

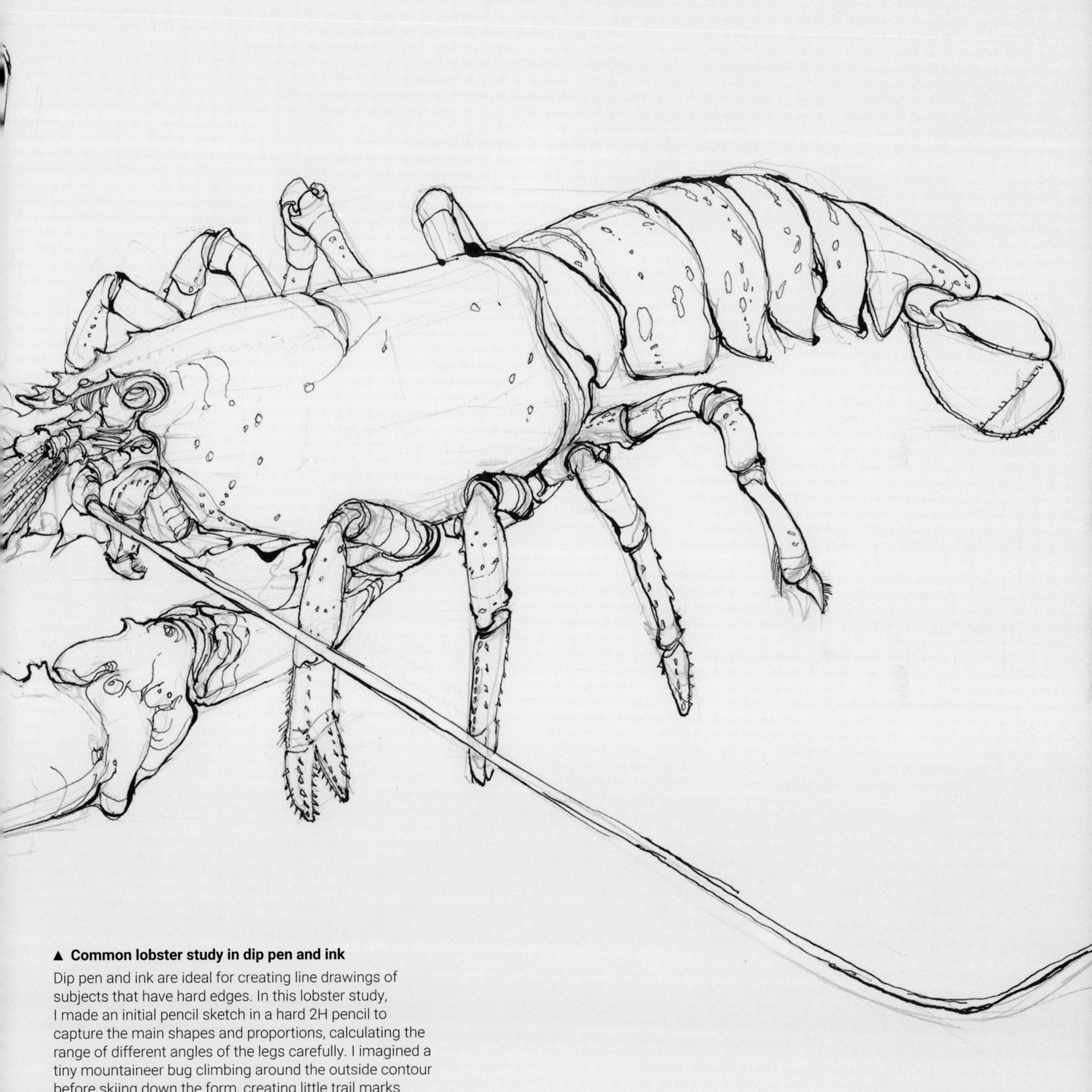

▲ Common lobster study in dip pen and ink

Dip pen and ink are ideal for creating line drawings of
subjects that have hard edges. In this lobster study,
I made an initial pencil sketch in a hard 2H pencil to
capture the main shapes and proportions, calculating the
range of different angles of the legs carefully. I imagined a
tiny mountaineer bug climbing around the outside contour
before skiing down the form, creating little trail marks
that model the form. I tried to vary my line from a light
decorative pattern and spike mark to darker structural
delineation using the faint ghost 2H line as guidance,
but I did take another look at the subject and make
adjustments to the underlying sketch before turning
to the dip pen and ink.

Line Essentials

The line is my primary means of communication in a drawing, so it is worth taking time to find out what marks your drawing implement can produce to create visual interest. Experiment with a variety of lines in your drawing while you try to capture anything from a gelatinous jellyfish to a sharp piece of flint. A line can be delicate and precise, or it can be bold, expressive and even emotional. The artist's mood and personality can be transmitted through line, so let's look at the different types and see what they can bring to your drawings.

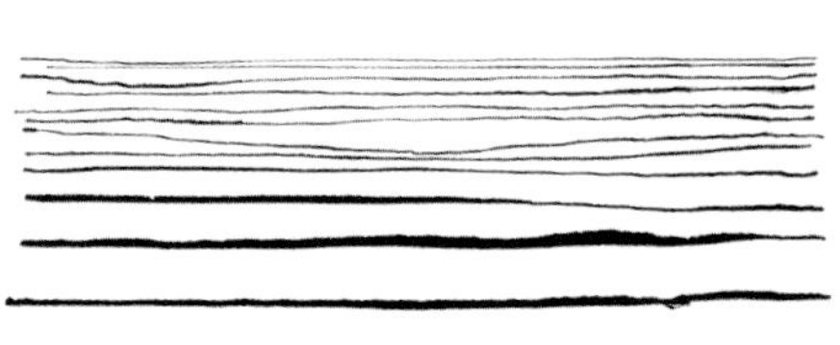

Horizontal lines

Fields, gently rolling hills, lakes, rivers and ocean scenes have strong horizontal lines. By incrementally widening or decreasing the space between these marks, you can create the impression of depth. Lines that run horizontally give the impression of calmness and rest.

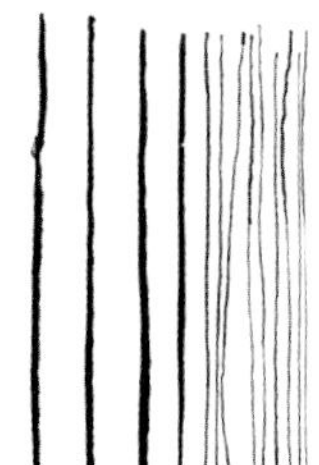

Vertical lines

Vertical lines, such as tall trees, frequently convey a sense of height because they are perpendicular to the earth and stretch upwards towards the sky. These, too, can suggest space and distance by incrementally changing the gap between them.

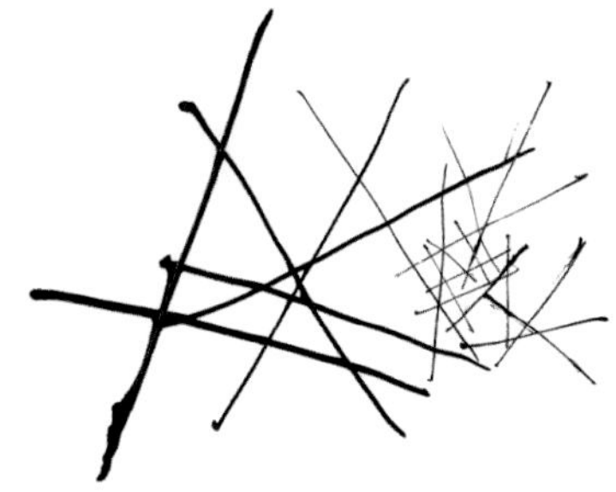

Diagonal lines

When we look at the natural world, we can see that lines are rarely truly vertical or horizontal but instead are a sea of subtle angles. Diagonal lines create the illusion of movement because we read them as unstable, either as about to fall or as already falling. Extreme opposing angles create dynamism and excitement.

Pencil line

Dip pen and ink

Line weight

Line weight refers to the thickness of a line – whether it is broad and heavy or fine and delicate. An individual's personality plays a vital role in the marks they naturally gravitate towards creating. The variation in line weight, just as with variety in tonality, can add visual interest to a drawing. Line weight is affected by the amount of pressure applied to the drawing implement – or, in terms of a brush, by diluting the ink or paint with water compared with heavily loading it with saturated pigment. Line thickness can create emphasis, making part of the drawing more dominant. Heavier lines appear to advance towards the eye, whereas light lines recede.

Type of mark

The type of mark you create should aim to capture the subject's qualities. The veins of a leaf might be delineated with a light touch, whereas the trunk of an oak drawn with a bold emphasis. Flick marks from the wrist could attempt to capture the fur on a squirrel, while fluid wavy lines could suggest the tentacles of a jellyfish.

Fur flick marks created from the wrist

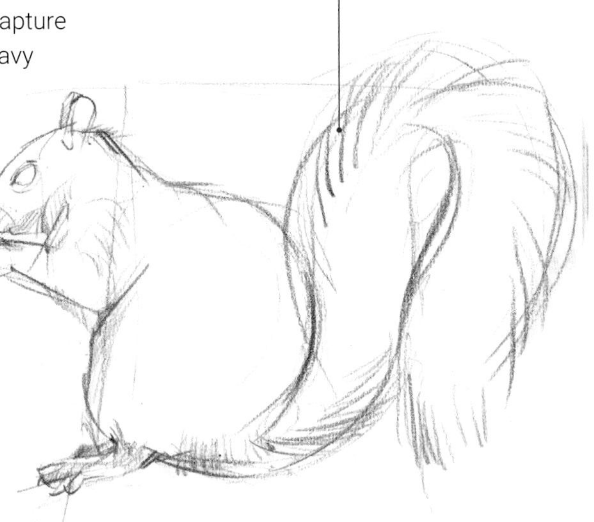

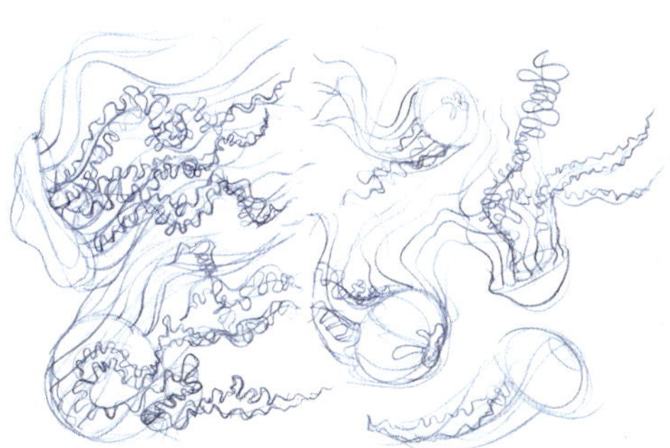

Fluid lines

To capture movement, ensuring that your studies are not too stiff and wooden, fluid lines are essential. Capturing a jellyfish bloom is the jazz equivalent of drawing in an aquarium – a world in which there doesn't seem to be a right way up or upside down.

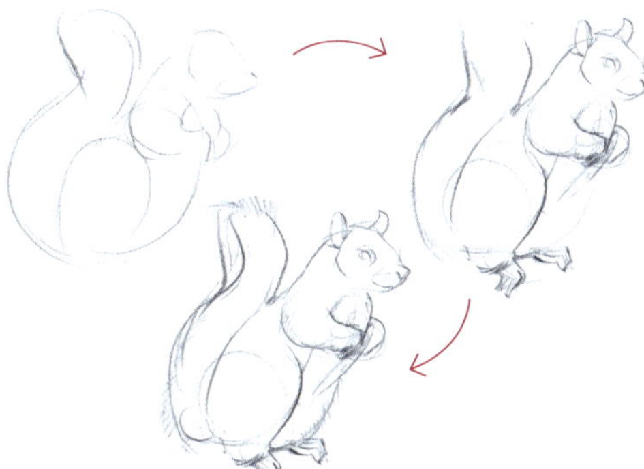

Construction

Build confidence before committing to delineating the edge.

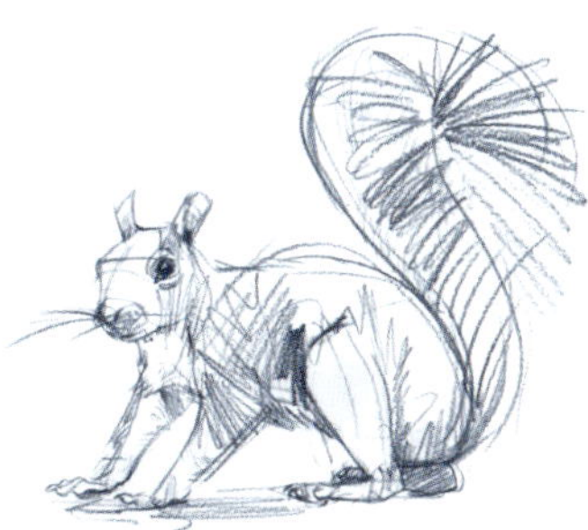

Emotion

Certain types of lines can conjure up different emotional responses in the viewer in an abstract way. As well as being a necessity to capture the creature before it leaps away, the fast, vigorous lines of a field sketch created quickly can be a conscious choice made by the artist. I also find the quiet line of precision can be equally moving.

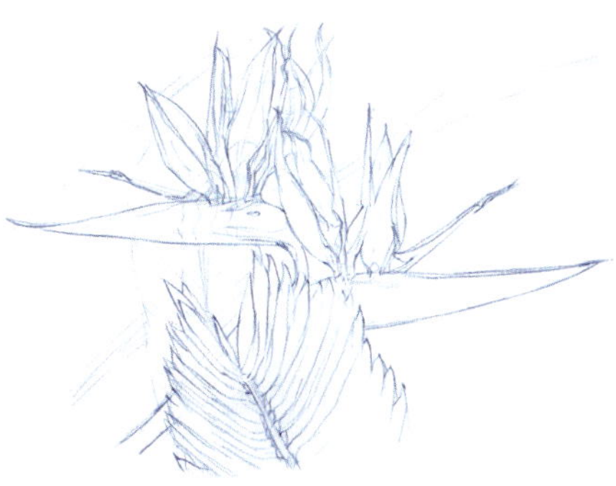

Colouring pencil drawings

Along with graphite pencils, I draw with high-quality, waxy colouring pencils. Drawing with colours feels like a new beginning and helps you get past any negative feelings towards a graphite line. Practise regularly to create a quick sketching style that incorporates a variety of line styles. Combine contour, hatched lines (see pages 80–1) and textural marks to develop a shorthand style to use anywhere, from plein air to museums, aquariums and zoos.

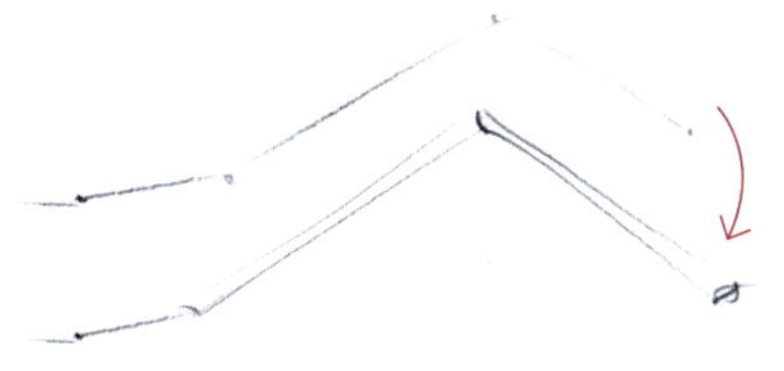

Skeleton and structure

You can use skeletal lines to plot out and plan your drawing. A concave mark can give the feeling of structure and support, from a butterfly to a giraffe's legs.

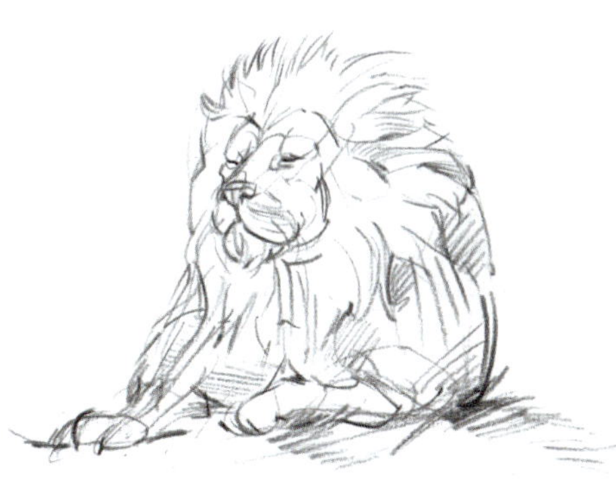

Character

Combinations of different abstract lines can combine to capture the subject's character and emotional state. Try to empathize with these characteristics as you sketch, such as a male lion's pride.

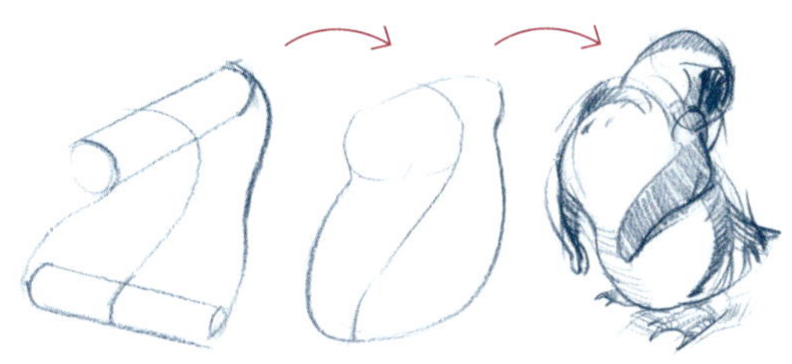

Elasticity, torque and tension

Create dynamic torsos in action by energizing bent shapes. In 'contrapposto', the figure's shoulders twist against the hips to create a dynamic twist of the torso. This gives life to static figures, imbuing them with a natural sense of movement, which might equally be seen in a penguin, for example.

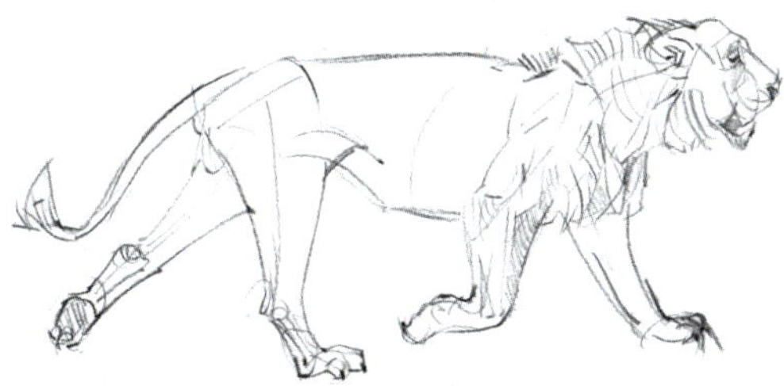

Gesture

A gestural line is an energetic sketch of an animal in action, created in seconds.

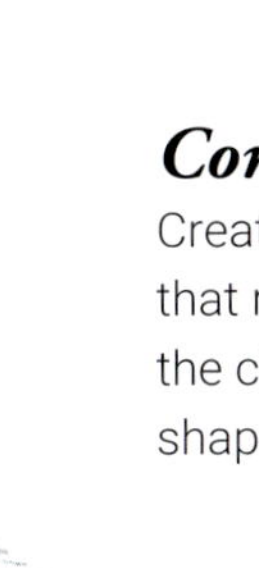

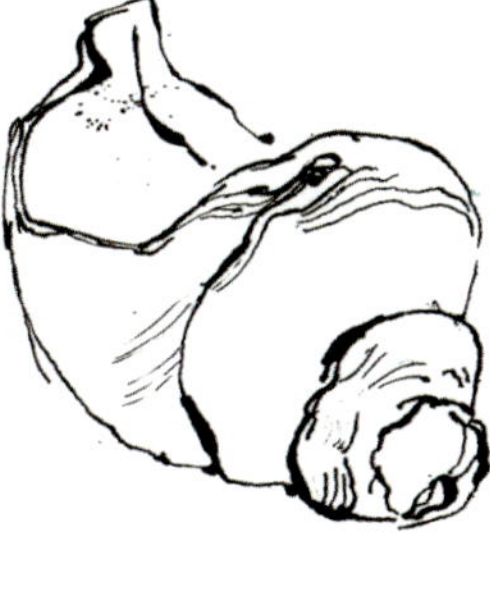

Contour

Create heavy lines that really bite into the character and shape of the form.

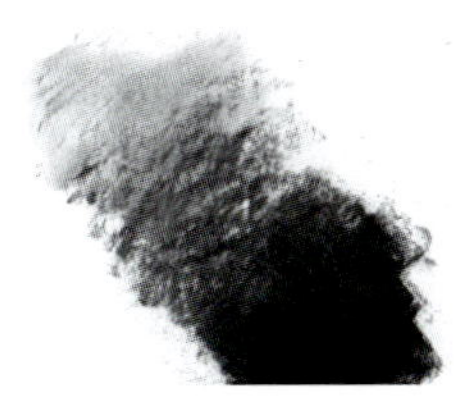

Atmosphere

Charcoal can make very light or intensely black lines with a host of mid-range tonal values, all of which can create different moods.

Contour Drawing

Your hand and eyes need training to create accurate reproductions of the world around you. Start by making a contour drawing – such as of a plant – whereby the form is cut out from the background with an outline. Then add further information, such as the inner contours of folded leaves. Finally, add small details, such as the delicate veins of the leaves, but do not add any shading. The main goal of these exercises is to train your hand and eyes to have synchronistic movement.

Drawing is, in part, a process of learning to see rather than following the assumptions we have stored in our minds. A good way to capture characterful lines is to take a line for a walk along the contours of your subject by imagining a pioneering beetle walking around the edge before exploring the inner terrain. Look at the subject longer than the paper – just flick your eyes over to monitor proportions.

Beetroot

Characterful beetroots make an excellent, readily available subject to sketch with its bulbous edible root, spindly trailing tail and wilting leaves offering contrasting forms and textures that give it a somewhat fairy-tale character.

Beetroot (*Beta vulgaris*)
The beetroot flavour, with its distinct colour and strong earthiness, is either loved or loathed. The beetroot came from coastal regions of Eurasia and was initially considered animal feed. The Greeks and Romans used the root and leaves as both food and medicine. Its powerful red dye has been used for centuries to colour fabric, hair and even food.

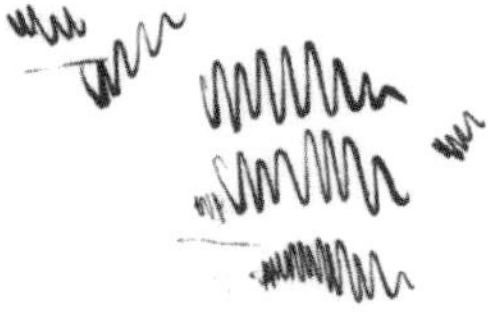

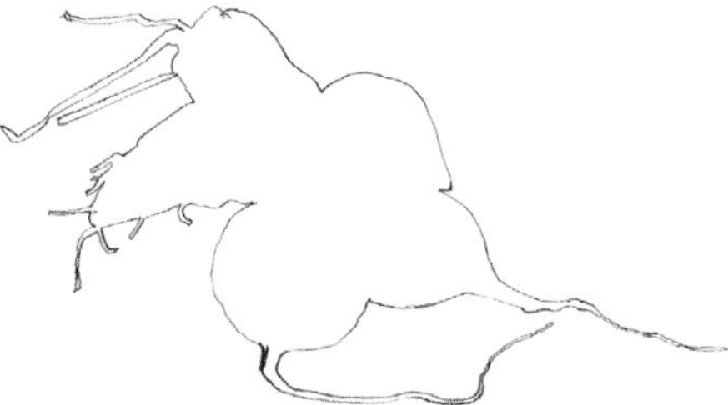

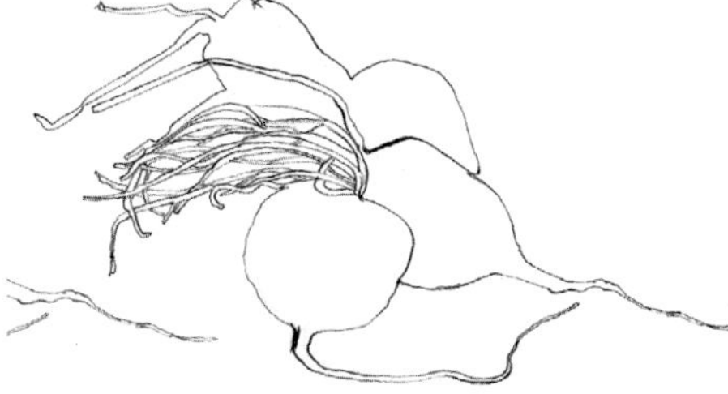

1 *Warm up with your dip pen nib by creating little squiggle marks on the corner of your page. The initial steps with any new medium can feel daunting at first, and the ability to create fluid lines with a medium that many find a little scratchy comes with practice, helped by using a high-quality ink.*

2 *Create an outline that cuts the form out from the background. Dip pen lines are strong, which is why they are favoured by cartoonists whose work appears in newsprint, where linear clarity is vital for image legibility, and their biting lines are ideal for scathing caricature portraits.*

3 *Overlap the lines to create the impression that one beetroot is in front of another. This is a simple convention loved by artists such as Henri Matisse, who, in his simple linear drawings, could imply with the slightest of an overlap that a shoulder was in front of a torso, a finger before a hand and the hand before the forearm, creating the illusion of both form and depth.*

4 *Draw inner contours that wrap around the beetroot, creating the impression of three-dimensional form. These lighter lines are topographic and can follow the growth rings of the vegetable, sculpting the illusion of form on the two-dimensional paper.*

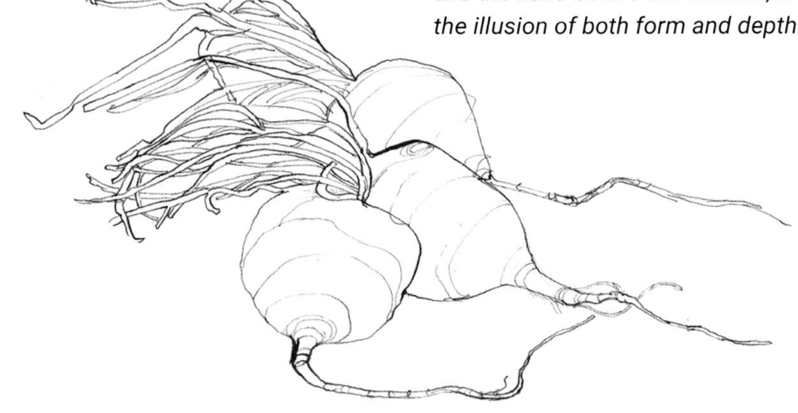

Ivy

Ivy was a popular subject in Pre-Raphaelite paintings, in which it was used as a decorative frame and created symbolic associations of ever-lasting life. With its heart-shaped lobed leaves, ivy is an excellent, readily available subject that offers the challenge of trying to capture the essence of its personality. Use a large sheet of paper so you can draw the plant in actual size and let your drawing grow to fill the page. Try your best to be honest in this exercise, capturing every nook and cranny, and sketch the veins that run like rivers breaking up into delicate streams with a finer line.

Common ivy (*Hedera helix*)

Ivy is an evergreen, woody climber that can grow to a height of about 100ft (30m). Its lobed dark green glossy leaves have pale delicate veins. The leaves of a juvenile plant have three to five lobes and a pale underside. On a mature plant, the leaves are oval or heart shaped.

Materials:

- 2B to 4B graphite pencil
- Large cartridge (drawing) paper or sketchbook
- Sharpener
- Putty eraser

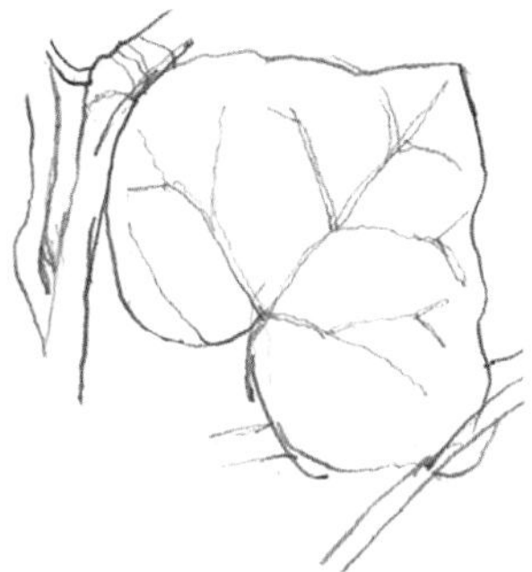

1 Place your ivy in front of you on a white piece of paper to avoid the visual noise of a background, and sit close to it. Choose a spot to begin mapping out your sprig – anywhere will do – and place the tip of your pencil on the paper.

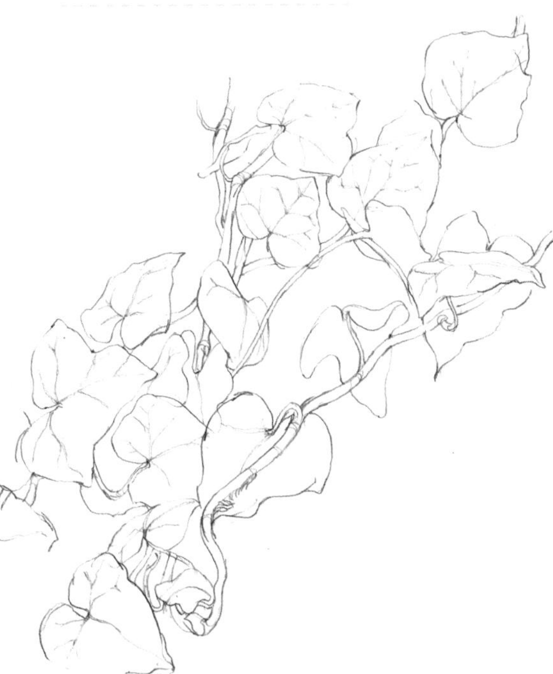

2 Imagine that the tip of your pencil is touching the ivy rather than the paper. Let your eye follow along the edge of the form as you move your hand in coordination. Try to get your pencil point to bite into the character of the form. Look at the ivy more than the paper, just returning a glance to keep the shapes roughly in proportion. Do this slowly and patiently, and avoid the temptation to speed up and make rough equivalents.

3 Not all the contours will lie along the outer edge of the leaves and twigs. There may be a folded leaf, for example. Draw these inner lines as precisely as the exterior lines and give them equal attention. Don't be afraid to have more than one go at delineating the contour. Even in some paintings by Edgar Degas, it is possible to see several lines as he searched for the character of a leg. Don't worry about the exact proportions. Practice will take care of this over time.

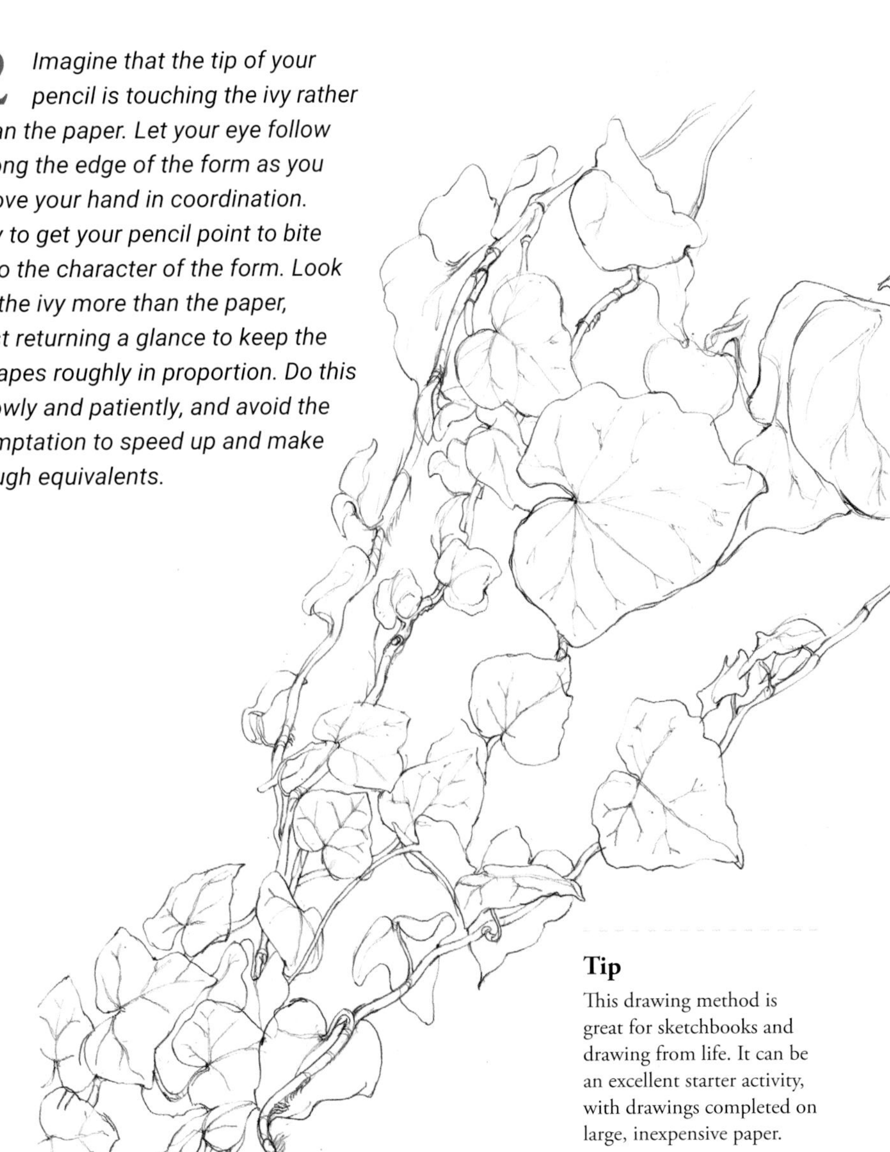

Tip

This drawing method is great for sketchbooks and drawing from life. It can be an excellent starter activity, with drawings completed on large, inexpensive paper.

Descriptive Lines

Providing extra details about a subject can lead to a descriptive drawing. By expressing light, shade and texture, your drawing will take on a more three-dimensional shape and realistic appearance. Successful descriptive drawing requires both honest observation and the ability to control your media to create marks that capture what you are witnessing. The emphasis should be on the quality of your line and textural nuances. Look regularly at the subject and quickly flick your eyes between the subject and the paper.

Starfish

With its wealth of detail, a starfish provides the perfect subject for a descriptive line drawing. Contour lines (see pages 40–1) cut out the overall form from space. More detailed lines, creating contrasting areas of rough and smooth textures, combine to show rugged ridges, spiky knobbly bumps and defensive protrusions. The overall effect is that the starfish looks three dimensional, although it is a drawing on flat two-dimensional paper.

1 *Start by handling the dried starfish to get a sense of its shapes and textures. Then, sitting very close to the subject, focus on your breathing while identifying a starting point. I find that descriptive drawings are created best in a calm state with keenly focused attention. Observe the organic shape of the starfish, with its undulating and irregular lines. They are likely to be flexible and lack a clear structure, and don't always take the same course.*

Materials

- Dip pen and ink
- Cartridge (drawing) paper or sketchbook

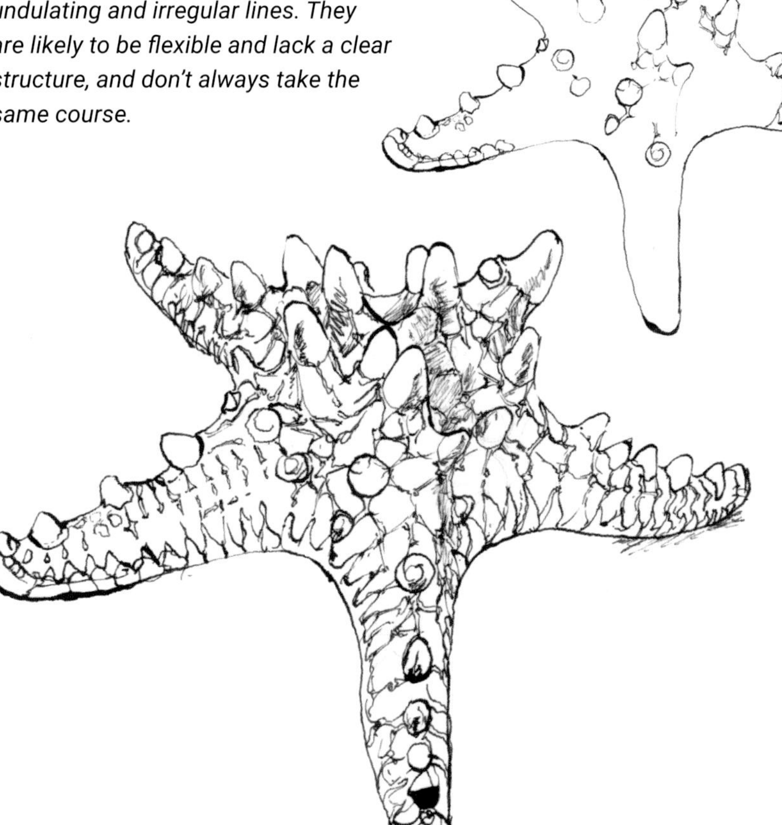

2 *When you are ready, imagine that the tip of your nib is touching the starfish and move it like a beetle walking around the silhouette and then exploring the interior landscape of the starfish. Start at the top and work down to prevent smudging, which I find is a good method when drawing with wet ink. Draw organic lines that are free flowing rather than geometric. As you draw, notice that the starfish has pockets of order and conventions of repeating tessellating shapes that break down into disorder and change scale.*

3 *Throughout the drawing, as you build on it use different types of marks for visual diversity. A line drawn quickly will have a more energetic quality than a slowly drawn one. Finally, add the smaller details, which will also help to give a sense of form.*

Scorpion conch

The surface of the shell of this sea snail has a number of spiny vertical folds, ridges and very fine encircling lines at its mouth. Shading can be created with a dip pen by repeating lines on top of each other.

Materials
- Dip pen and ink
- Cartridge (drawing) paper or sketchbook

Scorpion conch
(*Lambis scorpius*)

The scorpion conch (or scorpion spider conch) is a striking sea snail in which each finger of its shell resembles a scorpion's tail. It is detritivorous, meaning it is an organism that obtains nutrients by consuming detritus.

Tip

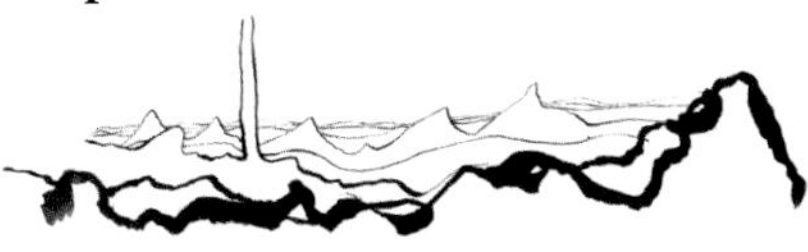

Experiment by creating an abstract landscape doodle. Make the lines in the foreground thicker and those in the distance thinner. Fatter, heavier lines will advance towards the eye while thinner lines will recede. Changing the amount of pressure you place on your drawing implement will modify line weight.

1 *Begin to sketch this gastropod by starting with the siphon, the tube-like structure protruding from its shell.*

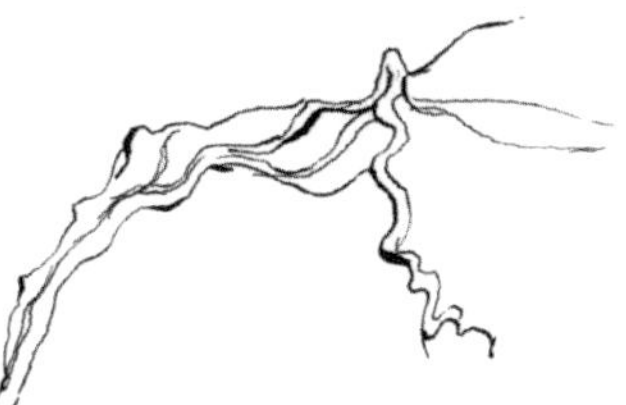

2 *Next, draw the contour line around the entirety of the shell, attempting to capture every nook and cranny of the undulating shape. Sketch in the interior contours, including the mouth opening.*

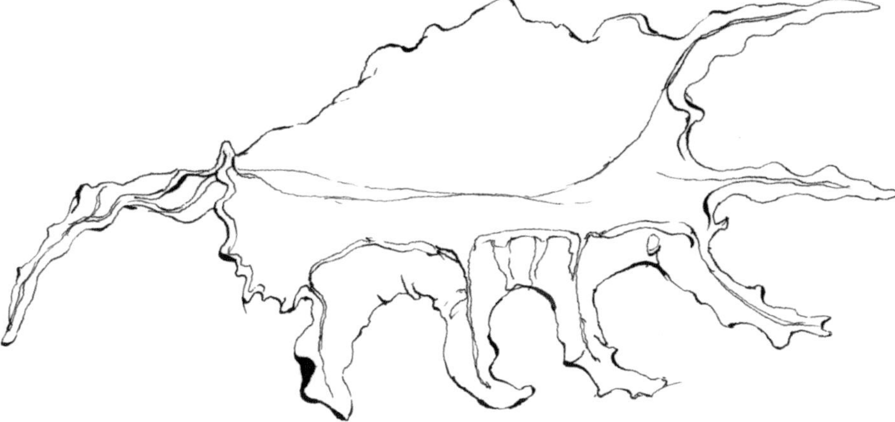

3 *To express volume, draw the ribbed, raised bands that curve around the body. Try to capture them with light, loose arching scribbles, starting at and working away from the aperture and gradually build on them, emphasizing the shadows.*

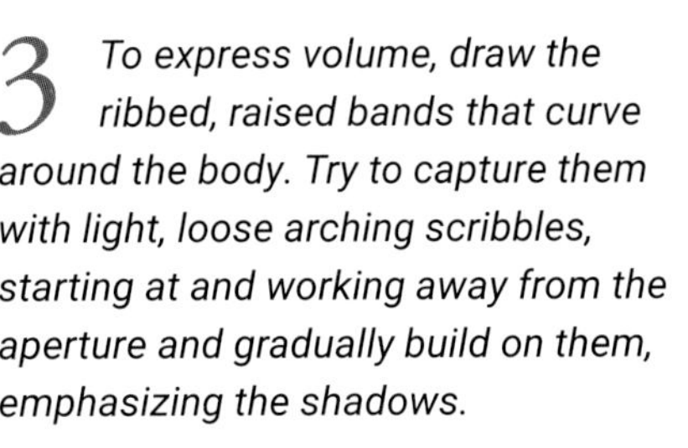

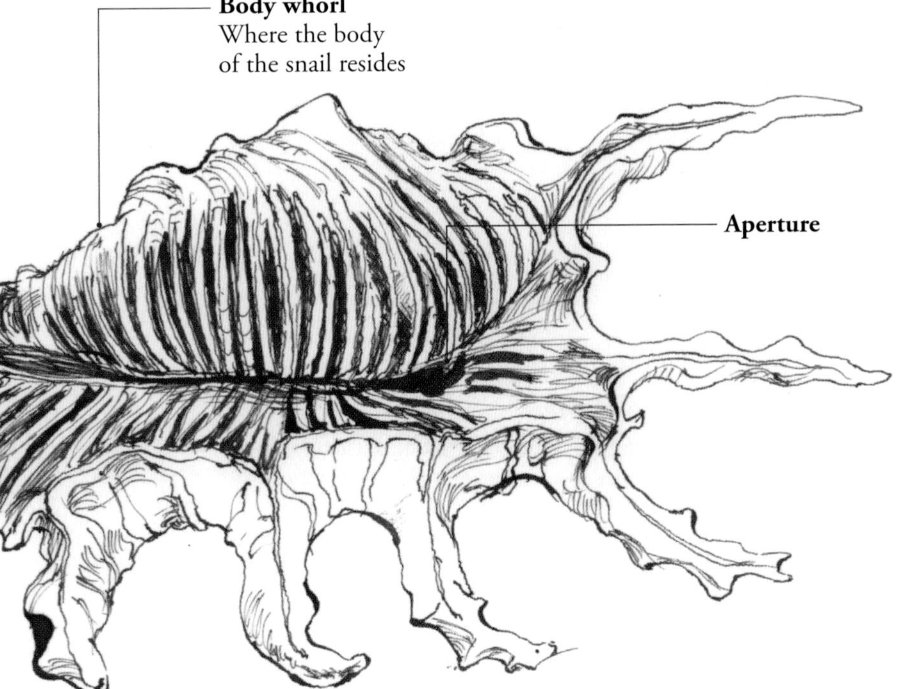

Construction Lines

Ghostly light construction lines can help you plan the subjects you want to draw by providing a framework that you can use to develop the rest of the image. Think of them as the frame of a house before the walls, windows and doors are added. I use construction lines in all of my drawings in a variety of ways. I draw construction lines lightly and they are always left in, although they tend to get superseded by the darker lines they provide guidance for. The more you practise these techniques, the better you'll become at constructing the objects you draw.

Fine-horned rhinoceros beetle

Placing a subject at a three-quarter angle below the eyeline, such as this beetle, creates a dynamic angle that gives the viewer a good understanding of the subject in three dimensions. Sketch a light frame – almost like measuring out a building plot – to help structure and organize the symmetrical body parts.

Materials
- Raw umber artist's quality colouring pencil
- Cartridge (drawing) paper or sketchbook

Five-horned rhinoceros beetle
(*Eupatorus gracilicornis*)
This beetle has four large horns on the prothorax and one extra-long cephalic horn. It has a pair of strong elytra to protect its delicate wings, which allow it to fly – although it does so clumsily owing to its size.

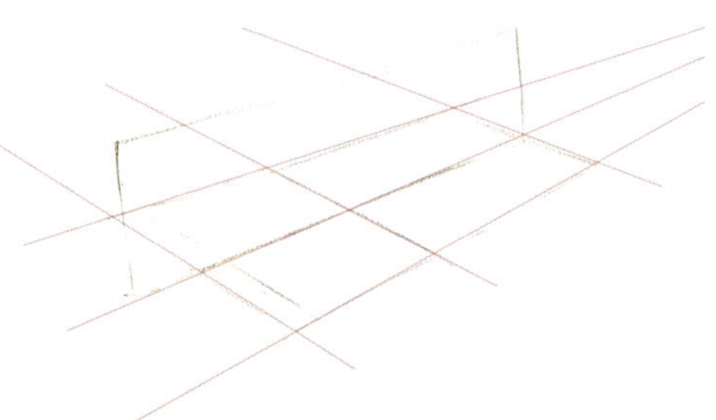

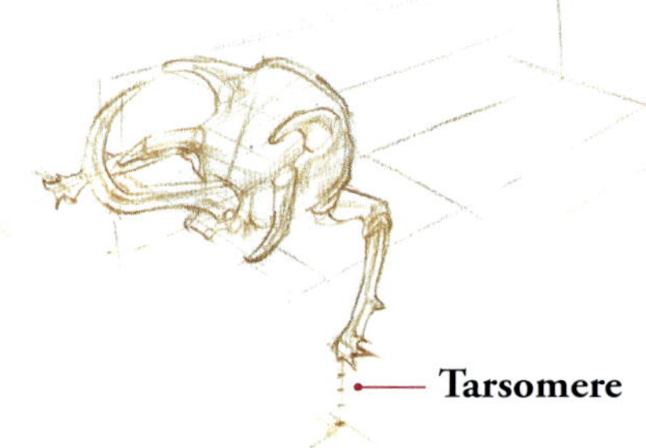

1 *Start by drawing a frame in multi-point perspective (see page 108) – this is when the vanishing points are off the paper – with divisions for the head, thorax and abdomen. Slice a vertical plane through the middle like a sheet of glass to create a scaffold to hang the bug on.*

2 *Next, sketch the head with its horn and wrap ellipse shapes around it to create cylindrical volume. Join the thorax (see pages 34–5 for insect anatomy) and make circles to plumb the horns into.*

3 *Add the legs by drawing them in segments. Initially, judge their angle and length by sketching in a skeleton line. Count the number of joints (tarsomeres) on the feet (tarsi), create four dots on the construction line and draw a light guidance line on the other side so the legs line up in symmetry.*

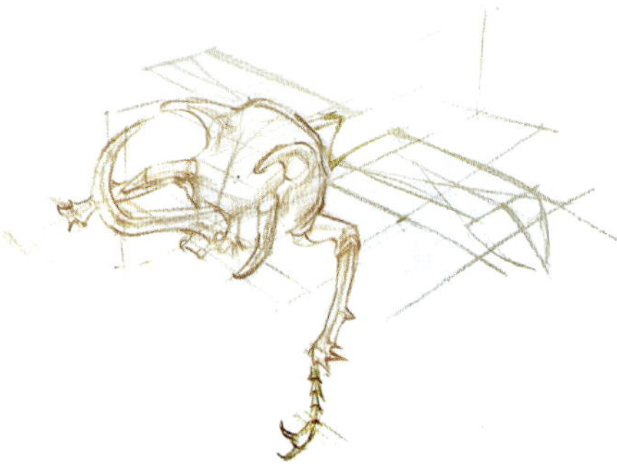

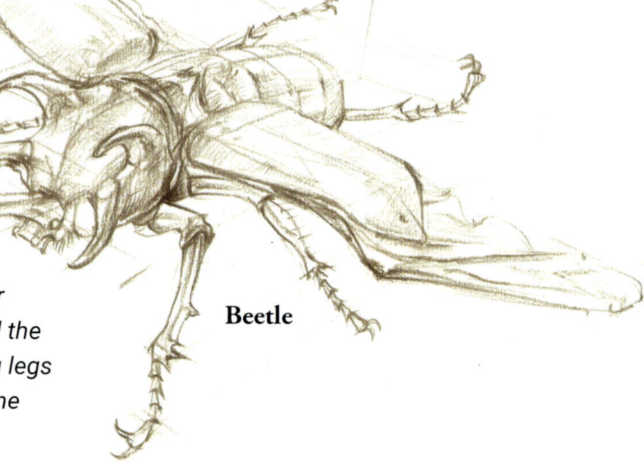

5 *Now draw the elytra and wings, starting with a rectangular shape and cutting the wing shape out.*

6 *Next, draw the gossamer wings, extending beyond the frames, and add the remaining legs using construction marks to line them up.*

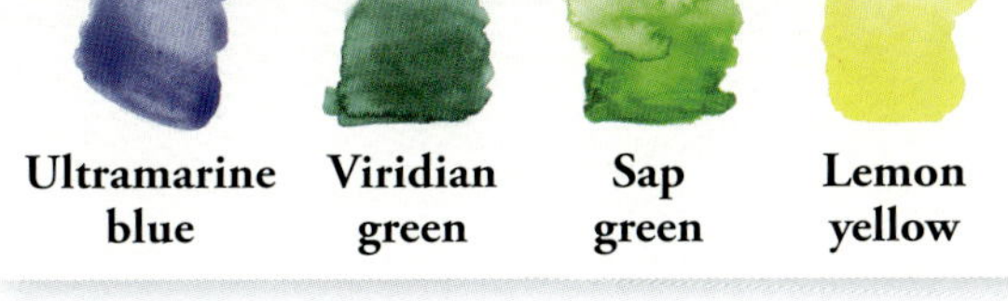

Drawing for watercolour

Preparatory drawing refers to any sketch of your intended subject made before beginning the actual watercolouring. It is critical to include only the boundary lines of shapes when drawing for a watercolour painting, allowing the watercolour to do the rest of the work. Rather than fill in the shape, I always draw, even with the brush. There are many types of lines: from thick, thin, zigzag, diagonals to the curly shapes of a pig's tail to explore, some created slowly, others fast. Lines are fundamental to my practice.

Silver birch

I always observe, draw and redraw, look and relook. I prefer to leave in working-out lines in the finished work, and sometimes it is impossible to see the underlying lines.

Tip:

Skeleton lines are the internal spine of a form. I use them to start a drawing where the subject is particularly thin, such as an insect's legs, the tentacles of a brittle starfish or a bird with a long neck. They are good for establishing the direction of travel and building confidence over positioning and the underlying shape.

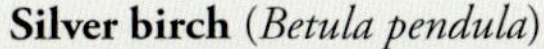

Materials

- Payne's grey artist's quality colouring pencil
- Watercolour paints (see swatches above)
- Cartridge (drawing) paper or sketchbook

Silver birch (*Betula pendula*)

The silver birch is a striking, medium-sized deciduous tree. They can grow up to 100ft (30m) high, and they have a patchy canopy with many sky windows between the leaf clumps and graceful, drooping branches. The snow-white bark turns dark and rough at the base as it sheds tissue paper-like layers.

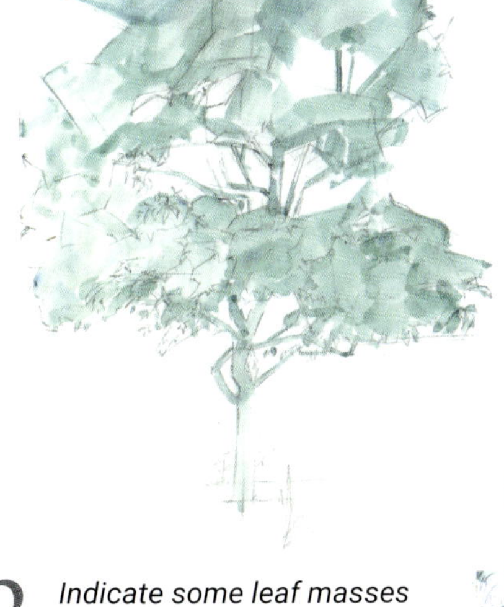

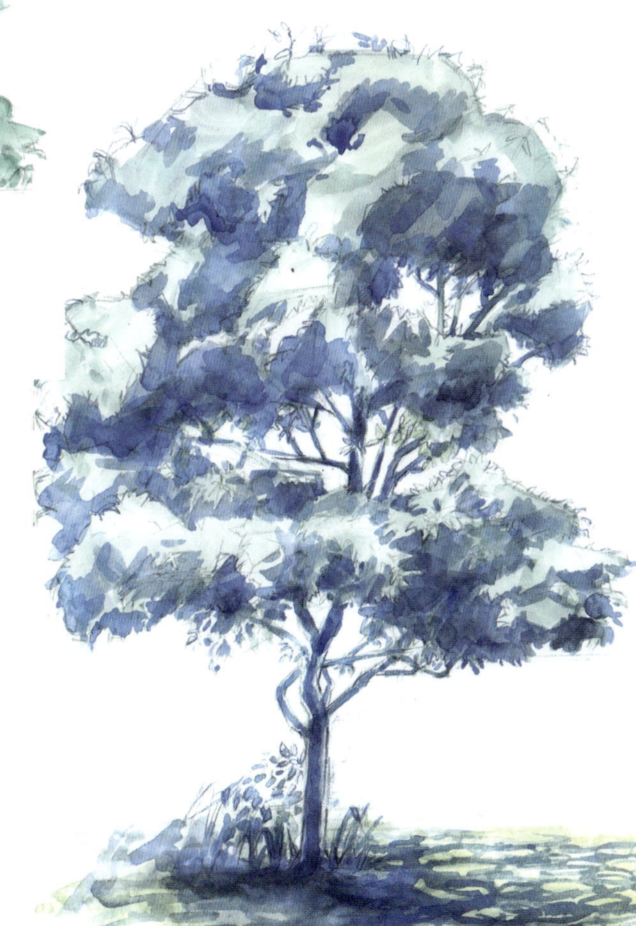

1 *Trees in foliage rooted to the spot in the middle distance will give you time to sit and observe the complex web of branches and leaves. Begin by selecting a point to start, sketching its positive and negative leaf window shapes and gaps between the branches (see pages 50–1). Hold up a vertical and horizontal and create comparative measurements (see pages 54–5) until the paper becomes peppered with small measurement dashes to help you judge the proportions. When drawing for watercolour, it is essential not to shade but just create a drawing of the leaf masses of light and dark clumps.*

2 *Indicate some leaf masses in front of others, and bathe some patches in shadow. Initially, apply a wash of the lightest and brightest colour over the entirety of the subject.*

3 *Next, return to the construction drawing beneath, which will give guidance to the areas of shadow. You don't need to stick strictly to these shapes, but observe again and redraw them with the brush.*

Shape

The profile of an object or subject against a background is recognized as its shape. This fundamental principle of art can portray a wide range of subjects in a drawing, in all of its immense varieties and sizes. All shapes are two-dimensional, having a length and width bordered by an outline in its most basic form. Shapes are commonly thought to have a closed contour like a trapped negative shape. However, I feel that there can be open shapes, too, such as the shape of the sky against the horizon.

Along with form (see page 74), shapes are one of the building blocks of any drawing and are created in the formative part of the work, and they can be the main focus. All shapes are essentially abstract, which, when combined, can create the appearance of something. They can be created by drawing the boundary of an object or through a change in adjacent colours, such as the pattern of a Friesian cow.

Shapes can be loosely classified as geometric and organic. Geometric shapes other than circles and ellipses are typically characterized by straight lines, angles and points. You'll find them everywhere in nature, from starfish, six-sided honeycomb cells, snowflakes, segmented fruit and shell spirals to spider webs and tree rings. Irregular, organic shapes can be characterized by being free-flowing, apparently orderless, such as ripples in water, twisted gnarled roots and billowing clouds to meandering rivers, the pattern on a jaguar and the myriad forms of coral.

We can respond to this breathtaking diversity with the type of mark we use to create shapes. It is much easier to get a sense of the character of a shape by studying your subject from first-hand observation. Shape contributes to the overall personality, from the spindly thin heron's leg to the mighty pillars of an elephant's leg. It can take time to tune in to these shapes, but after several warm-up sketches, you will begin to feel that you know your subject much better.

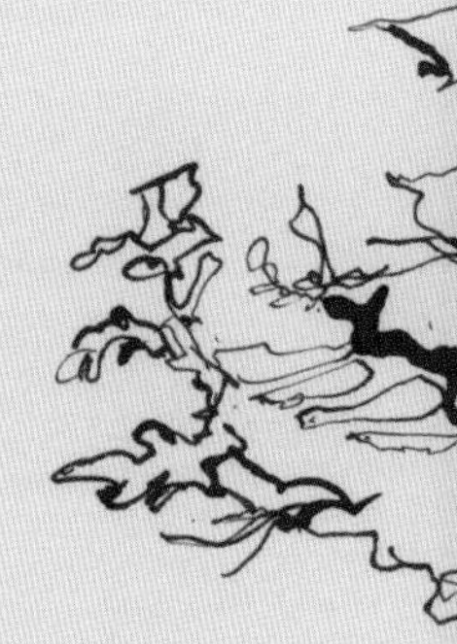

▶ **Oak tree in dip pen and ink**
This drawing is a compositional arrangement of shapes. I first identified a focal point: a window through the leaves to the blue sky, observing the negative shape. I did not attempt to draw individual leaves, but instead looked for clusters of leaves forming irregular clumps. For the leaves, I created an edge with a sketchy light mark. The shape of the trunk is delineated with a thicker bold line.

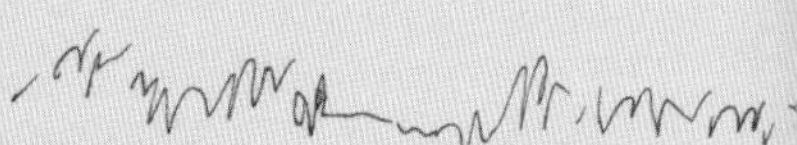

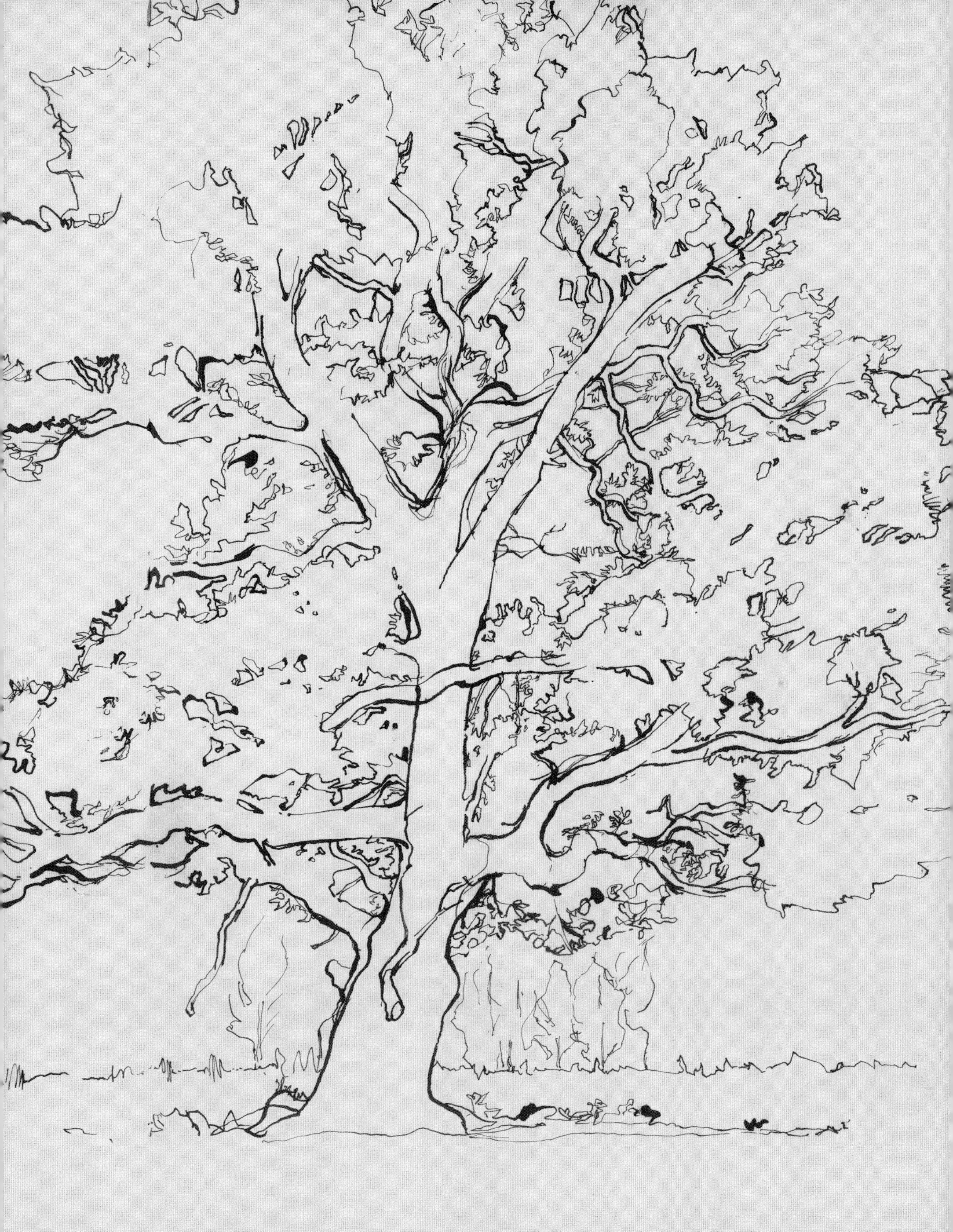

Shape Essentials

An important initial stage of any drawing is to become acquainted with the character of the two-dimensional, flat shapes that make up your subject. Capturing these shapes is key to expressing the personality of any subject in the natural world.

Organic shapes

Irregular, organic shapes come in a vast variety of guises, so try to develop a feeling for many different types, from hard and sharp flint to the softest ostrich feather. Careful observation of shape will help you capture the character of your subject. Touch the subject if you can to know it better. Their shapes can appear erratic, but artists should enjoy and capture these imperfections. Naturally, these shapes will differ slightly from one another even when they are repeated.

▼ Negative shapes

I created this drawing of bladderwrack by looking at the negative space as the positive (see pages 50–1). I found pleasure in walking the pencil tip around the undulating wobbly shapes as I tried to transfer this seaweed's unique personality to the page.

◄ Fearsome spikes

To capture the sharpness of cactus spines, I regularly sharpen my pencil to help me depict the tips with a flick mark.

► Abstract patterns in nature

Interlocking abstract liquid shapes of water ripples can be sketched with fluid curvilinear shapes that get closer together and smaller towards the horizon. Move your drawing implement by feeling the rhythm of the gently rocking water.

Geometric shapes

Geometric shapes come in a myriad of proportions. They can have numerous sides and corners and range from triangles, squares, rectangles, pentagons, hexagons, octagons, stars, snowflakes and so forth or can be completely round, such as circles and ellipses. These simplistic primary shapes are easy to understand. They can help construct both more complex geometric and organic shapes as well as forms.

Shapes in action

▶ Ellipses volumize form
Circles create organic construction lines.

▼ Combining shapes
Look for simple shapes in everything you draw, and combine primary shapes to create more complex ones.

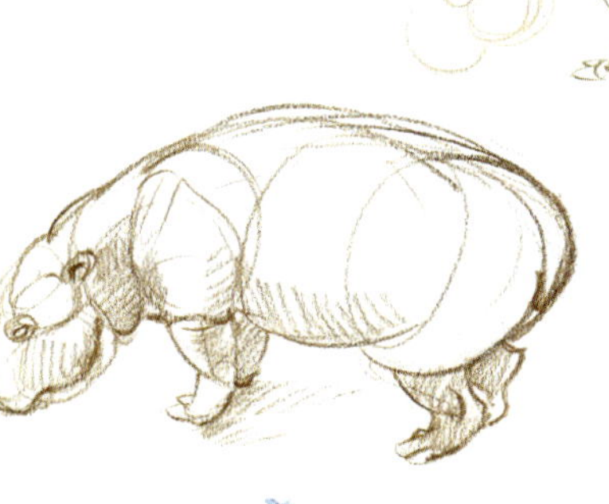

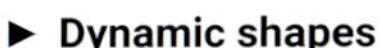

◀ Pentagon gizmo
A distorted pentagon can be used to structure a cat's nose and judge the distance between the eyes.

▶ Dynamic shapes
The converging lines draw the eye to the tip of a triangle and can move it through a composition. Triangular construction lines are useful in calculating the length and width of the beak.

Simple geometric shapes

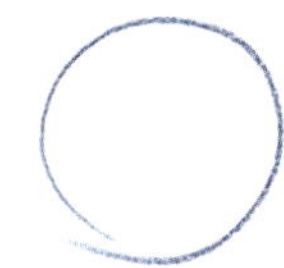

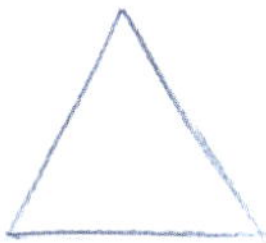

Circles and ellipses
Having no beginning or end, these shapes are associated with a sense of eternity. Planets are circular and the universe is elliptical. Because circles lack angles, they are softer than other geometric shapes. Circles and ellipses can be used as the building blocks of drawing many natural forms.

Triangles
Angular triangles create dynamic shapes that can create the impression of movement. An upright triangle represents stability and balance and is often used in composition (see pages 134–5). In contrast, an upside-down triangle creates a feeling of instability.

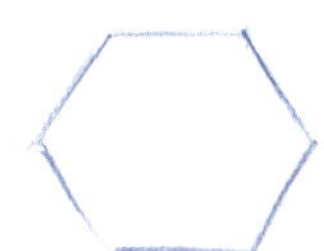

Squares
Squares and rectangles evoke feelings of trust, stability and authority. Divided into a symmetrical half, they become a valuable construction shape.

Polygons
Polygons are less common in nature but can dazzle the eye. Hexagonal cells in a beehive enable bees to efficiently use space using little wax.

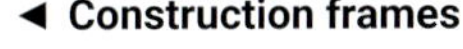

◀ Construction frames
Explore cubic box frames to make your drawings look three-dimensional.

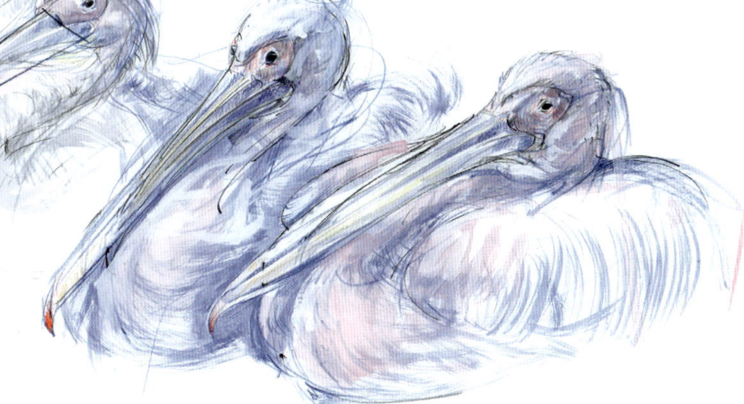

Negative and Positive Spaces

Creating clear drawings requires objectivity. We all have mental associations with the way objects appear, such as a violin or a chair. Learning to see them as positive shapes in space will make it easier to draw them as they actually appear rather than as how we think they should look. Drawing negative spaces will improve your proportions and ability to capture the character of the shapes. Trapped shapes will be easier to make sense of than open negative spaces that have no clear boundary. Start by working on one shape at a time and navigate your way around the entirety of your subject.

Positive shapes are the physical matter of the objects in a scene. White space, also known as 'negative space', is the empty space surrounding a positive space. It will allow composition space to breathe and give your eyes some space to rest. Negative shapes always appear further away from the viewer than positive shapes or subjects.

This drawing exercise is good for getting away from preconceived ideas of what you think your subject should look like. By concentrating initially on the negative space, the shapes of your subject will gradually emerge from the paper. I have carried out this tutorial with a bird of paradise flower, but it can also be done with any plant that has an interesting silhouette.

Bird of paradise

Every flower has its own personality. The bird of paradise flower, for example, has sharp spiky shapes compared with the softer arabesque shapes of an orchid. The way you move your drawing implement should be in sympathy with your subject's character.

1 *Start by drawing the shapes that surround your plant rather than the subject itself. I began this study by initially picking a focal point and sketching a jigsaw of small negative shapes, enjoying the interplay between the gaps and form. I tried to draw these shapes as precisely as possible.*

2 *From the initial area, move from shape to shape to unexplored territory, venturing from the trapped space to open space (see box, right). Try to draw neighbouring shapes rather than jumping around, keeping a close eye on proportions.*

Bird of paradise (*Strelitzia* spp.)
The bird of paradise flower, a native of South Africa, has banana-like leaves and bright architectural flowers. It is so-called because it looks a bit like a tropical bird.

3 *Allow the drawing to continue to take shape until the flower's personality emerges.*

4 *Add a sense of form by drawing light lines around the form, but don't add any shading.*

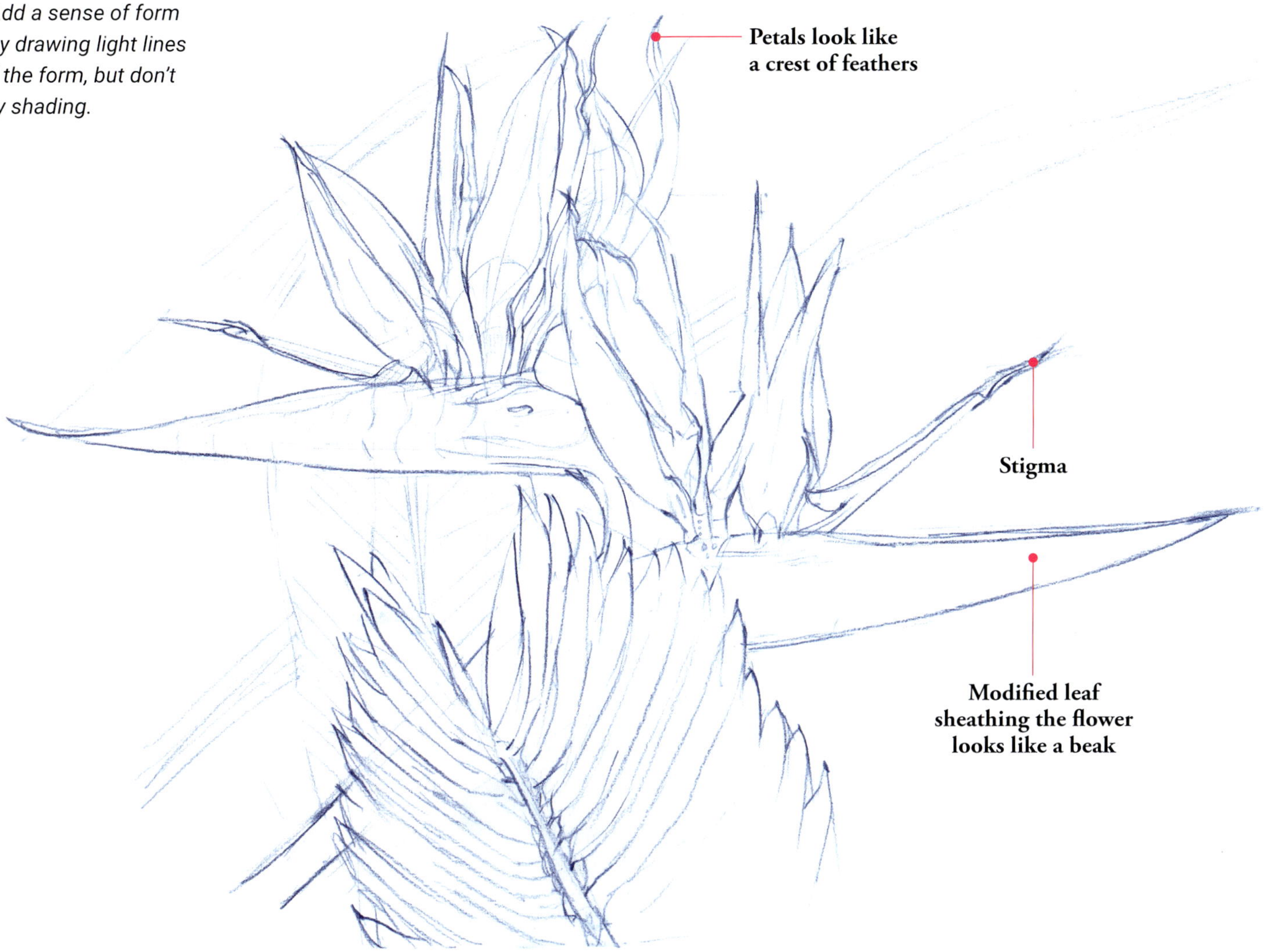

Trapped and open space

Trapped negative spaces refer to open spaces surrounded on all sides by positive shapes, whereas open spaces will have at least one free edge. Both trapped and open spaces create abstract shapes. Small trapped spaces are easier to understand than larger, more complex open spaces. Ask yourself, what does the shape remind you of? Is it a thin triangular shape, or perhaps roughly hexagonal or square? Is it an angular or a soft sinewy shape? These negative shapes capture the character of the positive forms and allow you to depict your subject by drawing space.

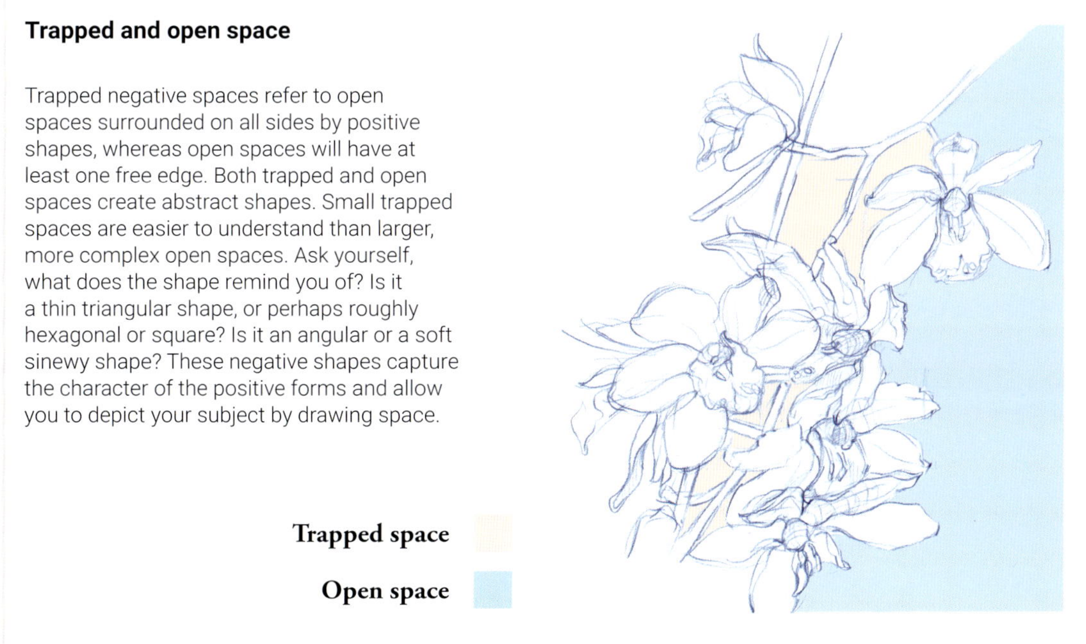

Trapped space

Open space

Sight-size Drawing

Getting the proportions correct of any subject can be a lifelong challenge, and when learning to draw it will be particularly tricky at the beginning. In life drawing, limbs can become too stretched like an elastic band and heads are often depicted too large. The sight-size method is a practical way to achieve accuracy by creating a drawing the same size as the subject. For me, this method works best when you can sit close to your subject – with faraway objects you will find yourself measuring tiny proportions.

The thumb-and-pencil method

There are a few tricks that are powerful tools to enable you to estimate the length and breadth of an object by comparing the parts against each other when drawing. One of them is the thumb-and-pencil method, which you can employ to estimate proportions and then check them with a fair degree of accuracy. This is done by holding your pencil (or wooden dowel, or thin paintbrush handle) in your hand and then holding it at arm's length between your eye and the object you plan to draw. Bring your pencil to your eye level and shut one eye. Use your thumb against the pencil as a gauge to measure the segments of your subject.

▲ Measuring angles

Fully extend your arm while holding your pencil either vertically or horizontally. With one eye closed, you can judge the angles of your subject by imagining a protractor attached to the pencil. You can check this angle on the page by placing a vertical or horizontal pencil against it.

▶ Incorrect posture

Be careful not to bend your arm or have the pencil on a slant. Both will distort your measurements.

▲ Correct posture

Close one eye and hold your arm straight.

Monstera monkey mask

Pot plants are a great still, unmoving subject with interesting shapes. Begin by plotting out the main shapes with light scant marks, then work your way to increasingly smaller shapes, gradually drawing everything together like a jigsaw puzzle.

Materials
- Black artist's quality colouring pencil
- Large cartridge (drawing) paper or sketchbook
- Sharpener
- Putty eraser

Monstera monkey mask
(*Monstera adansonii*)
Monsteras or Swiss cheese plants are known for their naturally occurring leaf holes, which some scientists believe allow sun flecks to reach light-hungry leaves below.

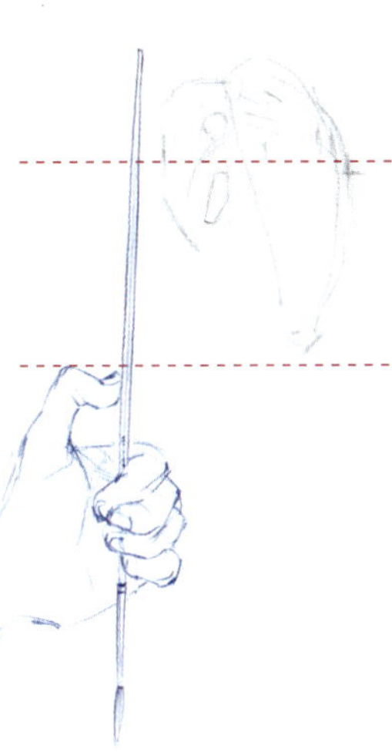

1 *Sit close to the plant and make some sight-size measurements, ensuring that you can fit the whole plant on the page. Spend a minute or two looking at your subject before starting a sketch. Carefully transfer these proportions onto the paper with dashed and crisscrossed marks. I prefer to use a thin upside-down, long-handled paintbrush to create longer measurements than a pencil allows.*

Compare the diagonal angles of leaf shapes by creating alignments across the paper

2 *Continually check the vertical, horizontal and diagonal alignments to help with proportions throughout the drawing process, always holding the paintbrush out in a similar manner. This method is like projecting graph lines onto your subject. The angle of the leaves can be determined by sketching the central vein. I sketch one leaf at a time, looking closely at the negative bean-shaped holes.*

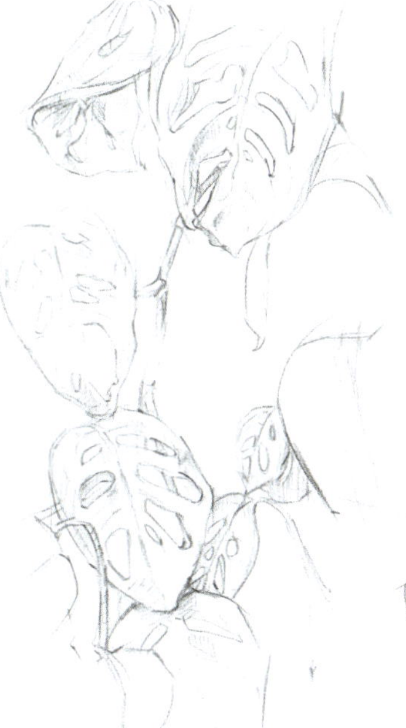

Hatched shading models the crinkles in the leaves and creates a sense of light by adding light's opposite: shadow

Darker shading pushes back into the shadows

3 *Particularly when plotting out at the early stages, continue to review and modify the shapes and leaf proportions.*

4 *Keep building up the drawing with perseverance and patience, and add tone with your preferred shading technique to emphasize the leaf forms and round stems.*

Comparative Measuring

Sight-size drawing can often result in tiny sketches. Comparative measuring means that you can draw at a more comfortable scale while still maintaining accurate proportions. The method involves taking one measurement, typically the length of a head, and using it as a unit to measure the size of the body and calculate its relation to other body parts.

Unlike sight-size, comparative measuring depends on scale, and it doesn't require that our drawings be the same size as the subject from your vantage point. You can draw as large or as small as you want. In comparative measuring, you will try to find the relative scale of any part of the subject to another. Do you need to know the length of the upper leg? Measure it on the subject and then compare it with another body part. The head is typically used as a measurement of scale on animals, but feel free to compare the scale of many other components.

Materials

- Yellow ochre artist's quality colouring pencil
- Light grey brush marker
- Fibre-tip fineliner
- Large cartridge (drawing) paper or sketchbook

Iguanodontia dinosaur (*Mantellisaurus atherfieldensis*)

This skeleton, displayed at the Natural History Museum in London, was reconstructed as a biped, but it is now thought that it would have been semi-quadrupedal, standing on all four limbs when stationary or moving slowly. The hand of each forelimb had a thumb spike, possibly to ward off predators, and the structure of the muscles inside its head indicates it had a long tongue. *Mantellisaurus atherfieldensis* lived in the early Cretaceous period, 125–110 million years ago.

Iguanodon skeleton

Sometimes I don't find it necessary to complete an entire underdrawing before adding the tone. With a proportional measuring frame structuring my sketching, I navigated my way along the dinosaur's body, sectioning off my focus on the challenge that each body zone presented. I intuitively swapped between the fineliner for linear qualities and a light grey brush marker for the tone. I worked my way from right to left, simplifying each item into abstract light and dark patches, going from an area I had understood to new territory, attempting to maintain proportions as the sketch grew. Note that the marker will stain the other side of the paper. You can follow these steps for drawing any dinosaur skeleton or other large-scale subject.

2 Now count the number of times the head fits into the body and guess at an appropriate transferable head scale unit that would mean you could fit the whole dinosaur across your paper, including the tail. For the iguanodon, nose to tail, I counted 11 heads. The distance between the head and the shoulders was about two heads, the end of the scapula five and so forth. Next, create short, vertical yellow lines horizontally across the paper by copying the new unit of measurement from your thumb to pencil tip. In my case I made 12 lines.

11

1 First, squint with one eye, which will stop binocular vision and flatten your view. With your pencil in your hand, hold your arm out straight to ensure a consistent unit of measurement. Slide your thumb along the pencil until it is at the tip of the iguanodon's horny beak and the point of the pencil is at the back of the skull.

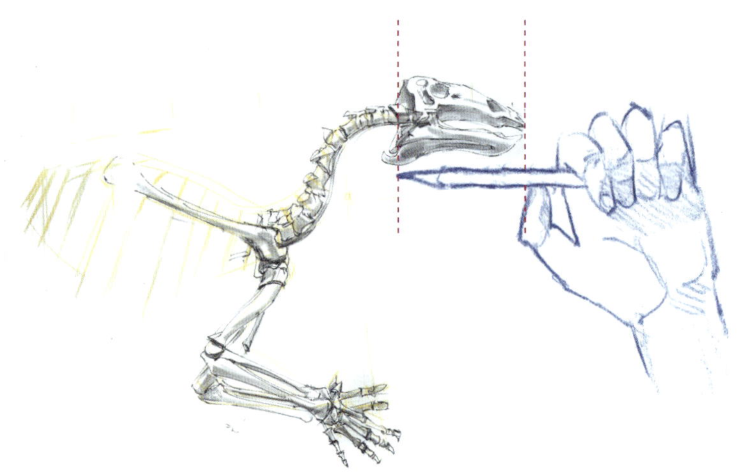

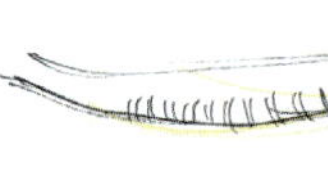

Holding up a vertical and horizontal

Look for comparative relationships. The tips of the fingers lie below the first two cervical vertebrae, the atlas (c1) and the axis (c2). The atlas allows for the rocking of the head and the axis the rotation. They can look a little different from the other cervical vertebrae. The atlas in some species can be as wide as the skull.

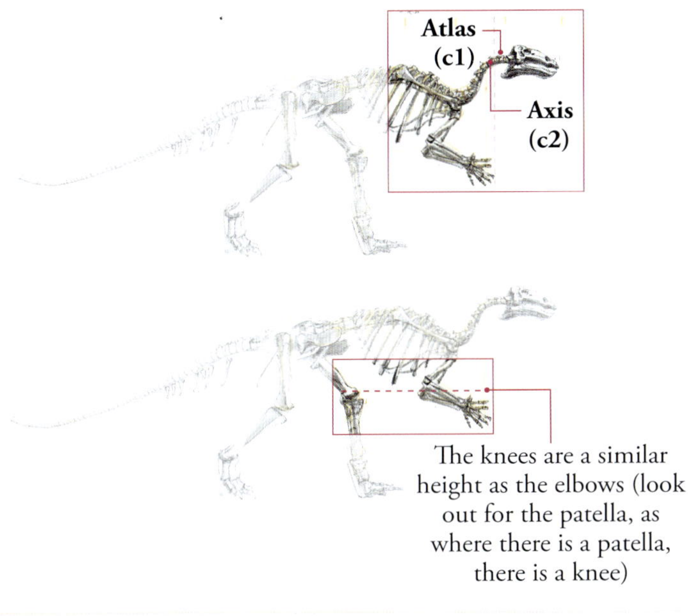

The knees are a similar height as the elbows (look out for the patella, as where there is a patella, there is a knee)

3 *Start working with a colouring pencil to sketch out a light armature before committing to an indelible fineliner mark. Break the iguanodon down into primary body zones and sketch nose to tail, shape to shape. Look out for landmarks, such as the shoulders, elbows and knees. By working in this way, you can break down the subject into mini-challenges, such as the head, the neck, the thorax and so on.*

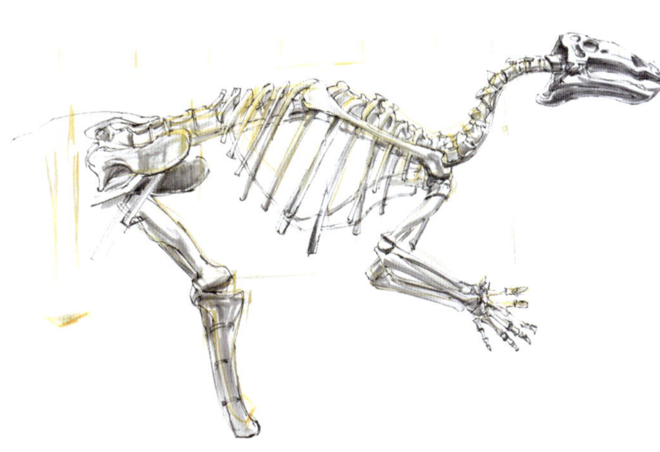

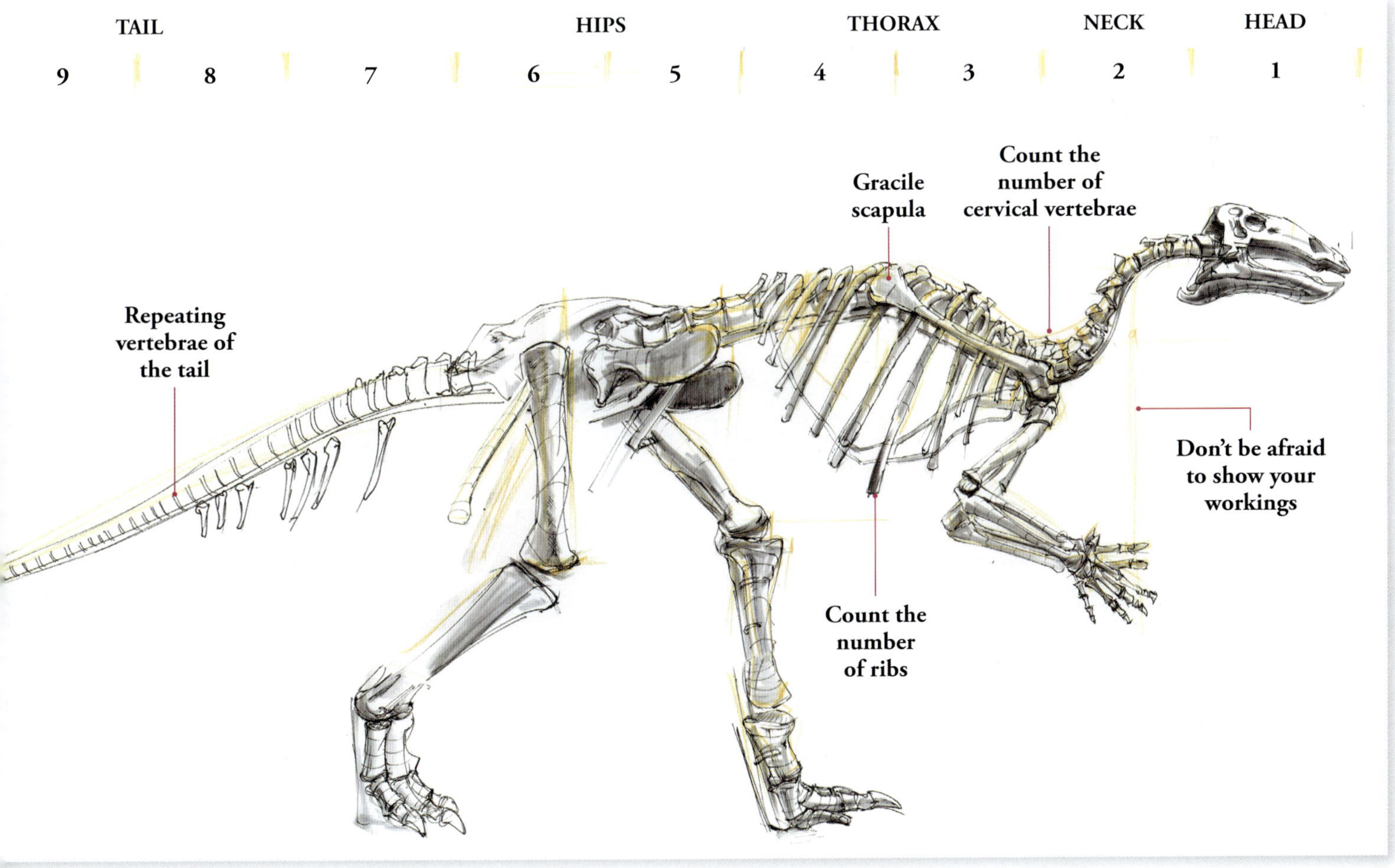

TAIL			HIPS		THORAX		NECK	HEAD
9	8	7	6	5	4	3	2	1

Gracile scapula

Count the number of cervical vertebrae

Repeating vertebrae of the tail

Don't be afraid to show your workings

Count the number of ribs

Drawing Giant Animals

Sketching giant animals is all about managing scale. Being close to these two giants during a museum visit, I chose a sight-sized approach for both the blue whale and the moa (opposite). Careful planning at the initial plotting-out stage is essential to ensure toes and tails can fit on the page. The easiest angle to judge proportions is from a side profile view. The skeletons themselves will really introduce the mechanics of the animal to an artist. Be on the lookout for unusual angles that can challenge your sketching skills and introduce you to new ways of looking at a familiar subject.

Natural history museums often suspend cetacean skeletons from the ceiling, which you can sit beneath to capture dramatic diving poses. Held like a puppet on a string, a rod is placed beneath the central vertebral column that acts like an armature for all the other bones.

Materials

- Indigo artist's quality colouring pencil
- Large cartridge (drawing) paper or sketchbook
- Sharpener
- Putty eraser

Blue whale skeleton

In this foreshortened view, the massive barrel of the chest is dramatically compressed and the rostrum appears elongated. I frequently flicked my eyes from viewing the subject to the page as I attempted to tackle the whale's structural make-up, taking lots of sight-sized measurements.

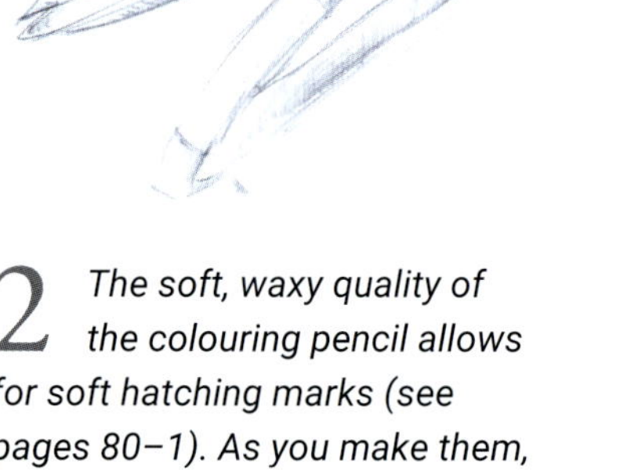

1 *Sit on a sketching stool beneath the suspended skeleton, where you will have a dynamic viewpoint. Begin your sketch lightly as you search for the character and proportions by looking at both negative and positive shapes. Try to get an understanding of one area and let the drawing grow from there, creating darker tones as the picture progresses like a photograph in a developing tray.*

2 *The soft, waxy quality of the colouring pencil allows for soft hatching marks (see pages 80–1). As you make them, purposefully angle them along the various planes of the bones.*

A rostrum is a beak-like structure that is found on some cetaceans

3 *Patiently observe and build up the drawing until it takes on shape and solidity.*

Moa skeleton

Although it is generally taught to work up all the parts of a drawing at the same time, for me this isn't the case. I have seen examples of some of the greatest draughtsmen, such as Rembrandt, completely finish an area of an etching while other areas appear virtually untouched.

Materials

- Indigo artist's quality colouring pencil
- Light grey brush marker
- Fibre-tip fineliner
- Large cartridge (drawing) paper or sketchbook
- Sharpener
- Putty eraser

1 Begin by creating a light armature in a blue colouring pencil. To help capture the posture of the pose, measure the angles and proportions. Hold up verticals at the toes to see where they are in relation to the ribcage.

2 With the scaffolding in place, you now have a supporting guide to hang loose fineliner details. Work beak to tail, going from one abstract shape to the next. Squint to reduce the detail. Initially sketch the line and then add tone in tandem.

3 Work with both marker and fineliner, regularly swapping between them until the sketch is complete.

Tip

Markers are good dry media you can use in a museum without making a mess. The tip of a fineliner can create sketchy, dynamic marks and the brush marker can get the shading down quickly.

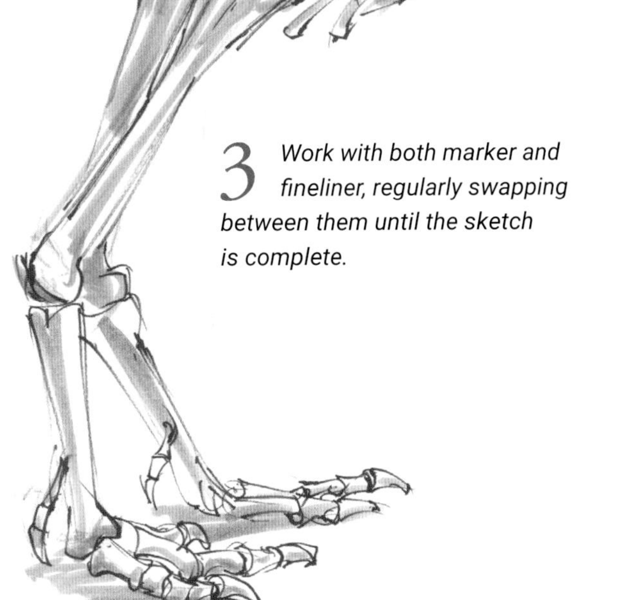

Gesture Drawing

Instead of focusing on the subject's appearance, gesture drawing focuses on what it is doing. To help you capture the dynamics of the subject's movement, you imagine doing it with your own body. Work quickly and with determination; it may feel like you're scribbling at first, but this is part of the process. You're not looking for a precise edge but rather the energy of the pose or line of action.

It takes a lot of concentration to translate an animal's unique shapes and movements onto paper. The best place to practise gesture drawing is directly through first-hand observation at a zoo, farm or aquarium. Working with live animals also creates a bond between the artist and the subject.

When sketching a moving subject there is a necessity to get the information down quickly. By speeding up, in the struggle to get your subject down on paper, your mark-making can create vigorous, spontaneous qualities in your sketch. This can bring a sense of dynamism to the study, which in turn can have emotive qualities.

A good understanding of the anatomy of your subject will support your action analysis and help you draw a convincing pose. Familiarize yourself with the pivot points of the skeleton and have a clear understanding of where the elbows, wrists and ankles are to help freeze the pose and articulate the limbs.

To begin with, I suggest working with a dark soft pencil, which is a direct and uncomplicated medium, and then you'll be ready to explore a range of different techniques. You will need to capture the essence of the pose in a few fleeting marks. Flick your eyes between the subject and your paper, and try to concentrate more on the subject than your drawing.

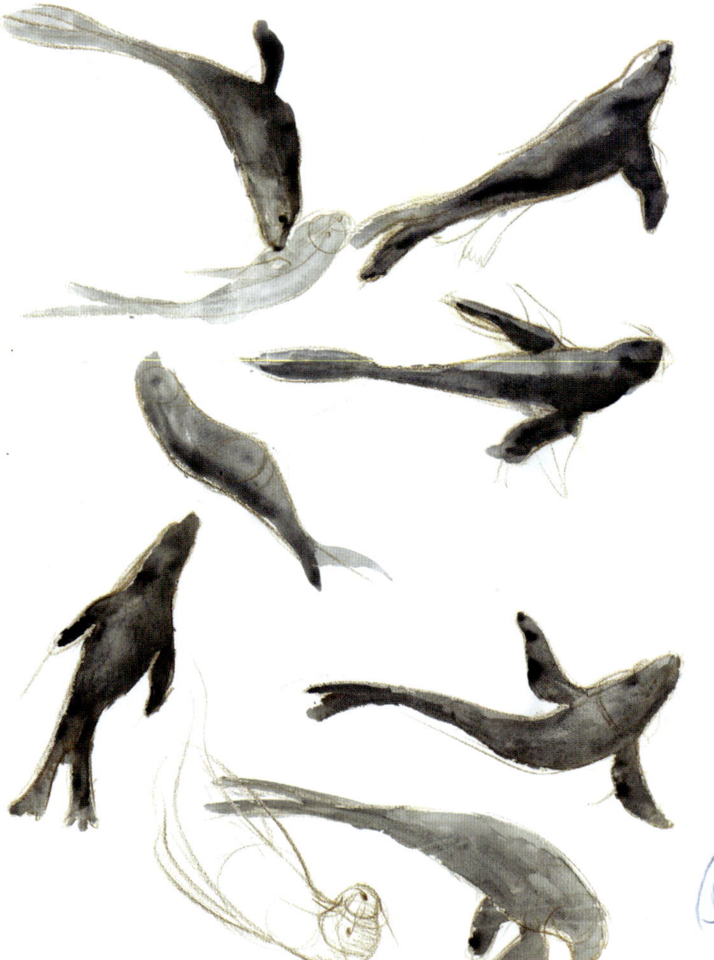

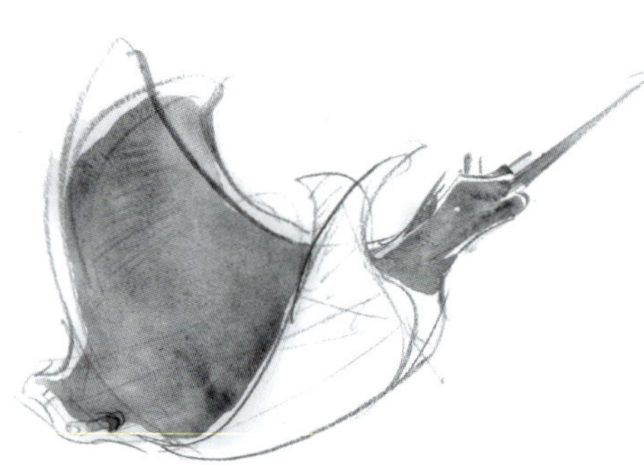

◄► Mixed media
Experiment with different materials and try something new. I used an ink wash with a granulating medium in these studies.

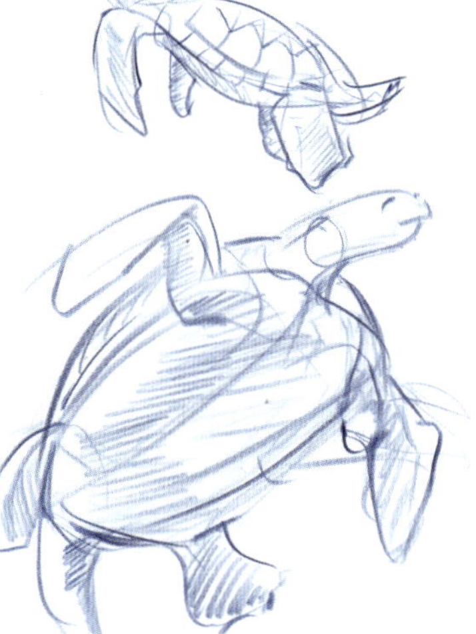

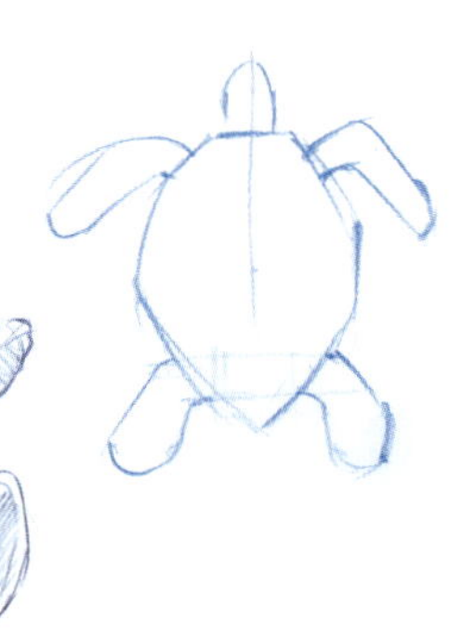

▼ Having an anatomical framework
Before beginning any study, you should create a body plan sketch, from nose to tail, by breaking the body down into simple shapes. This device, which I call a widget (see page 15), will allow you to rotate and imagine the form from various angles.

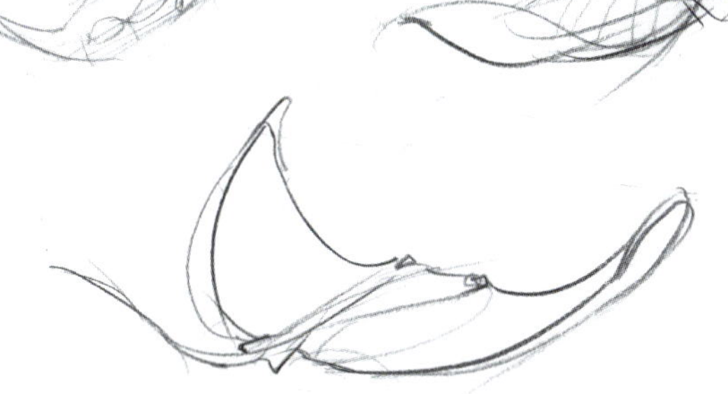

▶ Long lines

Create long rather than short lines to help express the gracile movement of cheetahs and other animals. To draw long lines, pivot from your shoulder, moving your entire arm, rather than making short movements with your wrist or fingers. Try to remember that you are not a camera; your drawing can be interpretative, almost an exaggeration, getting to the heart of the pose.

'People call me a painter of dancers, but really I wish to capture movement itself.'

Edgar Degas

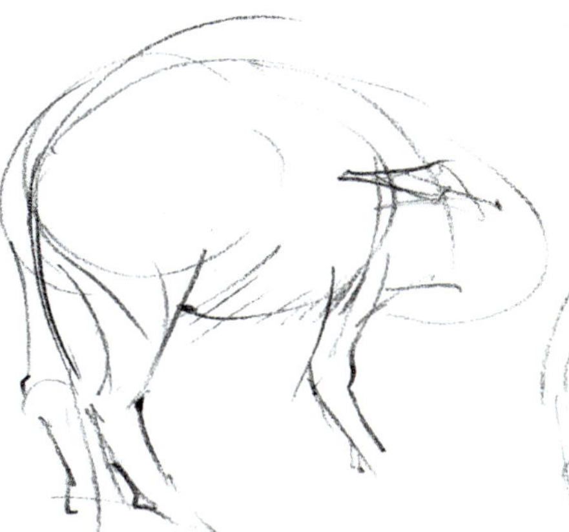

▲ It's the little things

Get a sense of the scale of the animals you sketch by drawing them at an appropriate size.

▲ Movement as dance

Think of the animal's movements like a dance and feel yourself going through the same motions. Keep your wrist and entire arm loose to create fluid lines.

▼ Revealing personality

Dive in and try to capture the character and posture of the animal. You will discover a lot of repetitive behaviours, such as preening. Markers can create quick brush marks that put shading down at great speed with vigour, which will capture the animal's energy.

▲ Basic forms

The time it takes to capture the pose may be longer than the animal maintains its pose. So practise developing visual memory and taking mental snapshots. A busy red river hog could be constructed with simple tube forms emerging from the body's elastic barrel. Don't be discouraged if you only have a few seconds to capture a sense of the pose and it results in just a few scribbles. You will still be gaining experience.

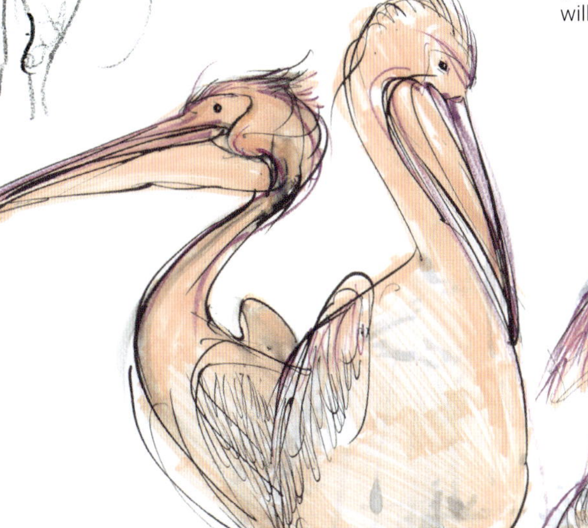

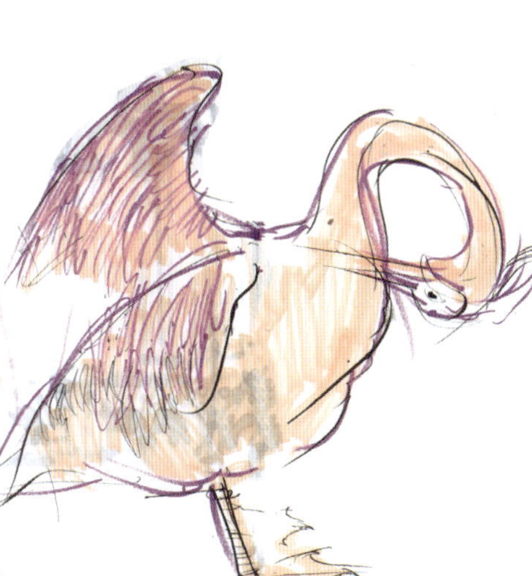

Animal Portraits

Drawings of people are not the exclusive subjects of portraits. A portrait drawing is typically an artistic depiction of a face that focuses primarily on the subject's personality and expressions. The intention is to express the subject's likeness, temperament and personality.

There is a thrill in getting acquainted with a new species while drawing. Before you start sketching, consider the animal's habitat and habits, and how its anatomy may have adapted to these conditions. I always observe an animal subject for a while before making any mark on the page, watching how it moves and looking out for any habitual movements. When drawing a live animal, I quickly switch from one sketch to the next, starting and stopping every time the animal moves, to make a study sheet (see pages 16–17). For this exercise, I made a study sheet of a sleepy fennec fox, although a cat, dog, rabbit and other pet will easily suffice as a subject.

Trying to capture moving or dozing animals from life will help bring the drawings to life, making the animals appear alive on paper. Wild animals are not likely to sit for a portrait, so the study sheet will result in a combination of many different views. Each pose will allow you to get closer to the animal's character, as you search for its proportions and shapes.

Fennec fox

Canids are a group of animals that come in a great variety of shapes and sizes, from the long-legged maned wolf to the short-legged sausage dog. Each species is distinct in shape and size, either through natural or human-made selection that results in specific characteristics. Amongst these are the individual personalities that you will really get a sense of when spending time with them.

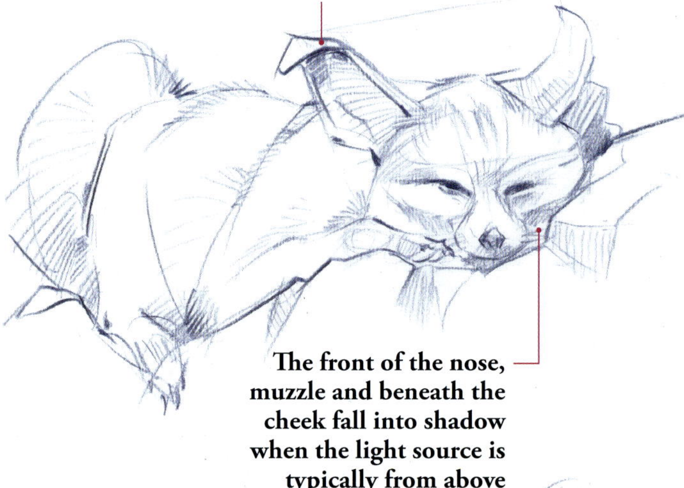

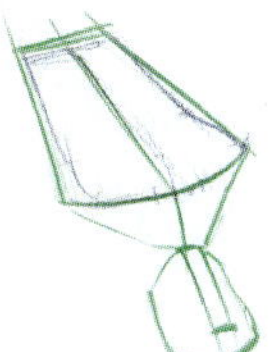

1 *Begin by creating the shape of the animal's forehead and establishing a line of symmetry. Make a triangular shape where the eyes will fit.*

2 *Make smooth ellipsis shapes to faintly create ghost lines of the cheeks and eyes. Sketch in the nostrils with a slit at the side, which enables exhaled air to come out of the side so that the fox can sniff fresh air and pick up new smells.*

3 *Finally, create shading with hatching (see pages 80–1), following the form and fur. Make lines that intentionally overlap to convey that one form is in front of the other: the head at the front, then the neck, torso and finally hindquarters.*

Study Sheet: *Fennec Fox*

A sequence of study sheet sketches introduced me to the subject's distinctive shapes. By breaking the head into a series of simple abstract shapes – I prefer to think of a head with a three-dimensional cranium and protruding snout rather than a face with two-dimensional eyes, nose and mouth – they can be combined to create a representational drawing.

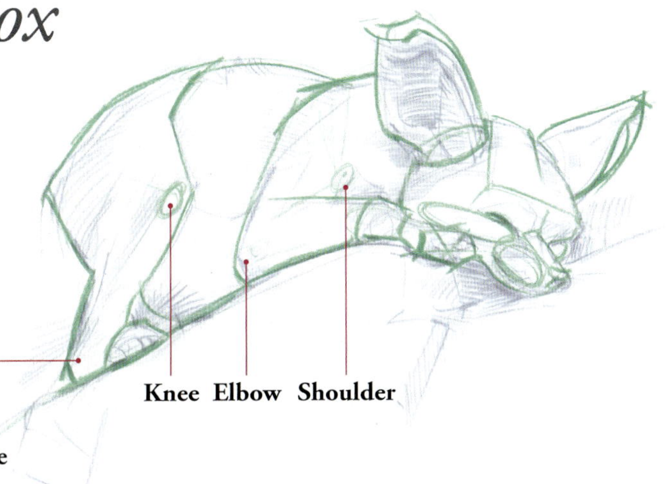

▶ Finding personality

Starting with the head, sketch the cranium by making a lightly drawn box and connecting a box to it to house the projecting muzzle. Work shape to shape along the animal's body until you get to its tail. Constantly evaluate the angles of the limbs and body and their proportions in respect to those of the head. You can do this by holding up a horizontal and vertical (see pages 52–3) and creating comparative measurements (see page 54–5).

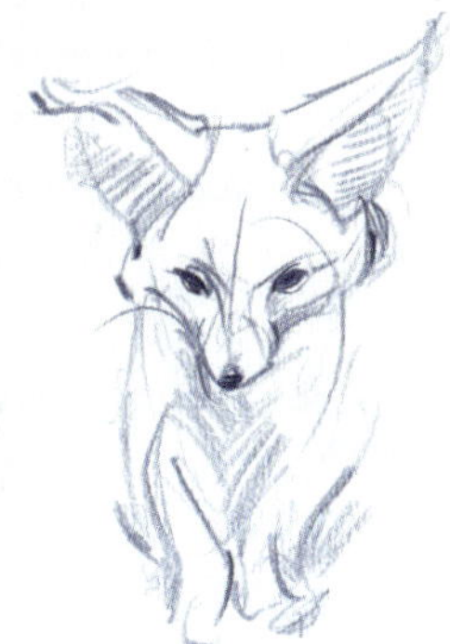

▲ Foot gizmo

Draw a pentagon with a cross in the centre. The front two toes are in front of the back two.

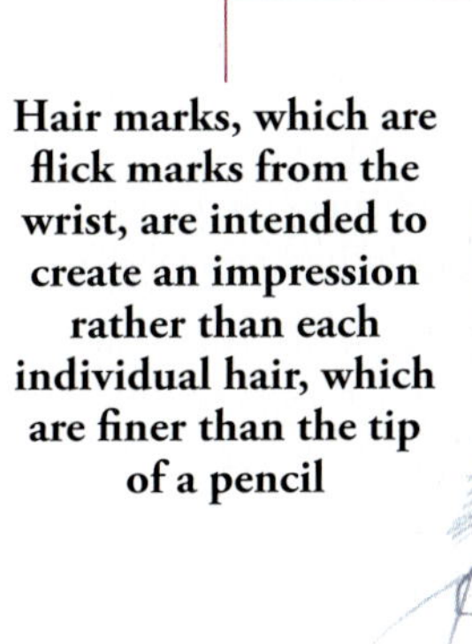

Hair marks, which are flick marks from the wrist, are intended to create an impression rather than each individual hair, which are finer than the tip of a pencil

Overlapping lines create the convention that one shape is in front of the other

▼ Familiarize yourself

Even the slightest change in pose can be drawn repeatedly in a study sheet as you familiarize yourself with the shapes of the eyes, nose, ears and paws.

▲ Warm-up

Quick warm-up exercises are helpful for acquainting you with the characterful shapes of the fennec fox.

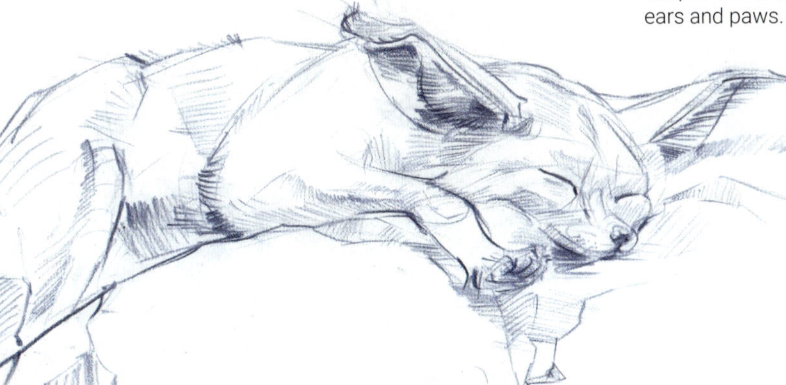

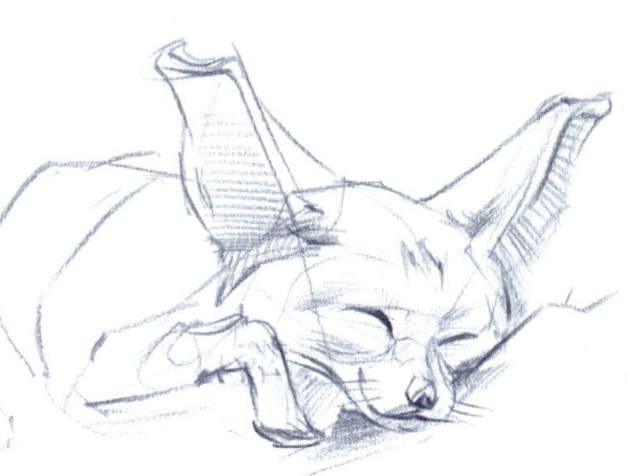

Tone

Whereas a line concentrates on the edges of the exterior or interior, tone refers to how light or dark an area is, and it addresses the surfaces and the whole of the subject. Tone plays an essential role in nature. When an apple turns red, its tone darkens, allowing animals that see in black and white to recognize that it is ready to eat. The orange pelt of a tiger appears to us to be an odd choice of colour for camouflage, but when seen in black and white, as its prey does, the tiger blends in seamlessly with the background. Penguins dress in a value pattern. Their counter-shading tuxedo uniforms help them survive in their aquatic habitat by blending in with the dark ocean depths from above and the shimmering sky when seen from below.

A true tonal drawing is devoid of colour: it relies on the artist's ability to translate the colours in a subject or scene into one of tonal variety, making it the artistic equivalent of taking a black-and-white photograph. Of course, tonal drawings can be created in various media and colours. In the Renaissance, artists such as Michelangelo favoured red chalk drawings, one of the earliest earth pigments. Michelangelo skilfully used sharpened chalk sticks and varied the pressure to create delicate nuances in muscular shading.

Tone can be created in a host of different ways, depending on the qualities of the media at hand. From cross-hatching with a dip pen to varying the pressure of the side of a small piece of charcoal to liberally scribbling with a soft pencil. Shading can be created informally with casual strokes or more mechanical cross-hatching or even dotting. Do what feels right to capture your subject, for example using a brush pen for a fast render or a pencil for shading at a slower pace. I tend to react to any subject through intuition rather than by method. Different media have different strengths. Wash work, for example, is suitable for producing large continuous areas of a single value, whereas charcoal can be graduated to make very light or intensely black tones.

▶ **Oak tree in charcoal**

Trees are a prominent feature in the warm climates of the temperate and tropical zones. Trees provide a myriad of microhabitats for countless animal species, creating a web of interdependent relationships that have evolved together over millions of years. The oak tree is no exception, being a giant in the world of housing biodiversity. In this charcoal drawing, I envisaged the trunk as a huge, three-dimensional barrel with tapering cylinders branching of this central column. Cast shadows from the branches wrap around the trunk and other branches as they sweep around the curved surfaces, which helps to express volume.

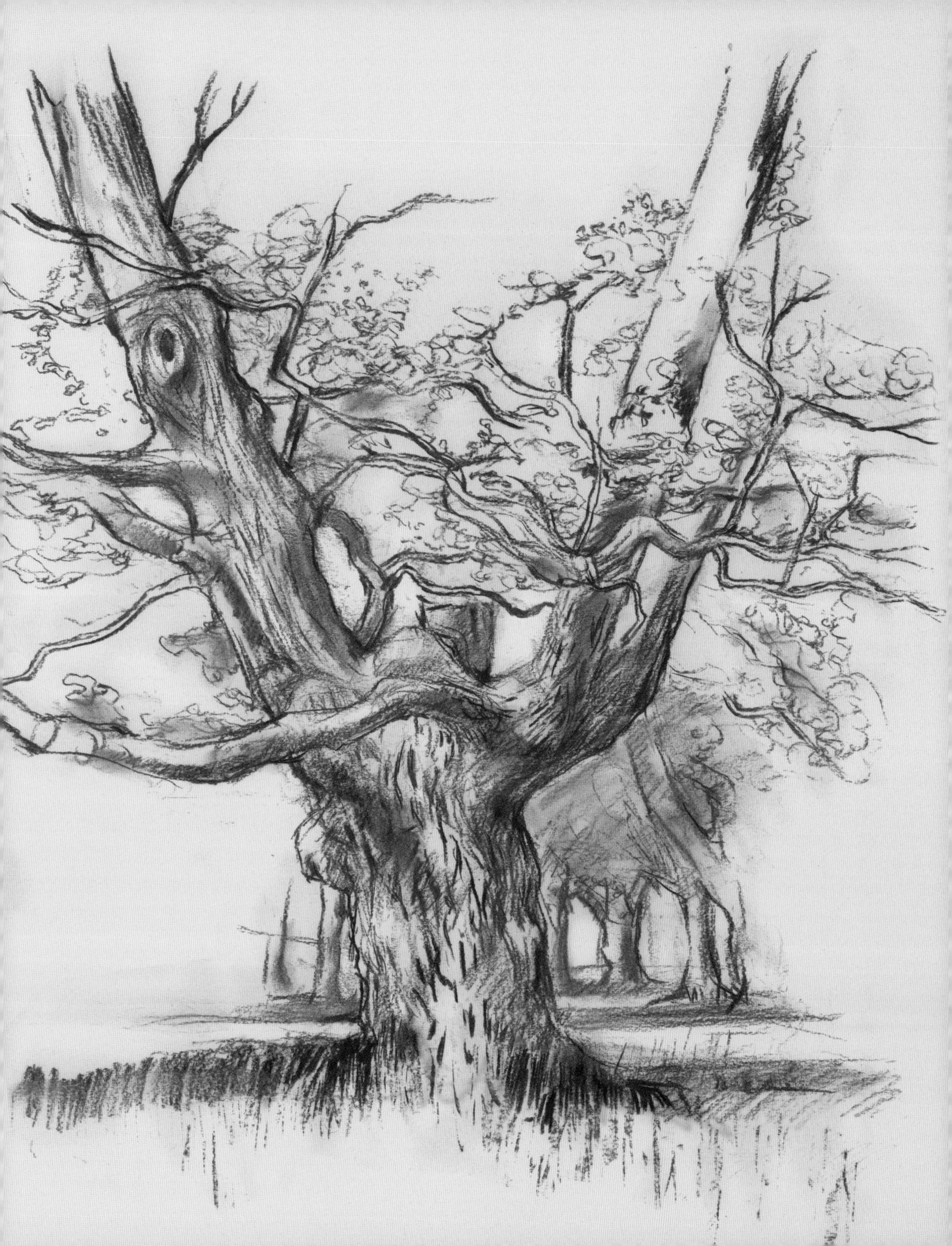

Tone Essentials

In drawing, tone (which is also called value) refers to the relative lightness or darkness of a colour. It is important to learn how to graduate your tones from light to dark, creating a subtle range of intermediate greys between the two. First, identify the areas of maximum light and maximum shadow and then make incremental steps between the two. Whether working on a landscape or subject, experiment by creating a variety in your tonal ranges.

Swatches of overlying ink in toned segments

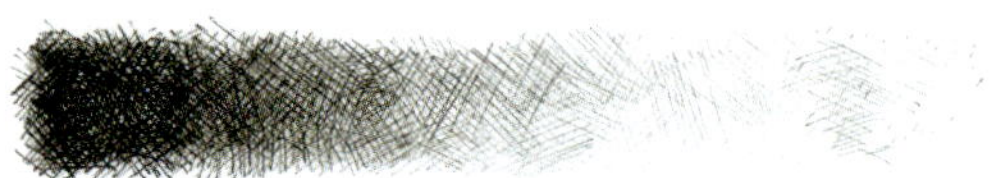

Cross-hatching with a dip pen and ink

4B graphite pencil

Ink

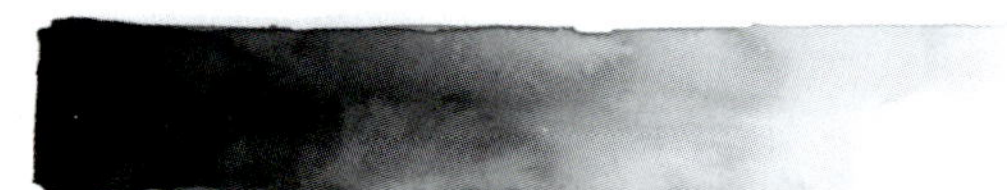

Watercolour

Tonal range

While I normally work with five tones, I reduce the tonal range to a minimum of three tones in certain sketching situations for simplification (white, mid-grey and black). In others, there might be as many as eight. When working on a drawing, challenge yourself by creating a variety of tones. You can adjust tones as you draw by changing the pressure you place on your pencil or other media or adjusting the saturation of the pigmentation. With watercolour and ink, add more water to lighten the tone and allow greater transparency, so you see more of the reflecting white paper beneath the drawing.

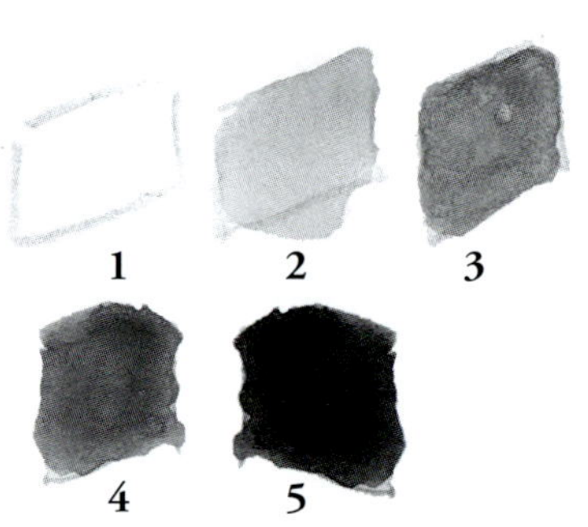

1 2 3 4 5

◄ Five-step tonal value scale
The majority of drawings in this book are carried out with a five-tone value scale that is easily manageable.

Local colour

Local colour is the colour of an object as seen in flat white light with no adjustments for shadow from a light source. Therefore, a dark red apple will have a darker tone than a light green one.

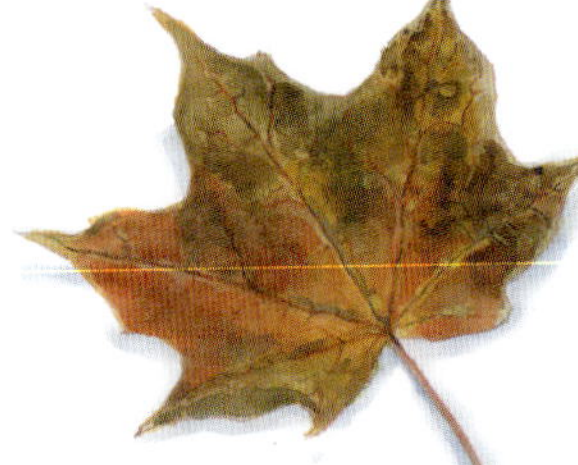

The stronger, the colour the deeper the tone

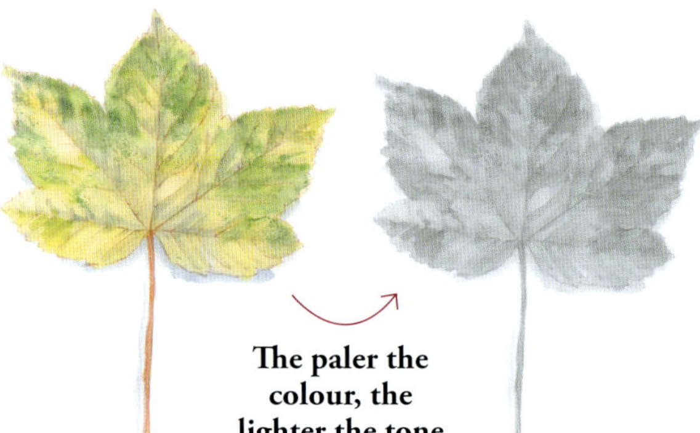

The paler the colour, the lighter the tone

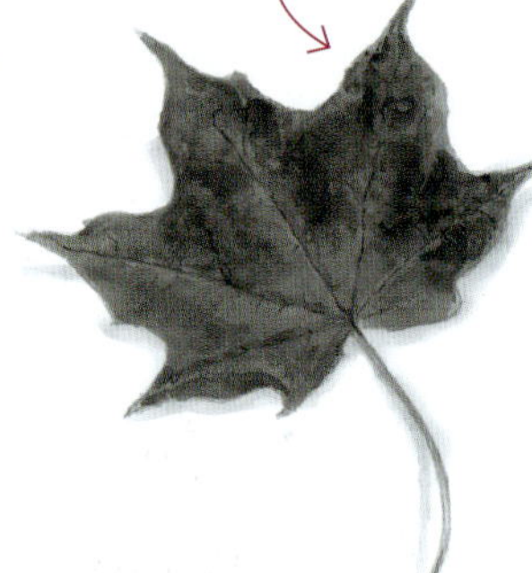

Tonal transitions

Tones can be defined by segments in a similar manner to painting-by-numbers, but more often they are created with gradients. It is worth spending time practising how to create smooth and even transitions in a variety of different media. A skilful blending of tonal transitions is satisfying and comforting to the eye.

Hatching and cross-hatching

Among the ways to create gradients is hatching, a technique that creates closely placed lines by using a zigzag motion (see pages 80–1). Cross-hatching goes a step further, using intersecting lines (see page 96). In both cases, the denser the line spacing, the darker your object will appear, and if the lines follow the contour of the object, they can create form and sculpt volume.

Wash

A drawing method that sits in between drawing and painting is a wash. When it is applied, the medium is wet. A wash can be created with brush markers, ink or watercolour. The tone is lightened with wet washes, such as ink and watercolour, typically by adding more water.

Light and shade

The illusion of light coming from the page is partnered with its opposite: shade. Learning to blend tones in the light and getting the relationship right for the dark shade tones captures light on the paper.

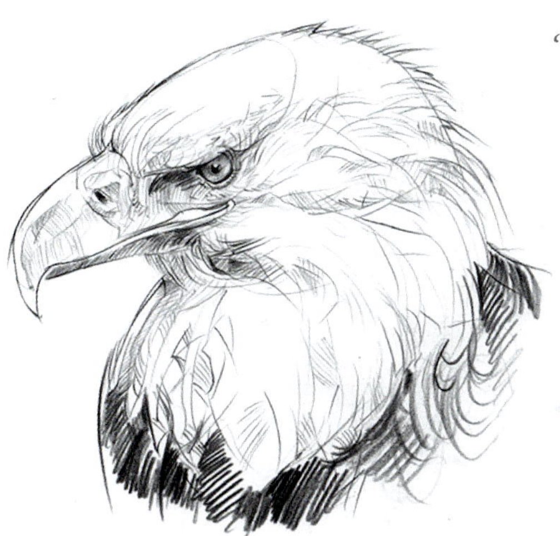

Tonal segments

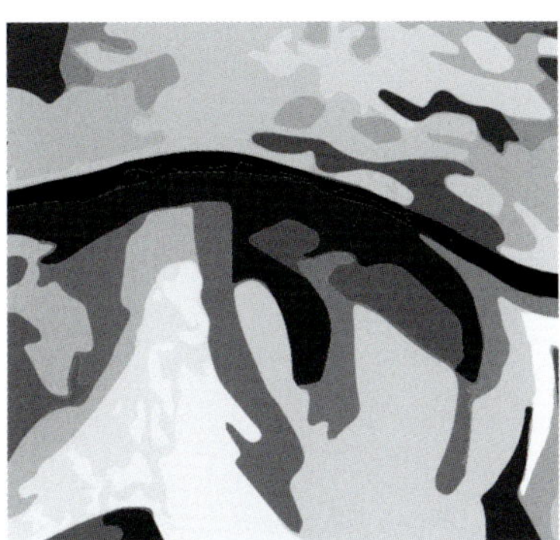

▲ Tone can be seen as interlocking puddles that are drawn shape to shape.

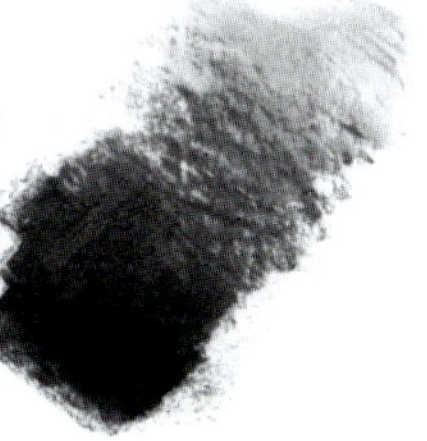

► Charcoal as a medium provides one of the most diverse ranges of tonal value, with rich velvety blacks.

▲ Graphite pencil
A sharp graphite pencil can create detailed shading.

► Overlapping
Darker tones can be created by repeatedly overlapping light grey markers.

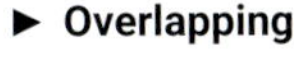

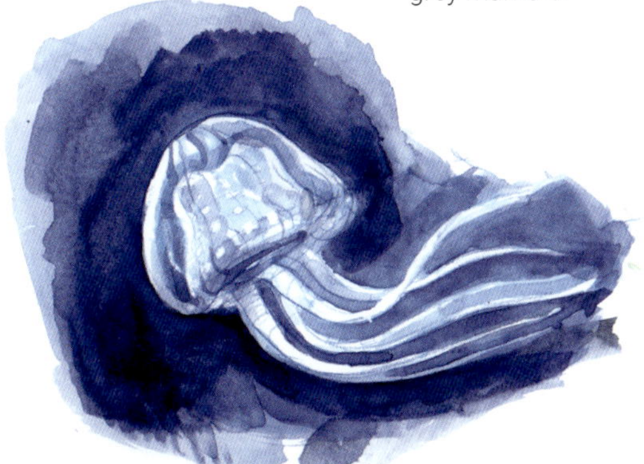

◄ A wash with shading
Bioluminescence can be captured with translucent washes of watercolour and ink. Denoting shade creates the illusion of light from the remaining bare white paper.

Making swatches

I will often make up little swatches before I begin to clarify in my mind what I am about to do. In field sketching, when using a mid-tone paper, I may reduce the range of swatches to four, including the paper itself.

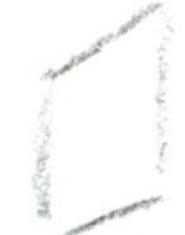

White fleece in sunlight created with white gouache

Shade of fleece as it turns away from the light

Fleece in shadow

Black socks of the legs

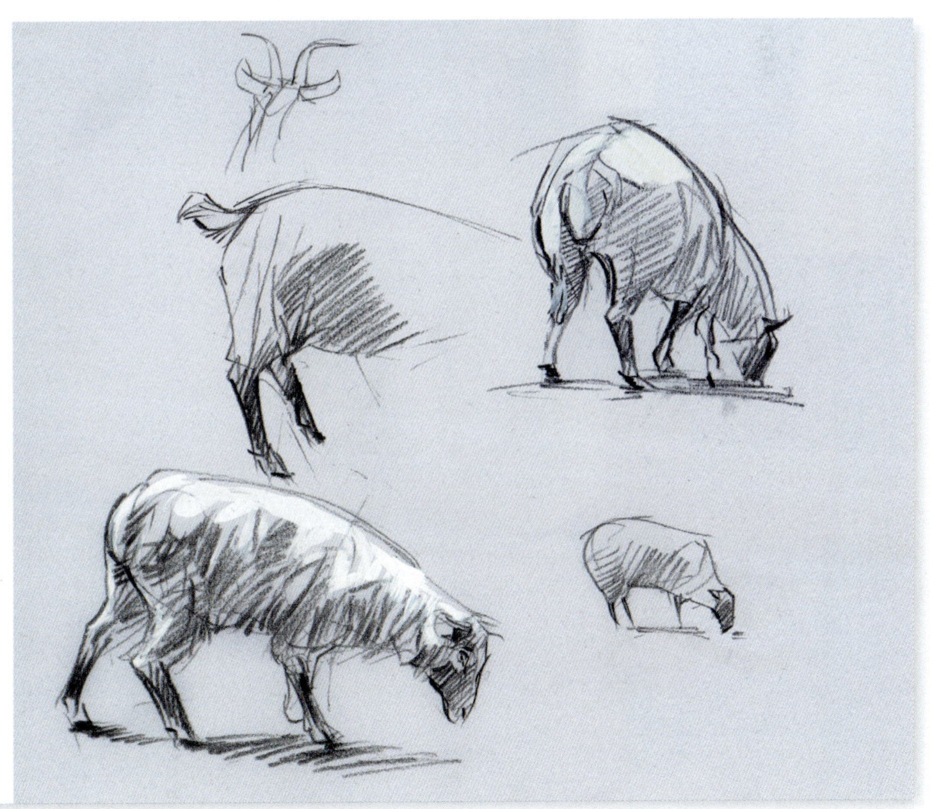

Light and Shadows

Without light, we would not be able to see, so it is critical to understand how we can capture it on the page. Whether noticeable or subtle, lighting helps bring depth and form to an image by providing areas of light and shadows. Objects in museums are often lit in such a way to emphasize their three-dimensional volume and to add drama to a piece to engage the visitor. Such is the case when we are creating a drawing. Lighting can also unify a drawing, ensuring that all the elements are imbibed with the same light source and brightness, such as creating early morning to late evening atmospheres. Lighting can bring romance to a scene and even turn an initially uninteresting subject, such as a beach towel, into a fascinating drapery study.

Tip

I always squint at my subject to help reduce visual noise and make it easier to see tonal blocks.

Lighting, which can come from different sources and directions and hit an object at different angles, plays an essential role in the tonal variety and lighting of the subject or scene. The direction or quality of light can enhance the feeling of form. In the evening, for example, the setting sun envelops subjects within the landscape, wrapping them with its golden light. This is in contrast to the flattening qualities of the midday sun.

In a high key image, such as a sunrise, all the tones are typically lighter than mid-grey. Whereas a low key image could be thought of as a nocturne, where the majority of tones are darker than mid-grey. There are, of course, many exceptions to this where images use a full range of tonal values. Some artists purposely limit their tonal range to create quiet, subtle still life images of everyday objects.

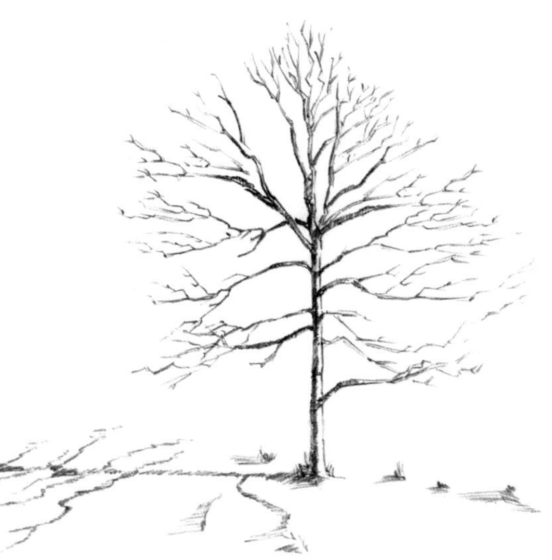

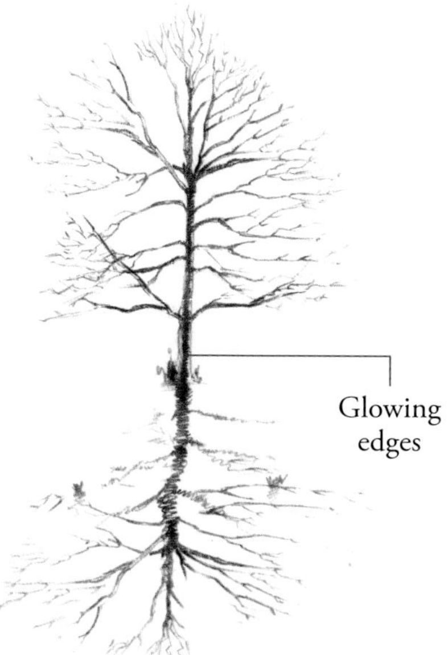

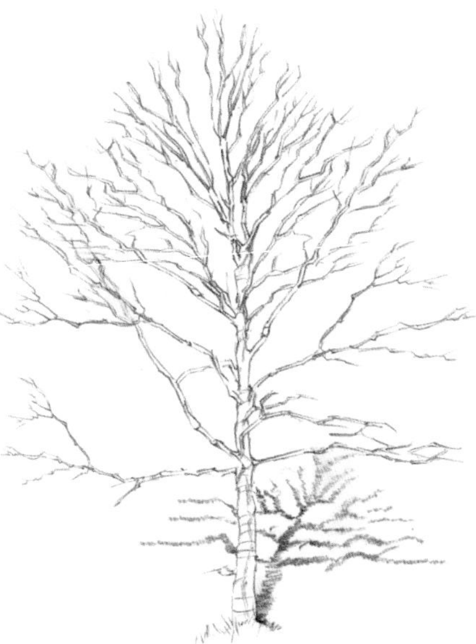

Side lighting

Light that strikes the subject from one side is called side lighting. It illuminates one side of the subject while the far side beyond its reach will be dark. The shadow is cast to the side. It is effective for expressing both form and drama.

Backlighting

Illuminating the subject from behind creates backlighting and places the it in silhouette. This often creates glowing edges on the subject, as the light peels around the form and shadows are cast in front of it.

Front lighting

Front lighting is when the light source is in front of the subject, such as when the sun is behind your back. This clearly illuminates the subject, although it can also flatten it as well. The shadow is cast behind the subject.

How to calculate shadows

While most sketching situations call for simply capturing the shadow shapes in front of your eyes, knowing how to construct cast shadows for compositional purposes is a valuable skill to have. Since light travels in a straight line, shadows created by an obstacle that are projected on planes will follow linear perspective rules. To establish the 'foot' of a light source, draw a point that represents the light source, then draw a perpendicular line to the horizon. To calculate straight-line cast shadows, simply draw a direct line to its principal junctions with the object. A round or organic shape can be orientated in a frame placed in two-point perspective (see page 108).

You can use a square frame to place a circle within it and calculate how the cast shadow would fall on the ground.

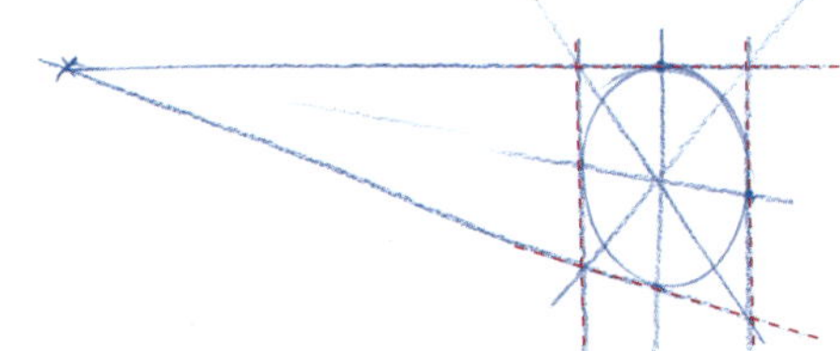

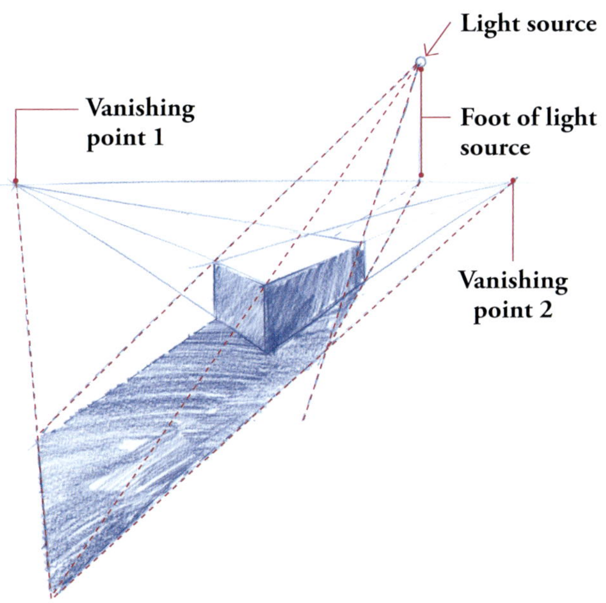

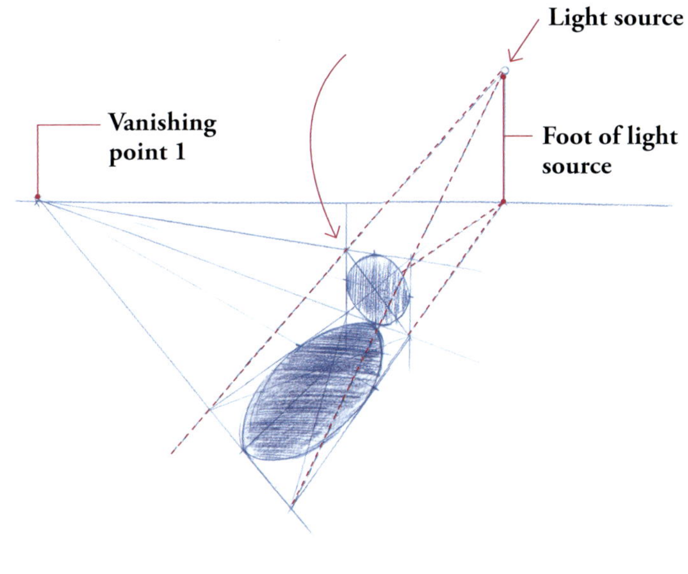

Core shadow

The core shadow is a dark band that appears where light and shadow meet. On round objects, reflected light from other surfaces means that the darkest shading is not on the edge of the form.

Primary form shadows

Notice that cast shadows have a softer edge than the forms of most solid objects.

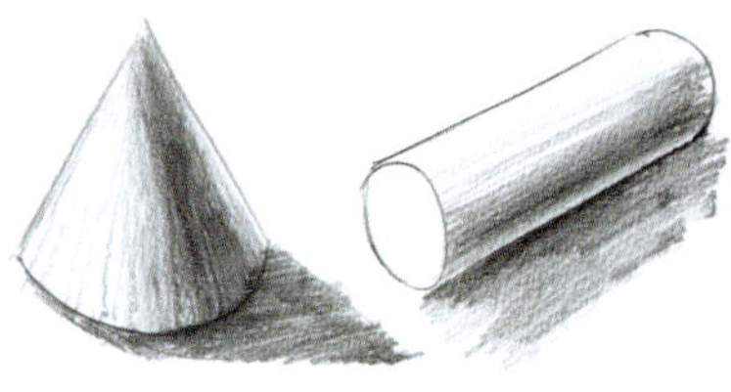

Shadow of form with a gradient

Curved forms will have a gradient shadow as the light reaches around them.

Uniform shadow of form

Forms that have flat planes will have a consistent, uniform shadow rather than a gradient.

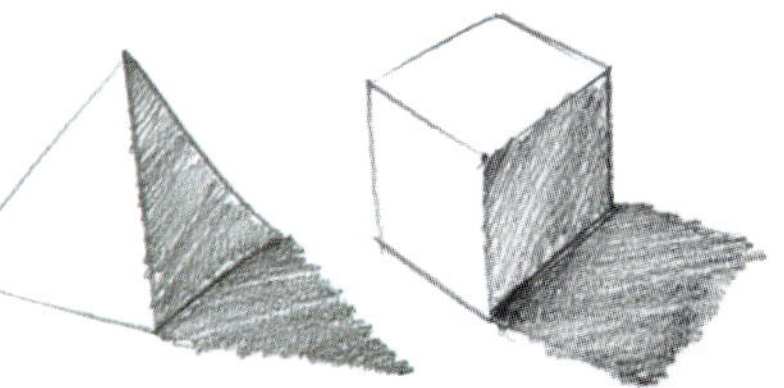

Using Mid-tone Paper

Toned paper is ideal for field sketching animals with a black and white livery. Either a neutral mid-range grey or the toothed side of brown wrapping paper is perfect for the job and avoids the glare of a white page on a sunny day. Tonally, you will be starting at the middle of the mid-tone paper value and going up or down.

The pelts of many animals are a striking black and white, such as tuxedo-wearing penguins, a dazzle of zebras and the European badger. You can create studies where the pelts pop from the paper by creating studies on mid-tone paper with artist's quality colouring pencils.

Colobus monkey

The black backs of African Colobus monkeys are dramatically adorned with long white fur, which can create striking images when drawn on mid-tone paper.

Materials

- Black and white artist's quality colouring pencils
- Large mid-tone pastel paper (or sugar/construction paper)
- Sharpener
- Putty eraser

Colobus monkey (*Colobus* spp.) The name 'colobus' is derived from the Greek word for maimed because, in contrast to other monkeys, colobus monkeys do not have thumbs. Colobus come from Africa, and they are part of a group of primates known as the Old World monkeys. Their striking black fur contrasts with the long white mantle, whiskers, bushy tail and beard around the face. The Eastern black-and-white or mantle (*Colobus guereza*) is distinguishable by a U-shaped cape of white hair running from the shoulders to the lower back, whereas the Angolan black-and-white (*Colobus angolensis*) has white hairs flaring out only at the shoulders.

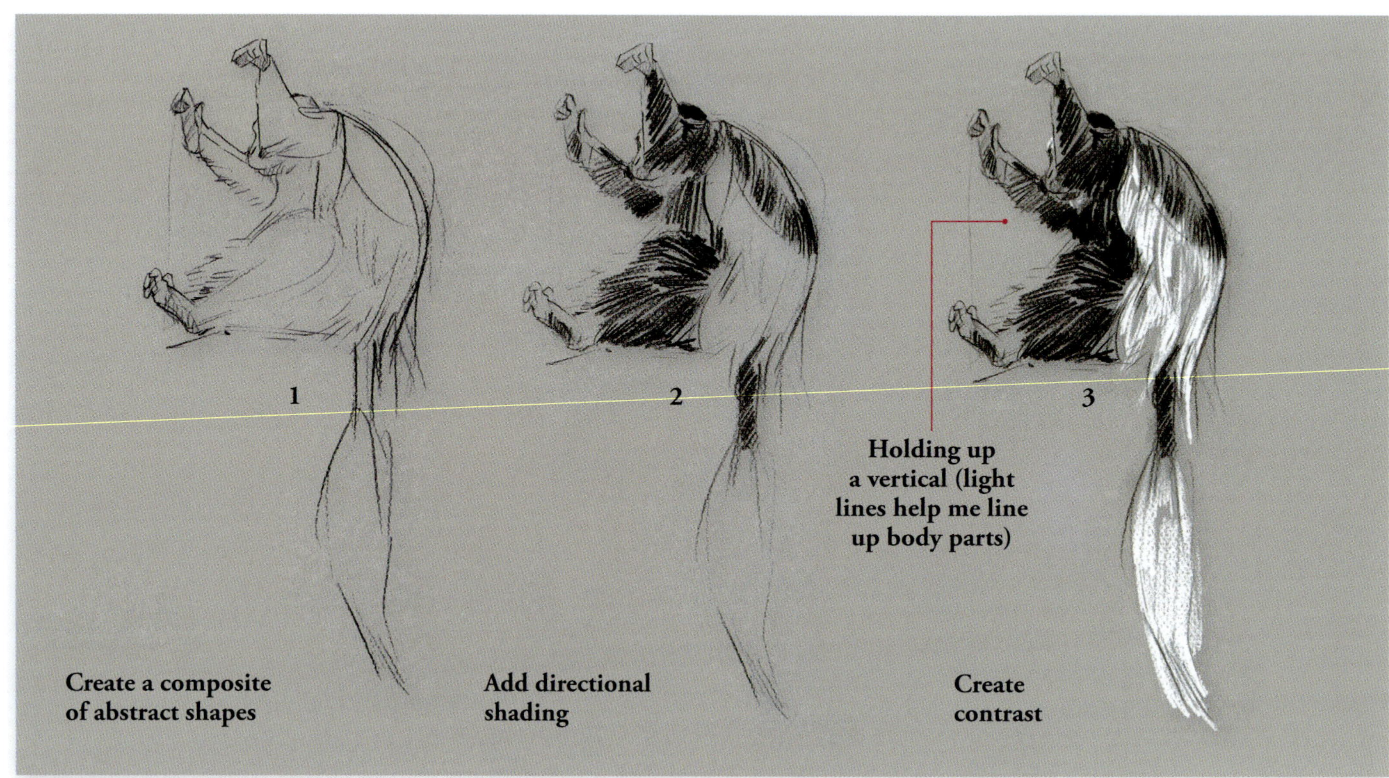

1 *Begin with a loose sketch that captures the main pose, posture and proportions, keeping a keen eye out for shapes that capture the unique character of the colobus monkey.*

2 *Next, begin to shade, attempting to capture the movement and direction of the black areas of the pelt.*

3 *Add some sparkle and vivid contrast by applying white with gusto, following the flowing lines of dangling white fur.*

Study Sheet: *Colobus Monkeys*

In this study sheet, I tried to draw the adult monkeys the same size to appear as a troop and interacting with each other. Notice how their tails drop vertically beneath them like bulbs. Each time the animal moved, it presented me with a new set of shapes, like walking around a sculpture and creating a fresh sketching challenge.

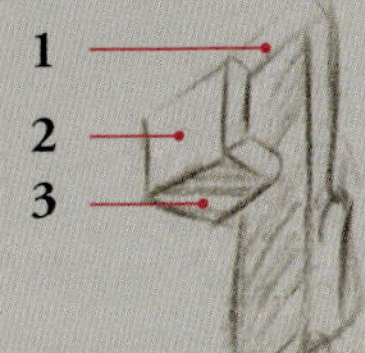

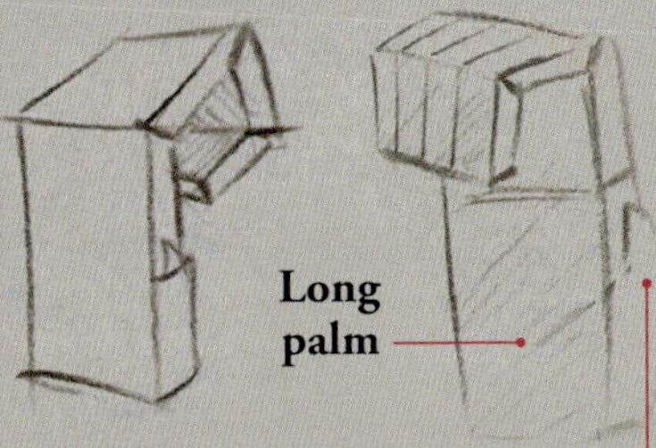

▶▼ Head widget

Drawing different parts of the animal's head, such as the ears, cheek and nostrils, at different angles will help build a good understanding of its structure in your mind. You can combine these forms to help you understand what the head will look like from different angles.

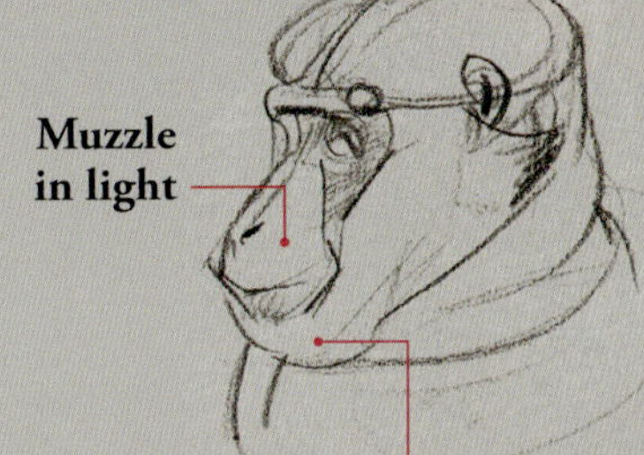

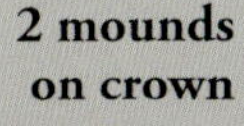

▲ Hand widget

I break the hand down into the main shapes of the palm and three little sections of the fingers and thumb. I combine the four fingers into one articulated block before segmenting it into individual fingers. Count the number of phalanges in your fingers, and see the similarities between yourself and our broader cousins.

▼ Abstract shapes

Forget your preconceptions about the shape of familiar forms. Try to see your subject as a set of abstract shapes put together to become readable as an animal, a bit like piecing together a jigsaw puzzle.

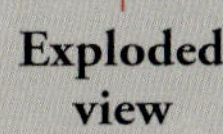

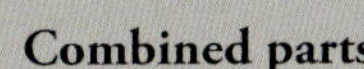

Combined parts

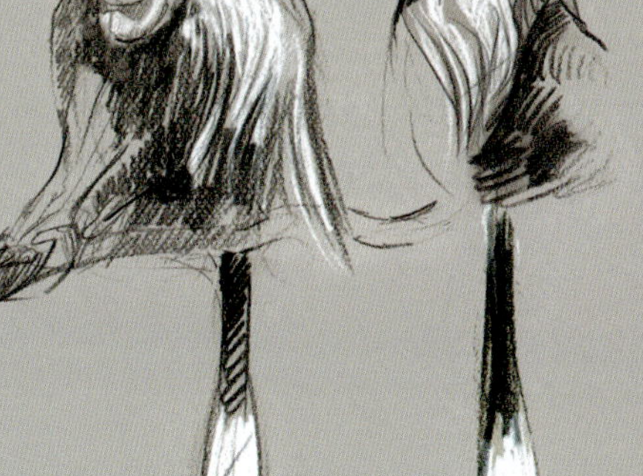

▲▶ Playful interactions

I tried to vary the height of the monkeys to create the impression that they were climbing up and down the canopy layer playfully. Play is as essential in design as it is in growing up for mammals.

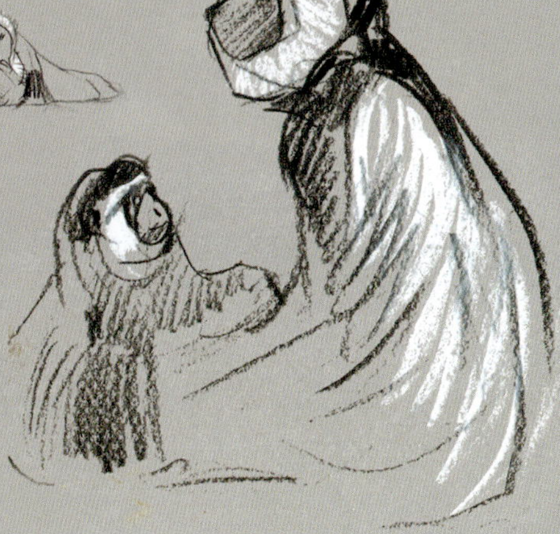

Chiaroscuro

From an Italian term that literally translates as 'light-dark', chiaroscuro involves the use of strong contrasts between light and dark, often from a single light source that affects all the elements in a composition. The subjects are bathed in a dramatic light while their dark sides melt into the dimly lit backgrounds.

This method of creating images was popular during the Renaissance. It resulted in images with strong tonal contrasts that suggested the volume and modelling of the subjects depicted. Leonardo da Vinci used it to create a strong sense of three-dimensionality in his figures, whereas Caravaggio used it for dramatic effect. The seventeenth-century Dutch artist Rembrandt also recognized the power of chiaroscuro and used it to heighten emotional tension and drama in his artwork.

Materials

- Black artist's quality colouring pencil
- Cartridge (drawing) paper or sketchbook
- Sharpener
- Putty eraser

Indian rhinoceros
(*Rhinoceros unicornis*)
The Indian rhinoceros live primarily in northern India and Nepal. Indian rhinos appear even more armoured than their African cousins. Their segmented hide works as formidable natural body armour. The sunlight will catch these sculpted planes on a bright day, creating clear and interesting light and dark shapes.

Indian rhino

Drawing animals from life requires the ability to be able to draw them from all sorts of angles. Some animals are naturally curious and will want to stand and watch you as you sketch them. This rhino was facing me, placing its long nose in a foreshortened compressed view. This made it harder to judge the distance, for example, from the nostril to the eye. I tend to work from an eye tube and work backwards and forwards, breaking down the head into a set of abstract shapes.

▼ Sunlight direction
When you first start creating chiaroscuro drawings, it is worth drawing a small arrow on the page to identify where the sun is and ensure all the forms are uniformly affected.

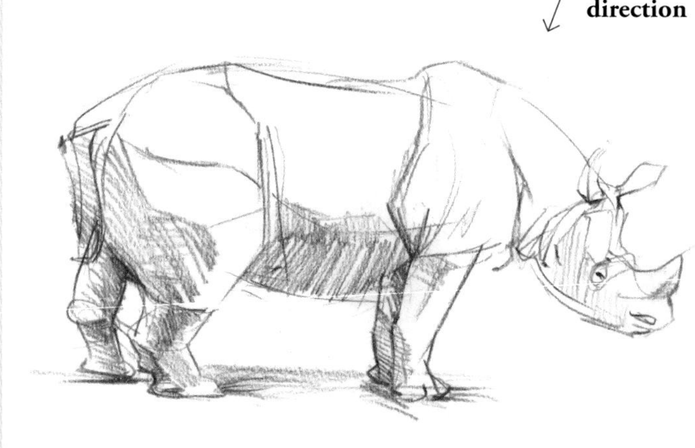

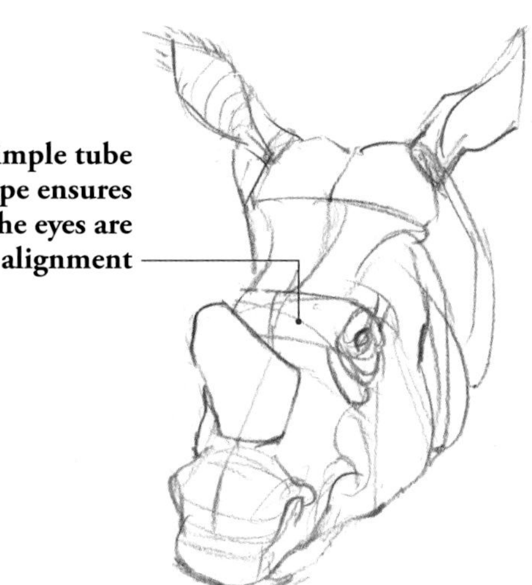

A simple tube shape ensures that the eyes are in alignment

1 *Begin by creating an initial line drawing with a bilateral line of symmetry. The horn is conceived as a simple cone shape.*

2 *Next, shade blocks of shadow with loose hatching marks (see pages 80–1) that follow the direction of the form. The zygomatic arch creates a bulge behind the eye.*

Study Sheet: *Asian Rhino*

The armoured plating of the Asian rhino creates powerful directional planes that, in a similar manner to a crystal, capture light or half-light or are in shadow. This creates chunks of shading that can be seen as abstract shapes.

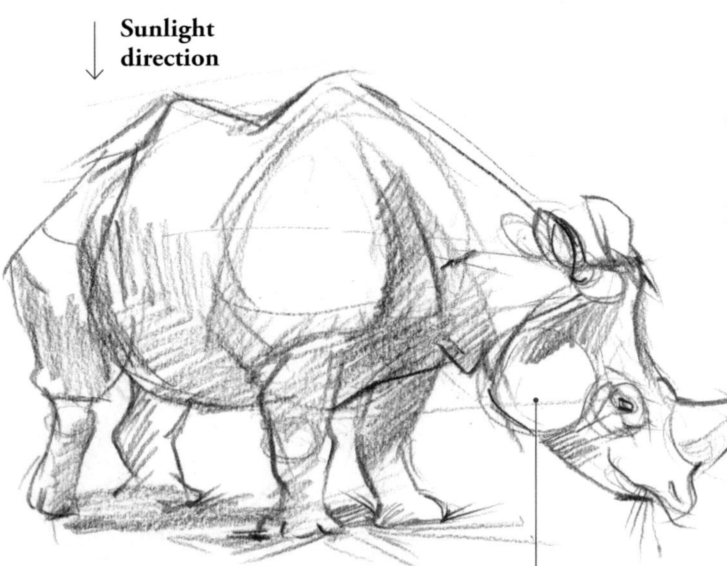

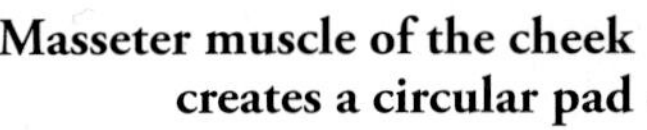

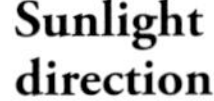

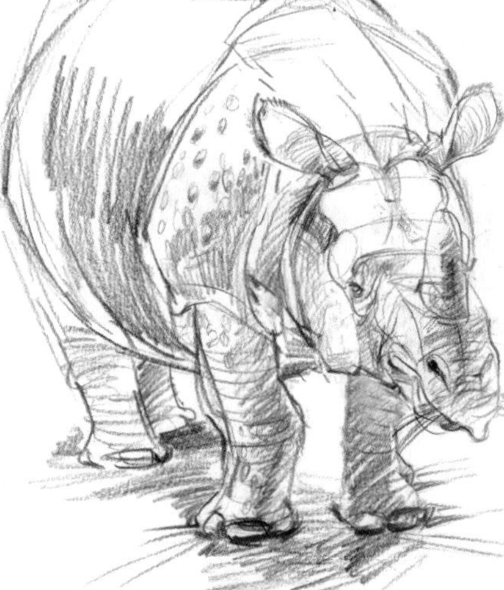

▲ Bathing rhino

Reflections, as well as shadows, can add visual interest and drama. Water reflections are typically closer and darker in tonality in normal daylight. Vertical lines are reflected with greater clarity than horizontal. I drew this mirrored image with less detail and included some suggestive watery marks.

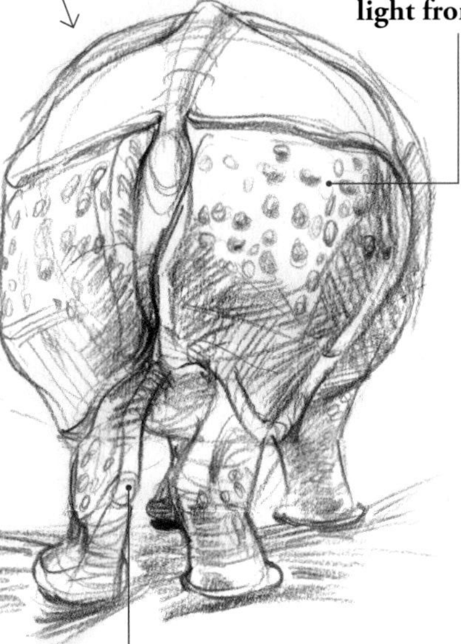

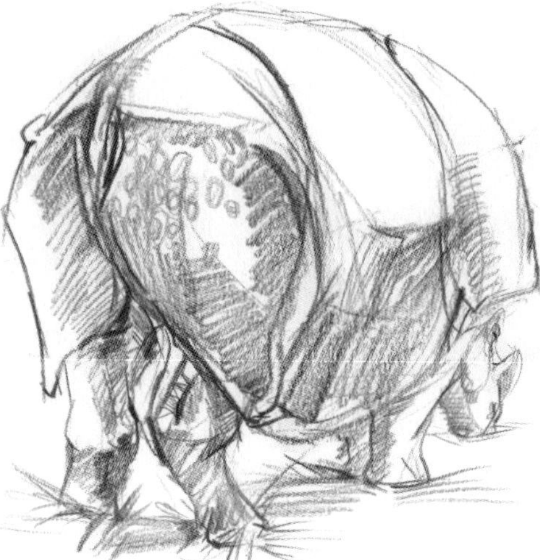

▲ Detailed observation

Capture details from different angles.

▲ Working out

I work from the closest section of the body and then draw shape to shape along the interconnected shield shapes.

Additive and Subtractive Shading

A drawing is often created by adding a series of lines to paper to form the subject, and this is known as additive drawing. However, a drawing can also be created in the reverse, by removing the medium – this is known as subtractive drawing. In subtractive drawing or shading, instead of creating form by adding shadows like you would in additive drawing, forms are created by adding light. Charcoal has the flexibility of both creating tones additively, by building it up with applied pressure on the stick to achieve dark, rich coal black shades, and subtractively, by cutting through a layer of charcoal with a putty eraser.

Materials
- Black artist's quality colouring pencil
- Charcoal
- Large cartridge (drawing) paper or sketchbook
- Putty eraser
- Pencil sharpener

Charcoal is often used in life drawing classes. Because it has no binder, it is easy to erase. This also makes it the perfect medium for additive and subtractive shading. The goal is to start by applying an even layer of charcoal to the paper, then using a putty eraser to remove areas of light. In this drawing, I also use a black colouring pencil to help pick out the details.

Harvest supper

Before the twentieth century, farmers would invite everyone who had assisted in the harvest to a large feast, known as the harvest supper, to celebrate the completion of the harvest. A basket of seasonal autumn vegetables creates a visual cornucopia of delight with different textures, glowing in russet hues. The first step in still life drawing is not drawing at all but setting up the arrangement, where I wanted the appearance that the basket had just been knocked over and its generous bounty spills forth towards the viewer. I lit the scene with a single light source in a chiaroscuro manner (see pages 70–1) to help dramatize the scene and express volume.

1 *Place a thin stick of charcoal on its side and rub lightly and evenly over the paper until the entire surface is a silvery grey. Then smooth out the charcoal using a tissue to lighten and unify it into a single tone.*

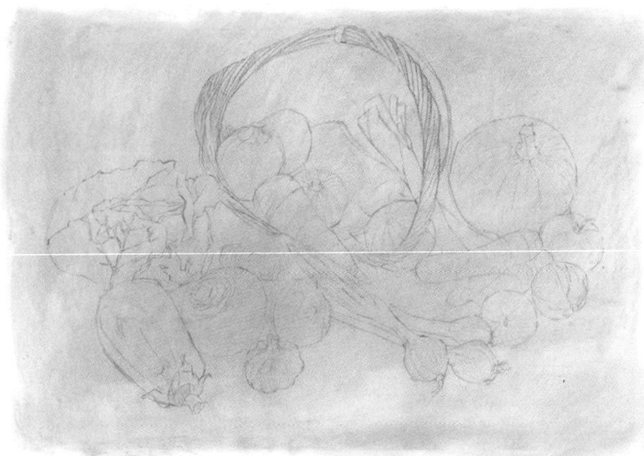

2 *Next, sketch out the main shapes, concentrating on proportions and the different characters that form the bulbous fruit and vegetables.*

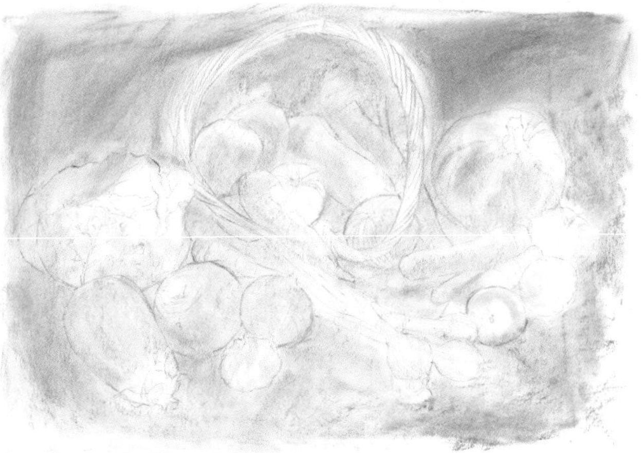

3 *Look closely at the still life and notice a pumpkin's skin is segmented into ribs, the onion's dry broken skin peels away to reveal the shiny onion beneath, the concentric rings on top of the turnip. Make a point in the putty eraser, then start erasing the whites, drawing subtractively.*

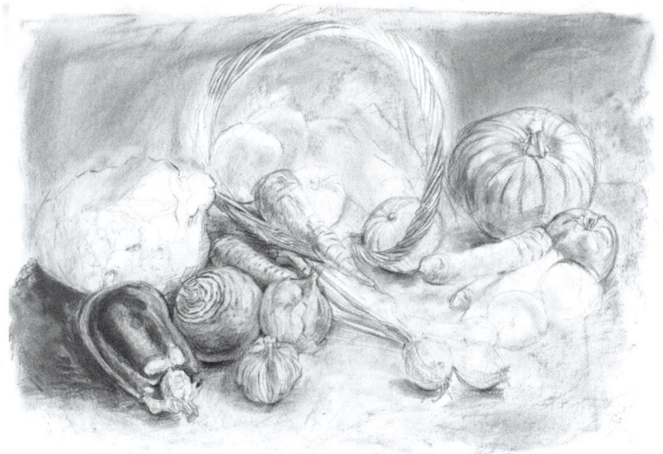 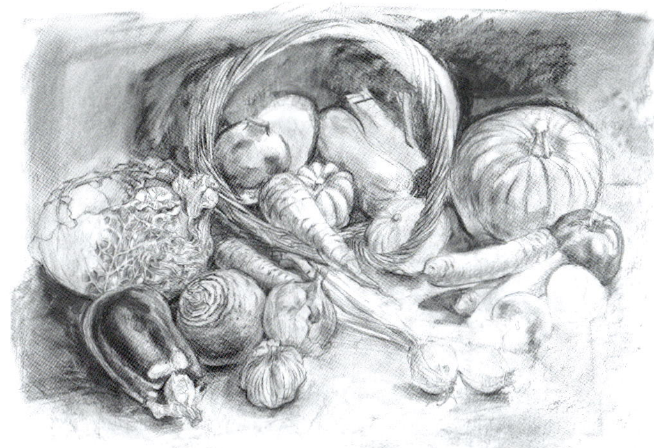

4 *Once all of the light areas are removed, begin working the dark areas with charcoal, referring to the still life for tonal values and textures. Manipulate the charcoal to sculpt the illusion of forms on the two-dimensional surface of the paper. Move from an understood area to new territory, working on the whole image like a photograph in a developing tray.*

Working with charcoal

To prevent smudging, place a piece of clean paper beneath your palm as you work. It is important not to be tempted to use a fixative too early, as this will prevent the putty eraser from removing the charcoal to get back to white.

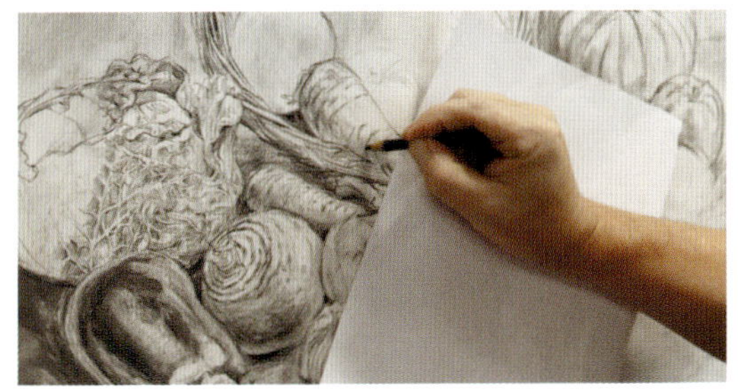

5 *Enjoy the imperfections of the fruit and vegetables using a sharp black colouring pencil to capture intricate details, such as the texture of the veined cabbage leaf. With the pencil's fine tip, it is possible to achieve greater detail. With such fine detail, I just try to create an impression of what I am looking at rather than a precise copy. Once completed, spray the drawing with a fixative so that the charcoal doesn't smudge.*

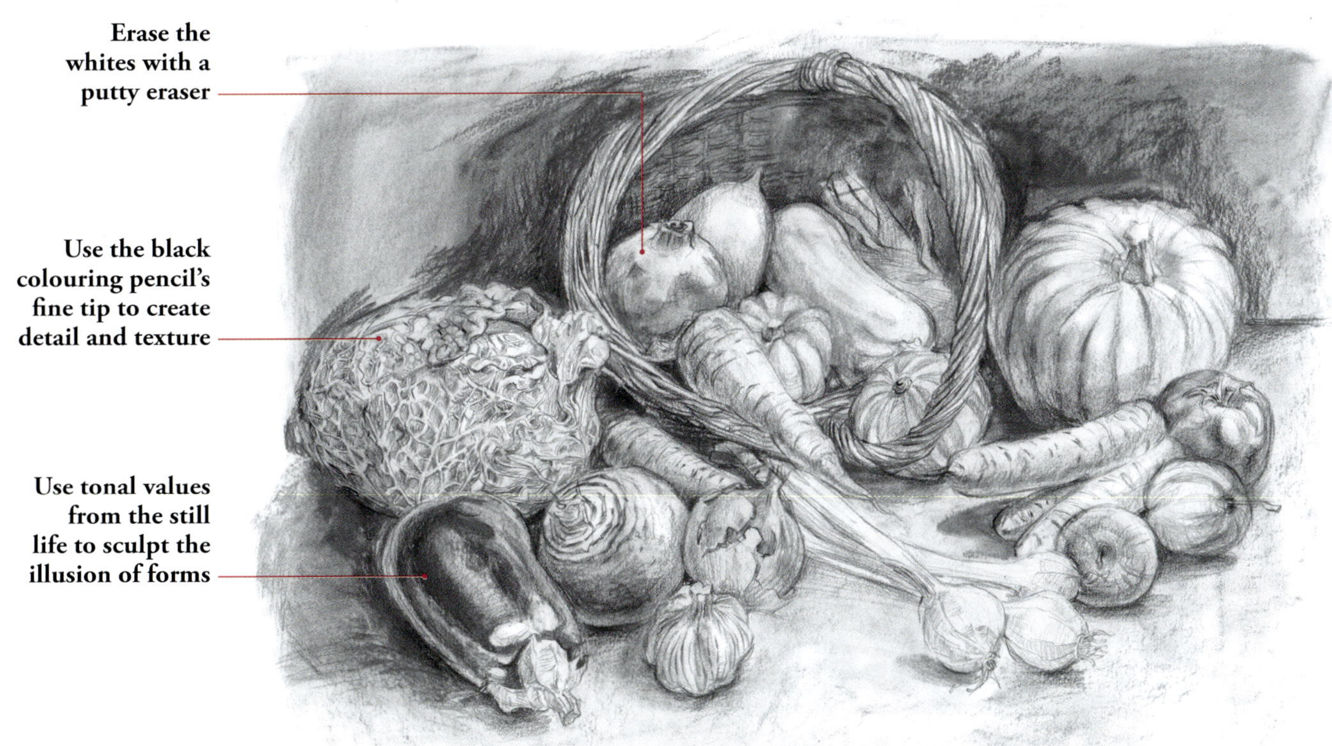

Form

Like space and the other formal elements of drawing, form is an illusion on a two-dimensional surface, but in this case giving the subject form helps to create the impression that it has three dimensions. By drawing lines, planes and shading, we can express solidity, volume and weight, which can also help create drama and impact.

A form can be solid, gas or liquid. We can further break the solids into two main categories: geometric and organic. Many forms in nature are highly geometric, from snowflakes and the petals on a daisy to orb-like apples and oranges and hexagonal honeycombs. Even some of nature's organic soft and pliable forms, such as the jellyfish or octopus, can still have geometric symmetry, despite their gelatinous nature.

Irregular, organic forms aren't symmetrical and don't have strict shapes or names. Organic forms appear natural and can be sculpted like a ball of clay. They can appear to flow and be unpredictable. They are found in abundance in nature: anything from sea sponges, coral and bladderwrack seaweed to potatoes, peppers and oak trees have organic forms.

To get an understanding of an object's form, handling it will allow you to quickly grasp its essential weight and mass, as well as its texture. A sharp flint shard will feel different from a smooth pebble. Running your hand under the tap will enable you to feel the water's liquidity in comparison to when it becomes solid ice at a colder temperature. You can feel a lightweight pine cone with your fingers and make sense of its intricate opening geometry of seed scales. Form can also contain energy, such as when cupping a frog in your hand, with it being ready to spring with powerful back legs. The elastic sinewy body of being alive versus the limpness of death are all qualities that we can capture in a drawing.

▶ **Prickly pear cactus in colouring pencil and markers**

This challenging subject is a member of the Opuntia cactus family, a native of the New World. They are identified by their broad, flat paddles and edible fruit. I used backlighting to help capture the form, which put the cactus primarily in silhouette, with ridges and planes catching the light. I wrapped a geometrical X-shaped mesh of spiny points around the cactus' lobed ears, keeping my pencil sharpened to capture the razor-sharp spines.

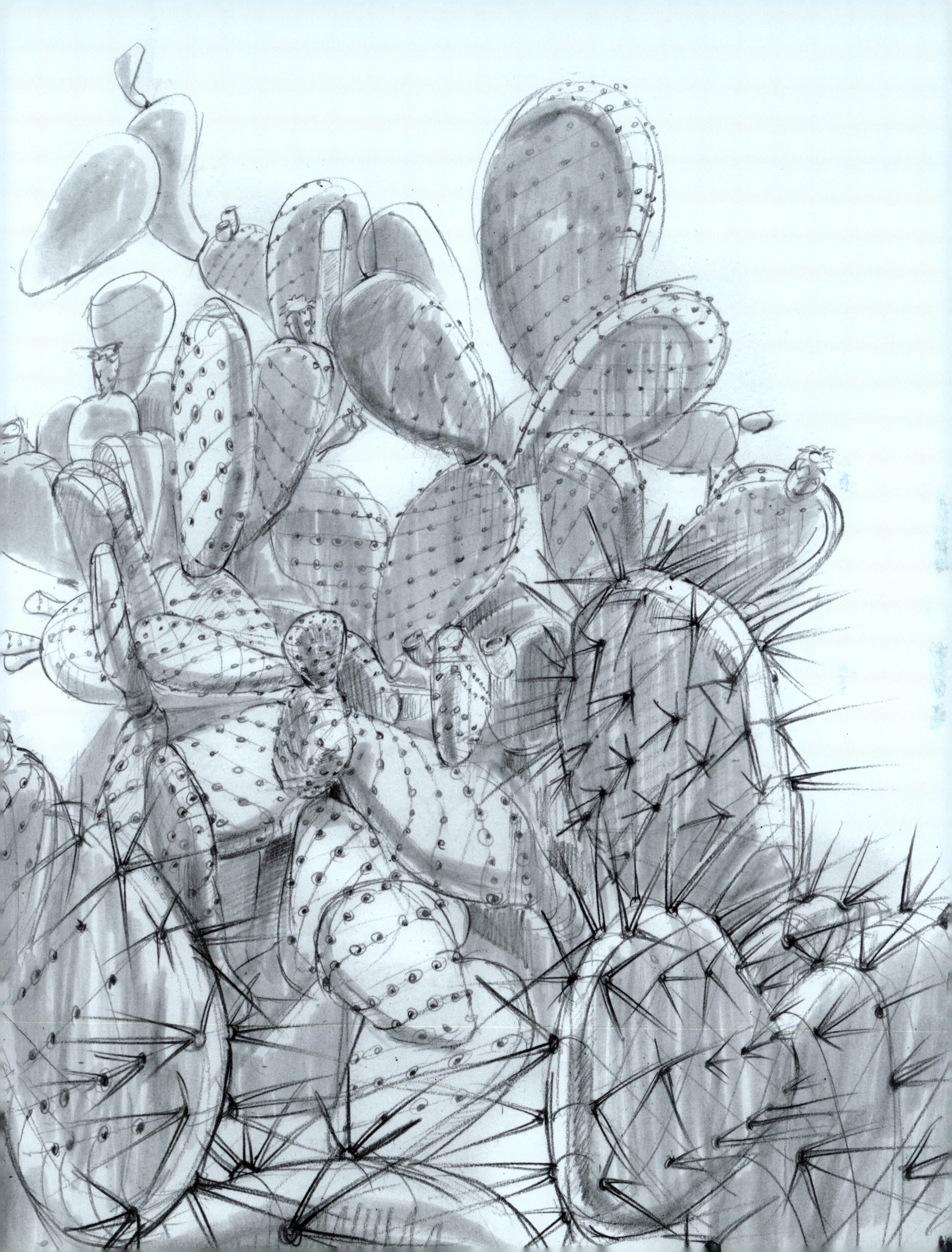

Form Essentials

You know how to draw the flat two-dimensional shape of a subject on paper, but how can you convey form, giving it mass and weight? There are a few tips and tricks that will help bring a sense of mass to your subject, giving a sense that a physical form is being sculpted on the paper.

Geometric forms

The primary geometric forms are the sphere, cube, pyramid, cone and cylinder. They are three-dimensional forms of the basic shapes (see page 49).

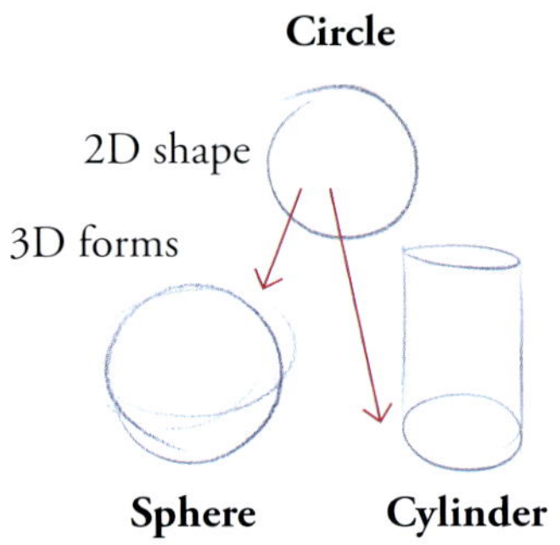

Circle

2D shape

3D forms

Sphere   **Cylinder**

Triangle

2D shape

3D forms

Cone   **Pyramid**

▲ Circles and ellipses

The flat circle transforms into a sphere with some implied modelling, or it can be stretched into a cylinder. Circles are a good organic option for constructing biological forms, such as a gorilla's head (see right).

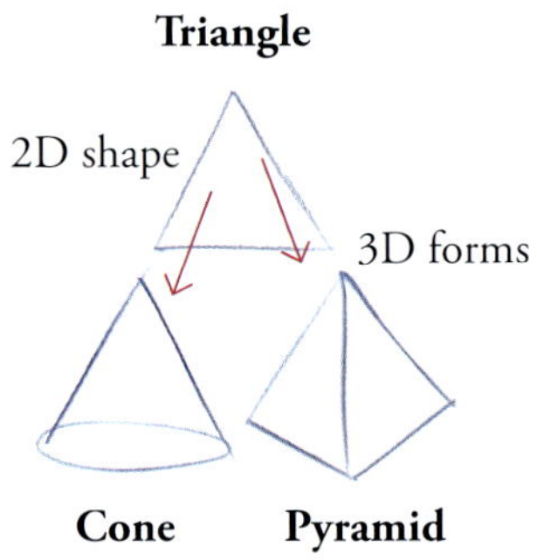

▲ Triangles

The upright shape of a triangle gives a feeling of stability, but upside down there's a feeling of imbalance. A triangle is the foundation of both the spherical cone seen in a carnivore's tooth or hump on a camel's back and the planar pyramid forms seen as bony plates on a crocodile's back.

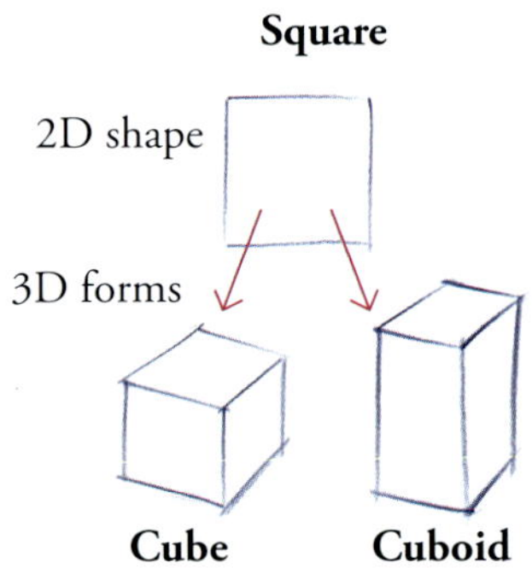

Square

2D shape

3D forms

Cube   **Cuboid**

Hexagon

2D shape

3D forms

Cubic   **Tube**

▲ Squares

The square gives birth to the cube and cuboid forms, which are ideal building blocks for constructing and organizing organic forms, such as a dog's head (right).

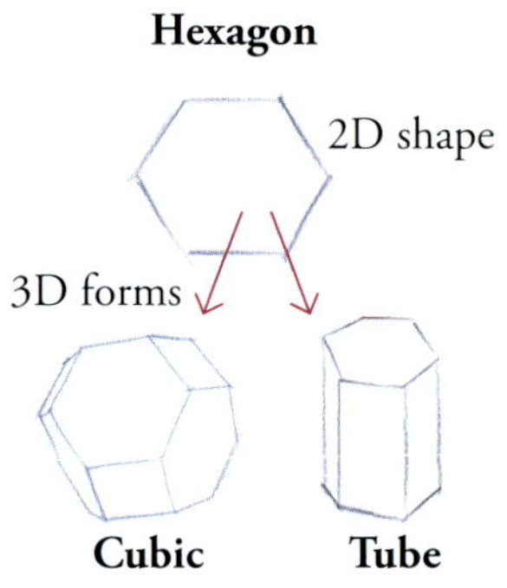

▲ Polygons

Polygons have three or more sides. Crystals are an example of naturally occurring three-dimensional geometric forms in nature. Quartz crystals often form hexagonal prisms.

Organic forms

We must consider form in its broadest sense when considering this element in nature. Clouds, for example, are forms of floating vapour, but the thick tree trunk of an oak is also an organic form. A rock structure created from a dark, rough stone has a solid form that carries great mass. However, forms in nature can also be delicate and light, such as a spider's web, swaying blades of grass and the skeleton of a decomposed leaf. And forms can be flat, such as sea kelp swaying in the sea, treated similarly to how Renaissance artists studied drapes as they waver in the water current. To help us organize these irregular, organic forms, boxes and spheres will provide good geometric frameworks.

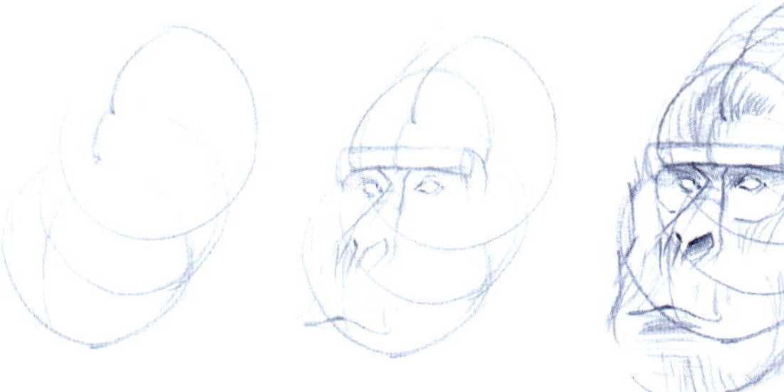

▲ Gorilla head

A more organic way of organizing the form of a gorilla's head is to begin with a three descending-circle widget (see page 15) with a tube for the ridge brow.

▼ Dog head

Draw a box and find the central line for the cranium, then add a smaller thinner muzzle box. The central line of symmetry is found by drawing an X.

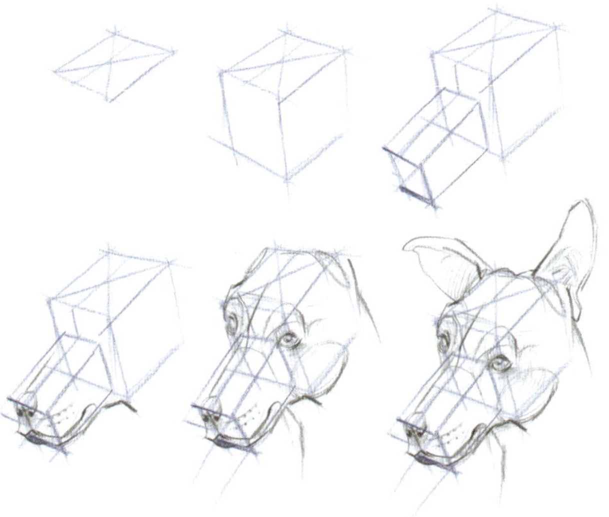

Creating form

Shading can be used to capture form. The most popular methods are drawing topographic lines and adding tonal shading. The process of shading is one of the most fundamental drawing concepts. We must be able to appropriately shade objects to convey the illusion of form in a scene. In addition, shading also implies light and its opposite shade, which is necessary to express the illusion of light coming from the paper.

Creating form with lines

Artists can use lines to express volume by drawing around the form, following its curves and planes. With a sensitive response to form, an artist can represent the form of anything from a hard, sharp shard of glass to free-flowing seaweed.

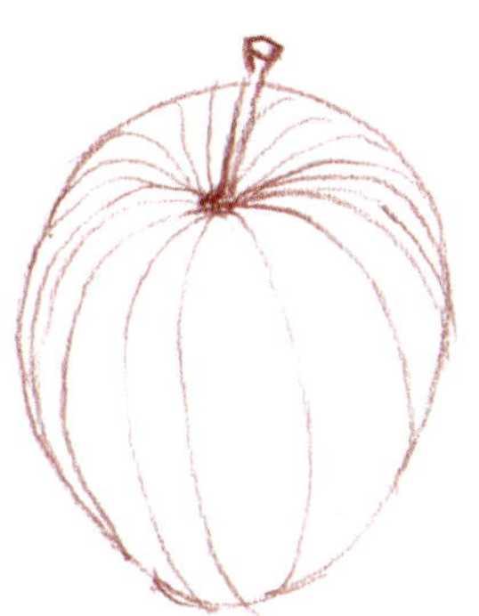

▲ Elliptical shading

The curved lines of elliptical shading helps to volumize the round orb shape of the apple.

▲ Planar shading

The directional lines of planar shading helps to describe the angles of the planes.

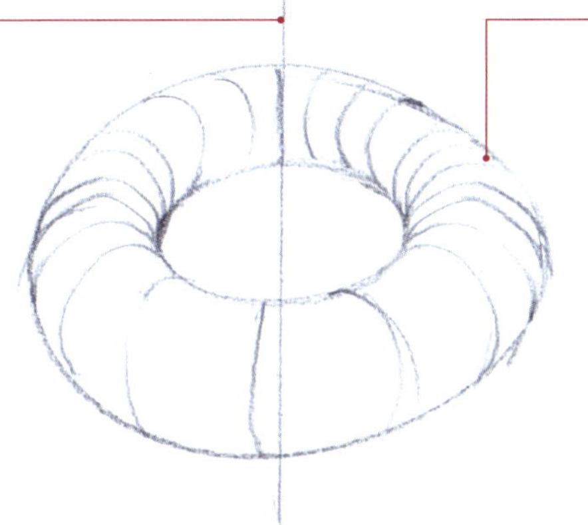

The turning point
Where the surface is directly in front of the viewer's eyes and the contour line appears as a straight line.

Compression
Foreshortening (see pages 112–13) creates an illusion that the contour lines are bunching up in compression as the form turns to face the eye. At this point, the ellipse contours are at their most open and roundest.

◄ Wrapping lines around an object

We can create the illusion of form without using light and shade by wrapping contour lines around organic forms. Notice how the contour line alternates in direction on either side of the turning point.

Creating form with tone

In addition to suggesting light (see page 66–7), tonal shading also reveals the appearance of form. Tonal shading can be added in a host of different ways, from cross-hatching to a loose wash (see page 96). I have a personal preference for loose shading rather than the more mechanical cross-hatching.

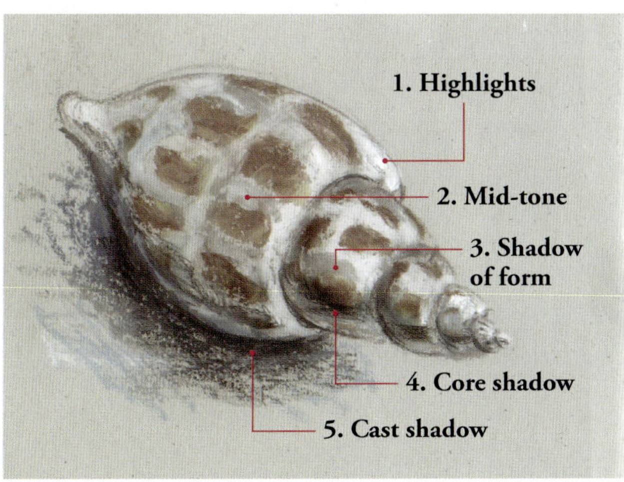

1. Highlights

2. Mid-tone

3. Shadow of form

4. Core shadow

5. Cast shadow

1. The highlights are the areas on an object where the light hits the object.

2. Mid-tones lie between the shadow and light values. They are lighter and brighter in pigment than everything in the darker shadow family.

3. The shadow of form is the part of an object that lies on the opposite side of the light source. It tends to have a softer edge than the cast shadow as the light reaches around the surface, so practise graduating your tone from dark to light in various media.

4. The core shadow is a dark band of shadow created by light reflected onto an object from the surface it sits on. There is no core shadow on the moon's dark side because there is no surface for light to bounce on in space.

5. Cast shadows bring drama to a study and prevent the subject from floating on the page. Drawing shadows requires thought about the light source, and cast shadows are no exception, so pinpoint it in your mind and even draw an arrow on your page. How dark the cast shadow is depends on the strength of the light source and the tonal value of the surface the object is sitting on.

Surface Textures and Decorations

In his classic book *The Elements of Drawing* (1857), the English art critic John Ruskin wrote, 'All drawing depends, primarily, on your power of representing Roundness. If you can once do that, all the rest is easy and straightforward . . . For Nature is all made up of roundnesses; not the roundness of perfect globes, but of variously curved surfaces.' Nature's forms are rarely based on regular geometric shapes. Rocks, plants and animals can have lots of lumps and imperfections that make their forms even more interesting to draw and paint.

Modelling or rendering is one of the best ways to sculpt forms on the page, where the strength of the light source dictates the contrast and tonal range. Surface texture and decorations can hugely assist in creating an illusion of form as they envelop it, wrapping around the three-dimensional structure, creating additional information to give the impression of solidity, volume and weight. The approach I take, whether in pencil or paint, is to build up many layers of loose shading. In these studies of pebbles, each form has a side facing the light and a dark side facing away from it.

Mark-making

As artists, a sense of familiarity comes with spending time with an object. Something about its proportions, shape and personality might draw you to pick it up in the first place. I often think of inanimate objects as characters, just as houses are. It might be a craggy, grizzled, scrunty root from a tree in a fairy tale or a smooth new bamboo shoot. The work of the drawing is to capture this character on the page like a portrait. Grit, pits and imperfections are excellent devices to suggest the coarse, grainy texture we feel when touching particular pebbles; they are also helpful in pulling form from the page. In this exercise, start broadly with your subject illuminated from a single light source. After massing out the form, add details with lines, scrapes and spots. Be creative with your mark-making to emulate the surface you can see and feel.

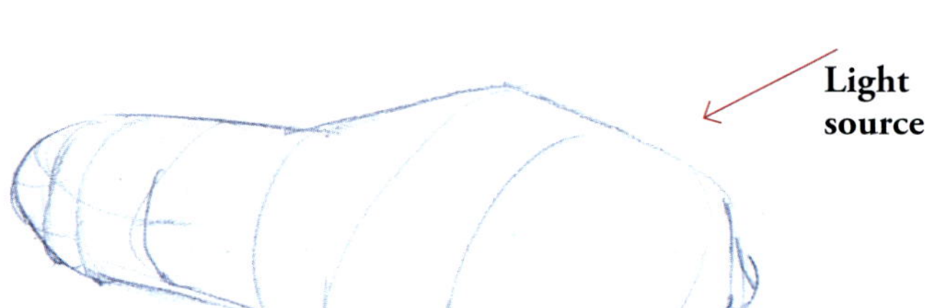

1 *Place your pebble by a window or under a lamp so that it is illuminated by a single light source. Create an initial sketch that suggests your subject's character, shape and proportions, then draw light lines around the form to suggest volume.*

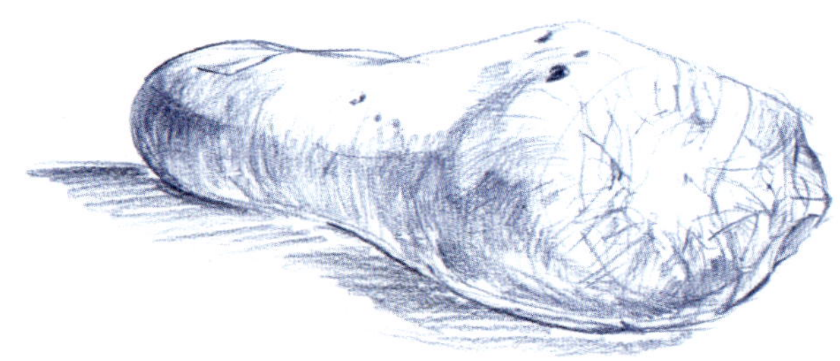

2 *Dramatic lighting can make the most everyday subject an exciting subject for a study. Begin modelling the pebble, coaxing the volume out of the paper by creating marks that follow the form.*

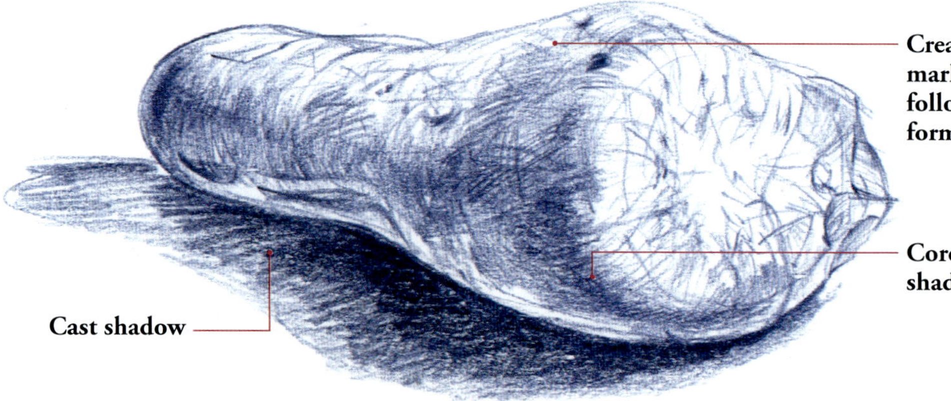

3 *Use the full range of tonality available to you. Capture the imperfections that bring interest to your subject. Use these dints, dings and cracks to help model the form.*

Surface decoration

In this rock study, quartz veins cut through black shale created in ancient geological activities. This decorative detail is attractive to the eye and also helps to give volume to the form; it can also be used to help express light and shade. I am always looking for ways to create the illusion of form, depth, light and shade on the paper. The way an object is lit can add drama to the subject and help express its three-dimensional qualities.

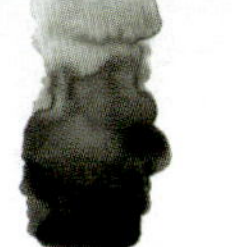
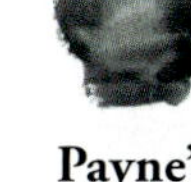

Materials
- 2B graphite pencil
- Watercolour paints (see swatches above)
- Cartridge (drawing) paper or sketchbook
- Sharpener
- Putty eraser
- Candle wax

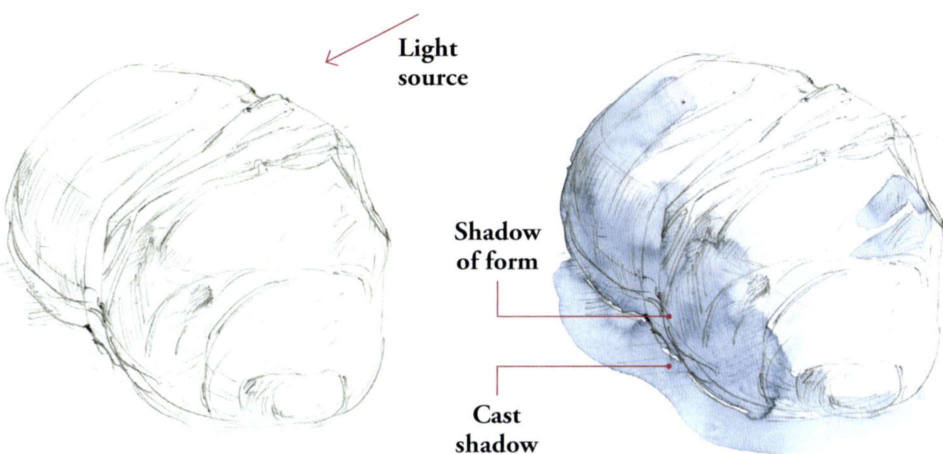

1 *Define your light source, then create a light pencil sketch. Quartz veins in the blue-black shale follow the form and help to express the physicality of the pebble.*

2 *Use a French ultramarine to place in both the shadow of form and cast shadow in one go. Now use a sharpened slither of a candle to make resist lines; these will emulate the pebble's texture on the thicker bands of white. It is important to place the shadow colour before adding the wax as you won't be able to add them afterwards.*

3 *Mix the smoky grey colour of the slate in the light by using a mixture of Payne's grey and ivory black. Squint your eye to reduce detail and paint in your initial modelling over the whole pebble. Ensure that you are continuously looking and drawing with the brush rather than filling in your initial sketch. Simplify the tones you see into two shades: the colour of the pebble in light and the one in the shade. Finally, beef up the shadow with more concentrated paint.*

Capturing light

When we draw a simple cube, it can look featureless and flat. However, when we add shading it can take on a monumental appearance. Practise adding value by creating a range of tone from coal black to a smoky grey. It is partly the conviction with which we apply these simple activities that makes the work appear three dimensional. I have seen an apple drawn on the corner of a newspaper with a simple ball-point pen that was so convincingly round, I felt it could be picked off the page.

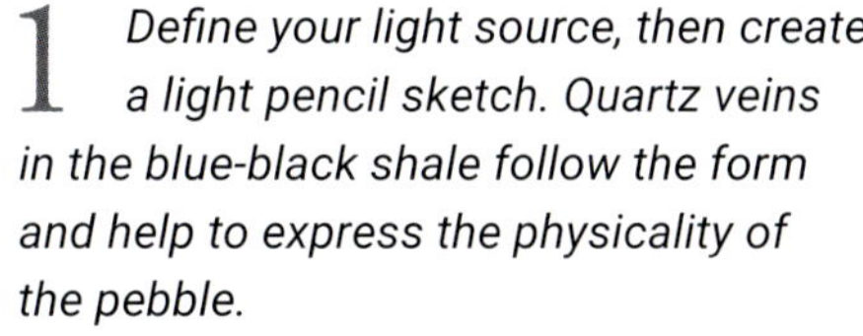

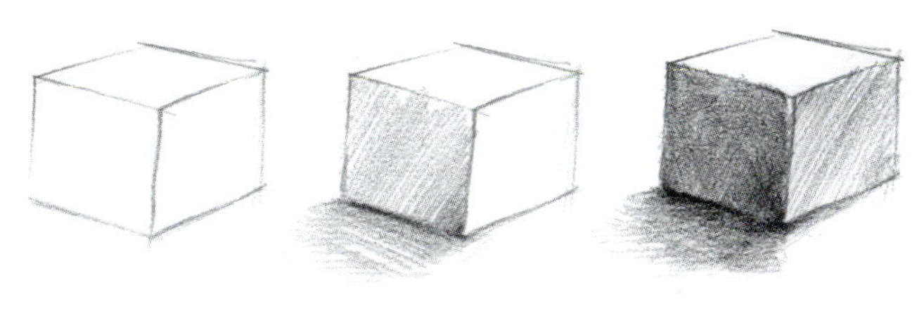

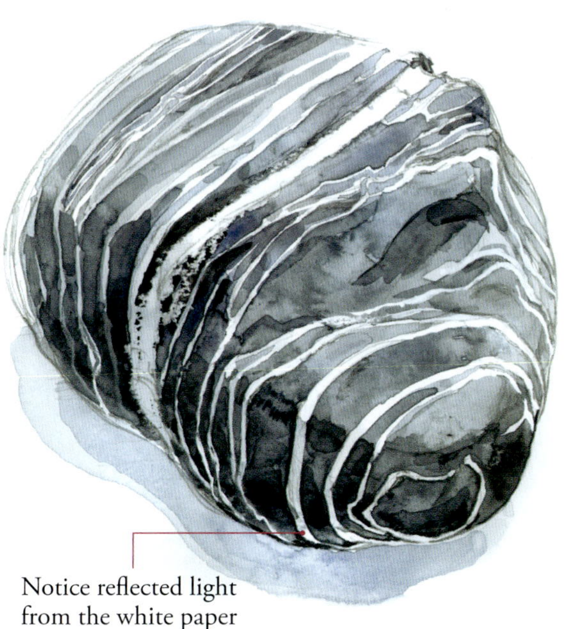

Notice reflected light from the white paper

Modelling with Line

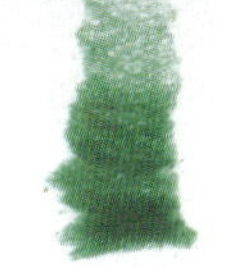
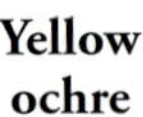

Permanent green   **Yellow ochre**

Drawing borrows the term 'modelling' from sculpture to refer to any graphic technique that creates the appearance of three dimensions. Form can be suggested by creating a zigzag movement of the pencil to create the parallel lines of hatching (see page 64). Strokes can be created in any direction. Those that follow the direction of the form will sculpt it and create the illusion of solidity.

In this tutorial, contour hatch modelling is used to emphasize the tactile three-dimensional volume of the cactus's smooth bulbous segments, which is contrasted with their fearsome defensive spikes. Hatching marks bend around the curvature of the segments, following the optical effects provided by a direct light and giving the form shadow; they also provide cast shadow.

Cacti can, at first, appear an intimidating subject. They can be unforgiving in getting their proportions right compared with the subtleties of sketching a face. Cacti are both organic and geometric simultaneously, following the mathematical laws of nature. The volume of the cacti's structures is evident through the natural contours surrounding them. I started from the crown and let my drawing grow organically by sketching shape to shape, working my way down to the base of the plant. I never feel restricted by my initial sketch and change and adapt it widely, particularly at the beginning.

Ball cactus (*Parodia magnifica*)

Cacti are a member of the succulent plant family. They have adapted to grow in arid climates, with little rainfall and plenty of sunshine. Their prickles turn them into an unattractive meal for many animals. The stems are green to photosynthesize food for the plant because spines can't do this. Cacti stems and ridges expand to store water for periods when rain is sparse. Most plants lose water every day through their leaves in a process called transpiration. Cacti, however, undertake this process at night when it is cooler to reduce the amount of water that is lost.

Materials

- Artist's quality colouring pencils (see swatches above)
- Cartridge (drawing) paper or sketchbook
- Sharpener
- Putty eraser

Tip

I often create the initial light underlying framework of the drawing in a lighter or different shade of colouring pencil.

Ball cactus

Various marks are employed to capture the different qualities of the contrasting smooth bulbous waxy skin and sharp spines. First, sharpen the pencil each time before trying to capture the sharpness of the spines, and then – when the pencil is blunter through use – turn to the ridges to create the shading by making hatching marks.

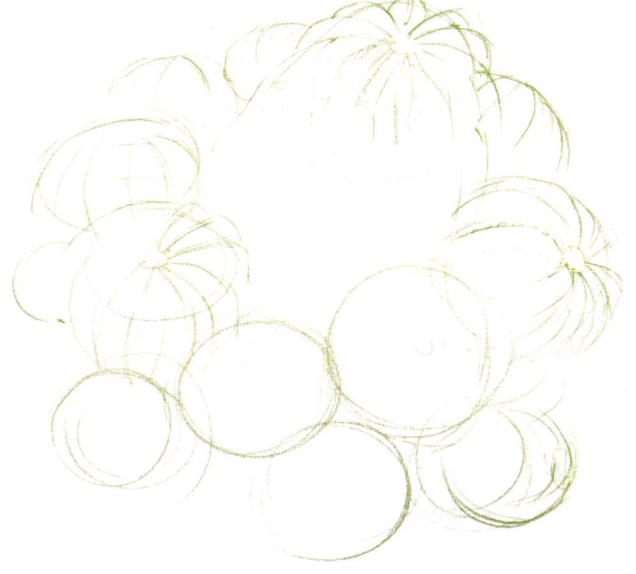

1   *Initially, concentrate on giving the cacti smooth, round shapes and sketch out their proportions. Use the natural compass hinges in your wrist and elbow to create a fluid scaffolding. This will be the initial architecture on which to hang the detail. Pick a neutral shade that will recede behind the second pencil work.*

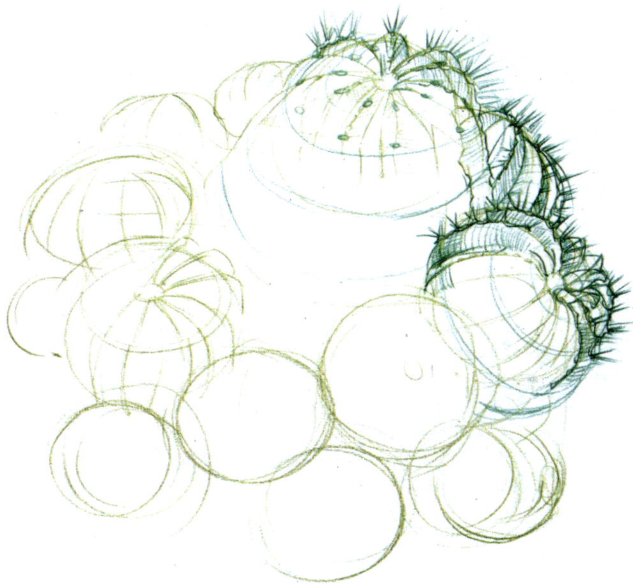

2 *Next, sketch from top downwards in a stronger, darker colour related to the cactus shade. Render the areas almost completely before moving onto new unfamiliar territory. Try to pull the ridges out from the orbs by creating directional shading, using hatching marks that follow the form.*

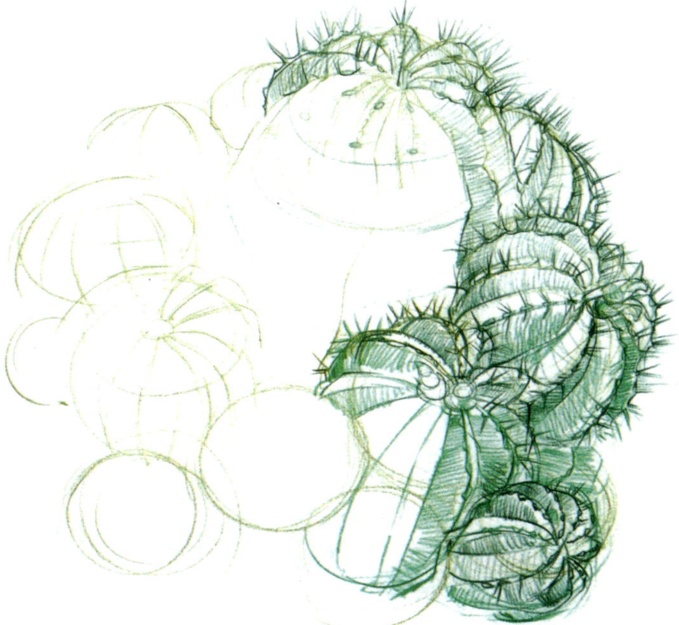

3 *Create flick marks to capture the sharp spines on top of the ridges, which are grouped in tiny clusters. You can sketch a small arrow in the corner of the page to indicate the light source and ensure all the elements in the study are affected uniformly by it.*

4 *Keep going until you feel that the drawing is complete. I sometimes leave the sketch a little unfinished to leave some white space, allowing the sketch to breathe.*

Creating zones of light and shadows

Separate your study into four basic tonal zones, based on the lights and shadows created by a single direct source of light. In graduating order, these should include a light zone, a light halftone zone, a dark halftone zone and a dark shadow zone.

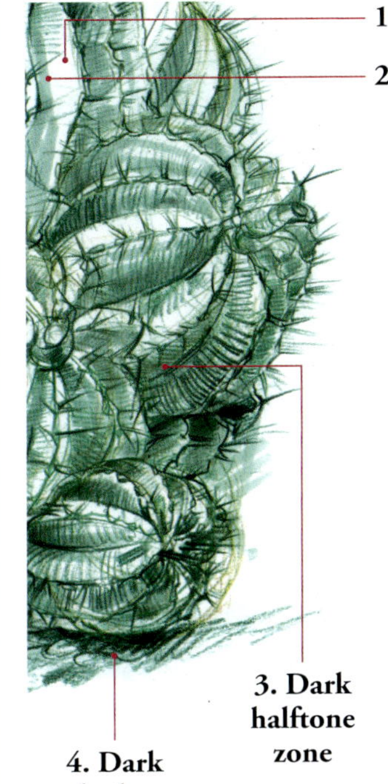

1. These parts of the form face the light source directly and are the brightest.

2. These are the transitional areas where the form initially turns away from the light. It is a light mid-tone value between light and dark.

3. Darker shading suggests planes more hidden from the light source on the underside of the cactus.

4. These zones have the darkest values, where the artist can really accentuate the mark, such as at the base.

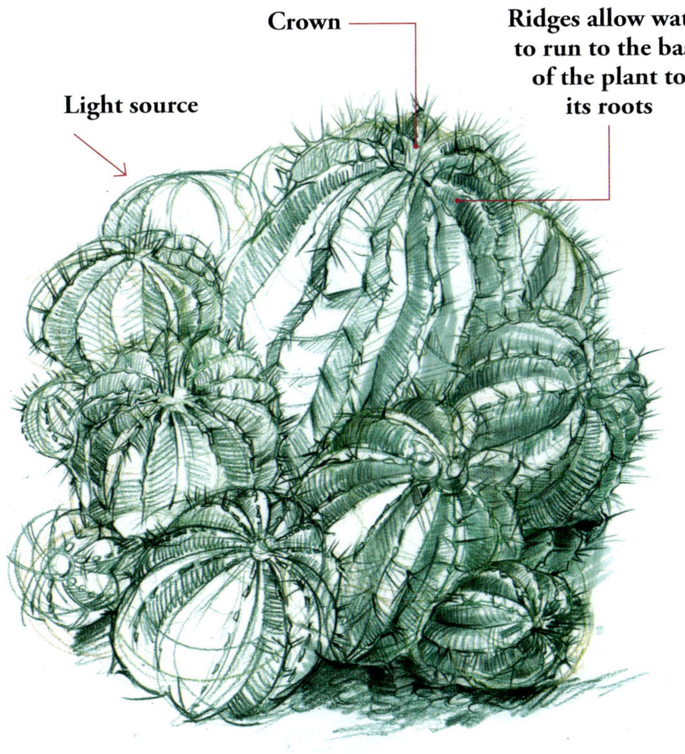

Planar Analysis

The dissection of a structure into flat planes is known as a planar analysis. This is a method that involves looking at a subject and breaking it down into faceted planes. Each plane is a flat surface and when a number of them are joined together they can create a form. A planar analysis drawing is best created from first-hand observation, where you can get a sense of the physicality of the form. If the subject is an object, pick it up and handle it to get a sense of the direction of the planes.

The planar analysis approach works hand in hand with a structural or constructive approach to drawing. The artist simplifies the subject into crisp, clean shard-like planes to create a volumetric shard-like image. Large planes on the form are drawn first, and then they are gradually broken down into smaller parts. The process could theoretically continue until smooth forms are created by tiny flat planes.

Glass animals

Live animals that are momentarily at rest can be dissected by eye. Imagine the body parts are made of glass. Being transparent, you can see the ellipses of the neck behind the head and so forth. Drawing through or seeing your subject as if it was transparent is an excellent approach when drawing animals from first-hand observation.

To begin drawing with this approach, reduce the organic volumes to their most basic geometric forms. The neck, for example, becomes a tube, the body a barrel and the legs a series of segmented tubes. Once the main body forms are set, use hatching to create the facets of planes on their surfaces (see pages 80–1). Details of tendons, muscles and fat can be implied with shading and tufts of pelt with flick marks of hair.

▲ Flint

A chipped piece of flint makes an excellent angular subject. Initially, create a drawing that has none or limited shading.

▼ Transparent camel head

The camel has a split upper lip with a groove that allows water to enter the mouth directly from the nostrils and prevents water loss by the camel. To generate bulging eyes caused by a muscle eye ring, incorporate the contour of a scuba diving mask.

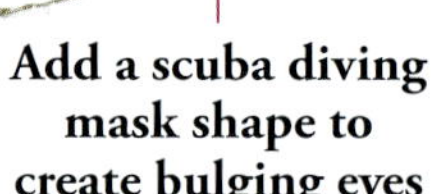

Create simple ellipses to plumb the ear tubes in

Add a scuba diving mask shape to create bulging eyes

► Camel from back view

Constantly strive to divide the subject into manageable body zones. Begin by drawing the area of the body closest to you; in this drawing, it is the back legs. The heel bone and Achilles tendon, which is joined to the gastrocnemius muscle, are particularly fun to model, and they create a feeling of elastic tension in the leg.

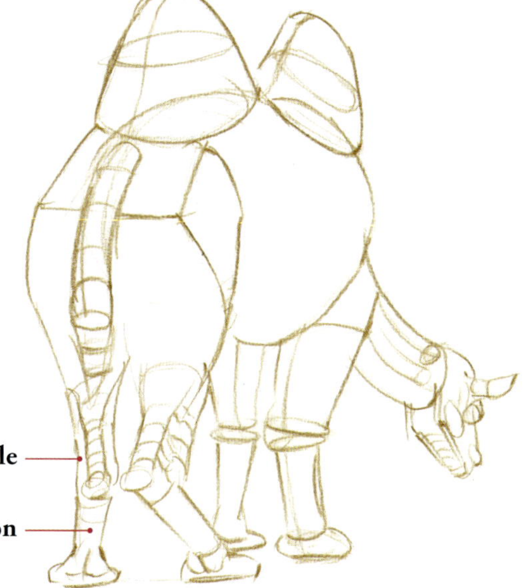

Gastrocnemius muscle

Achilles tendon

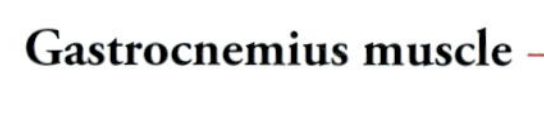

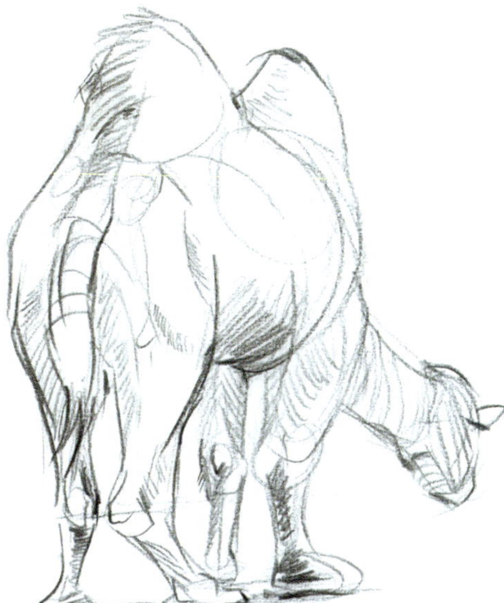

Alpaca

When drawing an alpaca, the ribcage can be envisaged as a large barrel and the limbs as simplified tapering tubes. You can see this idea in your own limbs. You can touch a finger and thumb together (or almost) in a grasp about your wrist, whereas this would be impossible around your upper arm. When the body is foreshortened (see page 112), these simple shapes are easily understood in compressed viewpoints.

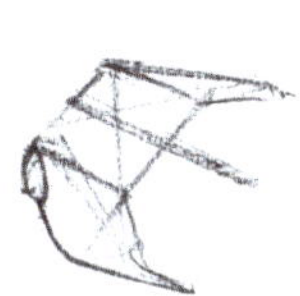

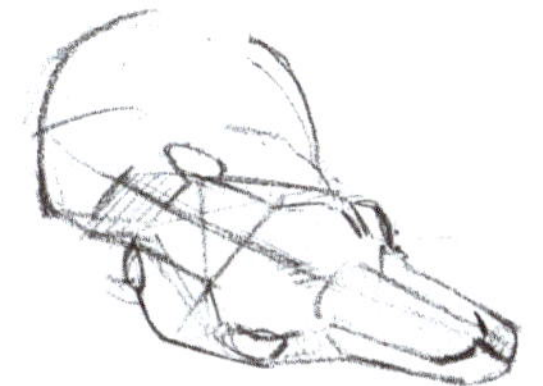

Materials
- Cold grey artist's quality colouring pencils
- Cartridge (drawing) paper or sketchbook
- Sharpener
- Putty eraser

Alpaca (*Vicugna pacos*)

According to DNA analysis, alpacas were domesticated by the Inca in the Andes Mountains in South America between 6,000 and 7,000 years ago and are descended from vicuñas, a type of camelid. Alpacas can walk on vegetation without damaging it, thanks to the soft padding under their even-toed feet. They have developed this adaptation because there is little vegetation in Peru's Andes, and their ability to maintain the grazing area is essential to their own survival.

1 *Start with the top of the head. A lightly drawn box with a bilateral line of symmetry slices the body in half and will enable you to align the left- and right-hand body parts.*

2 *Next, move the drawing forward by adding a projecting box for the muzzle, and then move back towards the neck, drawing a foreshortened tube.*

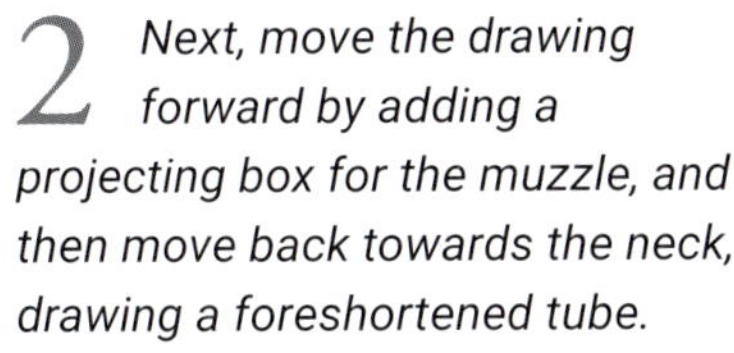

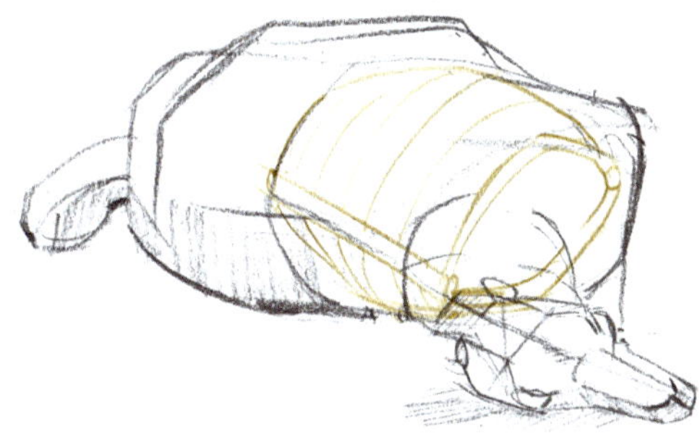

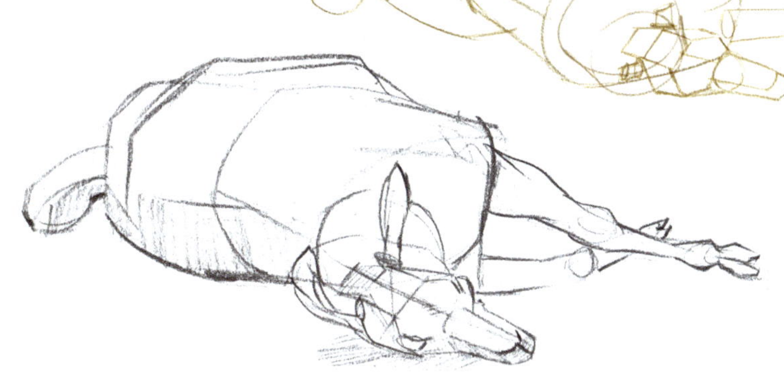

3 *Now bulk out the body, envisaging the mass of the ribcage beneath.*

4 *Work from the more prominent forms towards the smaller and add appendages, such as ears. When sketching from live animals, the amount of information you can get down on the paper will be dependent on the length of time your model holds the pose. This, however, can result in a lively mark and drawings that are full of life and personality.*

Planar shading

One of the valuable tools for modelling, especially on a muscular shark, is planar shading (see page 77). Sketching the shark simply as a tube would make it look tubby. However, if you look closely at its body, you will notice subdivisions of small geometric muscular planes, and drawing these can help express the animal's incredible power.

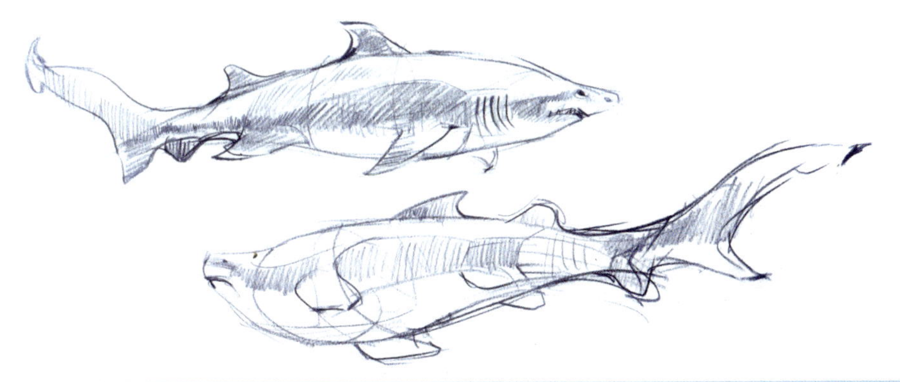

Three-quarter Views

Drawing three-quarter rear views will allow the artist to see all the body parts compressed in perspective. Two-thirds of an ungulate's body weight rests on its front legs when it is at rest. This enables the rear legs to take on more relaxed positions than the front ones, although they are always poised, ready to spring into action. Only rarely will the animal stand in a perfect profile view. Being able to rotate the skeleton in your mind's eye is a vital skill in understanding the articulation points and identifying various lumps and bumps on the surface, such as the head of the humerus bone or the patella of the knee.

What lies beneath is apparent on the surface

Having a clear understanding of the structure that lies beneath the fur, skin, fat and muscles of an animal is essential for giving your drawings a feeling of structure and weight distribution, and to stop them looking like a toy. Any animal can be seen as a combination of parts – a head, an arm, a leg and so on. These elements can be broken down further into simpler primary forms.

Developing your knowledge of the skeletal structure of a quadruped's legs, which creates a bridge-like structure supporting the barrel of the chest, is essential. From a three-quarters rear view you will notice the protuberance of the calcaneus, or heel bone, attached to the thick chord of the Achilles tendon. The carpals create a clear bulge at the 'wrist' and is a good point to look for a subtle change of angle of the lower leg, such as the slight knock-knees of ungulate youth.

Okapi

In these studies, the main emphasis is a play between the structural make-up of bones, the overlapping body masses, the folds in the skin and the flick marks of hair on the surface. Use the brown and white stripes of fur on the rump to model the form as they wrap around the buttocks and legs.

1 *I try to capture the feeling of trapped energy in the cocked spring of the back leg of an animal in my initial sketch.*

Okapi (*Okapia johnstoni*)
The okapi, also referred to as the forest giraffe, resembles a combination of a zebra and a deer. However, it is a giraffidae, and the giraffe's only living relative. The only place where the okapi may be found in the wild is in the Ituri rainforest in the Democratic Republic of the Congo. It has thick, oily fur to keep it dry in the rain. The brown and white stripes on its rump, which resemble streaks of sunlight passing through the trees, help it blend in with its surroundings. The ossicones, or short horns, of the okapi, are covered in skin and fur.

Materials
- Black artist's quality colouring pencil
- Cartridge (drawing) paper or sketchbook
- Sharpener
- Putty eraser

2 *Next I start to shade the surface detail and model the heel and Achilles tendon.*

3 *Cast shadow on the ground prevents the okapi from floating in space.*

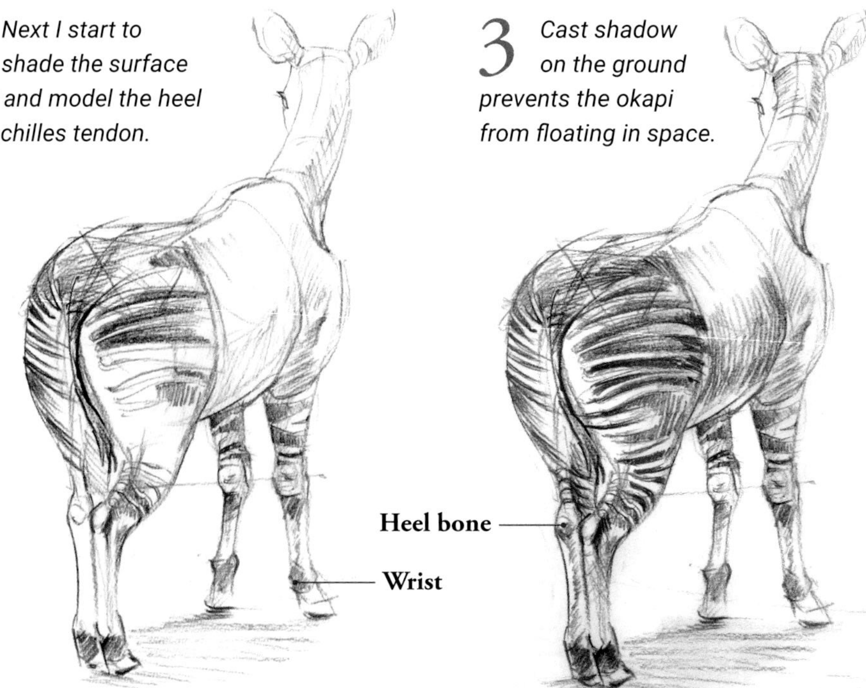

Study Sheet: *Okapi*

Wild animals will not sit for a portrait or the equivalent of Leonardo da Vinci's *Vitruvian Man*. You are at the mercy of their movements. A study sheet (see pages 16–17) is an ideal way of tackling this situation, and it will allow you to get to know your subject from lots of different angles.

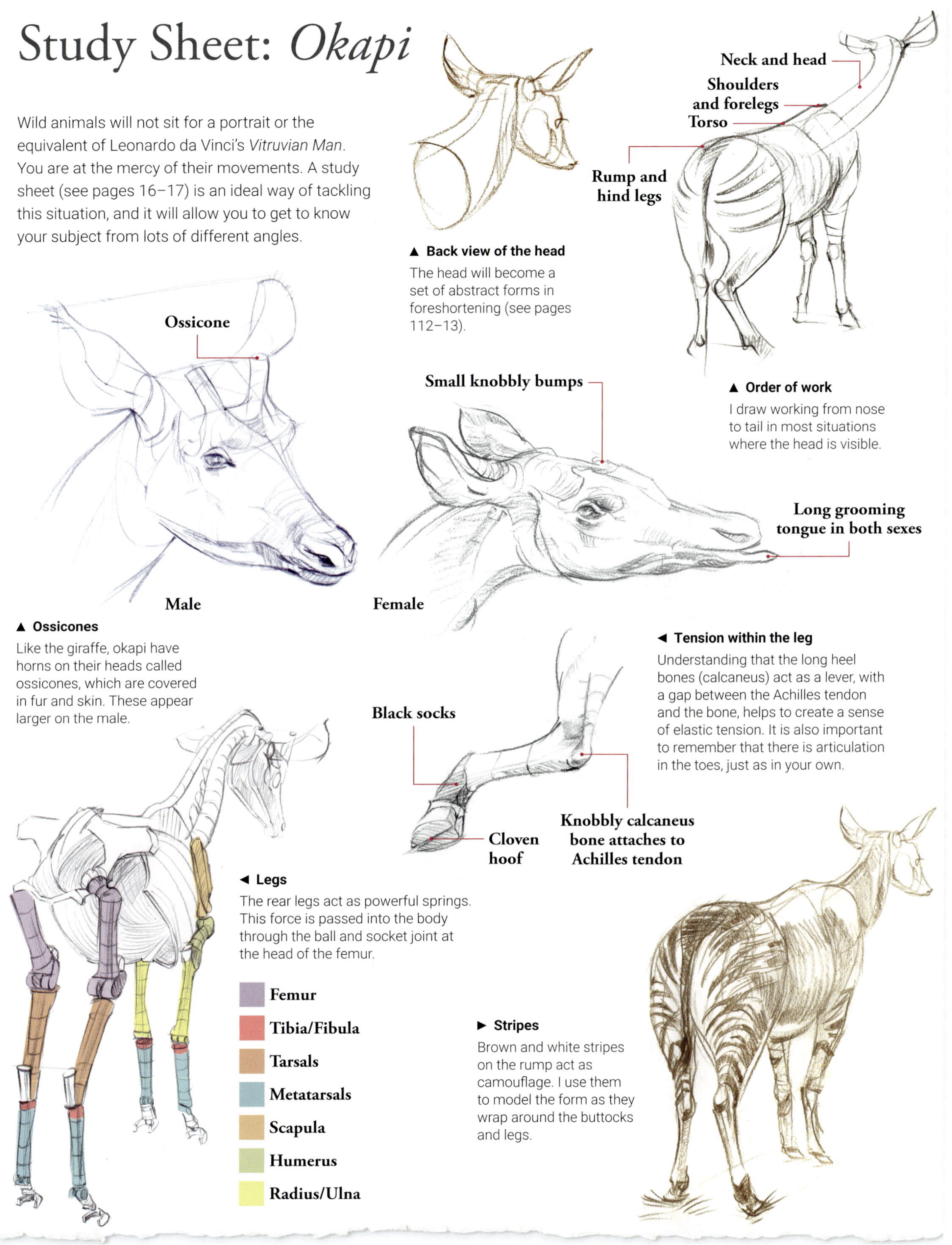

▲ Back view of the head

The head will become a set of abstract forms in foreshortening (see pages 112–13).

▲ Order of work

I draw working from nose to tail in most situations where the head is visible.

▲ Ossicones

Like the giraffe, okapi have horns on their heads called ossicones, which are covered in fur and skin. These appear larger on the male.

◄ Tension within the leg

Understanding that the long heel bones (calcaneus) act as a lever, with a gap between the Achilles tendon and the bone, helps to create a sense of elastic tension. It is also important to remember that there is articulation in the toes, just as in your own.

◄ Legs

The rear legs act as powerful springs. This force is passed into the body through the ball and socket joint at the head of the femur.

► Stripes

Brown and white stripes on the rump act as camouflage. I use them to model the form as they wrap around the buttocks and legs.

Perceived Mass

Mass is a measure of how much matter is in an object, and the challenge for any artist is to get the sense of a subject's mass and then convey it onto paper. I find it difficult to get a sense of mass from a photograph, but when I share the same space and get close to the subject, its shifting planes, mounds and bumps become far more apparent.

To get a sense of weight in your drawings, start by feeling your own body weight in the soles of your feet as they compact on the ground. Feel the force of gravity pulling you down to the earth. When drawing a subject with plenty of mass, marks can be emboldened at pressure points to emphasize gravitational pull, with the fat and skin of an elephant's foot, for example, splaying out as it impacts the earth.

Drawing with softer, darker colours and coarse textures helps create more sculptural drawings, where a sense of physicality is implied with vigorous shading marks carving out the form. You can get a sense of the enormity of an elephant's mass by observing it closely. Gravity pulls on the folds in the skin that drapes over its huge skeletal framework. Its legs are like pillars that support the barrel of the body, which is so heavy that the elephant cannot jump in the air.

Asian elephant
(*Elephas maximus indicus*)
As blood circulates through the vessels in the elephant's ear, it cools down and then circulates into the rest of the body, which helps cool the entire elephant down. As Asian elephants live in cooler temperatures, they have smaller ears, which also prevents them getting snagged in their forest habitat. All elephants are highly social animals and cannot be kept individually; they are ambassadors of maternal and paternal care and the shadowy wells of their eyes seem to hold many distant memories.

Asian elephant

When you come up close to an elephant herd, you get an overwhelming sense of their monumental physicality that needs to be conveyed on paper surface. Around the trunk and legs, I scribbled a rapid succession of loops that go above and below the eyeline (see pages 76–7).

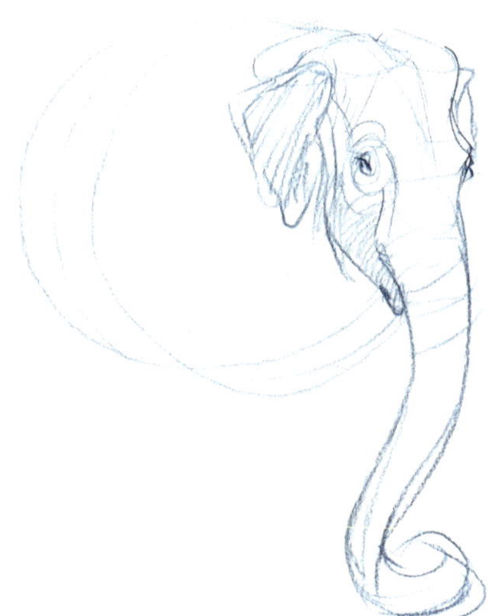

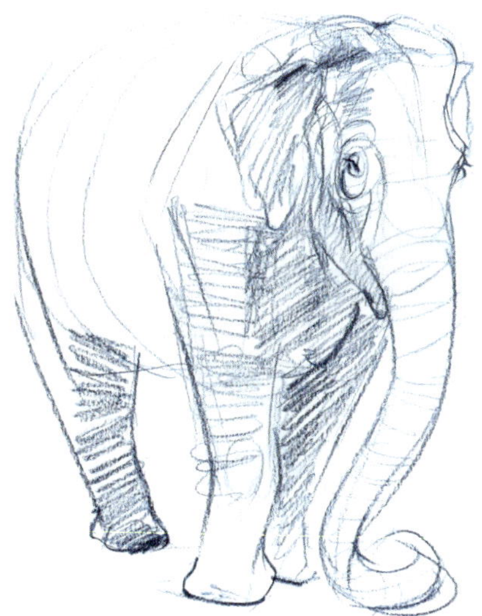

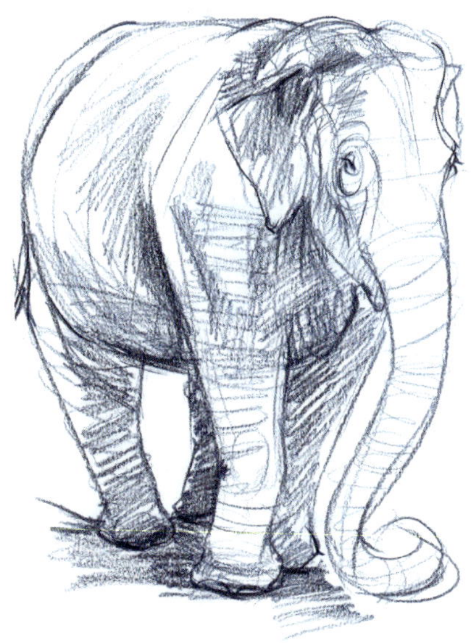

1 *Begin sketching at the head in a frontal view and then freeze the trunk in a gestural position. Asian elephants have a two-dome structure on the top of their head. Draw from front to back and start planning the volume of the torso by drawing circular loops.*

2 *Sketch light ellipses to suggest the volume of the trunk, being thoughtful about the angle that it tilts. By squinting at the elephant, you can reduce the detail and see the main blocks of light and shade.*

3 *Continue to shade with a loose underhand grip (see page 14) sculpting around the form in a chiaroscuro fashion (see pages 70–1). Adding a cast shadow will help express the massive bulk and anchor the animal to the ground.*

Study Sheet: *Elephant*

This study sheet (see pages 16–17) is about learning to hew like a sculptor and capture monumental forms in balance. Before drawing elephants in a herd, take a deep breath and simply observe them. Take a moment to immerse yourself in their world and see if you can pick up on their different personalities, from the playful child to the responsible grumpy parent.

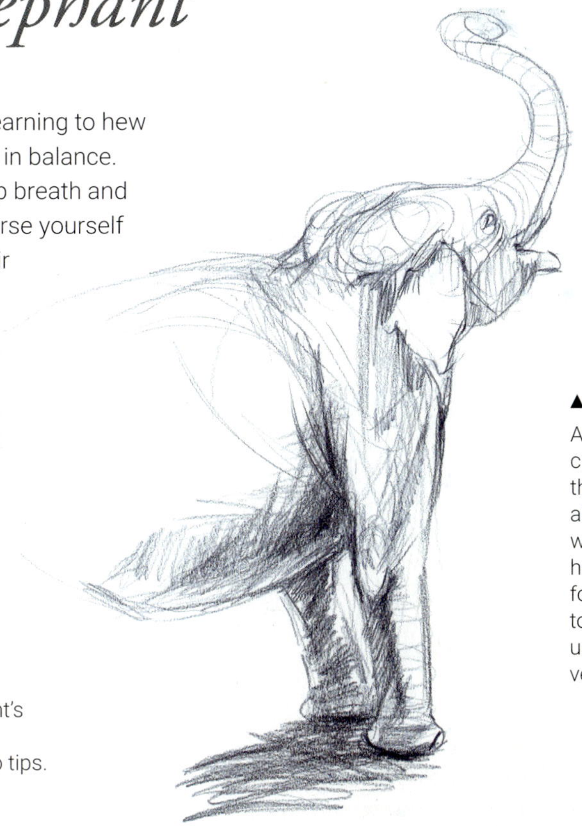

▶ Suggestive bulk

Create evocative scribbles to suggest the enormous bulk on the paper. Search for folds in the loose, wrinkled skin and draw the image as if you were shaping clay, almost kneading the pencil marks.

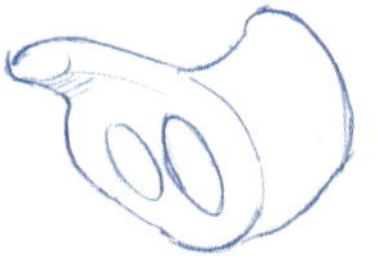

◀ Single tipped trunk

The tip of an Asian elephant's trunk has one 'finger', but African elephants have two tips.

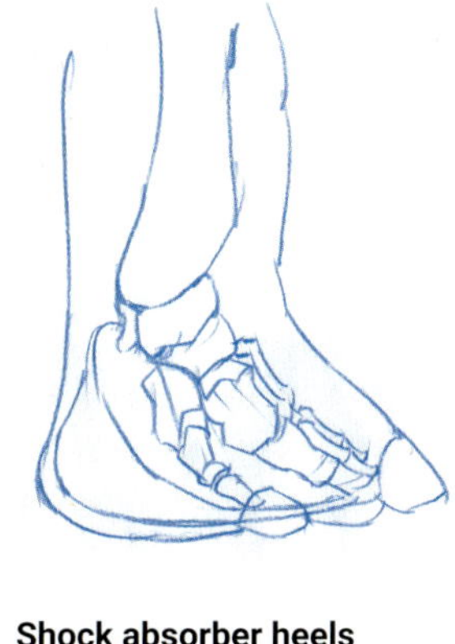

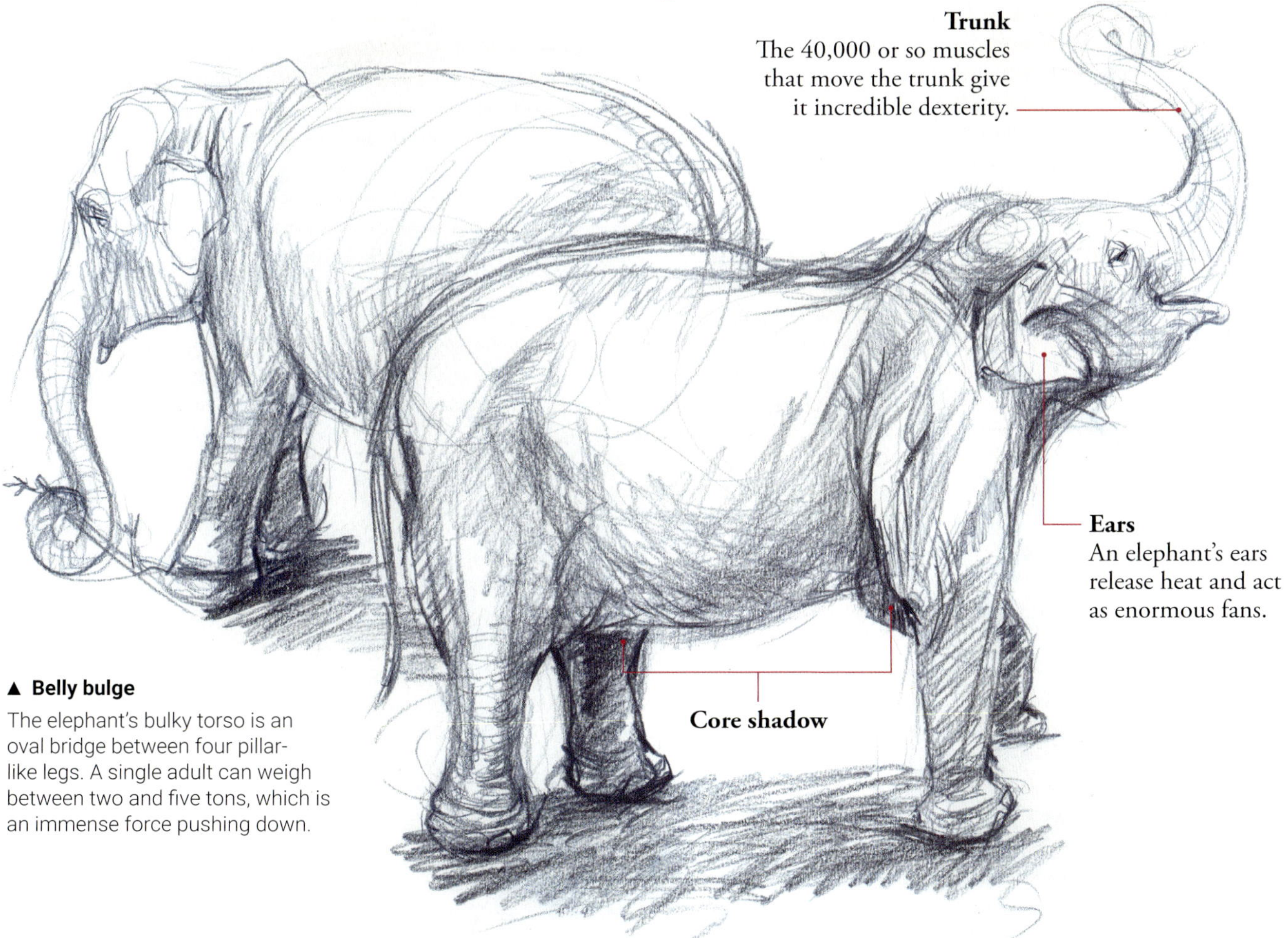

▲ Shock absorber heels

A wedge-shaped piece of cushioning soft tissue supports the heel, serving as a shock absorber. As the elephant puts its weight on each foot, you can see how it spreads out. Each elephant foot has five toes, but not every toe has a nail. The Asian elephant usually has four on the back, and very rarely five.

Trunk
The 40,000 or so muscles that move the trunk give it incredible dexterity.

Ears
An elephant's ears release heat and act as enormous fans.

Core shadow

▲ Belly bulge

The elephant's bulky torso is an oval bridge between four pillar-like legs. A single adult can weigh between two and five tons, which is an immense force pushing down.

Shape-to-shape Modelled Drawing

Skeletons can be an intimidating subject. The real challenge is to see through all the visual complexities to get down to the main underlying structure. This tutorial, which only works on static subjects, encourages you to see your subject as patches of dark and light shapes. Start from the nose and let your drawing grow organically by sketching from one shape to the next, working your way to the base of the tail as you create blocks of light and dark.

This method of drawing is relevant when the model is in a sustained pose and is lit by a clear, consistent light source, which makes it ideal for drawing in a museum. If you go to one, you will almost certainly only be allowed to use dry media, and you will have to get used to glancing through passing crowds.

In this exercise, focus on the subject and eliminate all background details to create white space, which will allow the complex web of bones to breathe. As you draw, contemplate your work almost as a mosaic of tonal shapes, working from an area that you understand to unfamiliar territory, and taking on each challenge one step at a time. I intentionally work from nose to tail, which prevents the ball of my hand smudging the soft pencil.

Giant ground sloth

These fossilized bones have the appearance of slabs of stone. Like in most museums, these bones were lit from above, a form of lighting that dramatizes the subject in a chiaroscuro fashion (see pages 70–1). You can create a more detailed drawing by working from direct observation. This will give you more information than can be gleaned from a photograph, which will flatten the form. The intention of this exercise is to create a drawing that evokes a sense of the three-dimensional form.

Materials
- Prussian blue artist's quality colouring pencil
- Cartridge (drawing) paper or sketchbook
- Sharpener
- Putty eraser

1 *Before you start drawing, spend time planning. Position yourself at a desired angle in front of the subject. Start with a series of light sight-size measuring marks and holding up vertical and horizontals to explore proportions, relationships and angles (see pages 52–3) to draw the head. If you find it a challenge to fit a large subject on the paper, draw out a light measured frame using comparative measuring (see pages 54–5). Look for landmarks, such as the length of the head and the distance from the top of the head to the elbow. Measure the height and the width of the skull.*

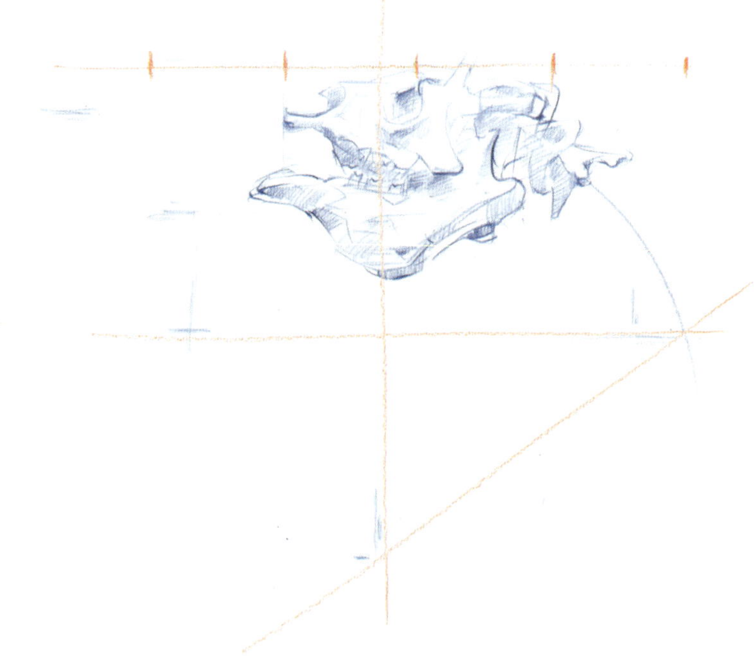

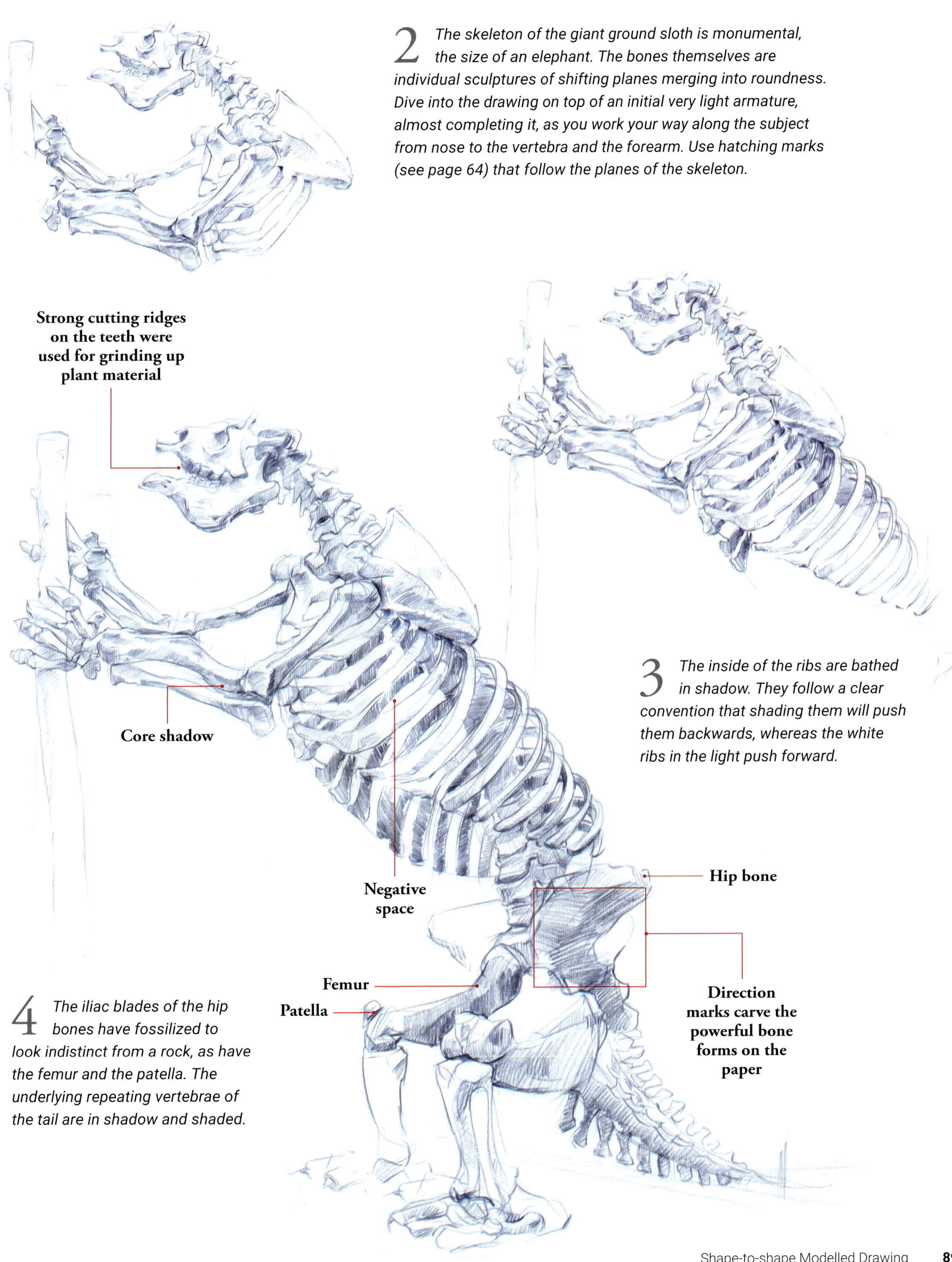

2 The skeleton of the giant ground sloth is monumental, the size of an elephant. The bones themselves are individual sculptures of shifting planes merging into roundness. Dive into the drawing on top of an initial very light armature, almost completing it, as you work your way along the subject from nose to the vertebra and the forearm. Use hatching marks (see page 64) that follow the planes of the skeleton.

3 The inside of the ribs are bathed in shadow. They follow a clear convention that shading them will push them backwards, whereas the white ribs in the light push forward.

4 The iliac blades of the hip bones have fossilized to look indistinct from a rock, as have the femur and the patella. The underlying repeating vertebrae of the tail are in shadow and shaded.

Colour

Humans can perceive colour when light waves strike an object and then reflect the object's local colour (or colours) to the optic nerve in their eyes. Colour can both unify and move the eye around an image. At least 75,000 years ago, artists created the earliest paints from a mixture of dirt, animal fat, charcoal and chalk, resulting in a basic colour palette of red, yellow, brown, black and white. Ever since, pigments have been developed alongside the evolution of art history's movements, allowing painters to experiment with new colours. Thanks to modern technologies, we now have interference paints that allow us to recreate structural colour – the iridescence found on a hummingbird's throat or peacock's tail that are so bright that it dazzles the eye and the imagination.

Colours create psychological reactions. Red, for example, implies dominance, power or even anger. The nose on a mandrill (a primate with colourful patches of skin) becomes a brighter shade of red as it rises through the ranks. Red can be a colour that creates an instant focal point as it draws the eye, such as a red jacket in a nineteenth-century painting by the British artist John Constable. The comforting colour of autumnal orange contains some of the power of red, but it is lightened by yellow. Yellow itself can evoke happiness and is seen in plenty in the sun-drenched paintings of the nineteenth-century Dutch artist Vincent Van Gogh when he captured the southern light of France. Green is clean and fresh; it is the colour of the chlorophyll in spring leaves and has positive associations. The twentieth-century Spanish painter Pablo Picasso had a blue period that evoked sadness, but blue can also be seen as a symbol of purity. Due to the scarcity of the original pigment lapis lazuli, only the most senior members of the Church, such as the Virgin Mary, were depicted in this hue of blue, resulting in spiritual associations that, in reality, were due to costs. Recessive blue bathes in the shadows of my coloured landscapes and is my most used colour. Finally, violet is a colour with perhaps more energy than blue. We might associate violet with royalty, luxury or even spirituality.

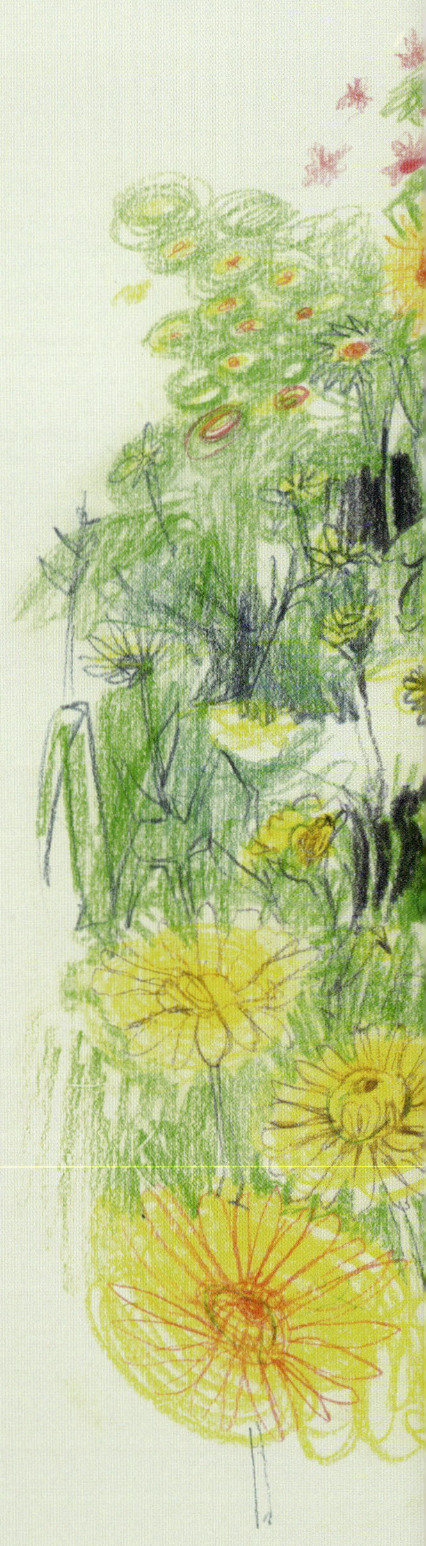

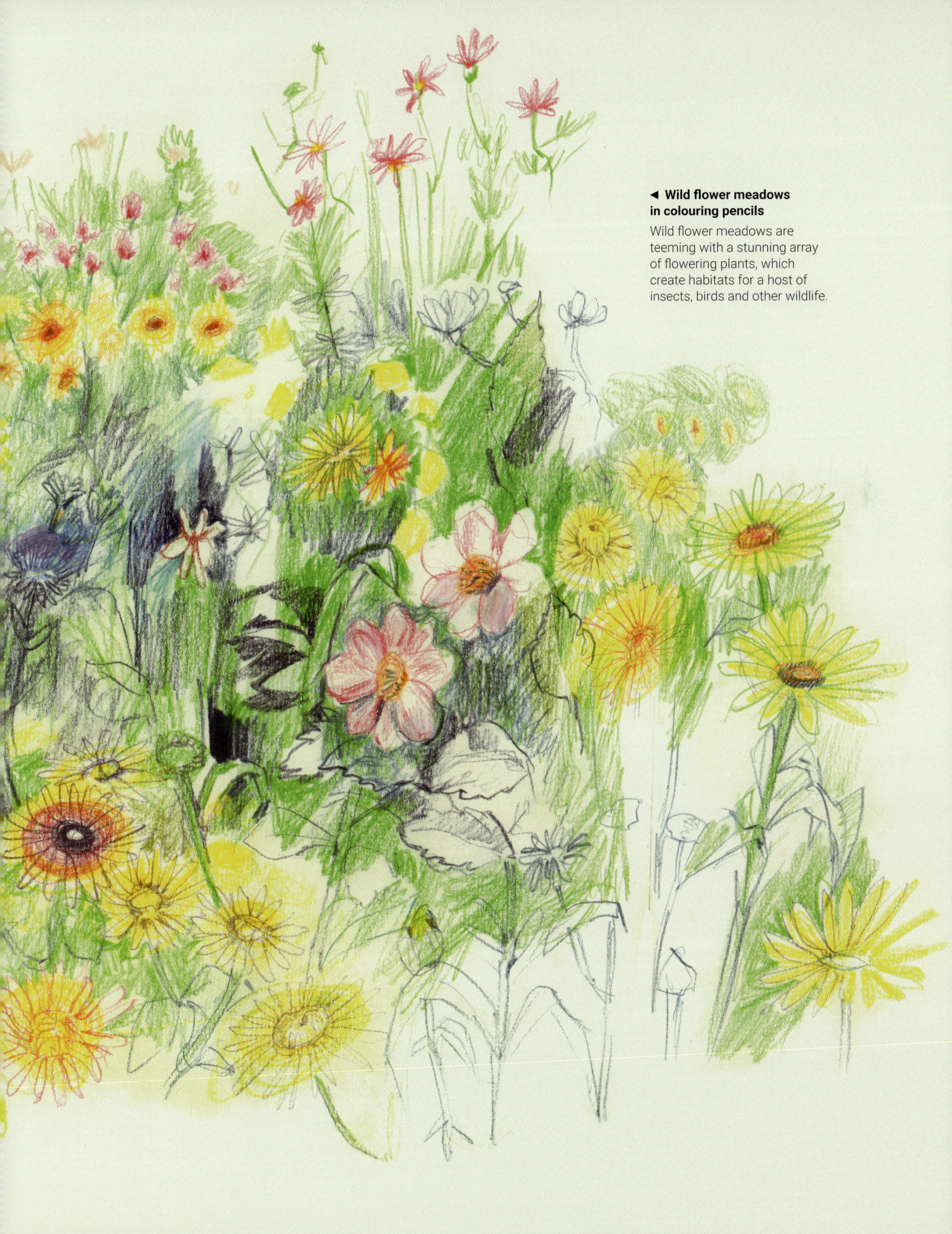

◄ Wild flower meadows
in colouring pencils
Wild flower meadows are
teeming with a stunning array
of flowering plants, which
create habitats for a host of
insects, birds and other wildlife.

Colour Essentials

It was Sir Isaac Newton who created the first colour wheel when he discovered the visible spectrum of light in around 1665. Newton passed white light through a prism and watched it fan out into a rainbow, and from this he identified seven constituent colours: red, orange, yellow, green, blue, indigo and violet. Today, artists' colour wheels are normally based on three of these colours, from which an almost infinite range of hues can be mixed. Different colours can be used to elicit a variety of feelings from the observer.

Additive and subtractive mixing

Adding the colours of light together is known as additive mixing. This colour mixing system uses red, green and blue (RGB) and is used in theatre lighting, television screens, smart phones and computer monitors.

However, when light is reflected from pigment, it is known as subtractive mixing – to remember this, think of starting with a pure colour. As different pigments are added, the wavelength's initial brilliance is subtracted until eventually you could be left with a dull black colour. Subtractive mixing comes in two main forms. The one we are interested is red, yellow and blue (RYB), which are used for artist's pigments. The other one, used for colour printing, is cyan, yellow and magenta (CYM), with the addition of black (K) to achieve a full range of dark values.

The primary colours

In subtractive mixing, yellow, red and blue are known as the three primary colours. This is because they can be mixed in different quantities to produce all the other colours in the wheel.

The secondary hues

There are also three secondary colours: orange, violet and green. These hues are created by combining roughly equal parts of two of the primary colours.

The tertiary colours

There are six tertiary colours; yellow-green, yellow-orange, red-orange, red-violet, blue-violet and blue-green. These colours are made by mixing a secondary colour with an adjacent primary colour on the wheel.

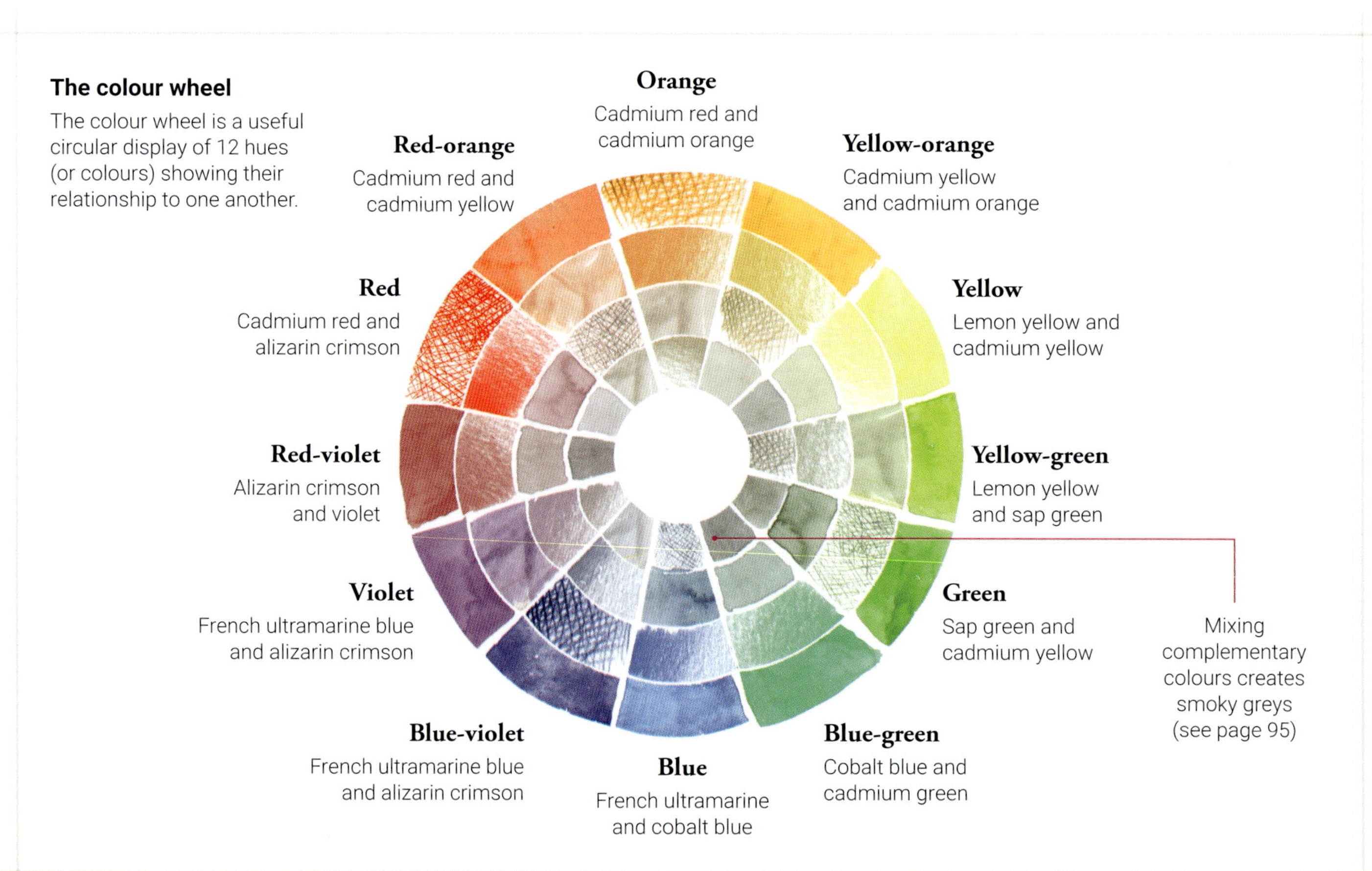

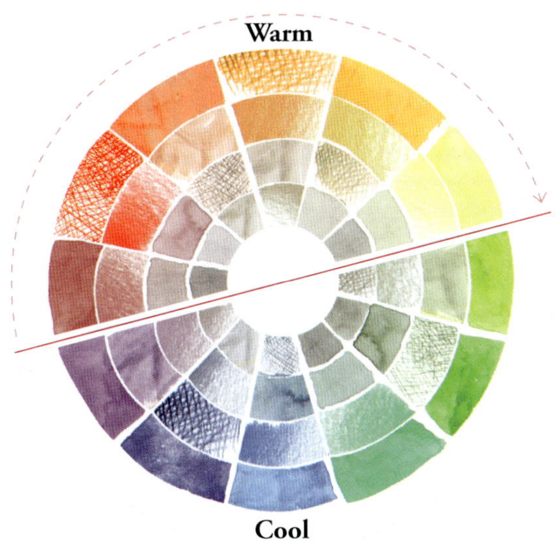

Warm hues are vivid and bright. They will seem to move forward in a drawing and exude feelings of warmth. Cool colours are calm and soothing. They will appear to recede within a painting.

Earth colours

The prehistoric palettes of the first artists were created from earth pigments. Red ochre is one of the oldest pigments on the planet and is created by the rusting of ferric oxide inside the clay. These ferric rich umbers and ochres, along with charcoal from the fire, were mixed with spit and animal fat, and applied to the walls, where they stained the porous rock surface. They are an excellent choice for an autumnal landscape.

Warm and cool colours

Changes in colour temperature and intensity can be observed in the atmospheric effects in landscape painting, where the colours of distant forms become colder, greyer and bluish and lighten in tonal contrast. Warm colours give the impression of coming forward towards the eye. In contrast, cool colours are referred to as recessive colours because they give the impression of dropping back. This will make them a good choice if you want to enhance the feeling of spatial depth in your painting.

Saturation and tone

The purity or brightness of a pigment is referred to as its saturation (or sometimes intensity). You can desaturate a colour by mixing it with its opposite colour. This is different than tone, where one colour of the same hue is naturally lighter than another, such as a cerulean blue being lighter than Prussian blue.

Tint

Any hue or combination of pure colours with white or water added to dilute it is referred to as a tint. Pastel hues are tints, for example. The tinted colour doesn't change, but it is paler than the original.

Blue tint

Pink tint

Shade

The opposite of tints are shades. These dark values are created by combining a colour with black. Navy is a shade of blue, for example, and maroon is a shade of red.

Navy

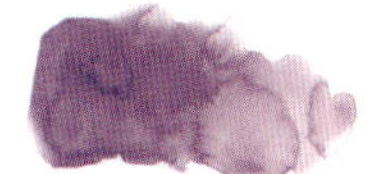

Maroon

Earth colours palette

Ivory black
A sooty coal colour, great for smoky greys when mixed with blue.

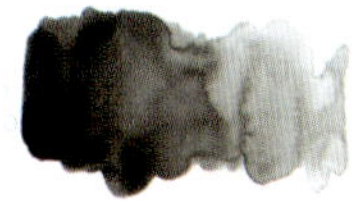

Payne's grey
A dark blue-grey. Eighteenth-century watercolourist William Payne created the mixture as an alternative to black.

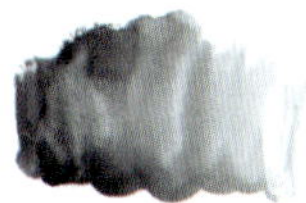

Yellow ochre
A natural, muted yellow-orange earth pigment composed primarily of clay coloured with iron oxides.

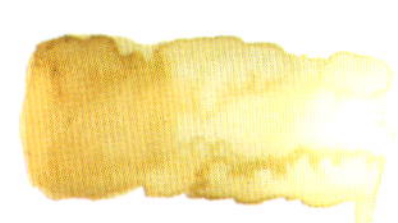

Raw sienna
A rich orange-brown pigment named after Sienna, Italy, where the pigment was sourced during the Renaissance.

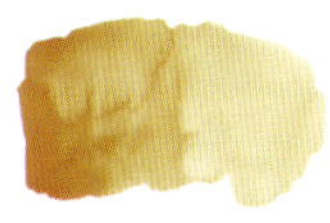

Umber
A rich, cool brown pigment made from clays; it is named after Umbria, in Italy, where it was mined.

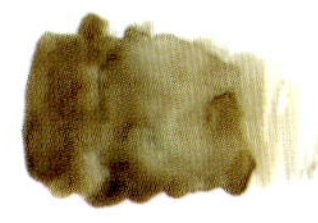

Burnt umber
A rich, dark brown pigment.

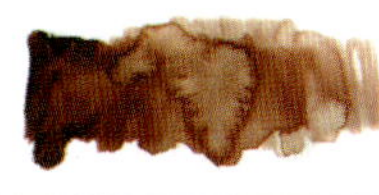

Terre verte
A soft, neutral emerald green colour. It was also known as Verona green as it was mined near Verona, Italy.

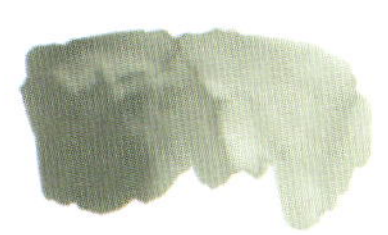

Colour Mixing

To achieve the colours you want from paints, pastels, inks or colouring pencils, it is essential that you understand how to mix colours together to be able to extend your colour range to match Monet's palette. You can learn which pigments to combine to create a variety of new colours, from the bright and bold to the subtle, grey and dark. You will find that colours lurk even in the shadows, and highlights can be tinged with subtle tints.

The rainbow

We love colour and devote a significant portion of our lives to admiring the beauty of colour in nature, in works of art and in the fashion we choose to wear. However, we can only see a portion of the entire spectrum, which we call visible light. Cone-shaped cells in our eyes that act as receivers can tune to wavelengths in only a relatively narrow band. Other animals have more receptor cones and can see colours beyond our range. These are typically animals with iridescent liveries, such as birds and butterflies – and the mantis shrimp can boast up to 16 different types of colour-based photoreceptors.

Colours of the rainbow

1. Ultramarine blue and alizarin crimson. 2. Ultramarine blue. 3. Cerulean blue. 4. Lemon yellow and cerulean blue. 5. Lemon yellow and cadmium yellow deep. 6. Cadmium yellow deep and cadmium red. 7. Cadmium red.

Getting familiar

There are a few key colours to note, from violet to red, which will help capture this bandwidth of dazzling vibrancy. Artist's quality paint manufacturers do not tend to sell the three primary colours and the selection of hues can differ between brands, so you need to learn to mix and match paint combinations from the classic artist colours available. There are violet blues, such as ultramarine, cobalt (a more primary blue), and a sky-blue cerulean. You can mix the latter with lemon yellow to achieve a bright lime green. Then there is a cadmium yellow deep, which can be mixed with a cadmium red to achieve a warm orange. There are also reds, from a blood-red cadmium red to the more purplish-red alizarin crimson. Whatever your choice of media, become familiar with these colours so you know how to pick the most appropriate hue for your mixes.

Extending your colour range

You will discover there is a limit to the vibrancy you can achieve by just mixing the three pure primaries without the aid of additional pigments. For example, a violet created with a primary blue and red will create a dull brown, whereas one created by an ultramarine blue and alizarin crimson is perfectly satisfactory. With time and experimentation, you can discover your own preferred combinations. Follow your heart and intuition to capture the sheer breadth and diversity found in the natural world.

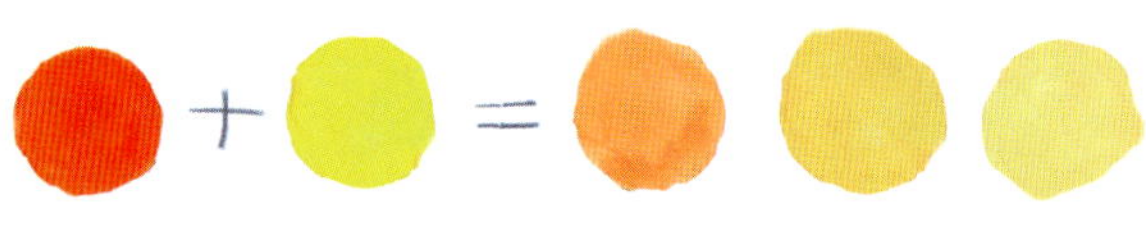

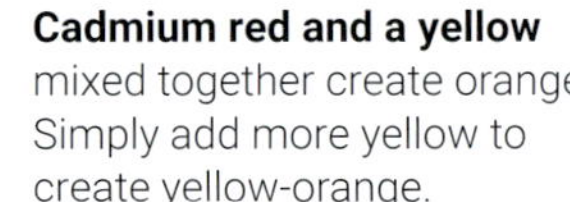

Cadmium red and a yellow mixed together create orange. Simply add more yellow to create yellow-orange.

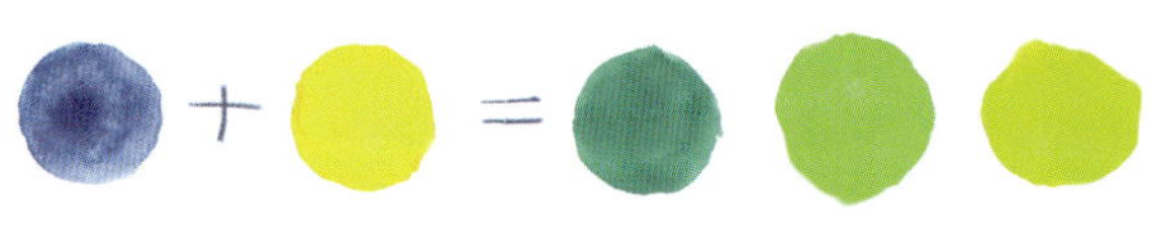

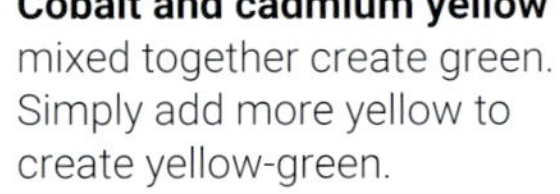

Cobalt and cadmium yellow mixed together create green. Simply add more yellow to create yellow-green.

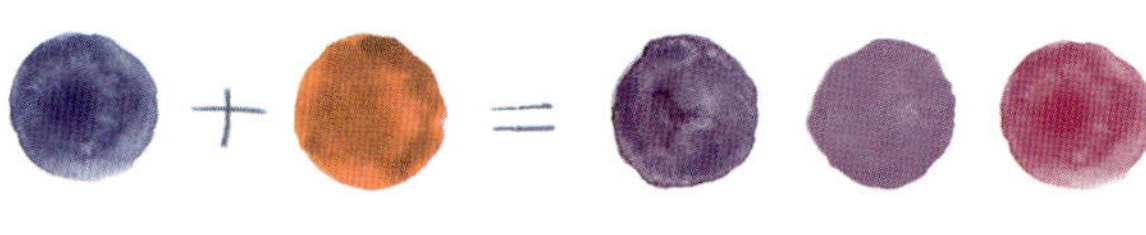

Ultramarine blue and alizarin crimson mixed together create violet. Simply add more alizarin to create violet-red.

Ultramarine blue, cadmium red and a yellow, such as lemon yellow, mixed together create brown to grey depending on the proportions of each colour.

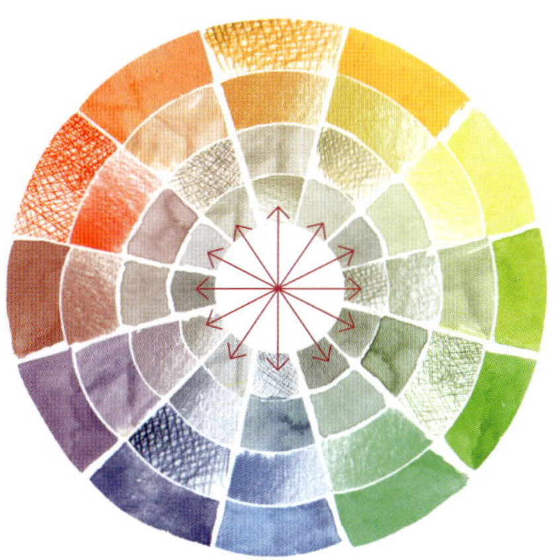

Complementary colours

All colours have opposites, just as black has an opposite in white. The complementary colour of the primary hues is created by combining the other two. Blue's complementary, for example, is orange, which is red mixed with yellow.

Colours in light tend to be brighter in saturation than colours in shade, and they are also lighter in tone. While black can be used in specific situations to darken tones, such as creating lovely smoky greys, overusing it can kill a painting. Instead, add the complementary colour: the more you add, the more desaturated the original colour will be.

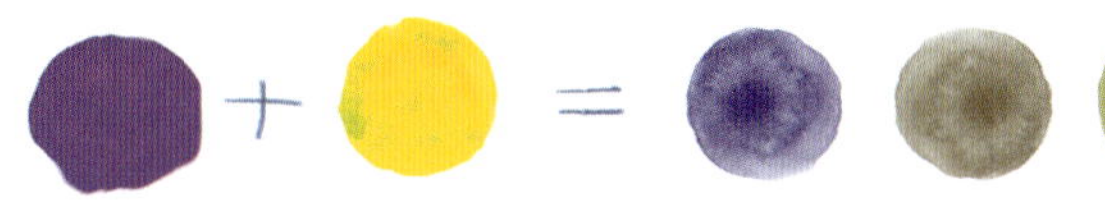

Violet and yellow

Yellow's opposite is violet, and they will cancel out the vibrancy of each other.

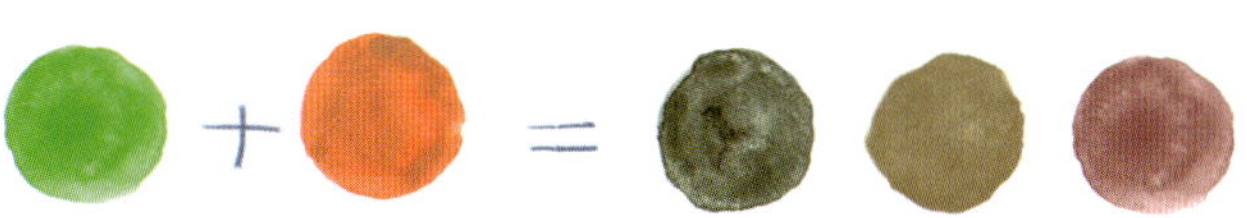

Green and red

Red and green are powerful complementaries. Think of the colours of Christmas to remember.

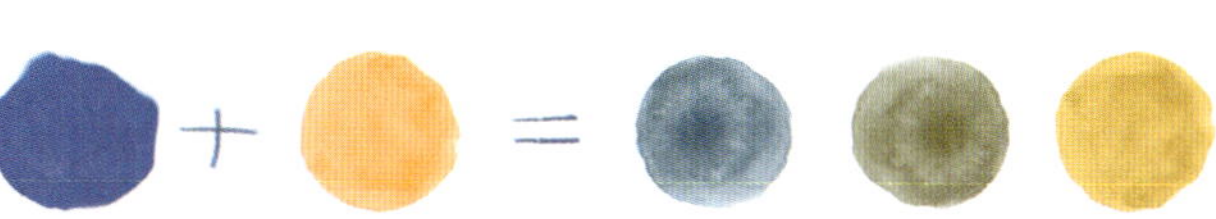

Blue and orange

Experiment by combining a varying amount of blue and orange to create a range of neutral tones. Think of a blue and gold macaw to remember.

Optical colour mixing

A type of optical illusion, optical colour mixing occurs when a viewer perceives colour in an image due to the mixing of two or more hues placed next to or near each other. The perceived colour is not the colour that exists on the surface. Instead, the colour perceived by the viewer is the colour that would arise from mixing the colours. If, for example, yellow and blue are placed near enough together on a surface, the viewer may believe that they are seeing green.

Pointillism

The most well-known artist who adopted optical colour mixing is Georges Pierre Seurat, a French Post-Impressionist painter who coined the term 'pointillism' to characterize his approach of juxtaposing dots of unmixed colours to form an image.

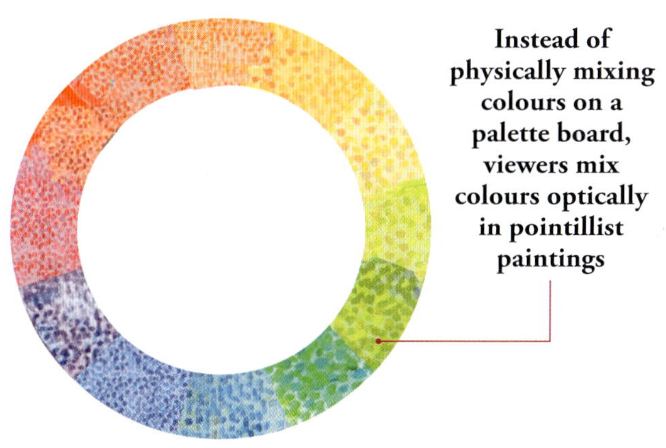

Instead of physically mixing colours on a palette board, viewers mix colours optically in pointillist paintings

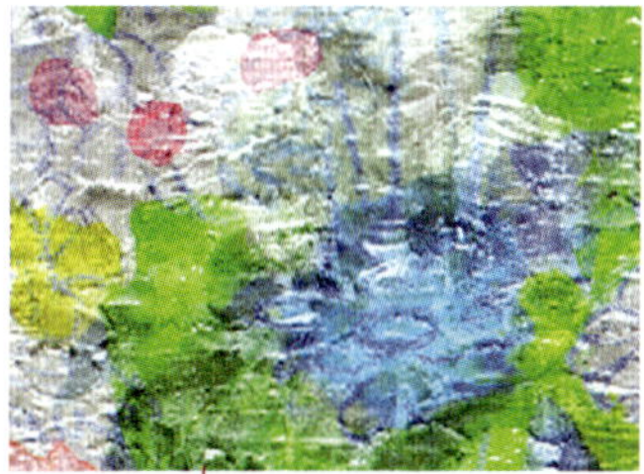

▶ Distant mixing
When viewed from a distance, the spectator sees the individual colours in a picture as one cohesive whole. The eye creates various colours that aren't present in the picture.

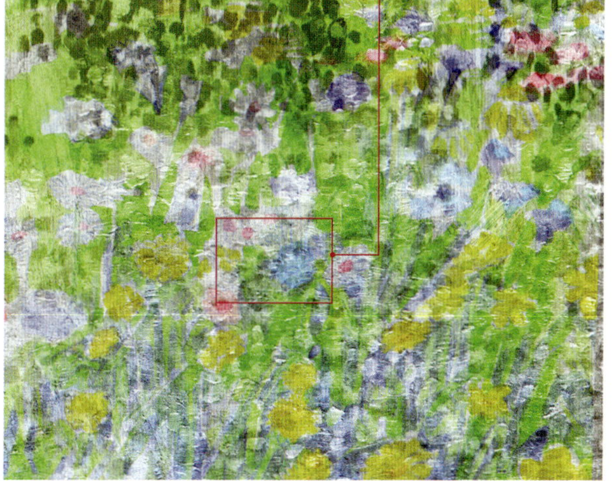

Colour with Pencils

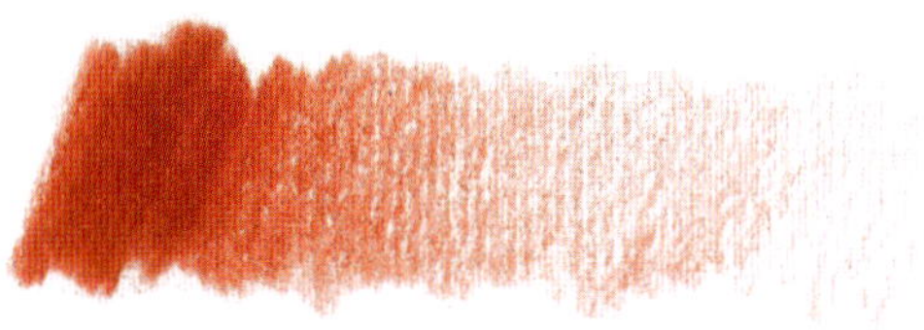

Colouring pencils were the first drawing material I started doodling with as a child. They remain close to my heart as a highly versatile, transportable and satisfying medium. There is a meditative quality to drawing with colouring pencils, plus there are no drying times to worry about. The colour of any single colouring pencil is unlikely to match the hue you are observing. The answer is to create the desired shade by mixing a combination of colours through layering them. At the heart of this technique lies a good understanding of complementary colours, rather than just adding black (see page 95), and my personal approach is to include a generous amount of ultramarine blue in the shadows to create an airy spatial quality. You can use a scribbly and scumbling approach with directional shading to shape the planes rather than using mechanical cross-hatching (see page 64).

Hatching

An approach that utilizes the tip of the pencil to create parallel lines on your paper is known as hatching. These lines can be vertical, horizontal or angled. Adding lines in different directions creates darker and richer tones – this is cross-hatching.

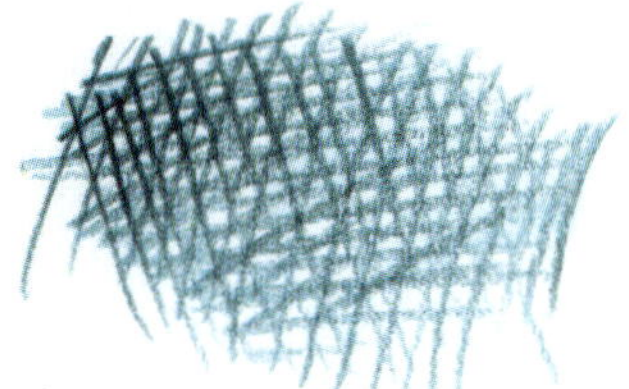

▲ Cross-hatching

Colouring pencil drawings are built up slowly by layering colours. In cross-hatching, the more lines cross over each other, and the harder the pressure is applied, the darker the value becomes.

Creating a gradient

Move your pencil back and forth in one continuous motion on the paper until you cover a small area. Simply lighten the pressure if you want to allow the white paper to show through.

Layering and scumbling

Don't feel limited by the number of colours in your pencil set. You can create more by overlaying different colours to produce new hues through visual optical mixing on the paper (see page 95).

Scumbling involves making a series of tiny overlapping circular motions of varying sizes to create shade. I try to vary my marks to create visual interest and combine merging layers, almost smearing them by using either the tip or the side of the pencil tip.

Yellow base colour

Green layered on top

Blue layered on top

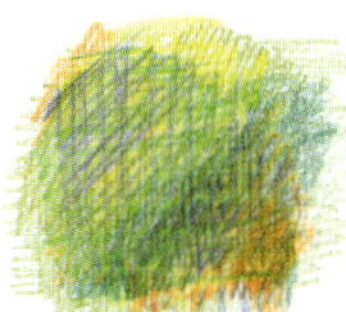

Orange layered on top

▼ Giving form

A red apple created with a combination of elliptical and planar shading (see page 77).

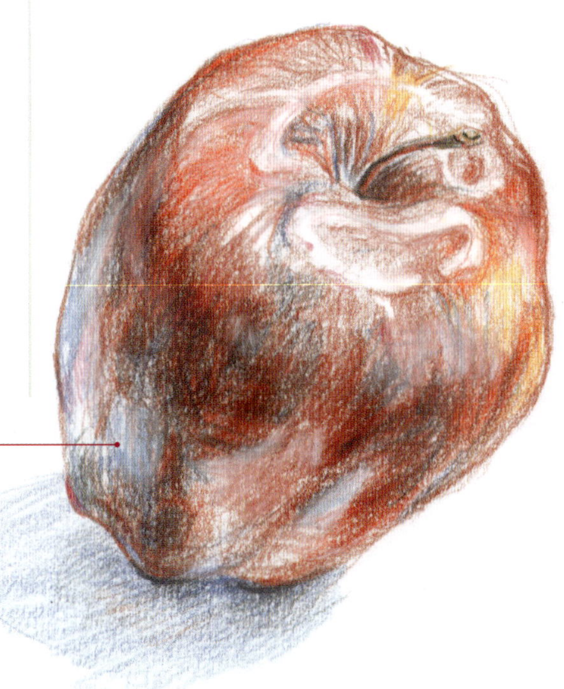

Reflected light can be added with a white watercolour pencil, which has a greater covering ability than a colouring pencil

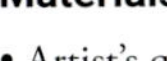

Blue violet	Ultramarine blue	Cobalt green	Phtalo green	Emerald green	Earth green	Light green	Lemon yellow	Cadmium yellow	Cadmium red	Alizarin crimson

Chiaroscuro apples

Apples have a long history in art, from appearing as a symbol of temptation in the garden of Eden to representing signs of autumn. They are an accessible and enjoyable subject to tackle in colouring pencils, using chiaroscuro (see pages 70–1).

Materials
- Artist's quality colouring pencils (see swatches above right)
- Cartridge (drawing) paper or sketchbook
- Sharpener
- Putty eraser

Apple (*Malus domestica*)
The first apples grew in Central Asia in southern Kazakhstan, the home of its wild ancestor (*Malus sieversii*), which has similar fruit with a diameter of up to 2¾in (7cm). Apples have been cultivated for thousands of years in Asia and Europe, and European colonists introduced them to North America.

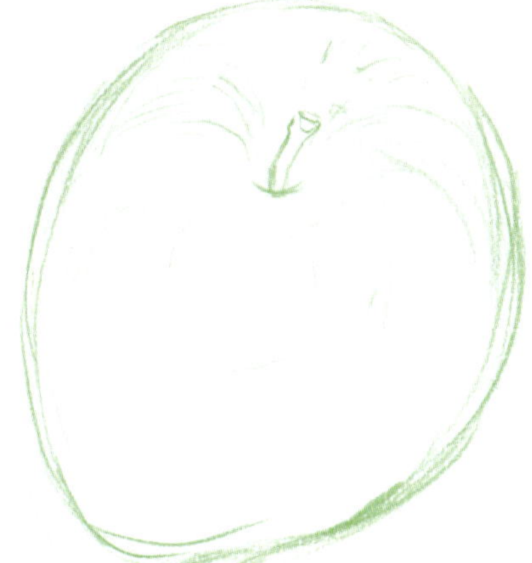

1 Begin by drawing the main shapes with the dominant colour of the subject, light green, and then start to volumize the form with a few elliptical marks.

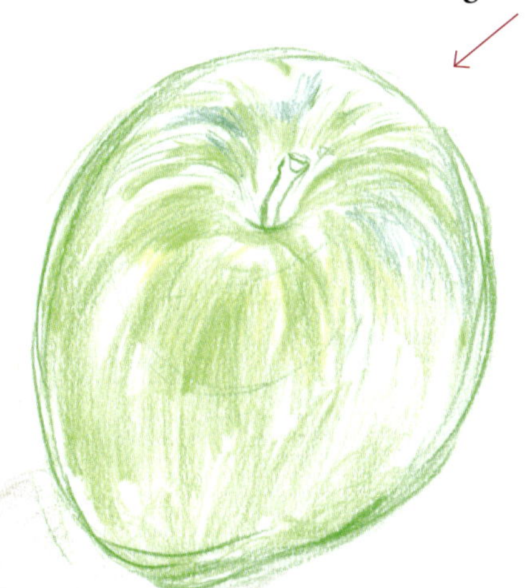

2 Next, add a layer of lemon yellow and more greens, switching between the pencil shades. Leave some gaps where there are red patches, which will keep them vibrant in the light. Observe the light and shadows.

3 Aim to put the colours where they belong, following the apple to get the appropriate tones and shape. Use a range of reds and wrap them around the sphere of the apple, coaxing it from the paper. Don't forget to follow the areas of light and shadows, including in the cast shadow.

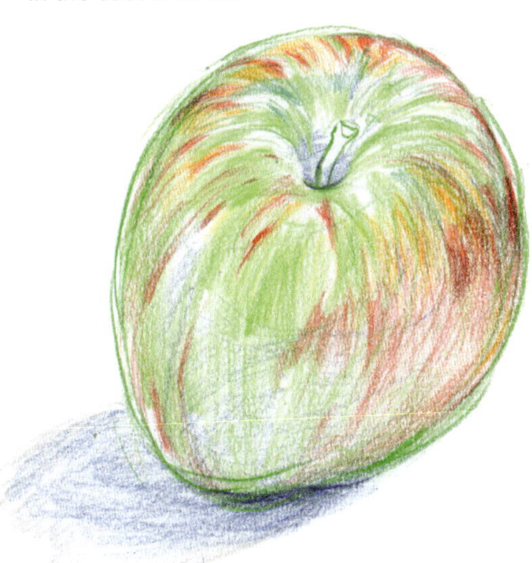

4 Finally, add more refined detail and bolster the shadows by layering ultramarine blue.

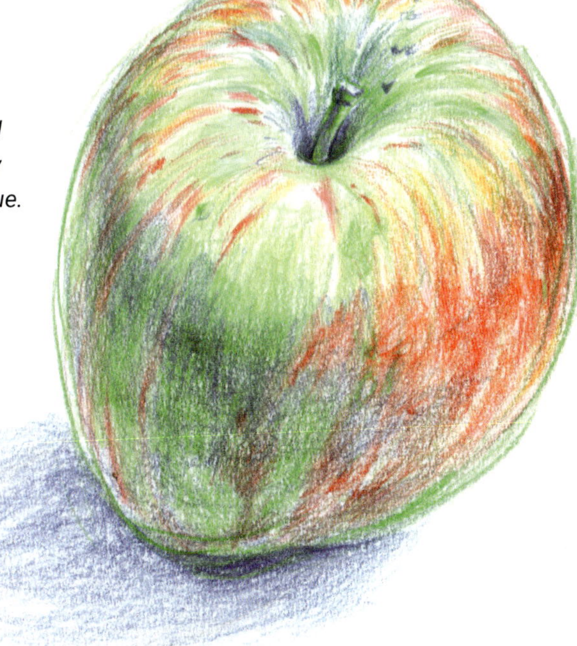

Colour with Line and Wash

Applying an ink wash to represent either monochrome tonal values, colour or a combination of both is a highly versatile technique. It can create lively studies when the brushwork is left clearly visible with spontaneous results. You can familiarize yourself with the medium's possibilities by experimenting with ink and working with its rich staining power. Inks are simply diluted with water to create lighter tones in the same manner as watercolour.

Line work

By using solely line work in ink, it's possible to define the edges of a form in the same way as drawing for watercolour, where shading is omitted to allow the ink to do the work of shading, creating tone, colour, emotive impact and atmosphere. The dip pen is a highly expressive tool, allowing for an extraordinary breadth in width of line. This has made it a favourite tool of satirical cartoonists, such as Gerald Scarfe or Ralph Steadman, whose spontaneous scrawling gestures created exaggerated lines that poked fun at their subjects.

Materials
- Indigo artist's quality colouring pencil
- Dip pen and colouring inks (see swatches above right)
- Cartridge (drawing) paper or sketchbook

Holly (*Ilex* spp.)
There are some 600 species of holly shrubs and trees distributed worldwide. Holly has green waxy leaves with wavy margins, tipped with spines and budded with bright red berries. This fruit is an essential winter food source for many bird species. Many hollies have evolved spikes to protect their energy-packed berries from hungry animals.

Holly

The leaves and spikes of a sprig of holly have specific qualities that lend themselves to dip pen and ink. A dip pen is an ideal tool for capturing the sharp spikes, and the liquid qualities of the ink are suitable for representing the waxy, shiny leaves. The aim of this exercise is to focus on intentional curiosity, with the artwork becoming a record of your observations.

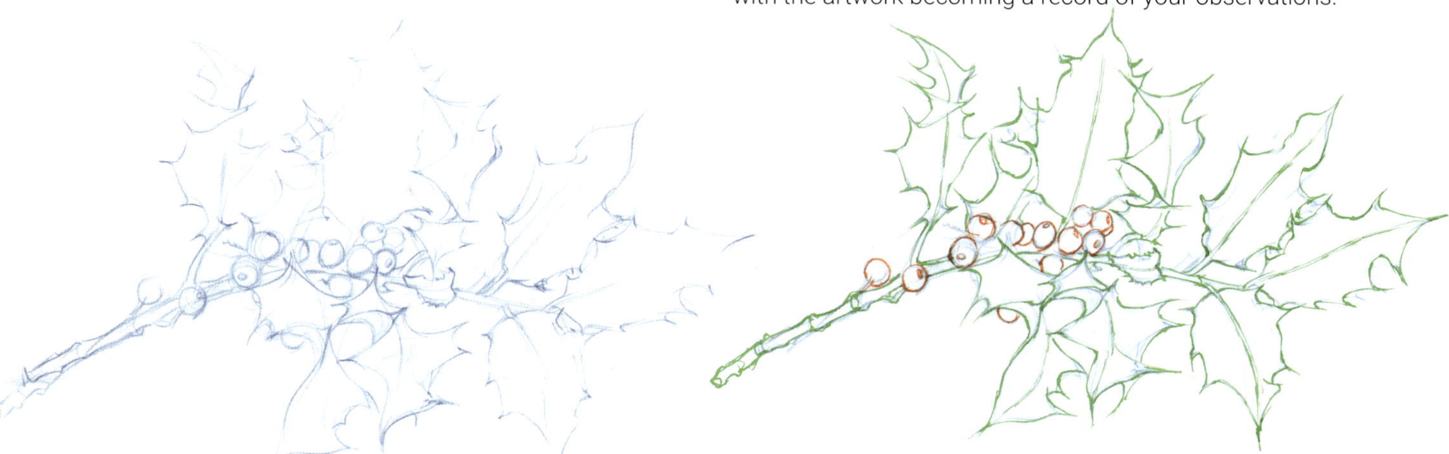

1 *Place a sprig of holly on a sheet of white paper to create a seasonal composition reminiscent of snow. Start the initial sketch in an indigo oil-based colouring pencil, a shade that will melt away into the background after adding the ink line. Choose a focal point, such as a single leaf, sketch the outline and central vein before moving on to each neighbouring leaf in turn. Remember to observe both positive and negative space.*

2 *With a dip pen, redraw the holly sprig in cobalt green and alizarin crimson inks. It is important to observe and draw the subject again, using the initial blue line merely for proportions, not as a traceable line. This second line will have more life and a feeling of structure. Create flick marks with your wrist to capture the sharp spines. I imagine the tip of my dip pen touching the contours of the holly leaves and taking my line for a walk, like a bug around the shapes, observing each nook and cranny. Try to capture the character of the twisted leaves with an accurate line that bites into the edge of the form. Look for imperfections, interesting broken bits and insect bite marks.*

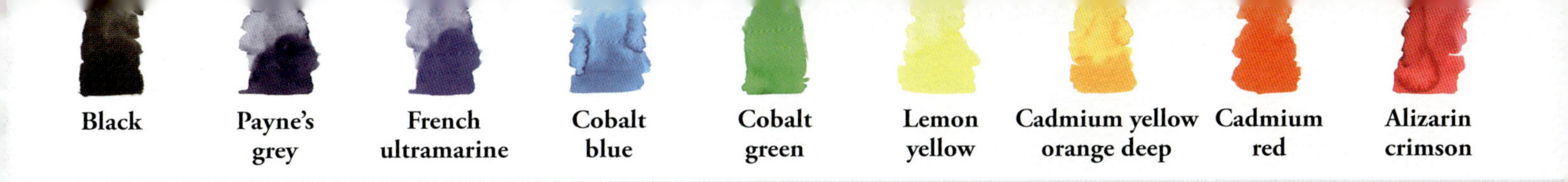

| Black | Payne's grey | French ultramarine | Cobalt blue | Cobalt green | Lemon yellow | Cadmium yellow orange deep | Cadmium red | Alizarin crimson |

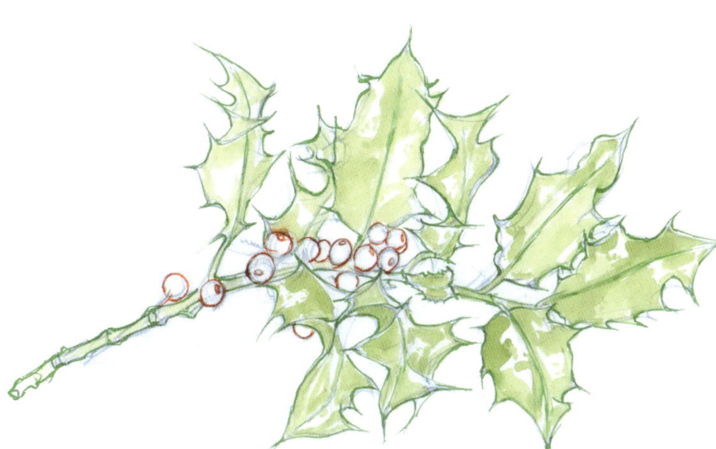

3 Next, mix the holly leaves' natural green body colour. Create little colour daubs on a separate scrap of paper to test the colour match close to the actual leaf. Keep modifying the mix until you feel close to the lightest and brightest shade. Most pure green pigments will need adapting to create an appropriate shade. Apply washes of the green ink to the leaves, leaving gaps to capture the reflections on and shininess of the waxy leaves.

4 Once dry, create bluish-green hues by combining cobalt green and ultramarine blue, then apply washes for the darker notes. Then add the lightest shades of the berries, using cadmium red and alizarin crimson.

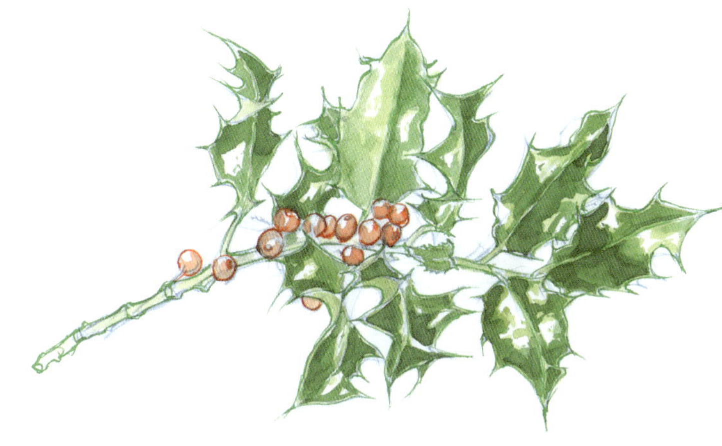

5 Use a bath of ultramarine blue to create the cast shadow and overlay it on the leaves to make the very darkest tone. At the same time, the shadow will unify the subject and the surface and stop the sprig floating in space. Finally, use an expressive flick of the dip pen with black to accentuate the spikes.

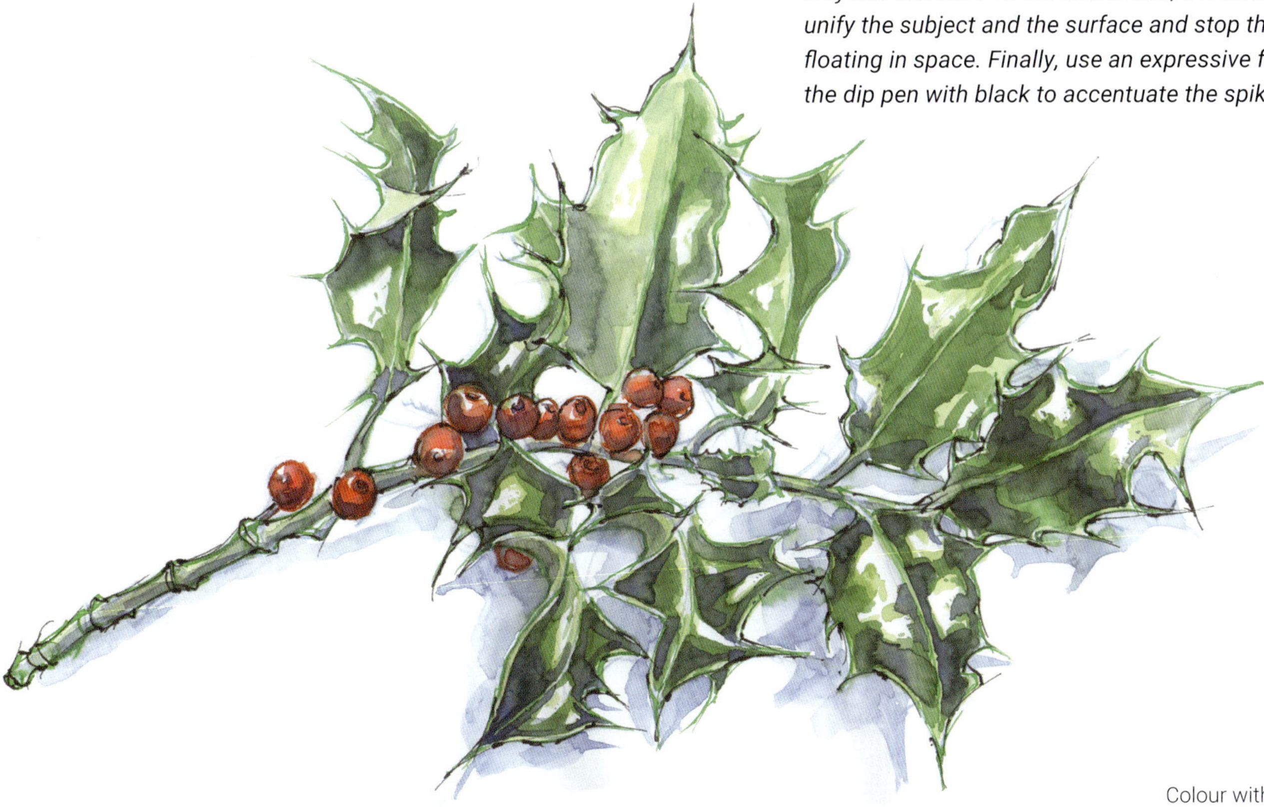

Colour with Pastels

With chalk pastels, you can layer and blend colours to create a comprehensive pallet, which is ideal for impressionistic artwork. I usually work with pastels on rough-textured paper, either sugar (construction) paper or the more expensive pastel paper. You can combine pastels with pastel pencils, which can be sharpened to a point in order to allow for a higher level of detail.

Before putting down the first layer of pastel onto paper, there are a variety of approaches for creating the basic outline and structure. Edgar Degas, the nineteenth-century French artist well known for his pastel drawings, often began his studies with a tonal underdrawing in charcoal or used an impression from a monoprint – created by ink wiped over a copper plate and being lifted off on paper. Drawing at a larger scale also helped Degas overcome the lack of detail possible with these crumbly sticks.

Scumbling

Layers of different pastel colours are used to create depth and volume in a pastel drawing. Try experimenting with your colour choices before committing them to your drawing. One way of applying the pastels is known as scumbling, which results in optical colour mixing, where adjacent colours are optically mixed and are perceived as a different colour (see page 95). To scumble, simply build layers in a scribbly circular fashion of one colour of pastel over another, working from light to dark. This is where the importance of the paper's tooth comes in, as the raised texture of the paper, whether it's a pastel paper or sugar paper, will pick up the material and leave the colour in the recesses between the peaks. In addition, as complementary colours cancel out each other's intensification without the need for black (see page 95), which can deaden a hue, you can build up layers using bright hues. These will be muted as they are mixed together by the eye. Final shading marks in pastel can be vigorous, almost coarse, adding a lively, energetic feeling.

Fixatives

Compared with oil paintings and acrylics, all pastel drawings remain a relatively fragile art form. However, you can seal in the pastels between layers by using a fixative, a type of adhesive spray. It keeps pastels and charcoal from smudging by glueing the particles of pigment to the paper. The fixative will also give the surface of the drawing a more abrasive tooth, ready (when dry) to hold a new layer of medium. Fixatives will frequently deepen and darken colours, so be prepared for this. You can use this darkening process to your advantage to achieve two shades of the same colour: one darker (fixed) and one lighter (unfixed), thereby extending your tonal range – but refrain from repeating the spraying process while adding finishing touches.

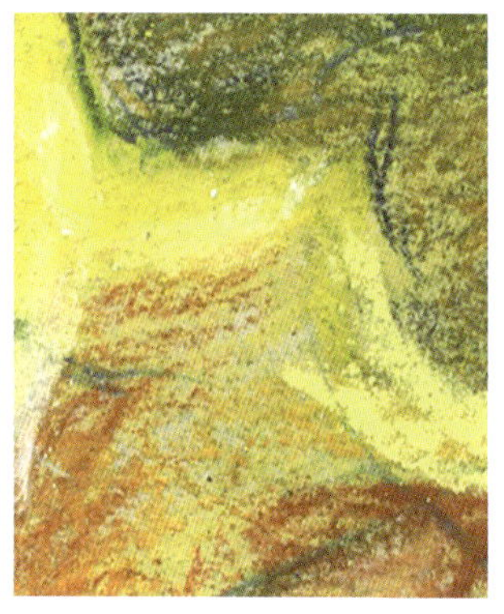

▲ Thrifty shades
Lightly apply second and further shades of scumbling in a circular (scumbling) motion over the base layer.

Maple sprig

1 *Begin by drawing the shapes with a blue pastel pencil. Start with a single leaf and sketch the outlines and some of the details of its veins. Then move on, from shape to shape, observing both negative and positive spaces. As with most drawings, this approach works from the broad to the detail.*

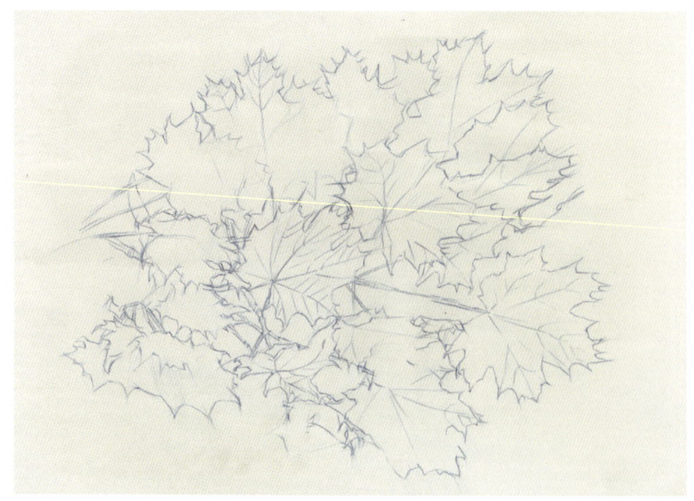

| Raw umber | Ultramarine blue | Sap green | Lemon yellow | Cadmium yellow light | Cadmium yellow deep | Yellow ochre | Burnt sienna |

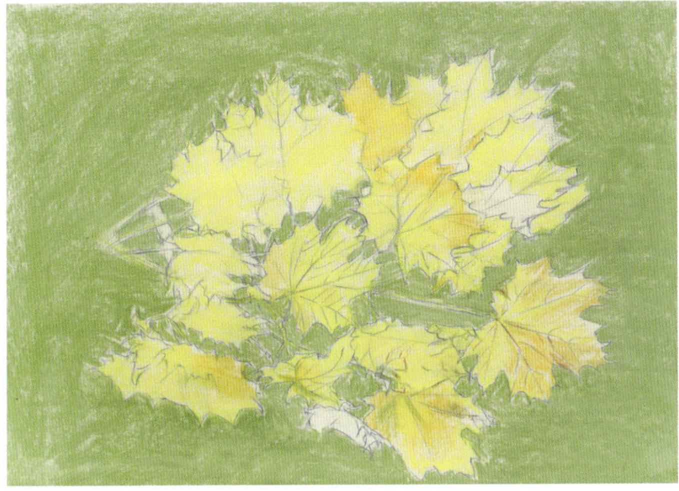

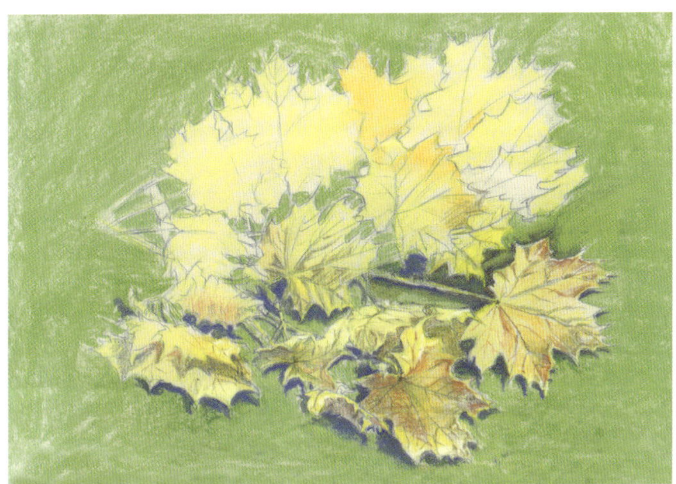

2   *Hold the pastel on its side so you can use the flat edge of the pastel to cover a wider area on the paper. Simply drag the side of the pastel, starting with lemon yellow, over the paper for the leaves, leaving some gaps for highlights, then add the background using a sap green. This technique is good for any large areas, such as the sea or skies.*

3   *Light captures forms that face the light, throwing the planes away from the light into shade and capturing the wrinkles in the leaves. To create the illusion of light catching the copper autumnal leaves, begin applying layers of yellows and browns. I used a pure ultramarine blue for the shadows. This was an interpretive colour, an exaggeration of the blue notes in the shade.*

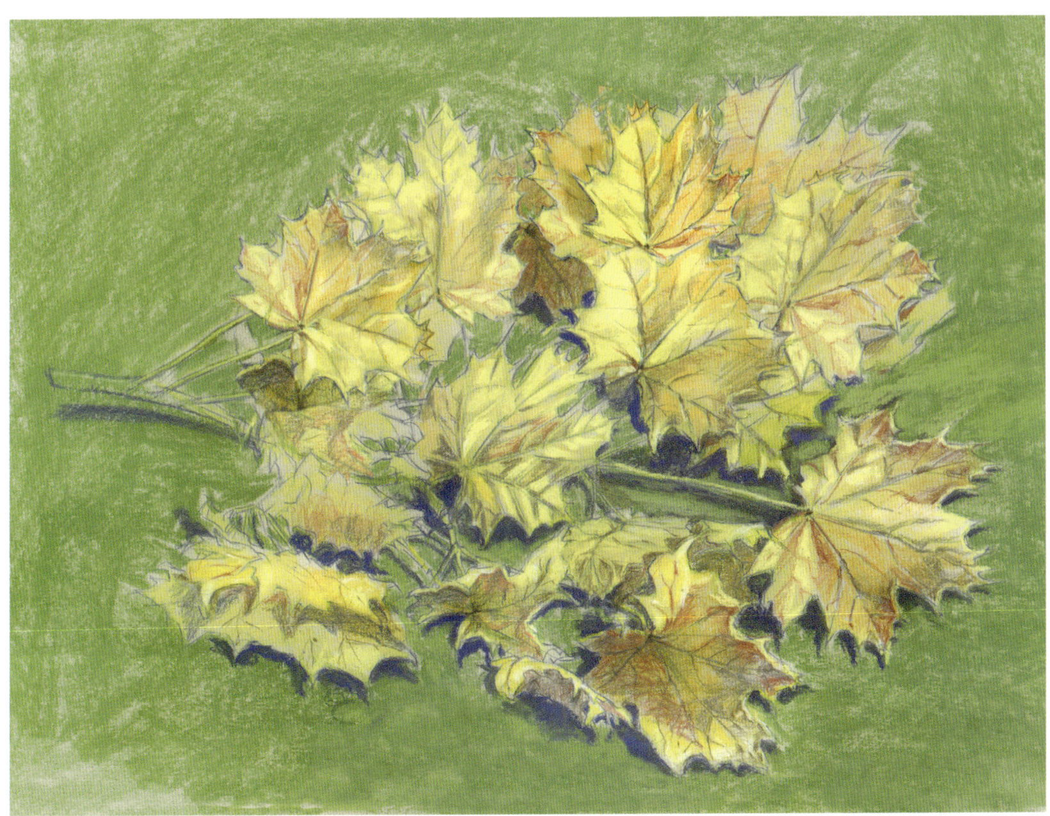

Tip

Before you begin the drawing, pick out all the relevant colours you want to use from your set of pastels and set them aside. Once you get started, you won't want to be wasting time hunting for a colour.

4   *The final stage is all about details, adding nuances and enhancing contrast. Tweak a highlight against a dark to enhance the feeling of light and shade. Under the leaves' veins there are tiny raised ridges that catch the light with a small shadow on their lee side. On top, these create furrowed grooves that are bathed in shade.*

Colour with Watercolours

Watercolour is both an accessible and portable medium to use. The lightness and simplicity of the materials required – a paint tin, water, paper and a few brushes – means you can carry your art kit anywhere. Watercolour paints are my go-to medium for staining drawings to bring them to life. There is pleasure in watercolour painting that comes from overlapping translucent washes that glow with a unique, vibrant luminosity as light passes through the paint and is reflected on the paper beneath. Professional artist's watercolour is the perfect medium for capturing arching rainbows, flowering meadows, shimmering hummingbirds, lush woodlands and coral reefs alive with spectacular tropical fish.

Drawing with brushes

I try to let my brush marks show in the final work. Life is in the brushstroke and has as much personality as handwriting. The artist's objective is not to create a photographic copy of what you are looking at but an interpretation. Vary your brush marks in relation to the size and quality of the subjects in a drawing to add visual interest. Always remain focused on your subject and draw with the brush rather than fill in a sketched shape.

Luminous colours

To achieve luminous shades, use artist's quality watercolour pencils in conjunction with paint diluted with the clearest water. Watercolour pencils become more vibrant when washes of water are dragged over the top. Both pencils and paint can be used in a free sketching manner or used with less water to create highly detailed natural history-style illustrations with fine brushes and sharp pencil points.

Royal gramma fish

This is a small, brightly coloured Caribbean fish that will require artist's quality pigments to stand a chance of capturing its striking livery.

Materials for both tutorials
- Indigo (and yellow for the trigger-fish) artist's quality colouring pencil
- Watercolour paints (see swatches below and above right)
- Cartridge (drawing) paper or sketchbook
- Sharpener
- Putty eraser

Royal gramma fish
(*Gramma loreto*)
This Grammidae family member is native to the Caribbean's deep-water reefs and dwells in dimly lit and large rockwork caves for hiding. It is a burst of bright complementaries, a violet anterior and yellow posterior.

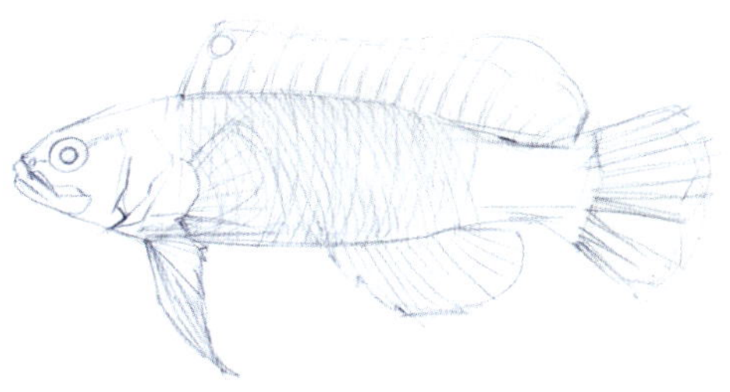

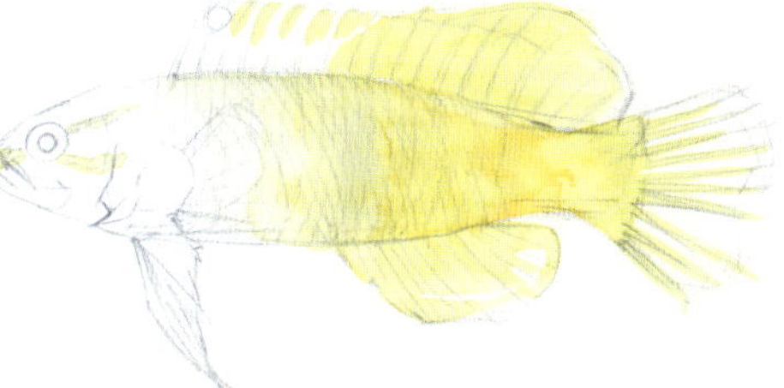

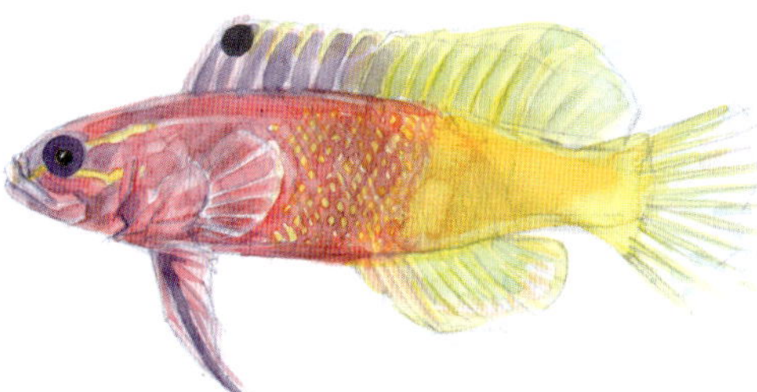

1   *Begin by making an initial sketch as accurately as possible; there is no need for shading as this is the work of the watercolour pencils and paint. Use a high quality indigo colouring pencil because the blue line will blend into the background.*

2   *Start applying the lightest and most vibrant watercolours to these to achieve bright, glowing pigment stains on the paper. Ensuring that your water is clear and your brush is spotless, combine lemon and cadmium yellow to create a graduated wash.*

3   *Next, mix varying quantities of shades around the magenta spectrum to create purplish hues. Rather than filling in the shapes, draw with the brush in an X-wrap pattern (see page 120). Allow the colours to bleed and create naturalistic happy accident effects.*

Black	French ultramarine	Lemon yellow	Cadmium yellow	Alizarin crimson	Magenta

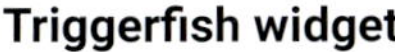

| Black | French ultramarine | Cobalt blue | Cobalt green | Sap green | Lemon yellow | Cadmium yellow | Cadmium orange | Alizarin crimson | Magenta |

Picasso triggerfish (*Rhinecanthus assasi*)
The Picasso triggerfish, or sometimes lagoon triggerfish, can grow to 12in (30cm) long and is found on Indo-Pacific reefs. The Hawaiian name for this fish is humuhumunukunukuāpua'a or just humuhumu for short, meaning 'triggerfish with a snout like a pig'.

Triggerfish widget

I usually doodle a widget (see page 15) before starting any illustration. This aids in comprehending the three-dimensional framework of my subject, preventing the image appearing too flat and ensuring I capture the bulging eyes.

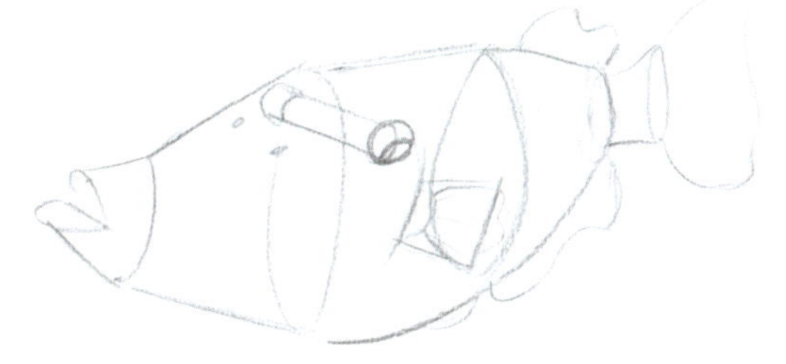

Picasso triggerfish

The background colour of this fish's livery is more subtle, but it provides a foil that makes the other, more exuberant colours pop.

1 Draw the outline and structure of the fish with watercolour pencils in the same colour as the paint you'll use, so the lines dissolve and disappear when water is added.

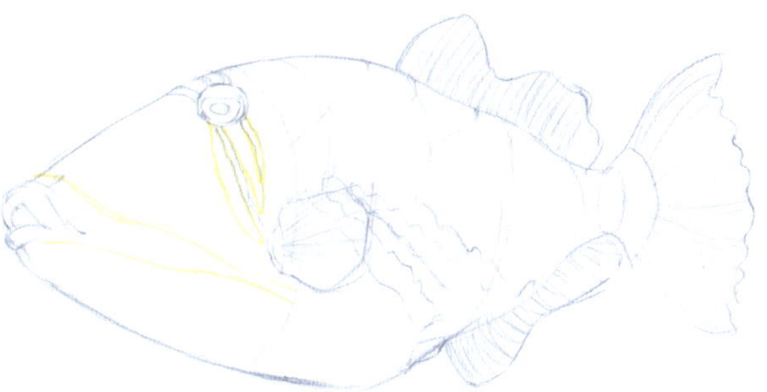

2 After brushing on the lightest and brightest shades, use ultramarine blue to create a tonal underpainting – it will create a sense of modelling.

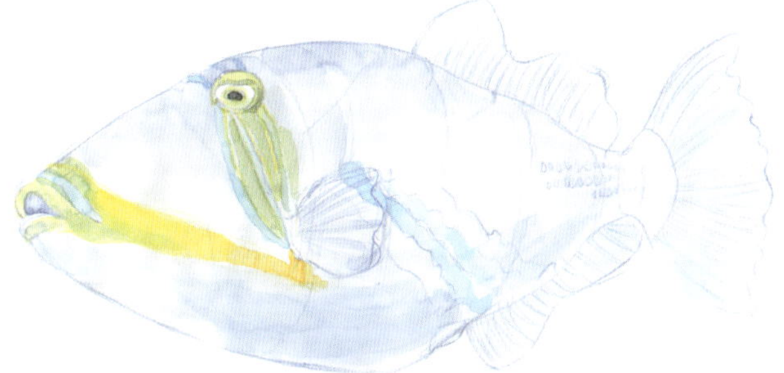

Tip
A visit to an aquarium with tropical fish can be a rich source of inspiration. However, sketching in the gloom can mean that it is difficult to judge the shade of colours. Rather than leaving field sketches in your sketchbook, try tinting them with watercolour paint and pencils. Remember to take photographs while sketching to gather as much information as possible to turn line work into full-colour studies at home.

Allow for highlights
Leave gaps of white paper around the eye to create the illusion of skin overlapping the pupil and to bring the eyes to life.

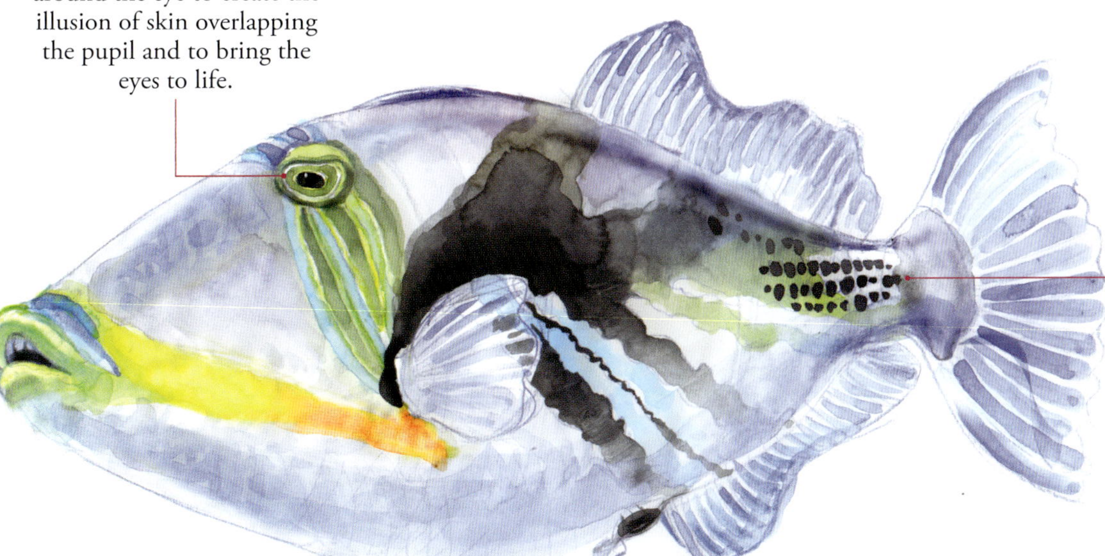

Disruptive spots
These break up the shape of the body to confuse predators.

3 Gradually work from the broad areas to the details using smaller brushes.

Space

There are many definitions for the abstract concept of 'space'. It can be any area, be it large or small, confined between objects or unobstructed and open. The space can be far away or near by. There also exist uncountable combinations of living elements in these spaces, both plants and animals, and inorganic elements that make up the earth's geology, such as rocks and minerals. In a desert habitat, for example, animal and plant life is sparse, and the environment in this space is primarily made up of non-living elements. Here, the focus of your sketches might be of the rocks, vast vistas and endless skies while only glimpsing the occasional animal. It is where space seems to be at its most expansive, with the sky filling the majority of the view.

Where water is more abundant, such as in the tropics, the organic element takes over, and the environment in this space is bursting with both plants and animals. Here, the challenge for the artist can be to simplify the incredible amount of visual information, such as when sketching in a botanical garden and looking through large leaves and tangled branches.

Artists use space to aid the viewer's comprehension of the subject and create drama, using a host of illusionistic devices to make the flat surface of the paper appear to have depth or even distance. Hold up a piece of paper. It is a fraction of a millimetre thick, yet the illusion of many miles can be created on the paper's surface. The illusion of space is usually implied: positive and negative spaces, open and closed areas, shallow and deep distances can conjure up the illusion of three dimensions on the paper's surface. To convey that something is closer to the viewer, you could simply make one thing larger than another or make it fainter to imply atmospheric perspective. For centuries, artists since the Renaissance have explored ways of representing pictorial space by using linear perspective. This has been refined over the years, which can now be seen in the dazzling effects used in the worlds of gaming and film.

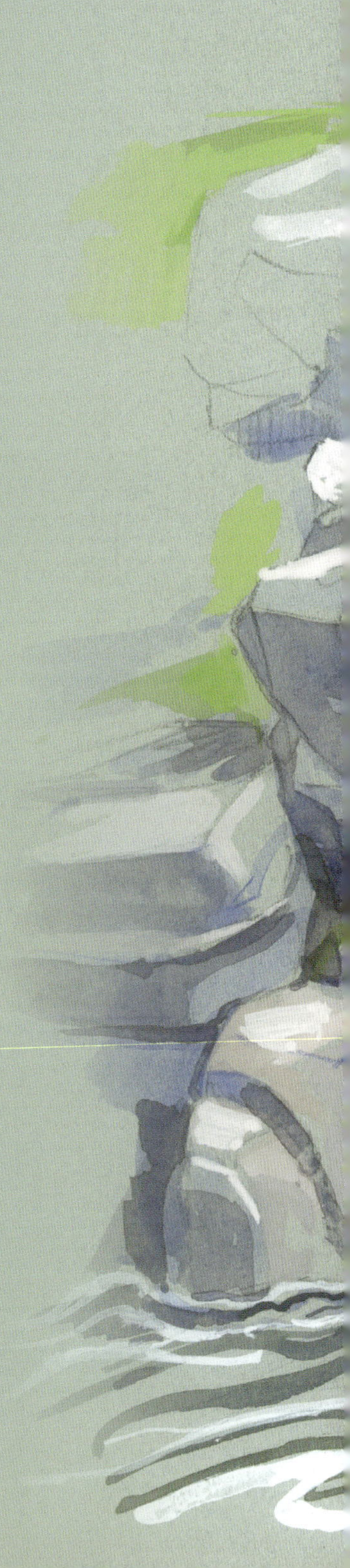

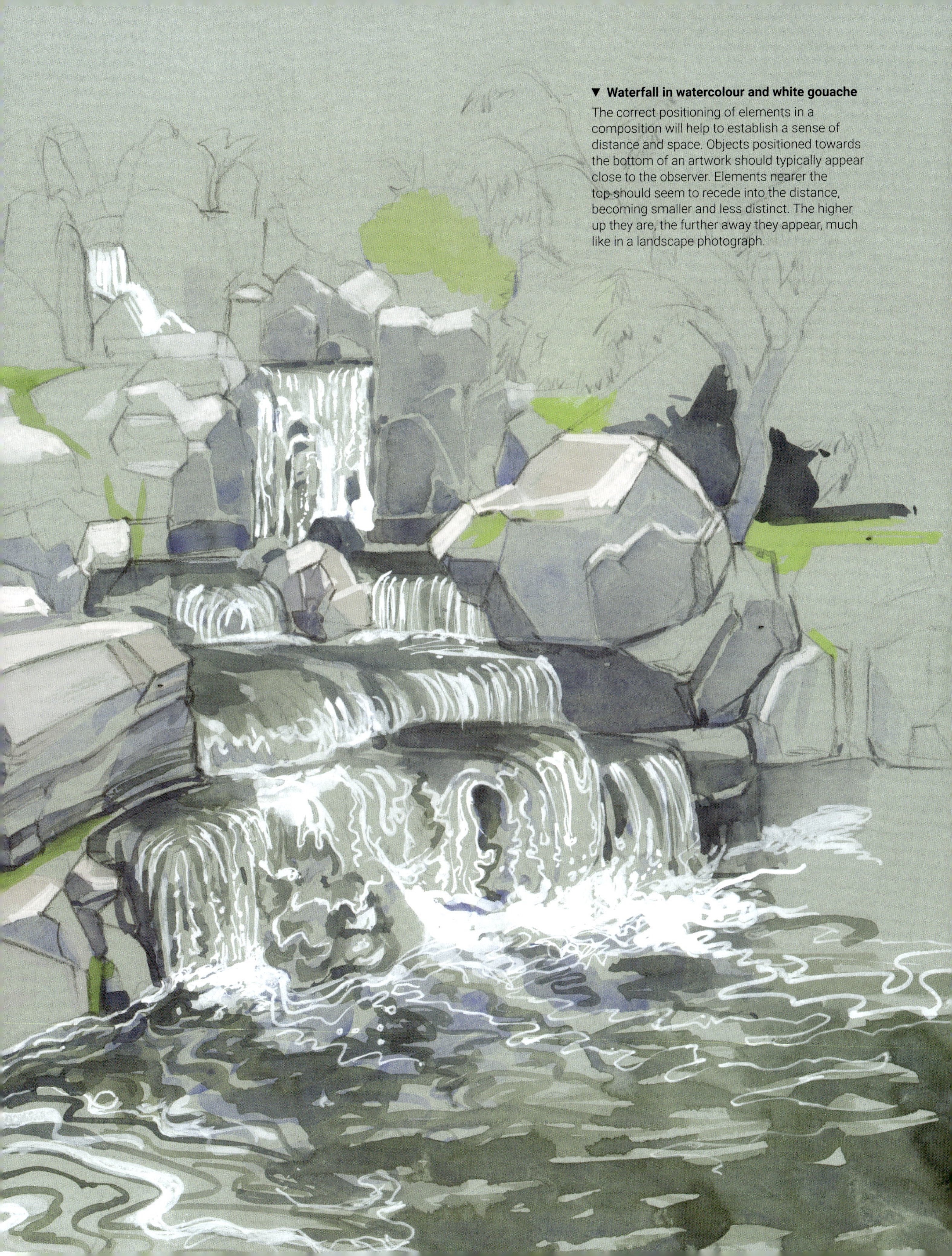

▼ **Waterfall in watercolour and white gouache**
The correct positioning of elements in a composition will help to establish a sense of distance and space. Objects positioned towards the bottom of an artwork should typically appear close to the observer. Elements nearer the top should seem to recede into the distance, becoming smaller and less distinct. The higher up they are, the further away they appear, much like in a landscape photograph.

Space Essentials

When we pick up a piece of paper, we can see it is flat, and if we turn it around, there is, of course, nothing behind it. However, one set of skills that every artist should acquire is the ability to create the illusion that this piece of paper is not flat but is a window in which we can visualize the three-dimensional world. Over centuries, artists worldwide have developed an array of pictorial conventions to imply depth and space.

One basic convention uses the simplicity of overlapping lines to indicate distance. In the illustration of the squares (see right), the image on the left implies two pieces of paper side by side on the same plane. In the second, the smaller piece of paper is clearly in front of the larger one. Another universally understood idea is the position on the picture plane: objects at the bottom of the drawing will appear closer to the viewer and those higher up will seem further away. This stacking up of elements in a picture can be combined with diminishing size and atmospheric perspective (see pages 110–11) to further emphasize the impression of space. Another visual device that most people will be familiar with is that of linear perspective (see opposite), when an element in the artwork with parallel sides, such as a path, converges to a vanishing point on the horizon. A good understanding of perspective will inform your broader practice, whether sketching landscapes, plants or animals.

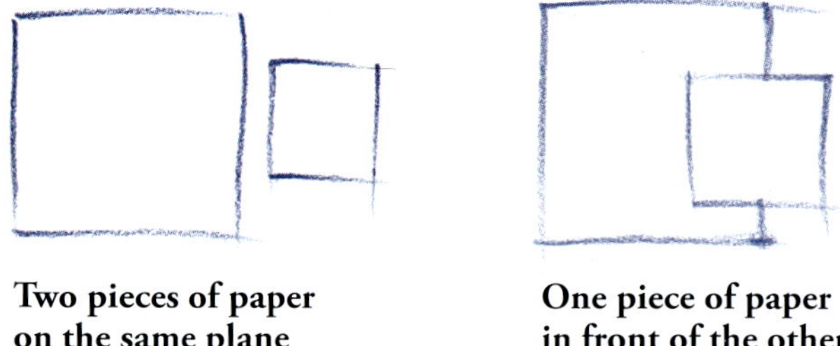

Two pieces of paper on the same plane

One piece of paper in front of the other

Diminishing detail

Objects that are further away should have less detail than those that are closer. There is a technique in photography called high-dynamic-range, which takes several exposures and can put the fore/mid/backgrounds all in sharp focus. However, we don't see this way, so objects in the distance are not as sharp. There should be moments of rest – a relief for the eye – in any study.

Diminishing size

One of the best uses of diminishing size is when an identical object is repeated, creating a clear comparison for the eye to follow from large to small, creating the illusion of vast distances. The trees in the illustration to the right become increasingly smaller as they recede from the eye. Also, the spaces between them will become shallower the further they are from the viewer. In other situations, organic elements such as clouds or trees may not be so identical. However, these will share similar characteristics that can be shrunk to convince the viewer that they are a varied part of a set.

Linear Perspective

One way to create the illusion of space on a two-dimensional surface is to use lines in linear perspective. Earlier perspective systems relied on a single fixed viewpoint with a single vanishing point, such as in the fifteenth-century Italian paintings by Paolo Uccello. Later, multiple vanishing points were introduced, allowing for a more naturalistic representation of a scene that is closer to how we actually see it. The four most common types of linear perspective are one-, two-, three- and multiple-point perspective. Perspective also helps with other techniques, such as foreshortening, where an object seems compressed in length (see pages 112–13).

Linear perspective is an element in art that strays into the mathematical branch of geometry. It can be applied to the three main parts of any linear perspective drawing.

Horizon line

This is eye level, or the height of the eye of the viewer. The viewer might be high up with a bird's eye view or low with the subject looming overhead. The horizon line is the first line to draw, and its height on the paper determines whether we will be looking up if it is low on the page, looking down if it is high up on the page, or have a more naturalistic viewpoint if it is in the middle of the page.

Orthogonals

The diagonal, horizontal or vertical lines of objects with parallel sides that recede to the vanishing point are known as orthogonals. These lines are sometimes called convergence lines for obvious reasons.

Vanishing point

A vanishing point is the final point where the orthogonal lines recede to in the distance. These tend to lie along the horizon line, (although there are some exceptions, such as during a meteor storm). Objects that are parallel to each other will recede to the same vanishing point, objects oriented at different angles will have their own vanishing points.

Above the eye level

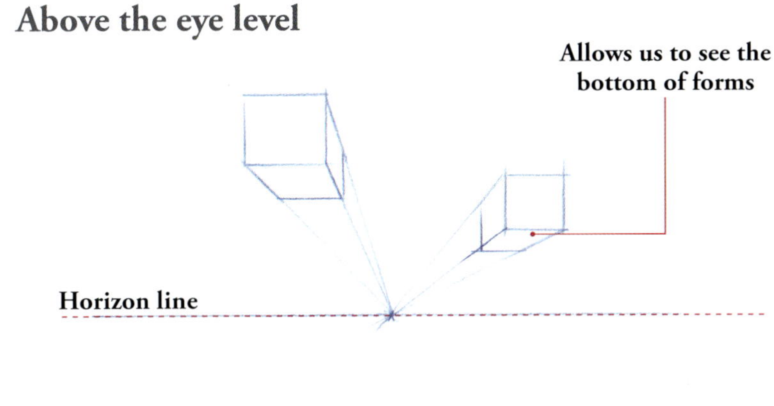

At eye level

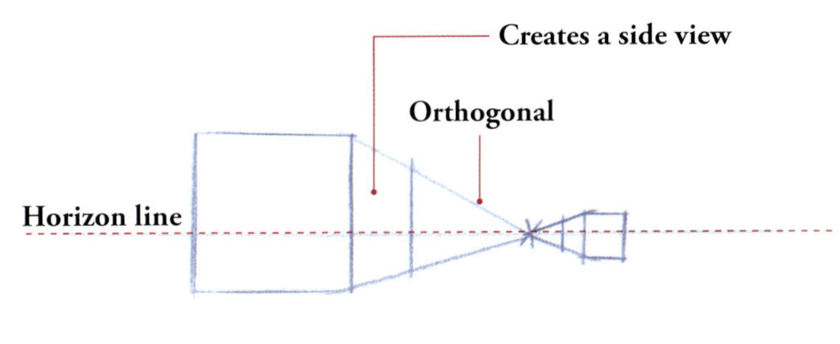

Below the eye level

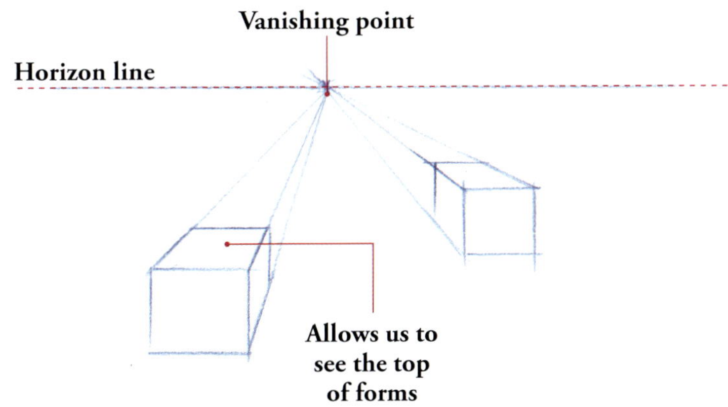

One-point perspective

A drawing technique known as one-point perspective shows how things appear to get smaller as they get further away, converging towards a single 'vanishing point' on the horizon line. It is the typical view you will get driving on a road.

Two-point perspective

In a two-point perspective drawing, two vanishing points are placed on the horizon line, typically the height of your eye line. These two points should be spaced out widely from each other to prevent dramatic distortion. Both vanishing points need not be on the paper, just as long as they are found on the horizon line. One might be some way off, and I often get students to attach their paper to a larger sheet to establish this point.

Three-point perspective

Imagine yourself looking either up at a very tall building or looking down from it to grasp three-point perspective. It is used to depict these extreme vantage points and can create a feeling of vertigo and dramatic space.

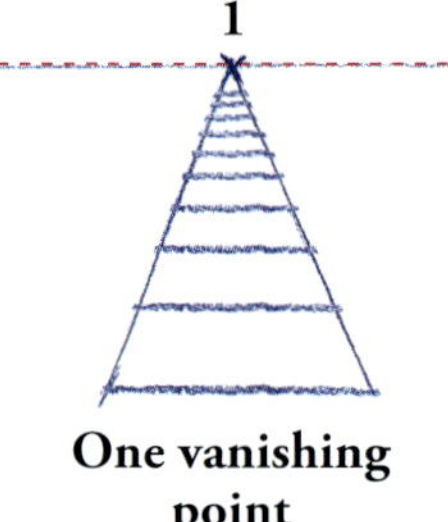

◄ One-point perspective

If you imagine standing on a railway line, the tracks would converge to a single point on the horizon. The sleepers would also appear spaced closer together and narrower the further away they were from you.

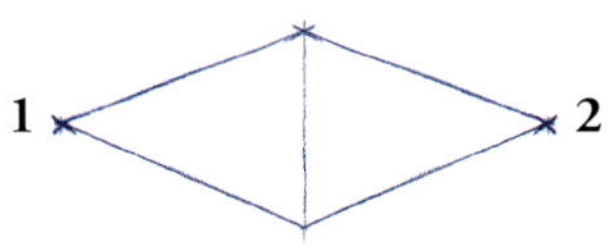

▲ Two-point perspective

If you take two railway tracks and turn them on their sides, you will have two-point perspective. You can then draw two additional vertical lines to create sides. Ensure that you keep your verticals straight and at 90 degrees to the horizontal line.

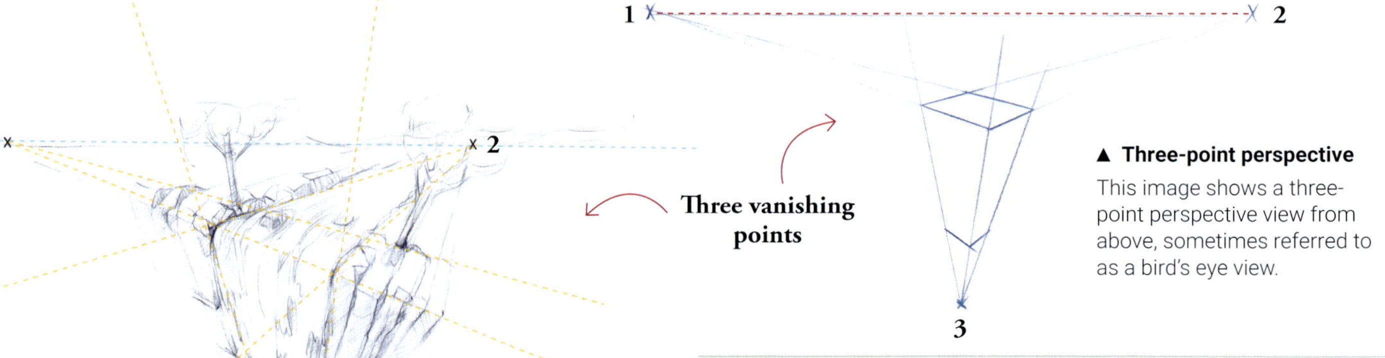

▲ Three-point perspective

This image shows a three-point perspective view from above, sometimes referred to as a bird's eye view.

Multi-point perspective

If the horizon line has more than three primary vanishing points, it is known as multi-point perspective. Perhaps surprisingly, this is the most common type of perspective we can see in the real world because not everything we see is aligned on a grid.

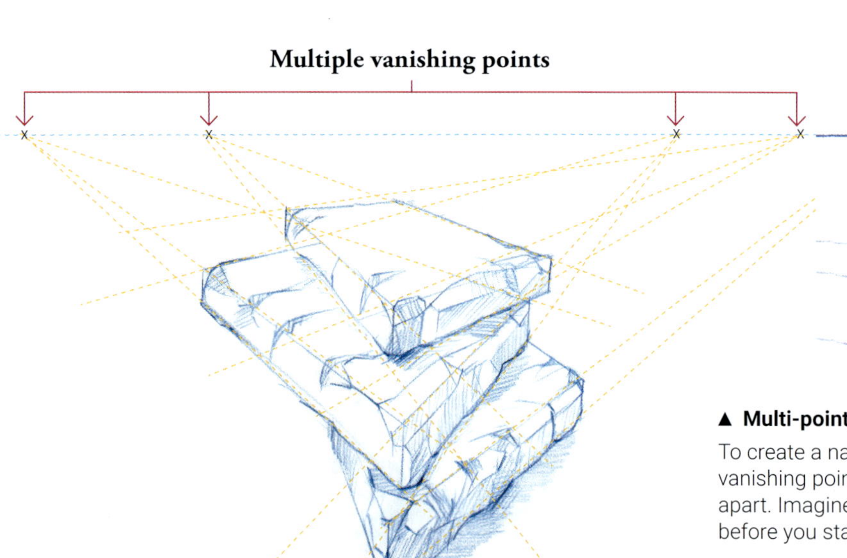

▲ Multi-point perspective

To create a natural feeling of perspective, the vanishing points will often be off the page and wide apart. Imagine the position of these vanishing points before you start sketching.

Using a grid

The plane of the ground can be divided into a perspective grid prior to drawing a landscape view. You should first find the halfway point between the foreground and the horizon. This section below the horizon can then be divided further several times by applying the same process. This grid will help create an initial sense of space when you overlay it with a one-point perspective drawing.

Early history

Around 1413, an Italian architect and one of the founding fathers of the Italian Renaissance, Filippo Brunelleschi, first demonstrated the geometrical method of perspective by painting the outlines of various Florentine buildings reflected onto a mirror. These outlines were followed beyond the frame of the mirror, where he noticed that the lines converged on the horizon line. This became a fundamental rule of perspective: lines that are parallel to each other will always converge to a single vanishing point. Look around you and see how many objects have parallel sides, and imagine where the vanishing point would be.

1 First, draw in the placement of the horizon line to divide that land from the sky. In this sketch, I have opted for using the golden ratio (see page 134) to create pleasing proportions.

2 Measure a cross from the ends of the horizon line to the bottom corners of the paper, then draw a halfway line (½). Divide the section between this line and the horizon (¼); repeat a third time (⅛). These proportions will radically decrease in width towards the horizon.

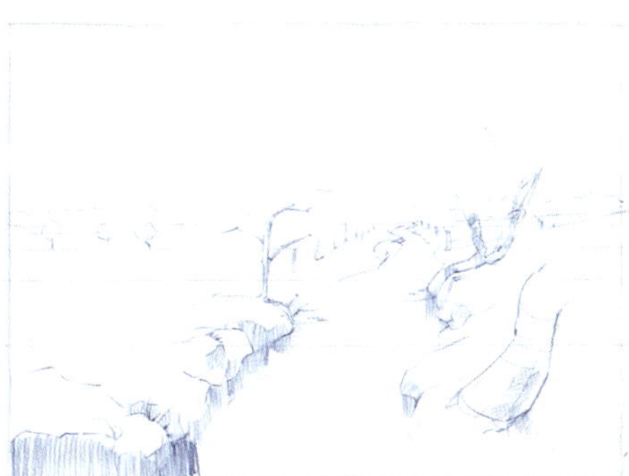

3 Choose a vanishing point on the horizon line, then sketch in a light version of your drawing, leaving parts of it incomplete to create white space that will allow the drawing to breathe. Give the trees in the foreground form, but flatten them off in the distance.

4 I tend to find it best to react with intuition, to start and then respond to what begins to form in front of you. Start with a few hatching lines here and there, working from light to dark to add more depth and form to your drawing.

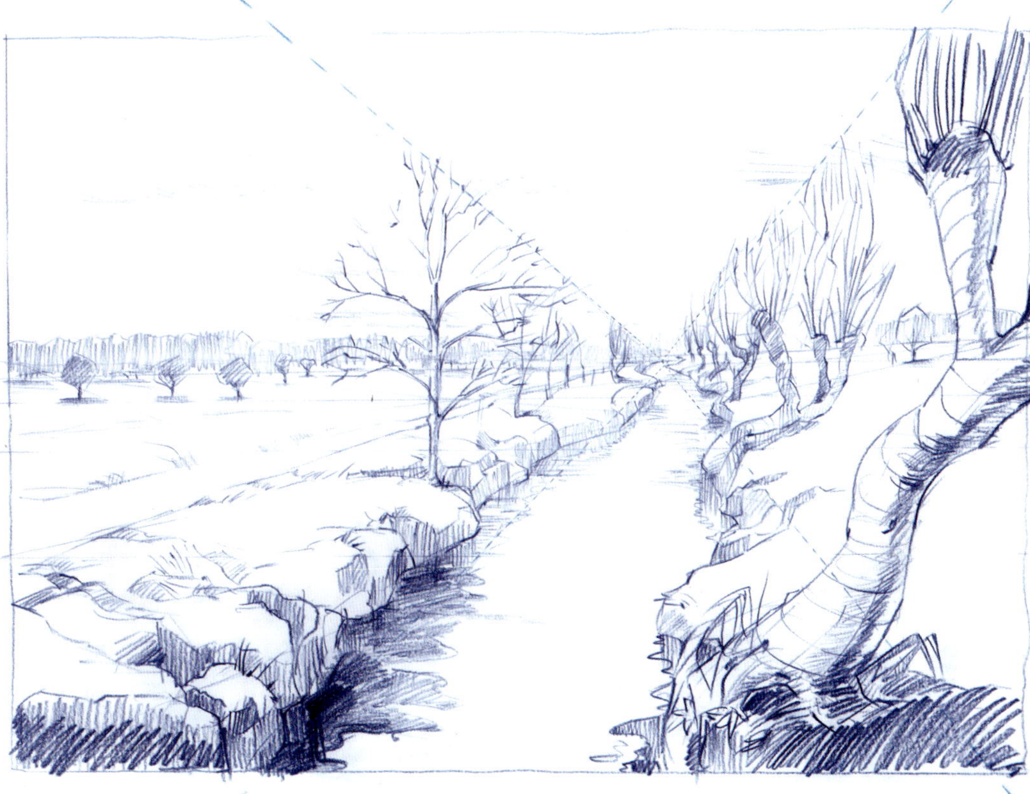

Atmospheric Perspective

The earth's atmosphere affects the appearance of distant objects, which is referred to as atmospheric perspective. Things further away are less distinct in detail. Their colour takes on bluish notes as they also become lighter in contrast. Observing these effects will aid spatial and moody qualities in your drawings.

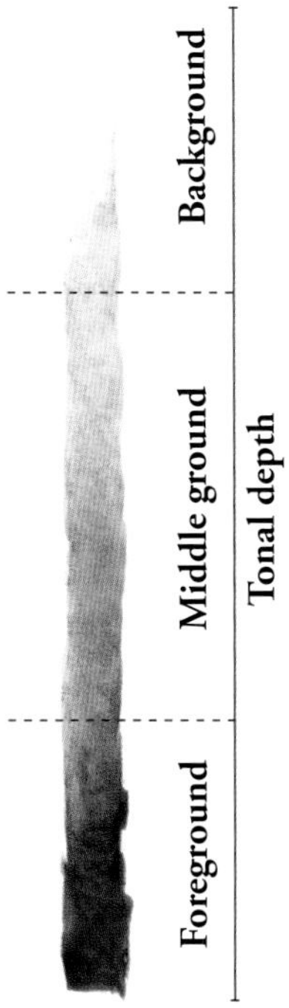

Tonal values in daylight compositions

Tones are graduated from high contrast in the foreground to lighter low contrast in the background. Shadows become lighter incrementally as they recede from the viewer in daylight views. In most compositions, the foreground is at the bottom of the page and is closest to the viewer.

Foreground

Colours in the foreground are at their strongest in tone and hue. To pull them forward on the page, create accents with significant contrast where the darkest notes play against the light. Add the darkest shadows and include the highest level of detail in this zone.

Middle ground

Shadows and dark-coloured objects will appear lighter in the middle ground than in the foreground. Use mid-tone values in the shadows.

Background

Tonal values in the background are at their lightest and closest in contrast. Objects in this zone have less detail and melt into neighbouring forms.

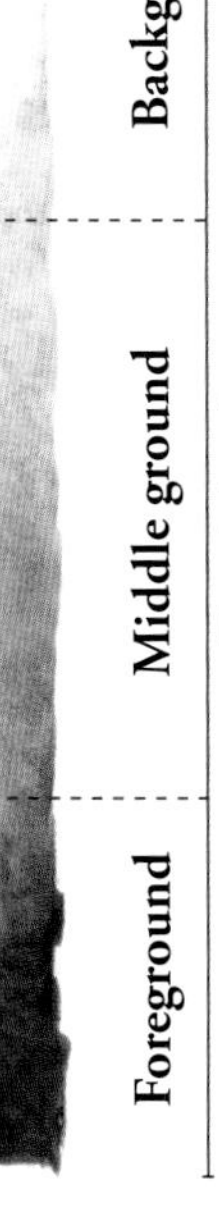

▼ **Cypriot mountains**

High viewpoints allow you to see for miles. When capturing vistas on this breathtaking scale, it is vital to pay close attention to the tonal values.

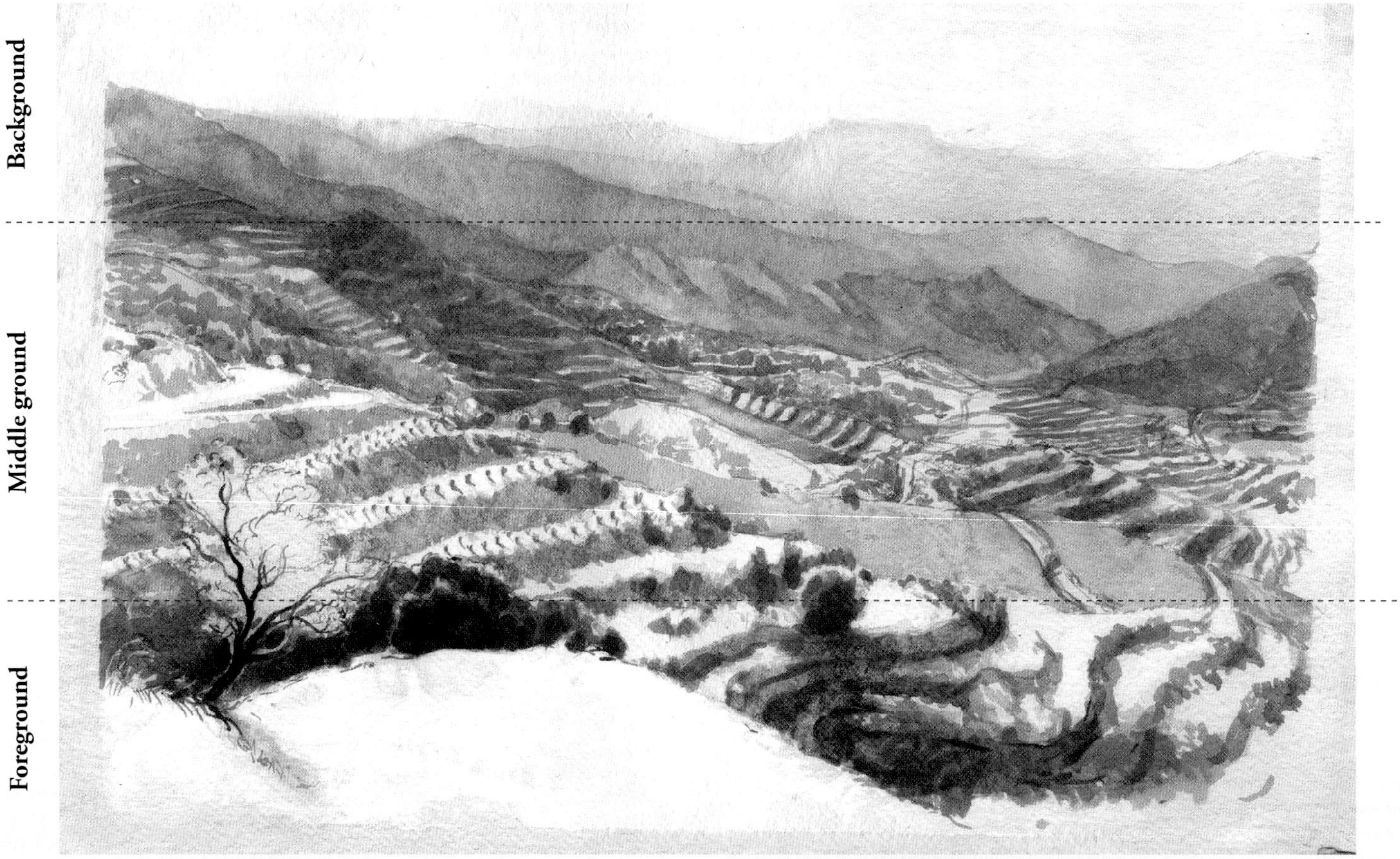

Colour values in daylight compositions

Objects and landscapes that are further away are cooler and bluer in colour temperature than closer scenes because of the abundance of water in the atmosphere. Distant colours lose some of their vibrancy due to moisture in the air and other particles will blend in more with the surrounding environment. Early morning mists and fog will dramatically increase the effects of atmospheric perspective. Blues tend to be warmer in the foreground and cooler in the background.

Foreground

The shadow colours in the foreground are at their warmest and darkest with plenty of plush ultramarine blue.

Middle ground

Mid-tones with cooler shadow notes distinguish the middle ground from the foreground.

Background

For shadows in the background, add cooler greyer blues, such as cerulean and cobalt, to the ultramarine blue mix and a touch of complementary orange to mute them.

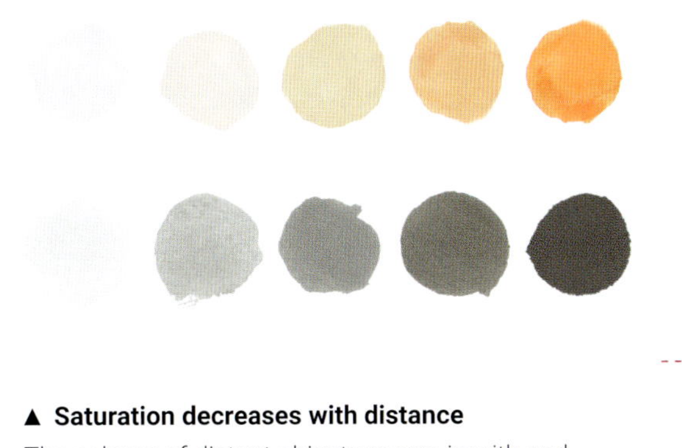

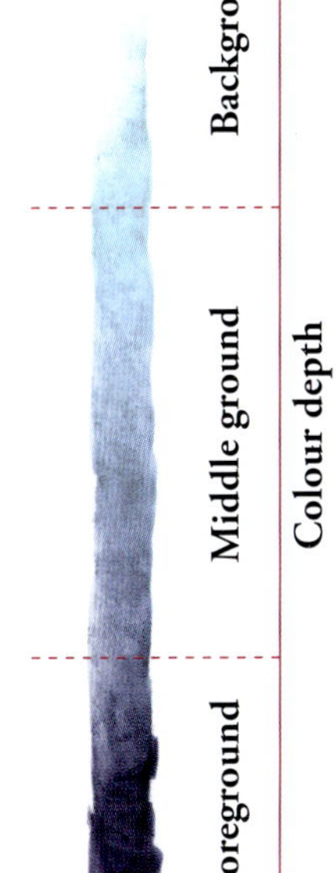

▲ Saturation decreases with distance

The colours of distant objects merge in with and take on some of the blue hues of the atmosphere. As a result, they lose their colour saturation. Another effect of atmospheric interference is that tones become lighter. Colour is far less apparent in monochromatic night scenes.

▼ Turner's view

For generations, artists have been inspired by this view from Richmond Hill, Surrey. It is known as Turner's view, as he executed studies from here throughout his career. The illusion of distance is enhanced by cooling and desaturating colours as they recede to the horizon.

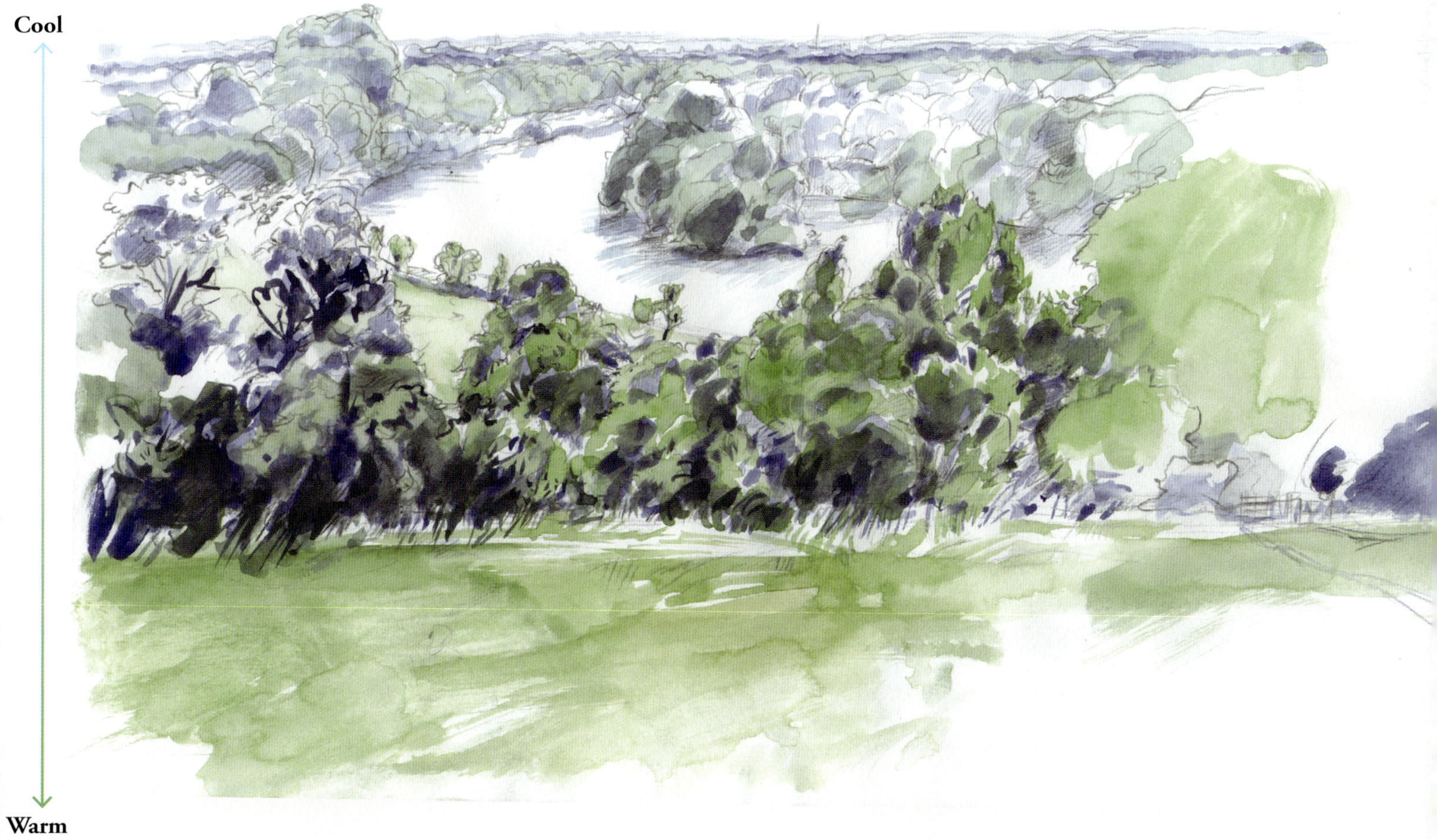

Foreshortening

One way to create the illusion of depth is for an object facing forward to recede sharply into the distance using a technique known as foreshortening. This concept first appeared in Renaissance paintings, with the Italian artist Andrea Mantegna being one of its pioneers – it is obvious in his *Lamentation of Christ*. Foreshortening is created by making the object shorter than it actually is, so it seems compressed as it faces the viewer.

The concept of foreshortening is one of the most challenging aspects of drawing to comprehend. However, most things we see are foreshortened to a certain extent. Look around the room you are sitting in and see just how few objects are truly parallel to your eye. If you hold an arm up towards you, it will appear shorter than it actually is (see box opposite). When you foreshorten an object in a drawing, it will appear more compressed than it is in real life and recede towards the background, as if it was shrinking. You'll find that sections in the foreground will overlap those behind it. For example, the feet in the foreground of a reclining figure will appear large in comparison to its head.

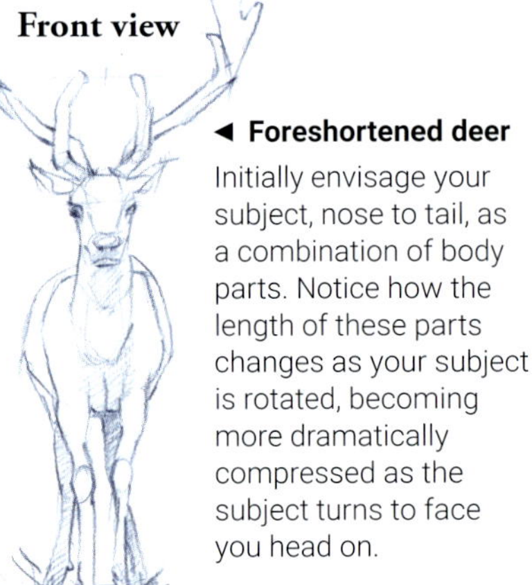

◄ Foreshortened deer
Initially envisage your subject, nose to tail, as a combination of body parts. Notice how the length of these parts changes as your subject is rotated, becoming more dramatically compressed as the subject turns to face you head on.

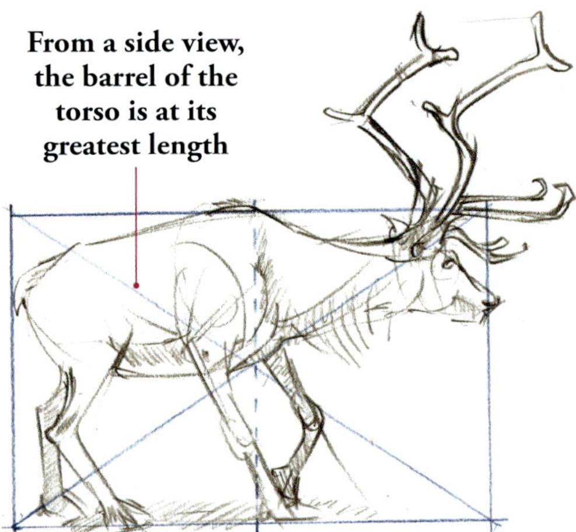

From a side view, the barrel of the torso is at its greatest length

From a rear view, the reindeer's rump appears larger than it really is

▲ Boxed proportions
By framing the side view of an animal or other object and using a cross to find a vertical centre line, you can help position it in a foreshortened view. Using the reindeer above, we can see how much of the reindeer would be to the right of the vertical line above right, or turn the box in the other direction as in the drawing below, far right.

► Resting reindeer
One of the easiest ways to conceive of foreshortening is an animal lying down, either facing you or away. The thorax and belly of a reindeer can be thought of as a barrel.

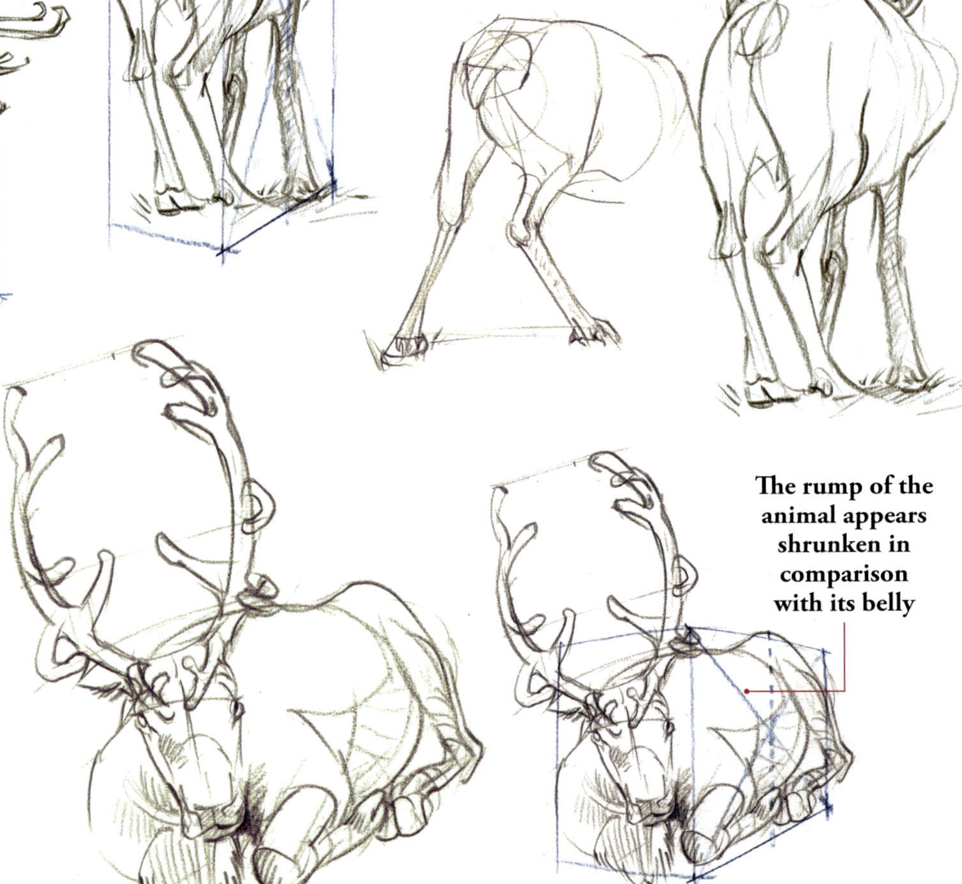

The rump of the animal appears shrunken in comparison with its belly

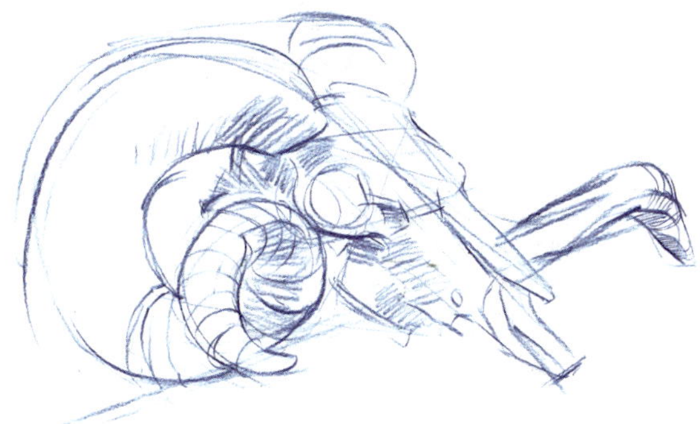

▲ Three-quarter foreshortening
Either facing towards you or away, a three-quarter foreshortened view is an attractive angle that provides plenty of information about the subject, allowing the viewer to get a sense of its three-dimensional form.

▼ Extreme foreshortening
Challenge yourself with extreme foreshortening poses to create the illusion that the form is emerging out of the paper towards the viewer, achieving a sense of depth.

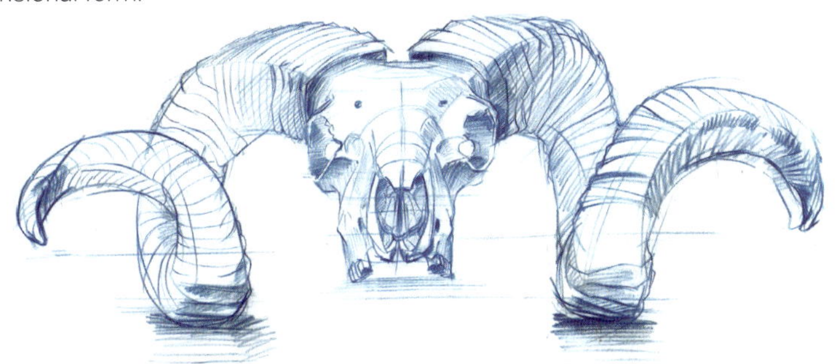

Foreshortening your arm
You can easily explore foreshortening by standing in front of a mirror. Simply hold up an arm straight from the shoulder to the side of your body, with fist clenched; here your arm is at its visually longest. Now rotate your arm so that your fist is facing you. As your arm rotates, it will seem to become shorter and more compressed, but there will also be a greater depth in space. Look in the mirror: with your fist facing you, you can barely see the arm at all, only the clenched knuckles.

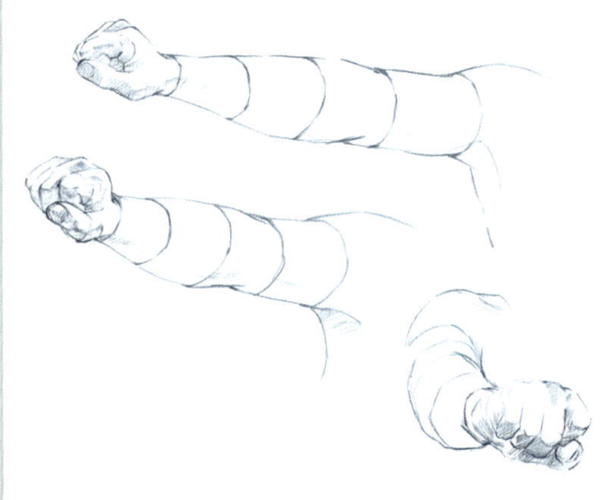

Sea urchin

In the natural world, many animals come in many shapes and sizes that defy the imagination, from the random shapes of sea sponges and coral cities to geometrical sea stars. Thousands are symmetrical, while many without a brain are not. Some forms, such as the pencil sea urchin, follow some seemingly initial order that can be broken down. Before I start, I always ask myself what is the best way to tackle the drawing challenge that the subject presents. The pencil sea urchin's spines predominantly radiate from a central point sitting in pockets on a raised ridge.

Materials
- Black artist's quality colouring pencil
- Cartridge (drawing) paper or sketchbook
- Sharpener
- Putty eraser

Sea urchin (*Eucidaris galapagensis*)
This sea urchin inhabits the coastal areas in the Galápagos. Being predominantly herbivorous, sea urchins consume algae and other coral reef-associated marine plants for food. Their feeding activities are crucial to maintaining the equilibrium of the reef because they free up space for corals to grow by removing overgrown plants and algae.

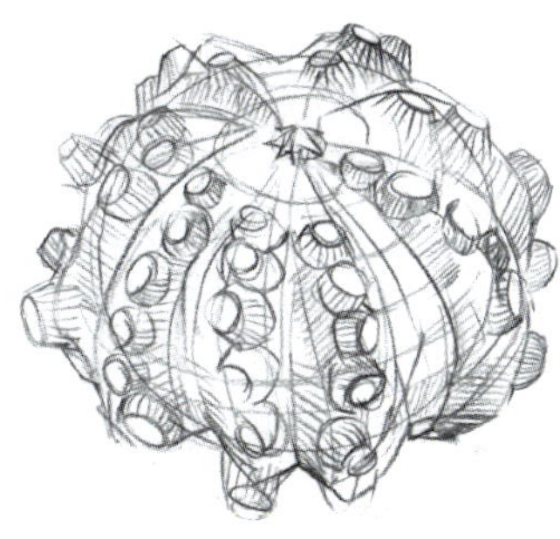

1   *Start by drawing the body of the urchin. Divide it into segments like an orange. Along the ridge of the raised divisions, sketch in the ragged line of adjoining cups.*

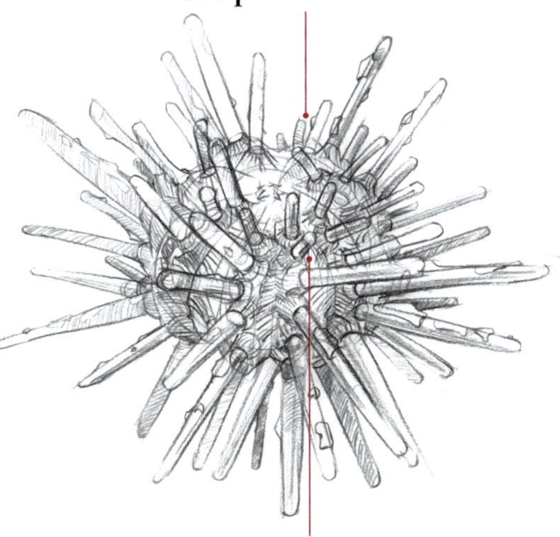

2   *Add in the spines at a multitude of angles – think of an orange covered in cocktail sticks that protect it from every angle. I like to shade the ones behind to push them backwards.*

Reclining Poses

Drawing constantly moving animals can be frustrating at times, so sketching sleeping animals provides welcome relief. It gives you time to slow down and study your subject, working from shape to shape, nose to tail, and to shade with more detail. The challenge is to find the correct proportions to create an accurate drawing of the subject. Reclining poses often bring the challenge of foreshortening (see pages 112–13).

Asiatic lion (*Panthera leo persica*)
The last remaining wild population of 600 Asiatic lions can be found within the boundaries of India's Gir National Park and the immediate surrounding area. These lions are smaller than their African cousins. The Maldhari population coexists in close proximity with the lions. The Maldharis revere the endangered Asiatic lions and by living peacefully alongside them have aided in their conservation.

Asiatic lion of the Gir

Because historically the lion has been regarded as the 'king of animals', it has been used to represent courage, nobility, monarchy, strength, stateliness and valour on coats of arms. Mediaeval heraldic artists placed the lion in different stances to express different meanings. A distinction is made between a 'lion couchant' – a lion lying down but with its head raised – to a 'lion dormant' with a head lowered and eyes shut.

Materials
- Cold grey artist's quality colouring pencil
- Large mid-tone pastel paper (or sugar/construction paper)
- Sharpener
- Putty eraser

1 *First, create cross lines for the bilateral line of symmetry of the eyes, ears and nose. By beginning with the eyes, I know that I have gone some way to capture the window of the soul. I often begin by looking hard at the shape of the eyes when visible. I find it encouraging to feel that I have something of the animal's spirit at this early stage that makes the animal feel alive on the paper.*

I tend to start with the head as it is easier to fit a body to a head than a head to a body

Viewed from the front, the lion's body appears short

2 *Next, sketch the whole body, reducing it to the simple primary forms: a barrel for the chest, tapering tubes for the legs and so forth.*

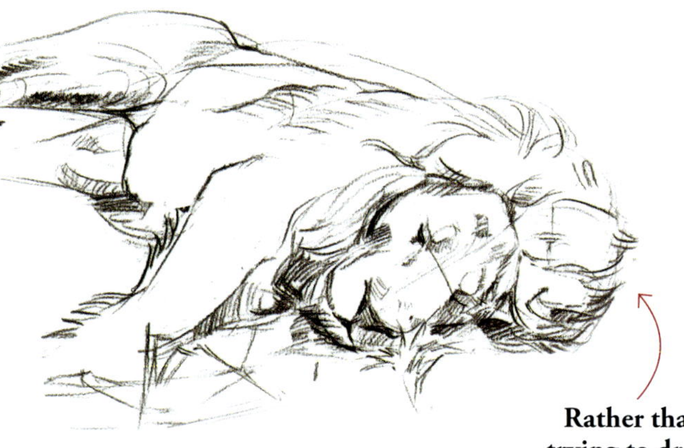

3 *Use darker lines towards the completion of the sketch. Apply those in the foreground more vigorously to push the forms forward.*

Rather than trying to draw every hair, I look for the main shapes of clumps in the mane

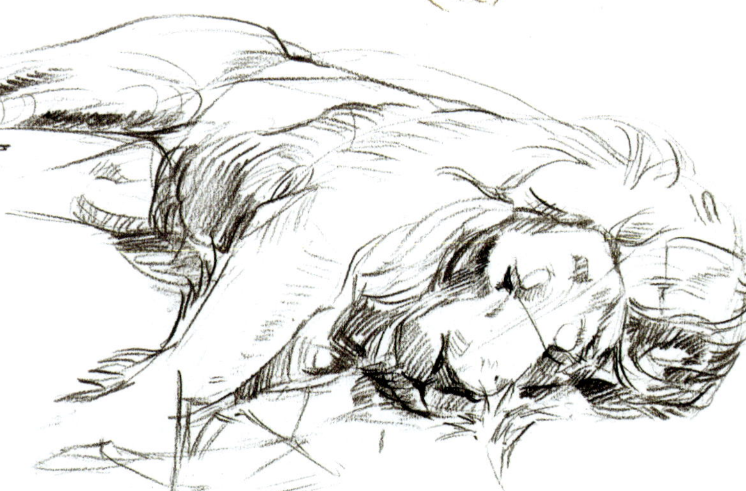

4 *Using directional hatch marks (see pages 80–1), looking for areas of light and shade, and angle them to follow the form.*

Study Sheet: *Asiatic Lion*

A sleeping animal allows you to draw a breath from the ferocity of capturing moving animals. Shapes can be more carefully studied and shading placed in with more precision, allowing you to look for delineation of the bones, muscles and tendons beneath the surface.

Lion head widget

It is important to get a sense that the muzzle is projecting. A good way to achieve this is simply to add a smaller box onto one for the cranium.

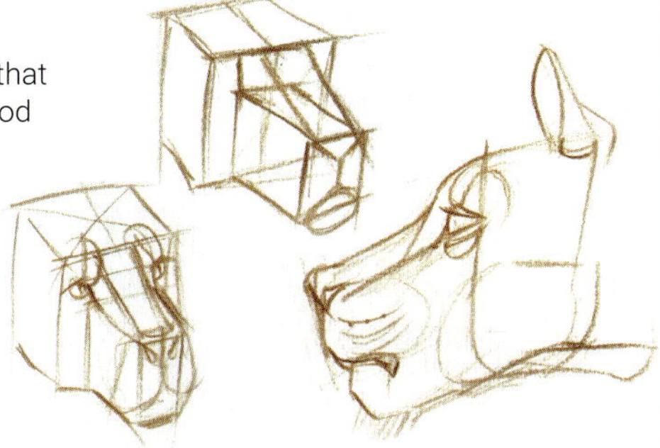

▼ Geometric simplification

Viewed laterally, a lion's body appears to be a long tube. The legs can initially be sketched as tapering tubes that get narrower from the top down, and then you cut into them to refine their shape and mass.

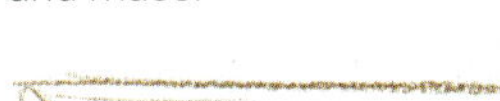

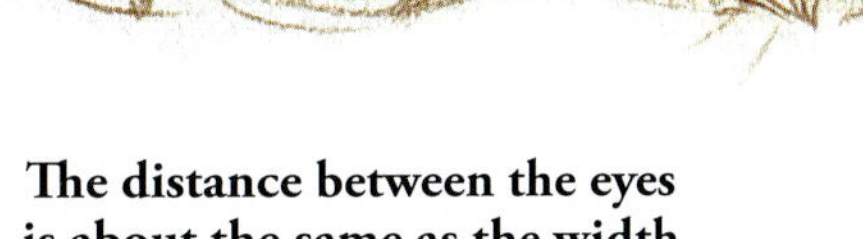

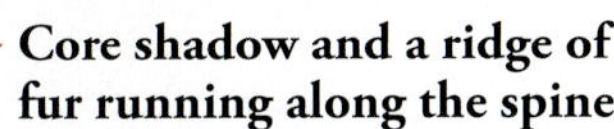

Core shadow and a ridge of fur running along the spine

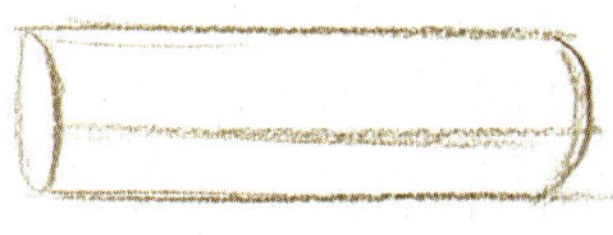

The distance between the eyes is about the same as the width of two more eyes

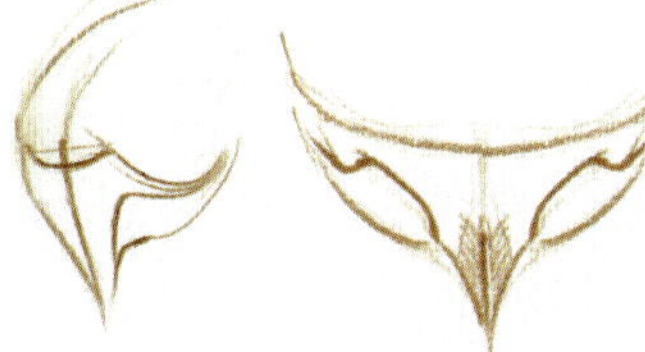

▲ Nose

After observing the lion's nose face on, I often create a little flat shape and then rotate it. Air is expelled from the slits to allow the big cats to sniff fresh air.

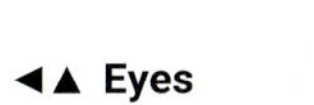

◀▲ Eyes

Notice how the eye changes shape when seen from the side.

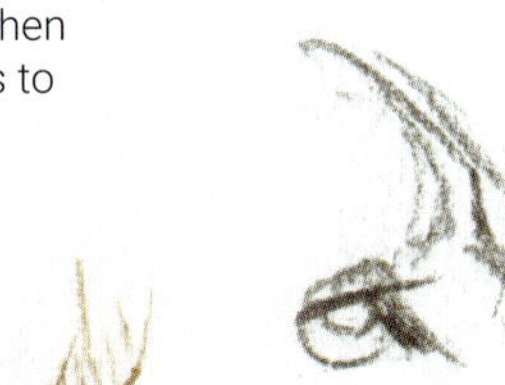

Dewclaw

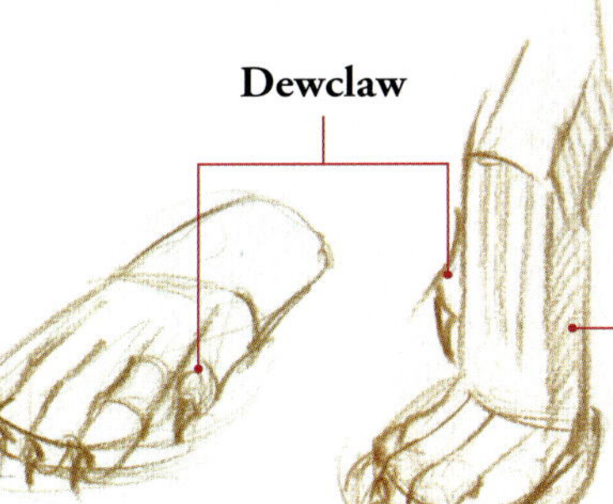

Left paw standing

▶ Paws and claws

Dogs and cats have five claws on their front paws, including a dewclaw that does not touch the ground when standing, and four claws on the back.

Right paw reclining

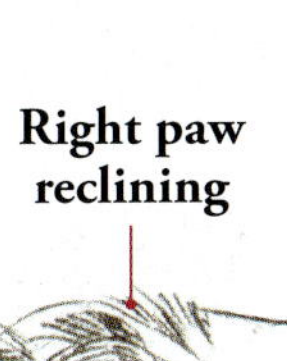

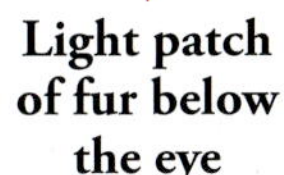

Light patch of fur below the eye

◀ Capturing pride

To capture the majestic mane of the male wavering in the wind, create long gestural lines.

Looking Through

The challenge of creating depth and space is not limited to the typical airy landscapes with a mosaic of scattered fields stretching to the horizon. In other locations, such as tropical rainforests, plants have taken over and evolved into spectacular lush vegetation with large leaves to harvest the sun's energy.

The vegetation in rainforests is so dense that only 2 per cent of the sun's rays can reach the ground. If you could visit one, your eyes would be met with a visual noise of diverse leaf shapes as you peer through larger foreground leaves to smaller distant ones. This scene can only be indicated with an impressionistic pattern (different leaves create different patterns) rather than botanical accuracy. It is not just in rainforests that this challenge of 'looking through' occurs: there are a myriad of other locations, from forest and woodlands to the subterranean habitats of caves.

You are not a camera

The job for the artist is to see through all of the visual noise in the rainforest to give an impression of it. Fortunately, plant structures can be slightly forgiving in that the viewer does not need to see exact proportions. Bear in mind that you are constructing an interpretation of what you are seeing, and certain plants will need to be implied with an impression or a shadowy silhouette in the background.

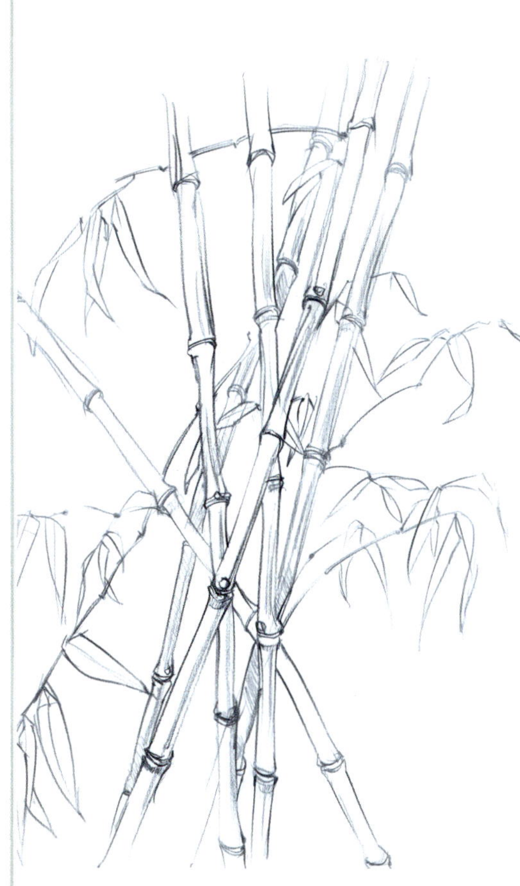

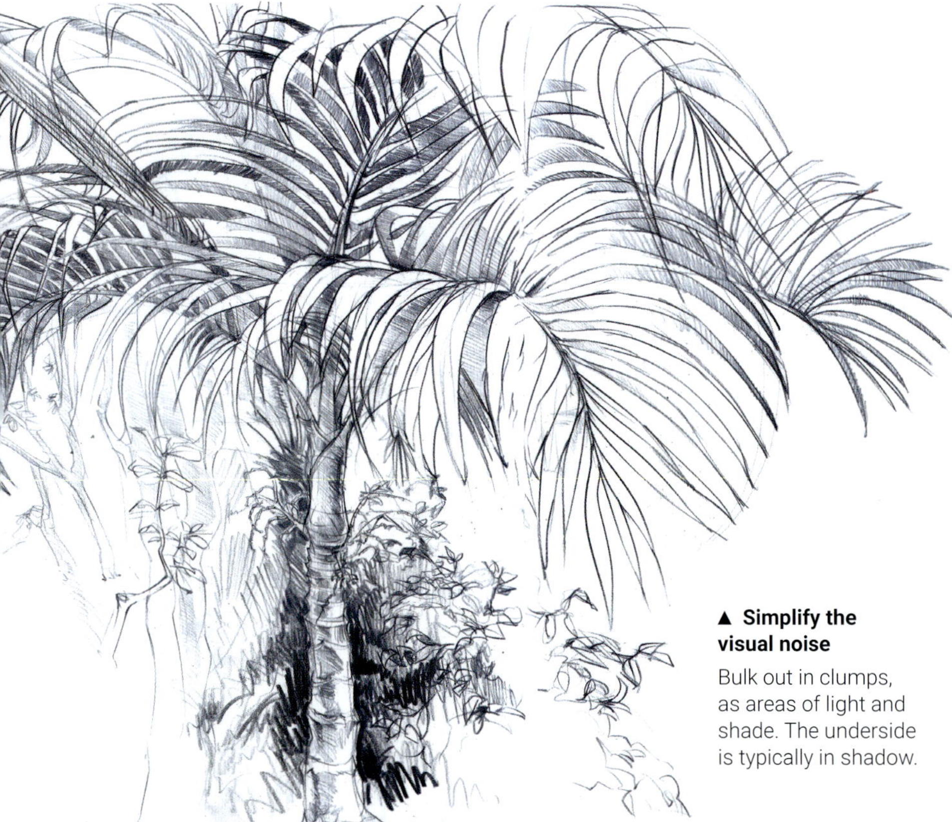

▲ Simplify the visual noise

Bulk out in clumps, as areas of light and shade. The underside is typically in shadow.

How to draw bamboo: seeing in segments

In a bamboo forest, the bamboo itself can be conceived as tube sections that join at slightly wider knuckles. Think of it as a playful game and create the impression that one stalk is in front of the other by overlapping lines.

Draw each segment of a plant stalk with a pair of curved lines. Notice how these slightly converge towards the middle and splay out at the joints. Draw a series of short curved lines across each joint that are either concave or convex, depending on your viewpoint. Join short tubes together to allow the bamboo stalks to grow piece by piece.

Notice how one piece of bamboo will overlap the other, creating a sense of depth. I added the highly characteristic leaves at the end on thin spindly twigs, trying to make a smooth transition between the under and topside as they curled.

Rainforests

For inspiration, you can visit your local botanical garden and enter the palm house, where the air is heavy, hot and humid, and the lush vegetation has grown to gigantic proportions.

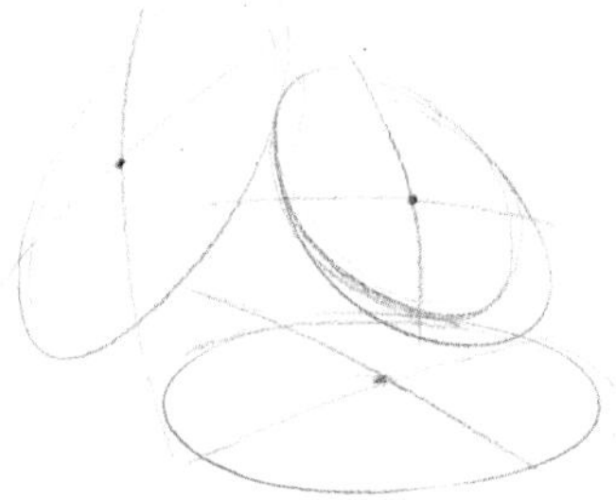

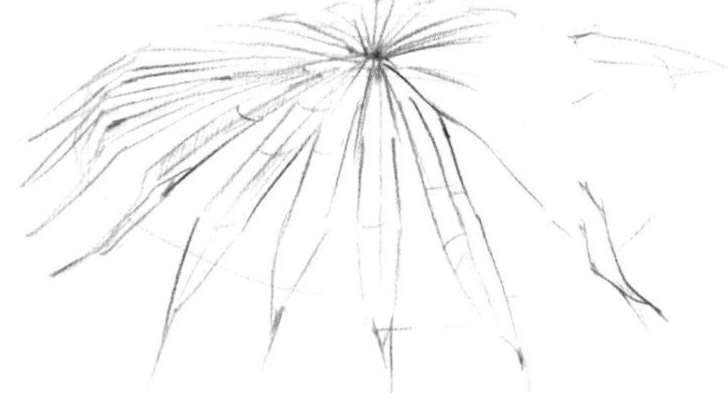

1 *Begin your sketch by creating a light set of loops with cross lines to structure large jungle leaves.*

2 *Choose a focal point, such as the core of the plant's leaf as a starting point and let your drawing grow, working shape by shape and navigating your way to the neighbouring branches and leaves.*

Rainforests

Rainforest cover only around 6 per cent of the world's surface, but they account for 50 per cent of all species, and they play an essential role in the survival of life on earth. Large leaves allow tropical plants to capture more sunlight energy, and a plentiful supply of water is converted into food for growth.

In a rainforest, it is a race to the light for plants. Those on the ground rely on capturing unpredictable shafts of sunlight, known as sunflecks, that break through the canopy. Little light falls on the forest floor, so plants here have vast leaves to capture as much sunlight as possible. Many plants have waxy leaves that help to repel the rain.

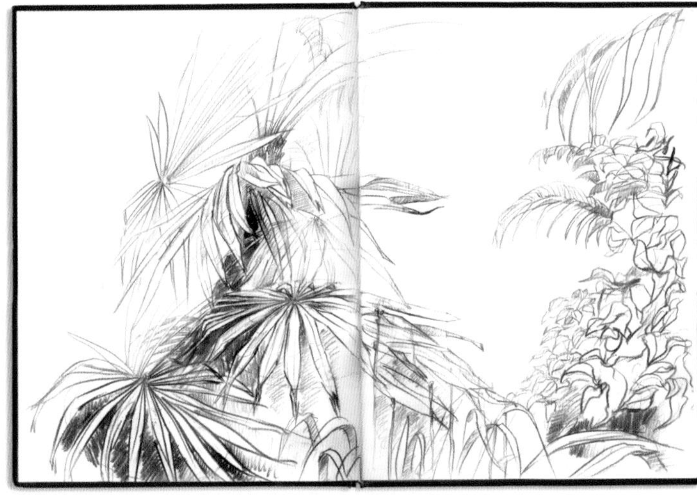

3 *Draw forms closer to you with a darker, thicker line to create emphasis and pull them to the front. Use lines that overlap to inform the eye that one leaf is in front of the other. Sketch leaves in the distance more lightly and with less detail.*

4 *Create characteristic shapes that attempt to capture the myriad of different shapes and sizes of jungle leaves. Draw individual leaves in the foreground and simply suggest clumps in the distance where there is less detail and contrast.*

Using contrast
Create high contrast in the foreground to project the leaf shapes forward to the viewer. I used a sharp pencil for the foreground and shaded the background when the pencil had become more blunt for softer, more atmospheric mark-making.

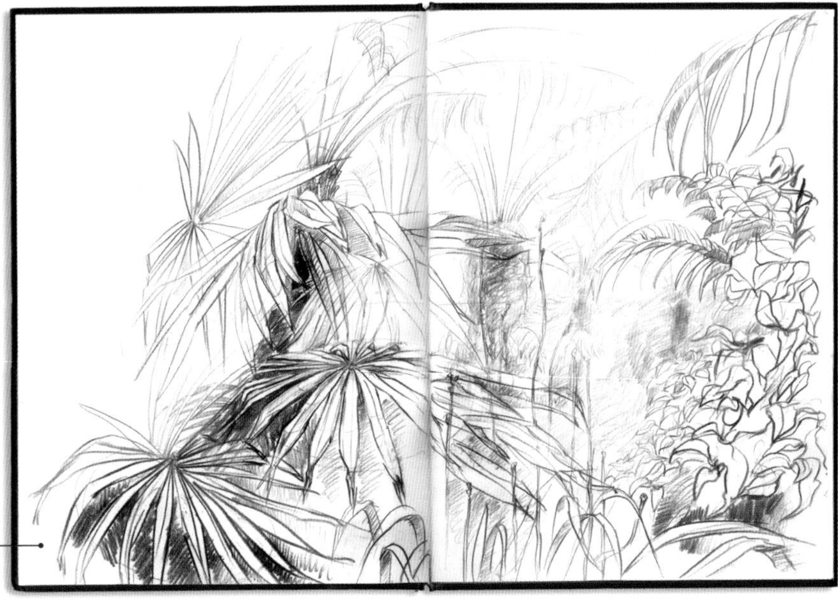

Pattern and Texture

A pattern is a design created by similar repeating lines, shapes, forms or colours. A single element that can be the starting point of any pattern is a motif. Regular and irregular patterns can be seen in both nature and manufactured artefacts. These can be symmetrical, like a butterfly's wings, or asymmetrical, like a cheetah's spots.

The tactile quality of a surface, such as the vanes of a feather or on coral polyps, is referred to as texture. As with pattern, texture can be regular, such as the gills of a toadstool or the strata of rock formations, or irregular. Texture is perceived in two ways: visually (through sight) and physically (through touch). If you're drawing an inanimate object, don't be afraid to pick it up before you start drawing to get a sense of its physical texture, closing your eyes and feeling, for example, the smoothness of a pebble contrasting against the rough geometric scales of a pine cone.

Pattern and texture are generally considered to be surface qualities of a subject, but both can also be observed as a quality of a group of subjects, such as a collection of pebbles on a beach, the feathers of a peacock's tail or the rings of an oak tree stump. You can utilize a host of techniques and approaches to replicate the patterns and textures in your drawings. This chapter will focus on fine-tuning your interpretations of these surface qualities and how to sensitively transcribe them to paper using various mark-making techniques.

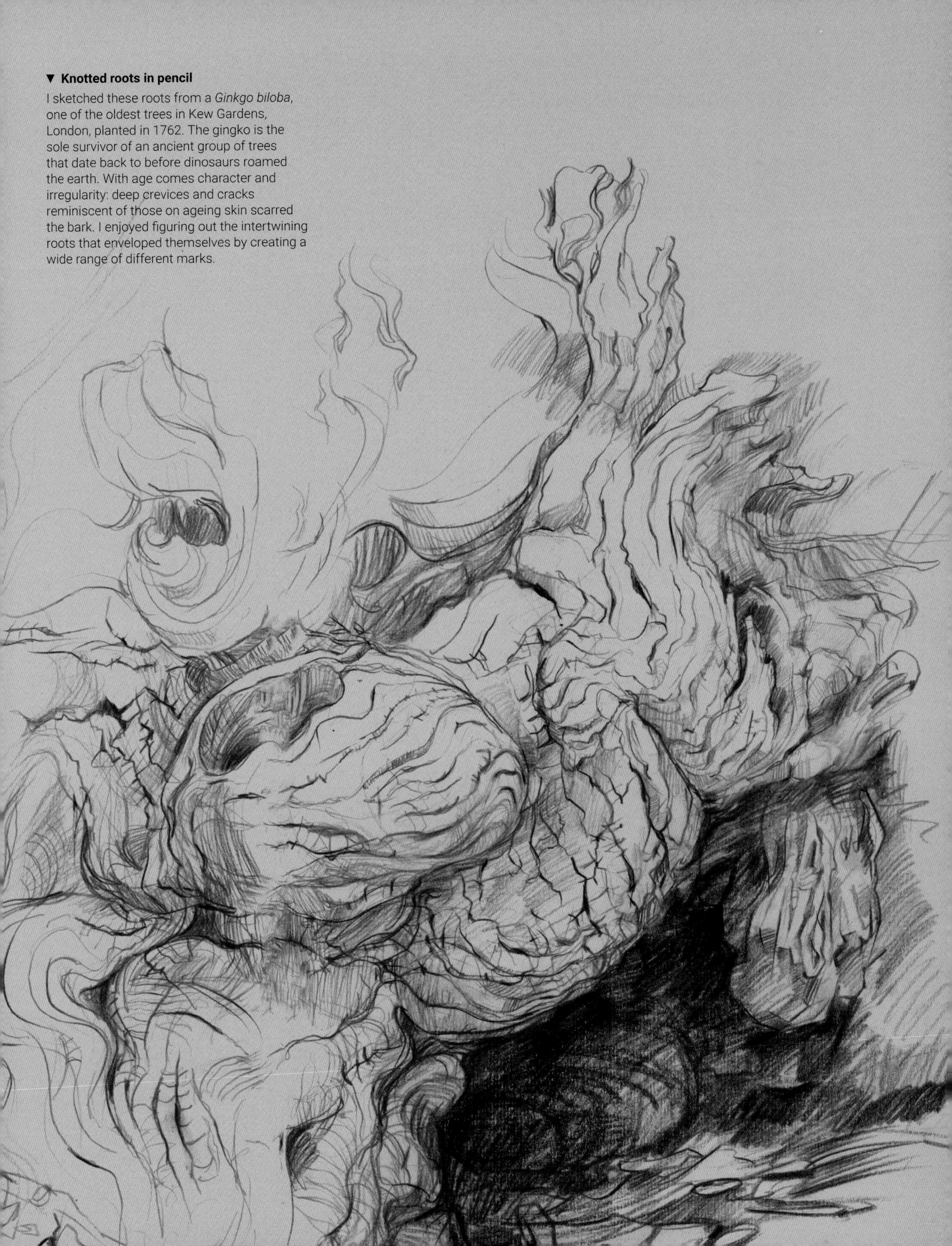

▼ **Knotted roots in pencil**
I sketched these roots from a *Ginkgo biloba*, one of the oldest trees in Kew Gardens, London, planted in 1762. The gingko is the sole survivor of an ancient group of trees that date back to before dinosaurs roamed the earth. With age comes character and irregularity: deep crevices and cracks reminiscent of those on ageing skin scarred the bark. I enjoyed figuring out the intertwining roots that enveloped themselves by creating a wide range of different marks.

Pattern and Texture Essentials

The wealth of different patterns and textures found in nature is vast. In trying to draw one, it is easy to make assumptions about a subject without fully appreciating its changing pattern. I suggest you carefully study, for example, the variety of spots on a leopard's coat or the diversity of cracks in an old oak's bark. Explore experimental and individual ways to imply both pattern and texture with your mark making, and even change your drawing media to more closely match to the subject's qualities, such as a wash for the shiny skin of a Koi carp.

Pattern

In nature, patterns typically seem to follow some geometrical order that are broken down or modified by organic interruptions or imperfections. For example, zebra stripes (which are as individual as a fingerprint) are not just straight vertical lines, they change angle at the shoulder.

I look for order in pattern using light tracing marks to create the geometrical frame for the placement of the pattern. These can interlock into a grid referred to as an X-wrap as a way to make sense of what can otherwise be chaos in free-flowing rhythmic overlapping lines, such as the scales on a fish or pine cone.

▲ Mirrored symmetry in patterns

Butterfly and moth wings represent perfect symmetry. An excellent way to visualize this pattern is to imagine the insect painted on a folded piece of paper.

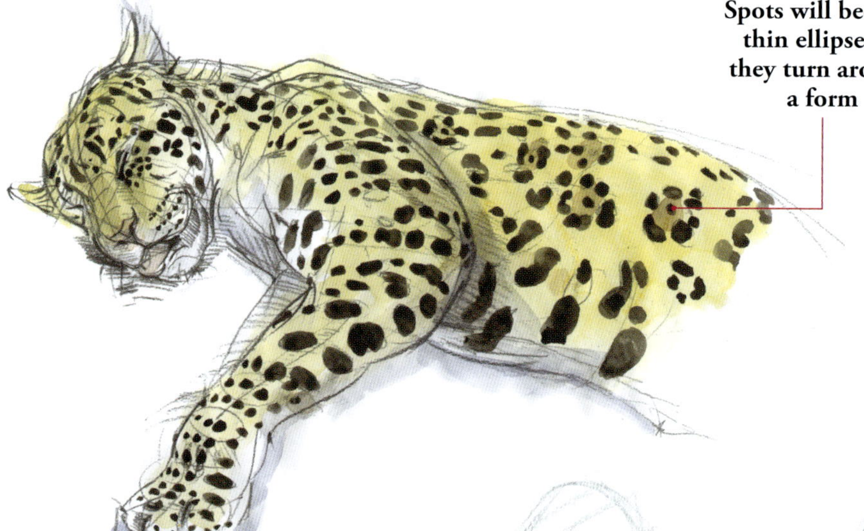

Spots will become thin ellipses as they turn around a form

◄ Variations on a theme

Rosettes are jagged black circles with tawny centres that appear on a jaguar's or leopard's coat. They vary significantly in appearance and shape, changing to small disc shapes on the head, resembling bean shapes, paw prints or ellipses. This sketch was created from life and watercolour was added from observing a photograph in the studio.

X-wrap

The interlocking spiralling shapes of scales on a pine cone can be plotted with an initial X-wrap. This is a criss-cross scaffold of opposing diagonal lines that acts as a framework for repeating geometric forms.

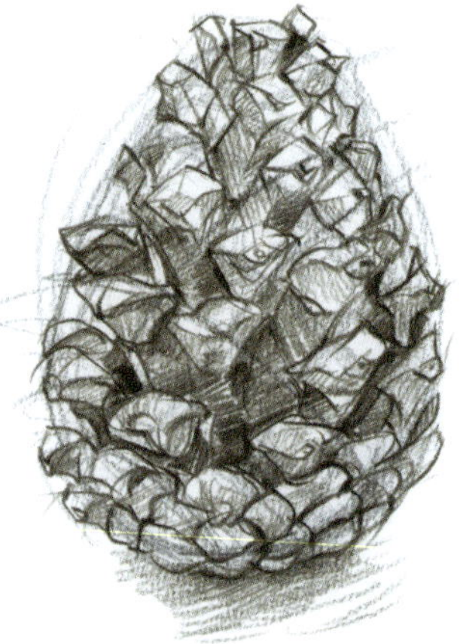

1 *Sketch out the main shape and central axis, in this case an egg shape, and create arcs that wrap around in the clockwise direction of the rows of scales.*

2 *Add a second series of arcs that run in the opposite direction.*

3 *Choose a scale and draw it in the corresponding position in the X-wrap, and let the drawing grow from there, shape to shape.*

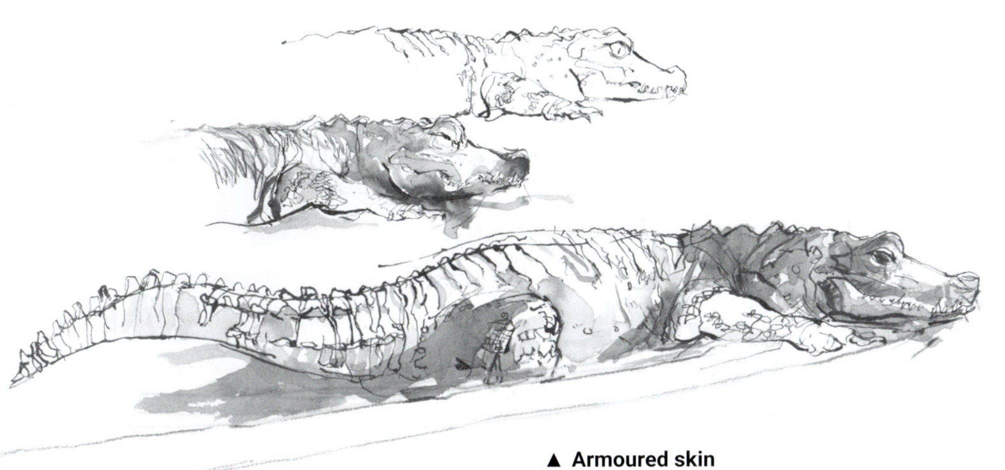

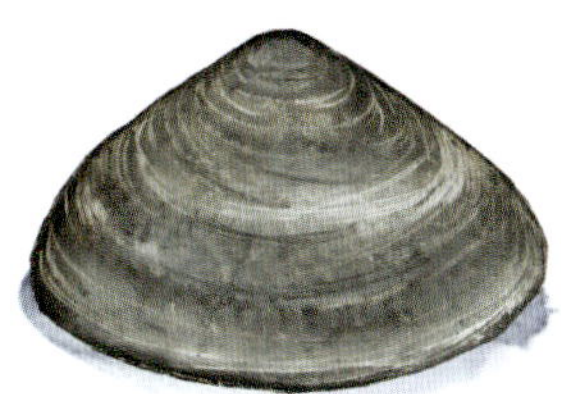

Sgraffito

Artists working on a two-dimensional surface use a technique known as sgraffito to produce a texture that might be inferred or actual. *Sgraffito*, which means 'scratched' in Italian, involves laying down a preliminary surface, covering it with another one and then scratching the top layer to reveal the underlying colour beneath. For example, scratching through layers of oil pastel with a compass point can capture the texture of the growth rings of a mussel.

▲ Armoured skin
The linear qualities of this sketch of a dwarf crocodile suggests their scaly skin.

Optical texture

Trompe l'oeil is a French term that means 'to deceive the eye'. It refers to a painting style that depicts an object or scene so true to life that it seems to be real, not just a painting on a flat surface. (This is also referred to as verisimilitude.) Well-known examples include a fly crawling on the surface of a painting and faux textures of marble painted on walls. Here's an exercise to try yourself: experiment with watercolour and ink to try to capture the impression of wet glistening skin. You can also experiment by using unusual painting tools and different techniques, such as rolling rags to create a crumbling effect or dry brushing (using a pigment without water) with turkey feathers to try to imitate marble. Sponges, knives, even fingers: there are no limits to the tools you can use to create textures.

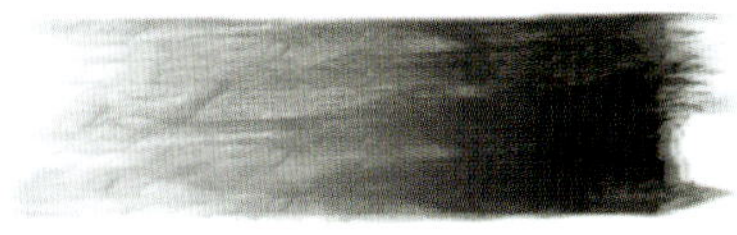

Sfumato

A technique that merges the edges of colours to create a gentle transition between colours or tones is known as *sfumato*, which is from the Italian meaning 'soft', 'vague' or 'indistinct'. It can be thought of as blurring. Charcoal and watercolour are excellent media for creating these soft transitions where you want a smooth texture, for example, between the light and shade on a cheek, as well as for a misty landscape.

Texture

Animals and plants have a host of different textures that will challenge your drawing ability. Imagine the difference between stroking a cat and a crocodile, or the sharp prick of a cactus to brushing your hand through wavering seagrass. Every subject you draw will have a texture, even the smoothness of glass-like ice. It would be impossible to cover all the examples, so be prepared to be creative and change your drawing media to meet the challenge ahead. The way you create shading is particularly important to suggest different textures.

Combine both pattern and texture together

Try to make capturing both pattern and texture second nature in your field study sheets. Both can be used to create highly decorative drawings that dazzle the senses.

▶ Hair marks
Look for divisions in the clumps of the pelt and create suggestive hair marks with flicks of your wrist. The hair tends to be longer and thicker in certain areas, such as beneath the neck on ungulates.

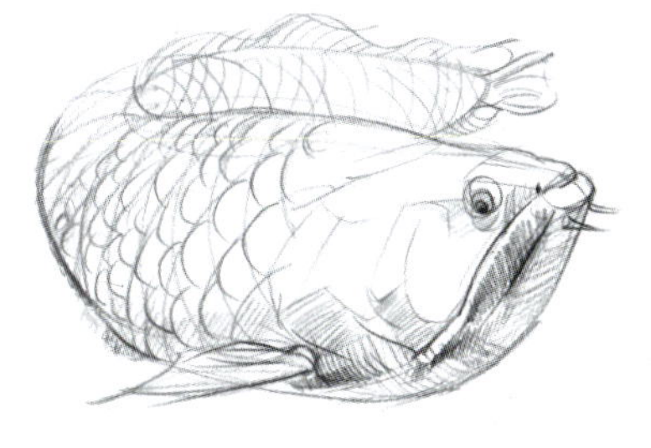

Contrasting Textures

While many creatures are predominantly a single texture – a cat's fur, a lizard's scales or the hair on a cow's hide – you'll frequently encounter subjects in the natural world that are distinctive through having two or more contrasting textures, and these need to be individually captured to portray the subject's essence. Replicating any texture on paper is a challenge to any artist's mark-making ability, let alone two, but paying close attention to each texture's details will allow you to create the illusion of different surfaces.

Soft tree fern

With spreading fronds above a thick trunk, the slow-growing soft tree fern makes a striking plant for an observational study. The texture of the delicate fronds contrast delightfully with the rugged teeth-like bark segments of its trunk. Think about the round strength and might of a tree fern trunk in contrast to the soft, feathery feeling of their fronds. Imagine both brushing against your cheek. How different do they feel? The way the dark, almost black wood contrasts with the unfurling, delicate leaflets makes them an attractive subject to draw.

In this drawing, both begin their journey with a ghostly structural underdrawing, which organizes the fronds as they splay out in a circular motion as well as the widening ellipses of the bark loops as they drop below eye level. Use lighter marks to indicate their fronds and darker, more rigorous mark-making to sculpt the architectural trunk.

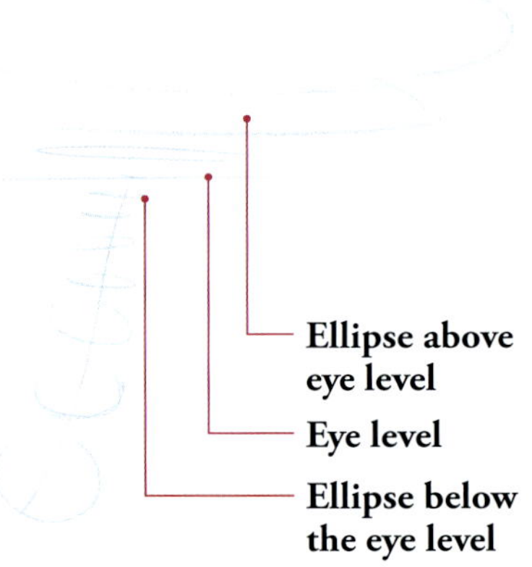

1 *Draw the light vertical line of action of the main trunk to act as the spine on which you can hang the massive trunk form and the lighter fronds. Surround this spine line with a series of ellipses, a small set of hoops that surround the trunk. Create larger, very light circular arcs massing out the foliage at the top of the palm to help give your sketch a three-dimensional feeling.*

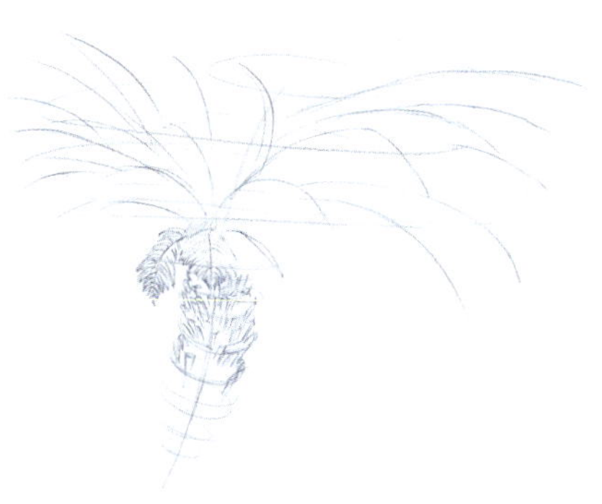

2 *Create a series of arc-like marks that radiate outwards to form the centre of the fronds' stalks or rachis.*

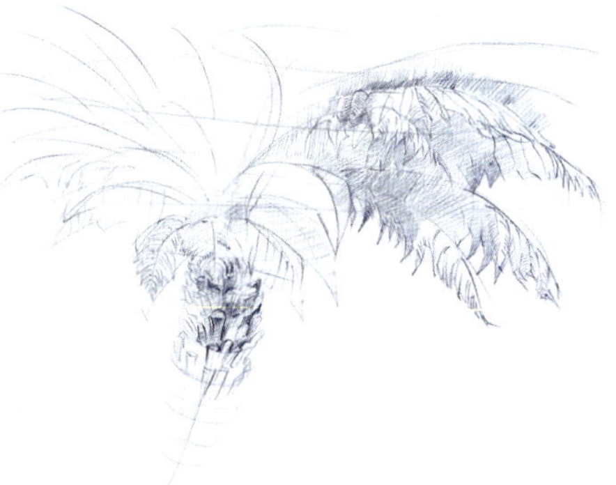

3 *Pick a starting point and start sketching the fronds to block in the main areas of shade. As you observe the fronds, reduce the visual noise in front of you by squinting at it.*

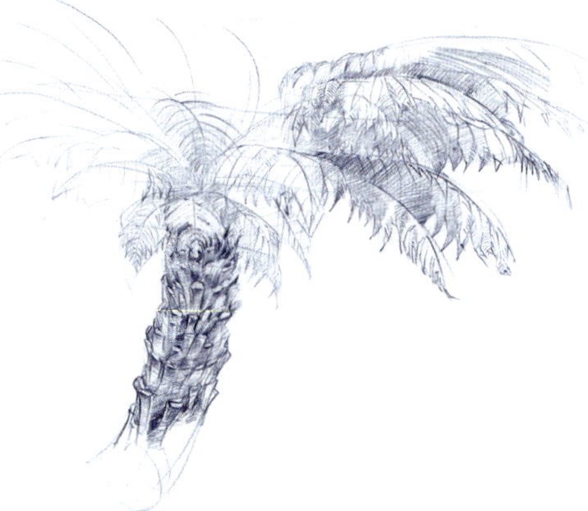

4 *Traverse like a climber across to new areas of your subject and let the drawing grow from an understood area, working across the fronds and down the trunk. Don't give up!*

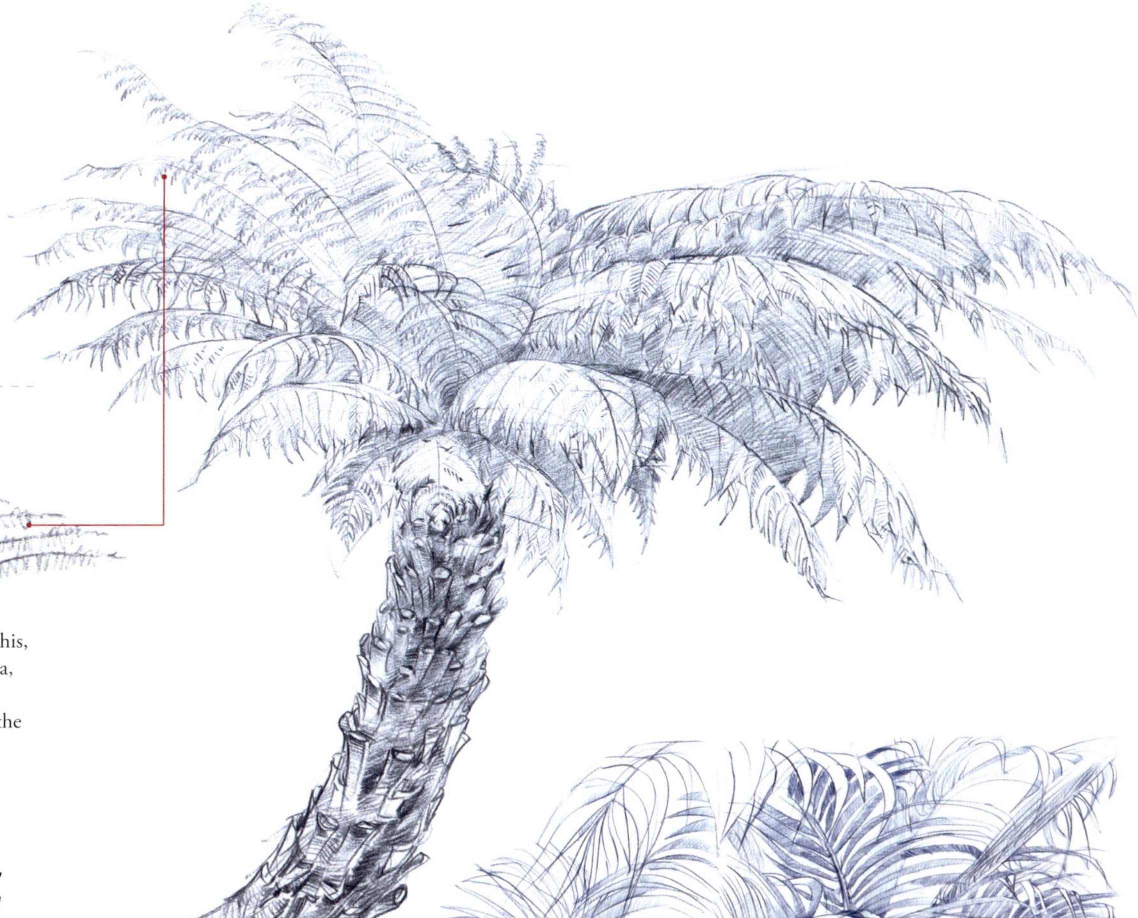

Tip

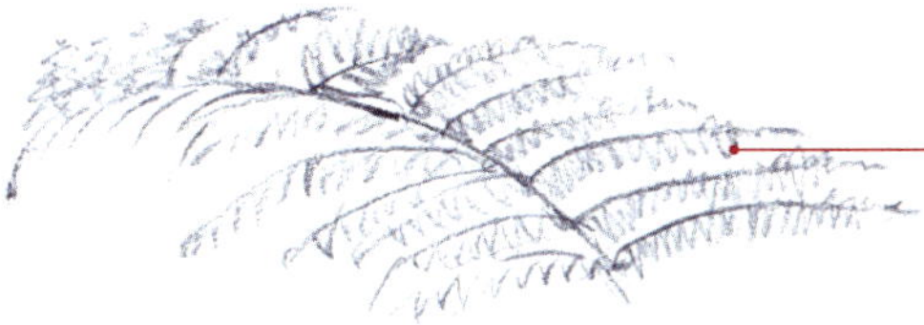

After sketching the arcs of the central rachis, sketch a series of smaller arches, the pinna, coming off the central rachis, then add zigzag marks to create the impression of the individual leaflets called pinnule.

5 *As the drawing progresses, add more rigorous shading to the bark to try to give the trunk some sense of muscular physicality compared to the wispy, springy fronds.*

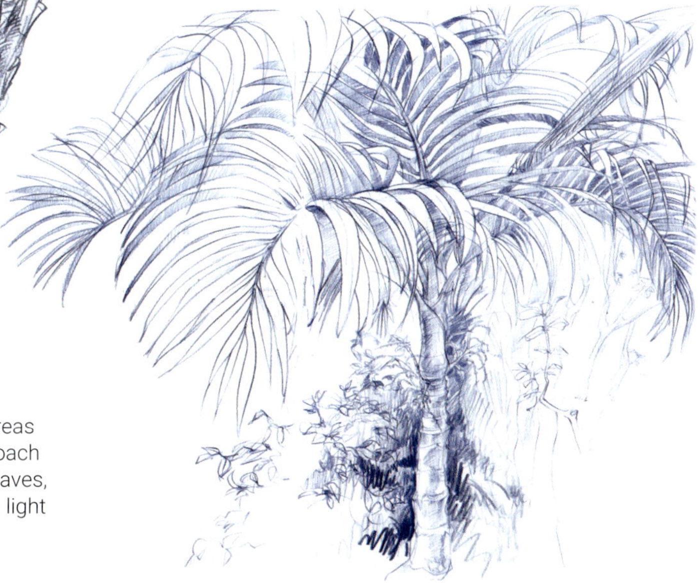

▶ Bulk out in areas of light and dark

Bulk out in clumps of fronds as areas of light and shade. A similar approach can be taken to sketching palm leaves, with the underside in shadow and light typically catching the top.

Frond

Having a comprehensive understanding of the anatomy of a frond leaf will give you an idea of how to accurately draw it as the form rotates, bends and appears in foreshortened positions.

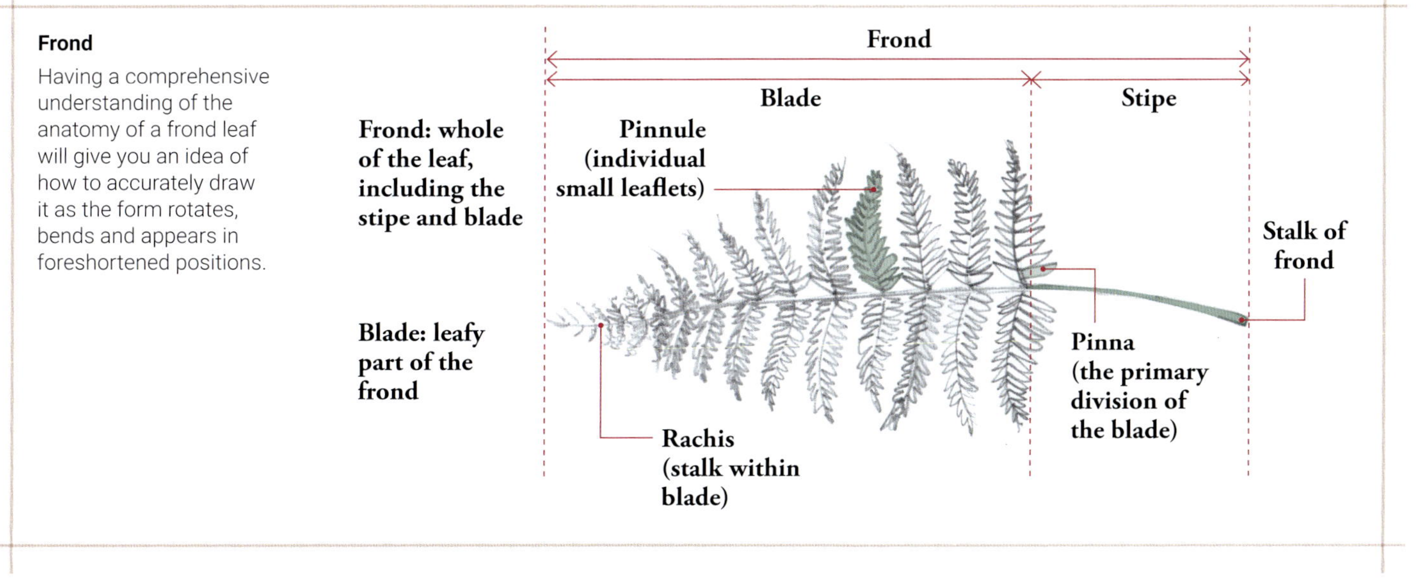

Body Markings

Stripes, spots and other body markings have an evolutionary basis that developed to help the animal survive. A harder-to-spot leopard (see page 120) will catch more prey, while a zebra's broken shape confuses predators, enabling it to escape. Stripes and dots are called disruptive camouflage because they help to break up the animal's silhouette. Having an understanding of this will help you as you draw these markings.

Animals that have stripes often have bilateral, or mirror, symmetry. This is useful to know because the stripes will line up when drawing the animal in front, rear and three-quarter views. The direction of the black bars of a zebra, for example, will help the viewer to understand the form beneath. When drawing stripes or spots on any animal, consider how they wrap around its bulbous rump and belly. Skin is elastic and stretches over the surface muscles, so think about how the head of bones beneath pushes into it, creating mounds and grooves that add shape to the stripes and spots.

Zebra

Native to Africa, zebras are distinctive single-hoofed mammals that live in herds. The bold black and white stripes of the zebra, particularly when the zebra is in a herd, confuse not only their big cat predators, such as lions, but also smaller pests such as mosquitos and flies. The stripes are created by white fur against the underlying black skin, which follow the form.

Materials
- Black artist's quality colouring pencil
- Cartridge paper or sketchbook
- Sharpener
- Putty eraser

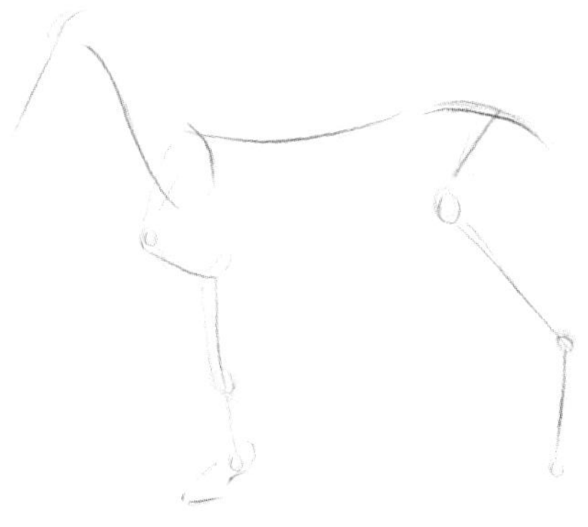

1 *Begin by sketching out a light armature of the skeleton. The forehead is flat, triangular and hard. Understanding the location of the pivot point is key to a feeling of articulation and can be denoted with a simple circle.*

Tip

Starting with a simple framework of landmarks will help to establish the proportions before committing to a more developed drawing.

2 *The zebra's legs are shorter than a horse's, and there is a change in the direction of the stripes at the shoulders. Look for other variations in the stripes.*

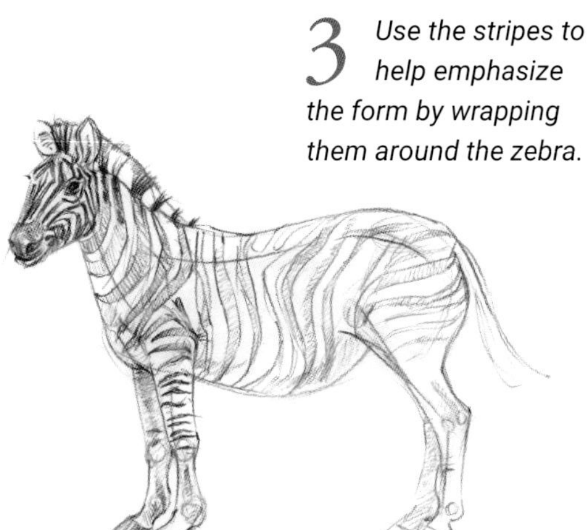

3 *Use the stripes to help emphasize the form by wrapping them around the zebra.*

4 *Build up a black waxy depth to your shading by adding more pressure to your pencil.*

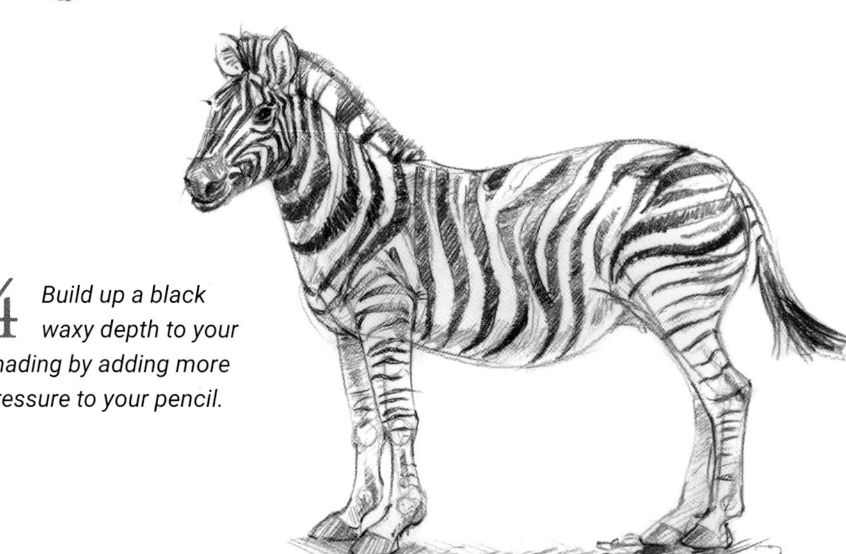

Study Sheet: *Zebra*

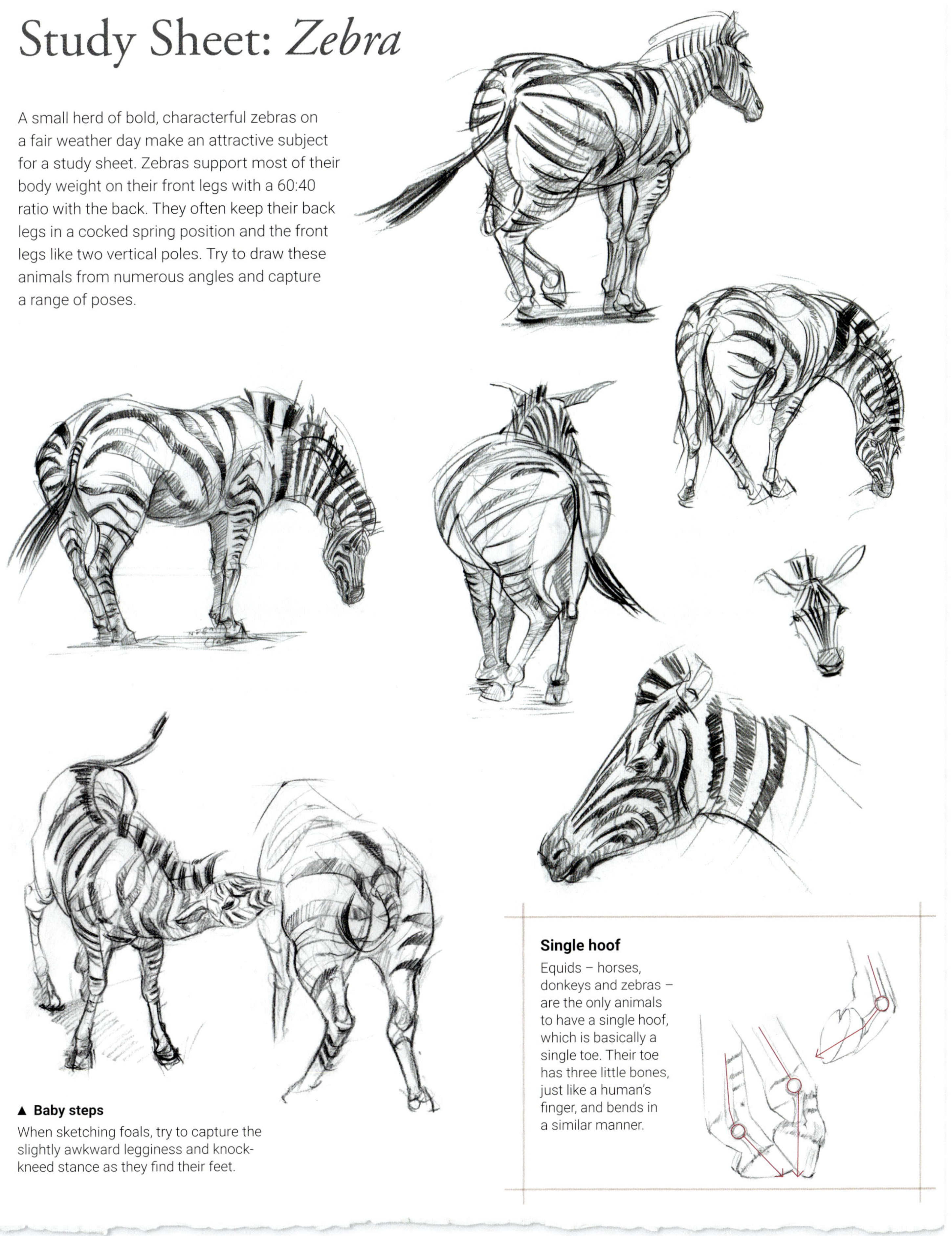

A small herd of bold, characterful zebras on a fair weather day make an attractive subject for a study sheet. Zebras support most of their body weight on their front legs with a 60:40 ratio with the back. They often keep their back legs in a cocked spring position and the front legs like two vertical poles. Try to draw these animals from numerous angles and capture a range of poses.

▲ Baby steps

When sketching foals, try to capture the slightly awkward legginess and knock-kneed stance as they find their feet.

Single hoof

Equids – horses, donkeys and zebras – are the only animals to have a single hoof, which is basically a single toe. Their toe has three little bones, just like a human's finger, and bends in a similar manner.

Scales

Fossil evidence shows that when sea creatures first began crawling and slithering onto land about 385 million years ago, their bodies were wrapped in a chain mail of scales. Early tetrapods retained these fish scales as a protective feature and evolved to flourish on dry land. Overlapping horny scales create protection from any angle that a tooth might penetrate while also allowing flexibility.

Tip

With more organic textures, where the textural shapes are more free-flowing and unpredictable, the eye can easily get lost in the chaos of shapes. It is often difficult to know where you left off and find again the exact location you were last drawing. In these situations, after lightly plotting out the proportions and main shapes, I pick an identifiable area and let the drawing grow from shape to shape.

Study Sheet: *Monitor*

Scales can be suggested by using the X-wrap technique (see page 120) to make a pattern on the reptile's back. The spaces between the lines can accommodate one scale each. This is both a quick and effective technique for organizing and distributing the scales.

Head widget

Familiarizing yourself with the fundamentals of form and using them to create a widget is a good way to warm up and get to know your subject.

Five fingers and toes on both front and back feet

▼ The neck

Simply envisage the neck as a flexible tube that has to be highly dexterous to catch prey.

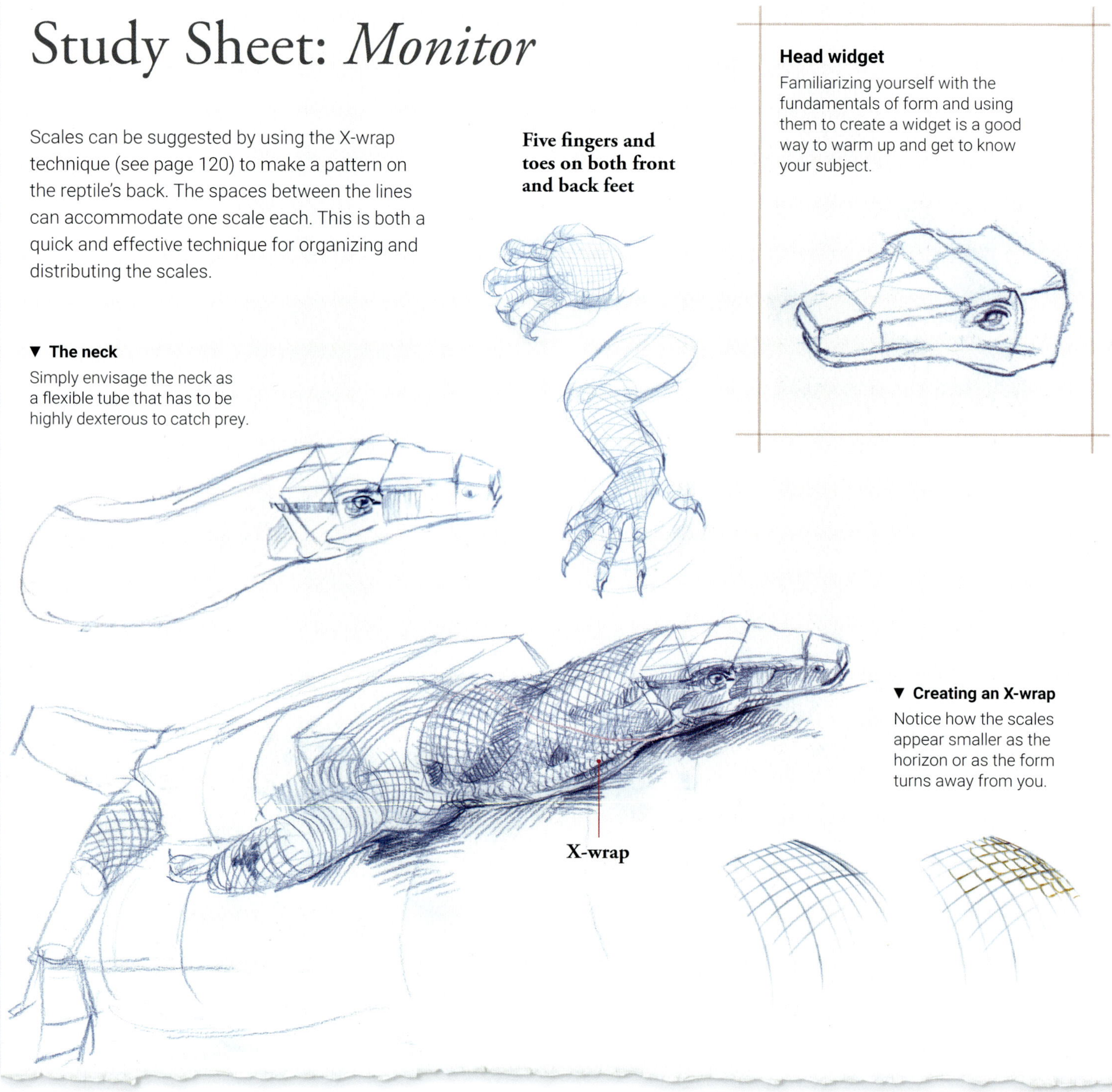

▼ Creating an X-wrap

Notice how the scales appear smaller as the horizon or as the form turns away from you.

Mindanao water monitor

A reptile in a zoo basking under a lamp creates the perfect motionless life model. Reptiles evolved from amphibians that began to lay hard-shelled eggs. They developed scaly waterproof skin, which stopped their bodies drying out and allowed them to pioneer onto dry land.

Materials

- Indigo artist's quality colouring pencil
- Cartridge (drawing) paper or sketchbook
- Sharpener
- Putty eraser

Mindanao water monitor (*Varanus cumingi*)

The Mindanao water monitor, or yellow-headed water lizard, is a lizard that lives in mangrove swamps and tropical forests of the island of Mindanao in the Philippines. They are carnivorous and not fussy eaters, consuming birds, fish, mammals, carrion, rodents, invertebrates, molluscs and eggs. They have mottled bright yellow and black skin that appears in stripes and splotches. To capture this camouflage, I shaded patches of scales by just filling them in towards the end of the drawing.

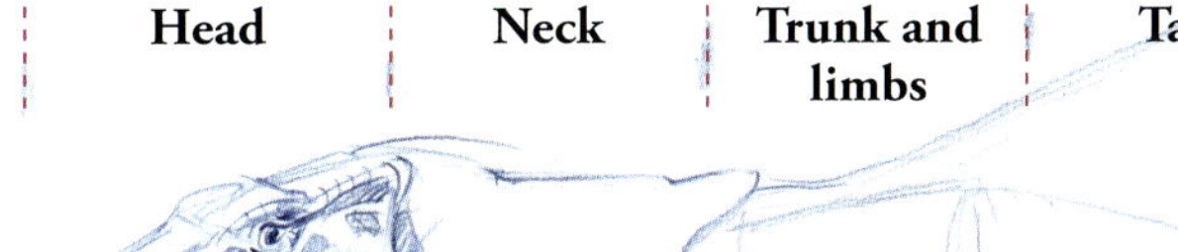

1 First, break down the drawing challenge into manageable parts. Using the head as a unit, create a comparative measuring scale across the page (see pages 54–5). Next, look for the subtle angles forming the lizard, ensuring that you don't default to the safe horizontal or vertical.

2 Use an X-wrap (see page 120) to allow you to sketch the scales without drawing every single one individually. Varying the direction of scales can help the viewer get a sense of the lizard's flaps of skin.

3 Next, create arcs in the opposite direction. I sometimes use an S-shaped curve, which happens when a cylinder is in perspective. Generally, I pick a single line of scales that identifies all the scales' direction of travel.

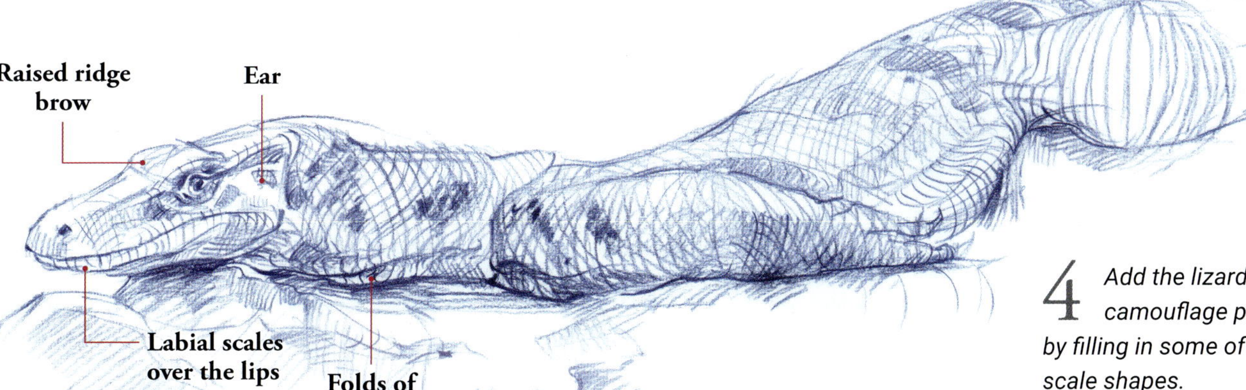

4 Add the lizard's camouflage pattern by filling in some of the scale shapes.

Hair and Wool

They may not always receive the same level of attention as facial features, but hair and wool are an important subject worth studying in their own right. Hair moves in clumps and waves in varying combinations of strands, creating curls, running flat or swirling to top notches, some following a general movement, others out of place. To help create the texture of hair or fur, remember what it felt like the last time you ran your fingers through your hair or stroked a dog, or imagine stroking your subject's hair.

It is best to conduct animal hair or wool studies while your animal is slumbering in the sun, which will give you time to patiently observe its character. The pencil strokes mimic the direction and length of the fur, which could be wavy or straight, dark or light in colour. Your shading's darkness should imply the darkness of the pelt. An alpaca's shaggy coat can range from white, to beige, brown and black.

Materials
- Black artist's quality colouring pencil
- Cartridge (drawing) paper or sketchbook
- Sharpener
- Putty eraser

Alpacas and llamas (*Lama* spp.)
Alpacas and llamas are members of the Camelidae family, which includes camels, and are primarily found in Bolivia and Peru. These domesticated species have wild cousins, the vicuna and guanaco. It's interesting to note that all four species may interbreed and produce fertile offspring. The shaggier, softer hair of alpacas is used to produce fleece in a wide range of colours, from white and light yellow to brown and black.

Woolly outlines

A rock with its hard-edged boundaries of form are clearly defined and can be sketched with a definite edge with a sharp drawing pencil tip. However, in these sketches, the boundaries of wool are less defined, and the character of the form is evoked from the paper with the blunt, soft tip of a waxy artist's quality colouring pencil.

Start of thoracic vertebrae and thorax

1 First, hold up a pencil vertically to judge the angle of the neck. Envisage it as a simple tube with a line of symmetry running down the central spine to the start of the thorax. Imagine the ribcage beneath in foreshortening, creating the bulk of the chest.

Tip

Before I begin a drawing, I sometimes reflect on who has done this type of drawing well. In this case, it was the sculptural sheep sketches of the twentieth-century British sculptor Henry Moore, who dedicated an entire sketchbook to the animal. Sculptors think in terms of mass, volume, weight and texture. Those elements translate even in their two-dimensional work. Henry Moore's scribbling line envelopes these animals, which are like clouds on legs but also with a sense of an underlying structure. 'Then I began to realize that underneath all that wool was a body, which moved in its own way, and that each sheep had its individual character.'

2 Follow the form with swirling curvilinear shading to give mass and volume. Look out for grooves and landmark gaps in the fleece, which will form in natural clumps. Notice how the fleece falls away into a central parting along the spine, all the way to the wide tail.

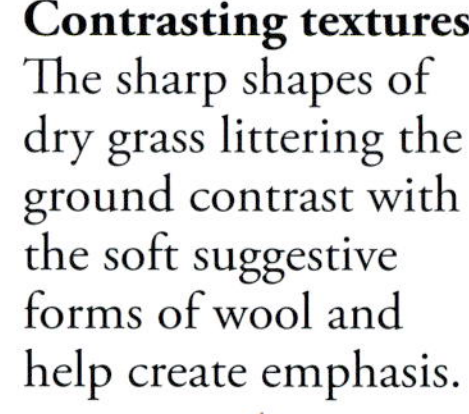

Contrasting textures
The sharp shapes of dry grass littering the ground contrast with the soft suggestive forms of wool and help create emphasis.

Clumps of fur

Rather than trying to mimic every single hair, which is often done in photorealistic illustrations – and which is an impossible task considering the tip of a pencil is wider than a hair strand – look for the main divisions in the clumps of fur. In this exercise, avoid mechanical, repetitive movements: free your arms to connect with the randomness of your subject and feel free to scribble.

1 Begin by laying down the posture of the animal, taking care with proportions and getting a sense of the hidden anatomy beneath the fleece.

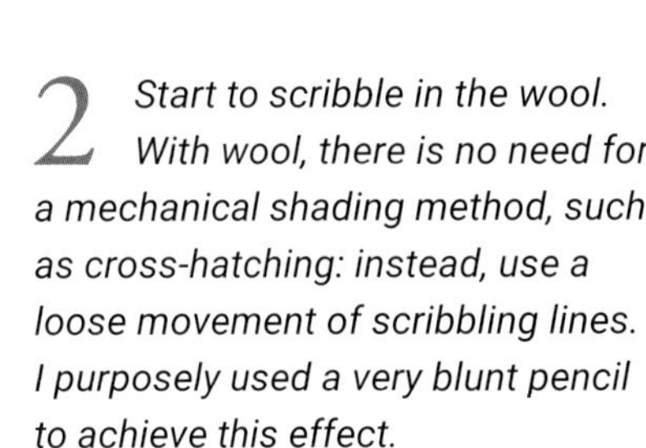

2 Start to scribble in the wool. With wool, there is no need for a mechanical shading method, such as cross-hatching: instead, use a loose movement of scribbling lines. I purposely used a very blunt pencil to achieve this effect.

Characteristic foppish alpaca hairstyle

Eyes bathed in shadow of light source from above falling on the fringe

3 Develop a feeling for fleece. Look for gaps in the pelt that are the edges of clumps, and look for the direction the clumps move in, especially over the eyes. To help suggest softness, reserve the darkest notes for the ground where the alpaca is resting.

Identify the darkest tonal values

Plumes and Feathers

Birds of all types make engaging subjects to sketch and can be seen both in zoos and on farms. They are a striking contrast between dinosaur-like sinewy, scaly legs and, depending on the bird, cascading opulent plumes that flow with no apparent order. When drawing plumes and feathers, we need to tune into the subject's character to create impressionistic marks that capture the feeling of them. Despite the apparent visual chaos of the plumes, it is essential to clearly understand the bird's skeleton of its arms and legs, which is the same archetype as flying birds.

Ostriches are inquisitive, bold birds that will stand still long enough for a portrait sketch, allowing you to tackle their whole body and present their unique sketching challenges. I was astonished to discover their feathers sprouted on both the front and back of the arm. After drawing a light armature I rendered it with a feather texture paying close attention to the patches of light and shade.

Ostrich (*Struthio* spp.)

The ostrich is the world's largest bird, with males growing to almost 9ft (3m), and they lay the biggest eggs. The males are black and white and sit on the eggs at night, and the females are brown and white and sit on the eggs during the day. The ostrich shares similar fluffy feathers as other flightless birds, or ratites, such as rheas and emus, but it is the only bird to have two toes.

Materials

- Prussian blue artist's quality colouring pencil
- Cartridge (drawing) paper or sketchbook
- Sharpener
- Putty eraser

Ostrich

Having lost the ability to fly, the feathers of an ostrich remain in a fluffy state ideal for display, warmth and incubating eggs. This shaggy appearance brings its own challenge. Try to create arabesque, buttery marks to model and conjure the feeling of the feathers. This is achieved as much through a feeling in the wrist to create rhythmic swirling marks as it is in observing the animal.

Ears

Knee

Heel

1 Begin with an egg shape and attach a simple tube for the neck. Look for key anatomical landmarks and articulation points. Be careful to keep in check the size of the head to the body, which is easy to get too big at this initial stage.

Scapula

Humerus

Radius ulna

Hand

2 After sketching out the initial forms, look through the visual noise of feathers to ghost sketch a skeletal construction line of the bones of the arm. Envisage the tail as a simple cone.

3 Next, with the main shapes in place, try to create velvety rich, loose shading that conjures the feeling of the plumes. Try to be creative with the marks you make to emulate the various feathery textures.

Study Sheet: *Ostrich*

These ostriches seemed most curious about me sketching them and confidently met my gaze. I barely took my eyes off them, just flicking my eyes to the paper to check on the proportions. A lot of the time I began these drawings with the giant eyes, the window of the soul, trying to get the animal to feel alive on the paper.

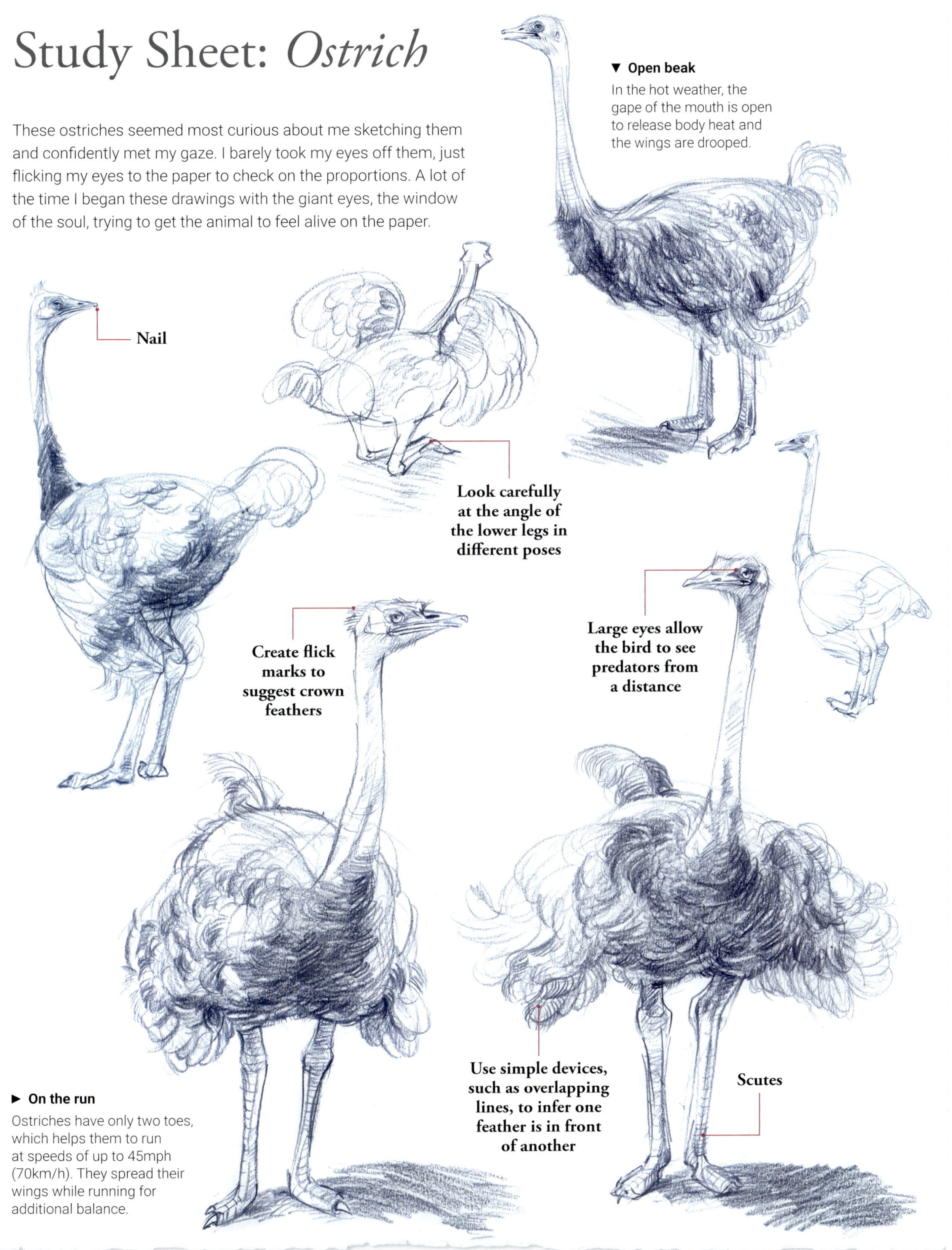

▶ On the run

Ostriches have only two toes, which helps them to run at speeds of up to 45mph (70km/h). They spread their wings while running for additional balance.

Composition

The way in which an artist can arrange a scene or study on the paper to maximize the drawing's impact is referred to as its composition. There are numerous geometrical aesthetics and approaches that can draw the viewer's attention to a drawing and guide it around its multiple elements, and using them sometimes gives the impression that the picture is harmonious or dynamic.

Most drawings in this book are created directly in front of the subject in a sketchbook. Personally, the smallest sketchbook I normally use is a large A3 (11¾ x 16½in) portrait-style book with a hard cover, which can be increased to twice this size if I sketch across two pages. Even so, one of my most frequent frustrations is not being able to fit the whole subject (typically tails and feet) or interesting elements in a landscape. This means that before I start any sketch, I always spend a few moments thinking about how the various elements will fit on the paper.

In composition, the major shapes matter more than the details. The preliminary drawing will determine how much sky or sea there will be and whether you can fit everything you want to include, so I always do some initial measuring before commencing a drawing (see pages 52–5). As there is no requirement to replicate an exact photographic representation, feel free to add, remove and rearrange anything you like. When drawing on the spot in a sketchbook it is unlikely that you will do as much planning as you would painting a more expensive canvas. Regardless, the same aesthetic principles will apply.

One principle is the golden ratio (see page 134), which has long been employed in architecture and art. This logarithmic spiral can be seen in many natural phenomena, from the curvature of a ram's horn to the arms of spiral galaxies to how an insect will approach a light source. The divisions and placing of key elements in drawings and paintings are seen to be aesthetically pleasing when arranged according to these proportions. Another principle used for arranging elements in composition is the rule of thirds (see pages 136–7), which is based on geometry.

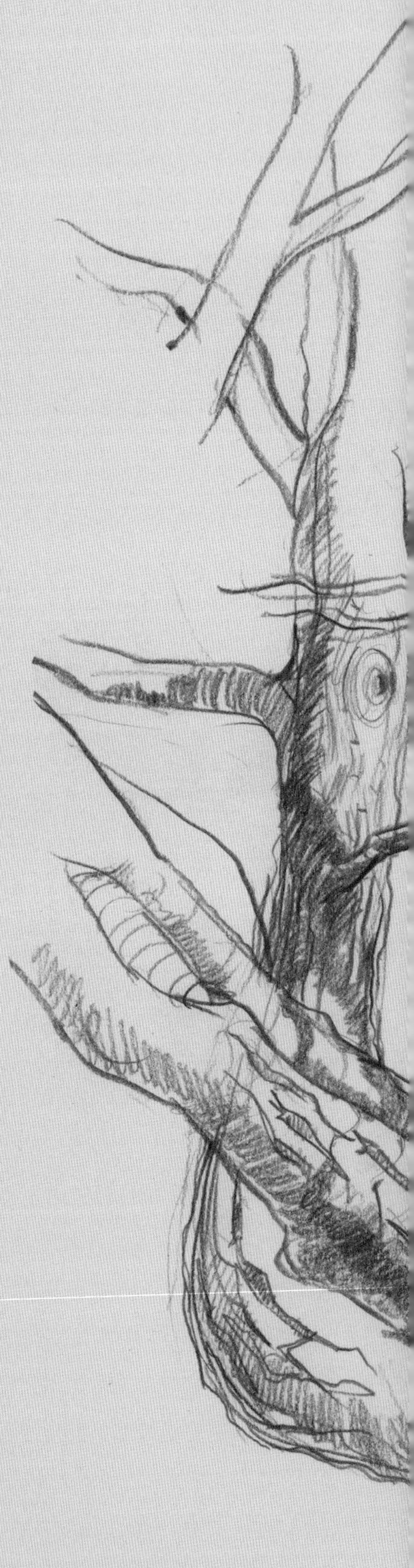

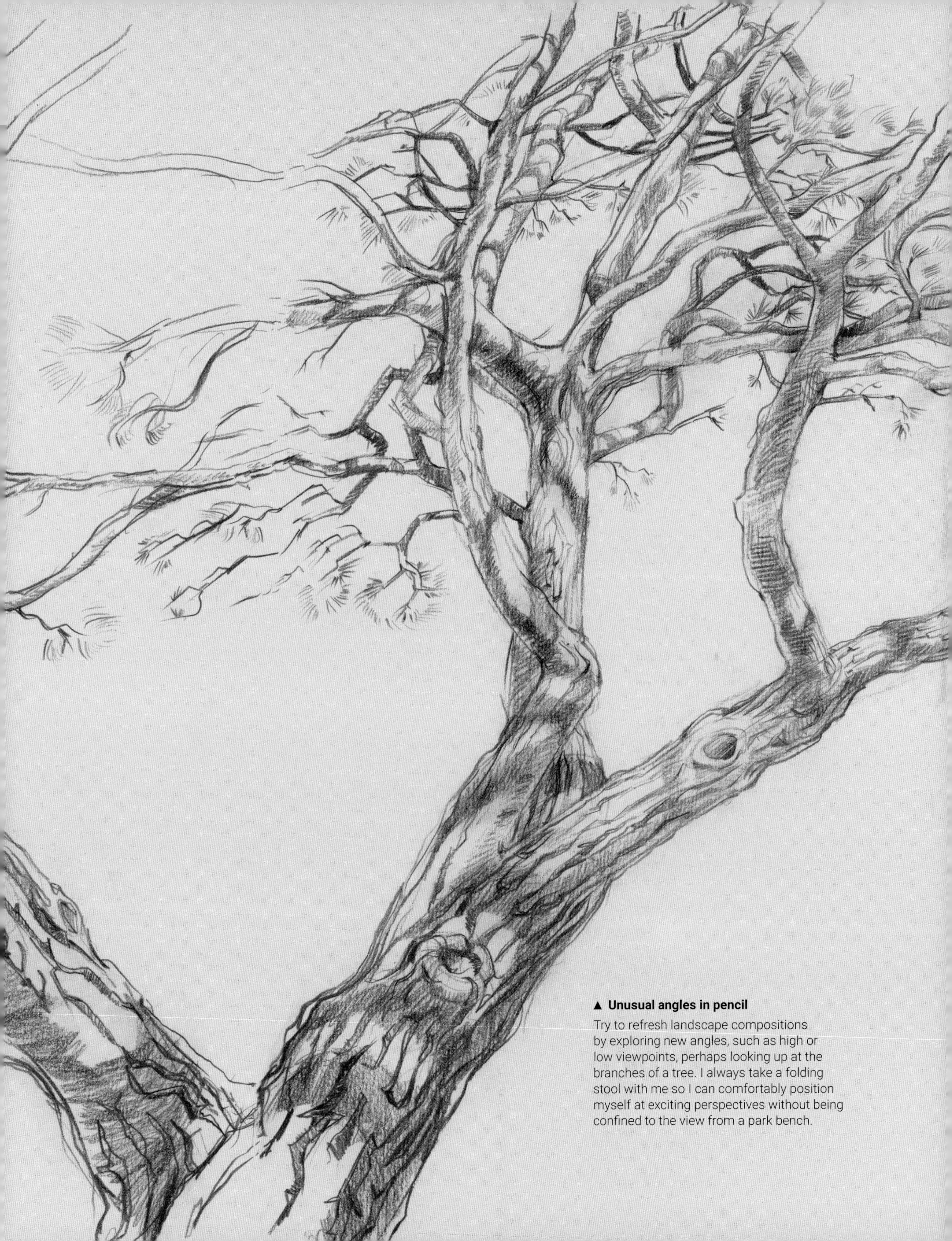

▲ Unusual angles in pencil
Try to refresh landscape compositions by exploring new angles, such as high or low viewpoints, perhaps looking up at the branches of a tree. I always take a folding stool with me so I can comfortably position myself at exciting perspectives without being confined to the view from a park bench.

Composition Essentials

Many artists have worked intuitively rather than carefully structuring their compositions and have produced beautiful drawings. However, it is essential to equally consider the planned and structured method. Here are some of the compositional ideas I have found to be the most helpful. These guidelines don't need to be followed mathematically and can be mixed and matched together.

Portrait, landscape or square?

Composition can inspire awe, drama, tension and dynamic action. A long or wide panoramic shot can tell us about the setting and give a sense of place, such as an expansive seascape. A close-up can reveal the character of a shell you might have found there or the emotion of a family playing with a dog on the sand. There are endless possibilities of focus in any location, so I suggest following your intuition while remaining open to new compositions and areas of focus. A sketchbook can be turned to accommodate either landscape or portrait, and three-quarters of the page can be used for square compositions.

Visual hierarchy

In a good composition, a viewer's eyes will be directed where to focus on the drawing, and in what sequence, by certain prominent elements that draw attention more forcefully than other ones, while other elements play supporting roles. If everything was the same size, the eye would have to compete for attention with each component. Including smaller items also aids in determining the size of larger ones.

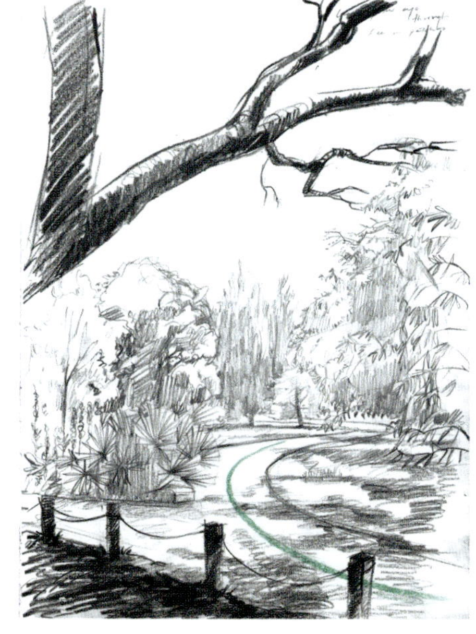

◄ C-shaped rhythm

This drawing's intended focal point, the distant tree, can be reached by following a C-shaped trail that carries the eye through the composition. Note that the silhouetted fence posts and tree bough in the foreground frame the subject and help create the illusion of depth.

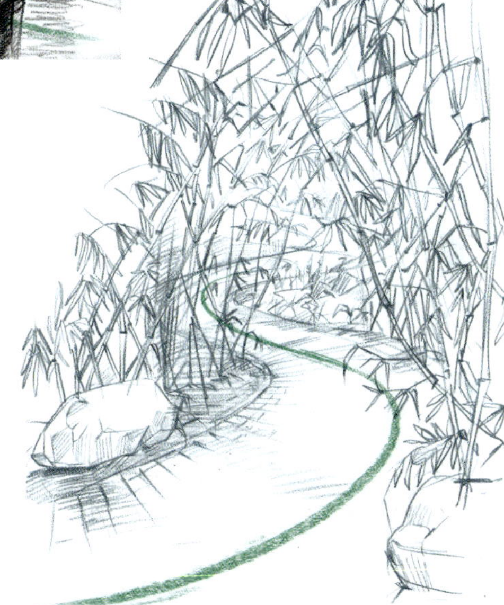

► S-shaped rhythm

Using an S-shaped rhythm will lead the eye gently through the landscape. It is a very effective technique with the artist leading the viewer on a gentle meandering journey through their drawing.

► The golden ratio

Artists have used the golden ratio to organize elements and divisions and to harmoniously distribute weight. Using these proportions can bring a sense of peace and tranquillity to a drawing, even if they are only loosely applied. The smallest portion – which is also where the viewer's attention will be focused – has a ratio of roughly 1:1.618 to the next larger portion, just as that portion does to the following portion and so forth. When you spiral a line through a golden rectangle, you will create a logarithmic spiral found in abundance in nature, from seashells to succulents to the eye of a hurricane.

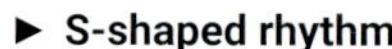

Golden spiral

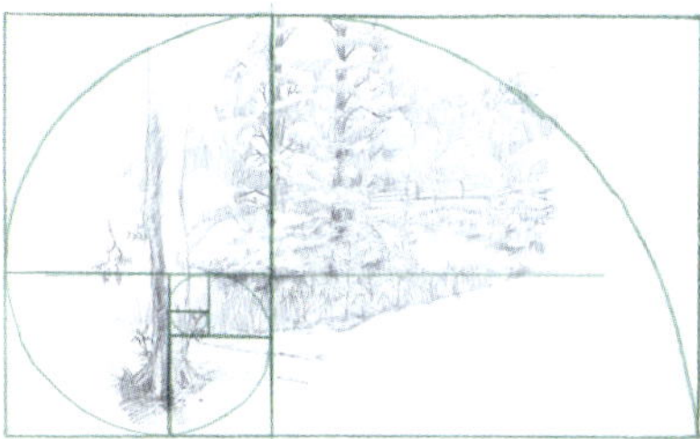

▼ Triangular

Renaissance artists used triangular or pyramidal compositions. They achieved harmony and balance by arranging the subjects into a solid overall geometric structure. To create a sense of informality, I positioned the focal point of the conifer off-centre and emphasized the contrast with dark shading. The viewer's eye is naturally drawn to areas where light and dark are in stark juxtaposition.

▶ The rule of thirds

Break a composition into thirds, vertically and horizontally, and then place the key elements of your image along these lines or at their junctions, and the arrangement achieved will be interesting, pleasing and dynamic. This is covered in more detail on pages 136–7.

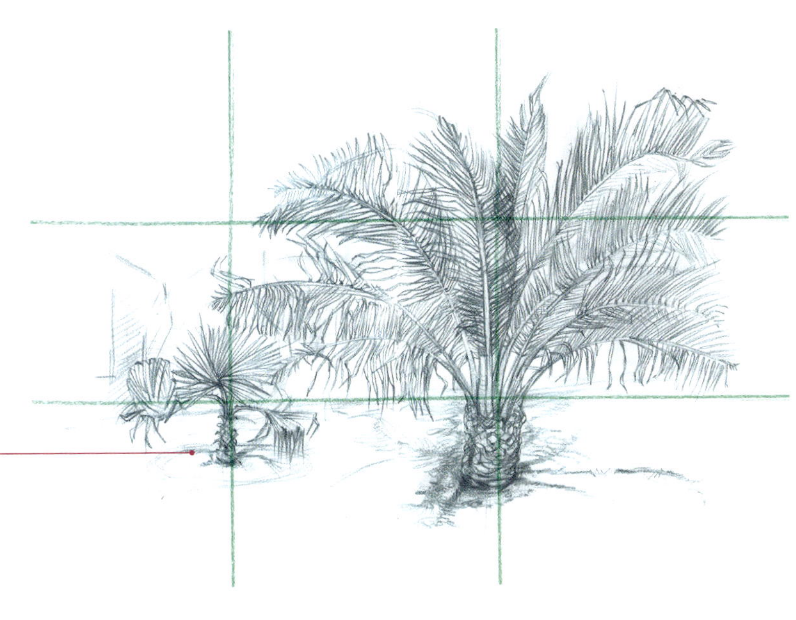

The smaller palm fern above provides a sense of scale for the larger one

▼ Scale

In anything you draw or design, always have a sense of scale at the back of your mind. A giant fish will make a fish tank look small and might be suitable for a portrait, whereas small fish will make a fish tank look massive and might be suitable for a scene composition.

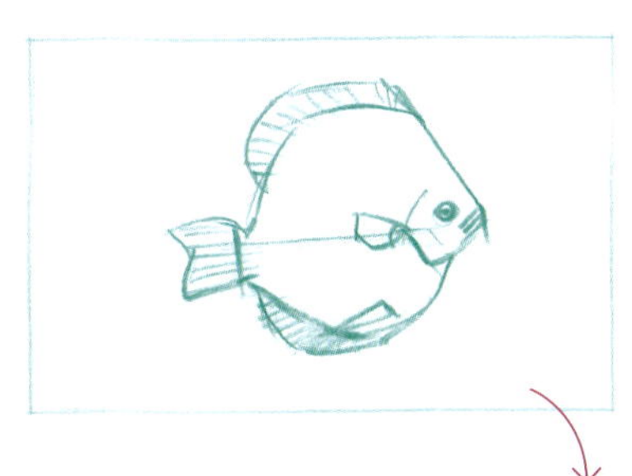

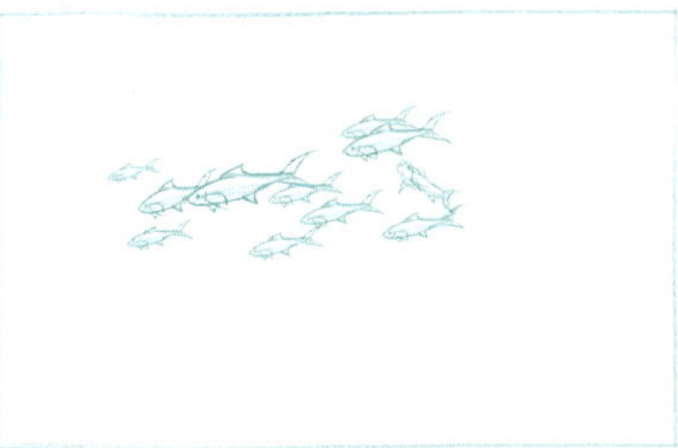

◀ Calm or agitated?

Horizontal lines can make up a serene arrangement, while dynamic angles can create a more energizing, agitated style.

▶ Cropping close

One exciting idea for creating compelling compositions is to zoom in on a fragment. Even the most familiar view can become a dynamic composition or an intimate portrait by zooming in close. After a field sketching trip, sometimes I spread all of my studies across a large table, then select one or two that have got potential for a composition. Interesting areas can be isolated by using two L-shaped pieces cut from mount board.

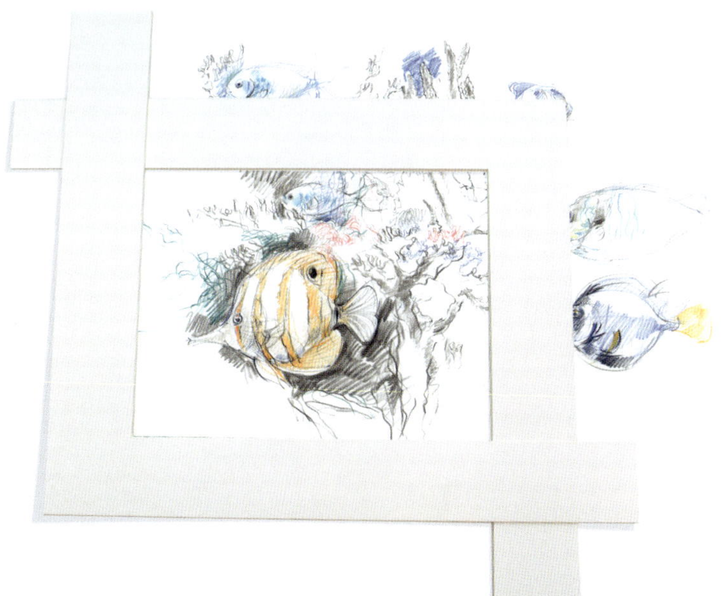

Rule of Thirds

Placing key elements in the centre is not always the best option and can create a lack of visual interest. A common way to organize pictorial elements is to geometrically divide the picture plane into thirds horizontally and vertically to create a stable and satisfying grid. This geometric framework then acts as a guide for the placement of the drawing's elements.

Asymmetrical designs appear more contemporary and often convey feelings of movement more than drawings with symmetrical designs. However, they are also slightly more challenging when it comes to unifying the elements in the design to give a feeling of coherence. Nevertheless, they create the perfect framework for variety.

Materials

- Light blue artist's quality colouring pencil
- Dip pen and ink
- Watercolour pencils and paints (see swatches above right)
- Large cartridge (drawing) paper or sketchbook
- Sharpener
- Putty eraser

Kew kitchen garden

The historic kitchen garden at Kew Gardens in London is a haven for wildlife and a visual and edible feast. On entering, there is an instant feeling of calm, wellbeing and sustainability as bees buzz about pollinating the fruit and vegetable plants. I was struck by the appealing composition: an oak trellis where fruit trees are trained to grow, bean poles and earthenware pots that created a jumbled charm. An organic network of gravel paths weaves between the beds creating attractive shapes, and I knew I wanted to sketch this scene instantly.

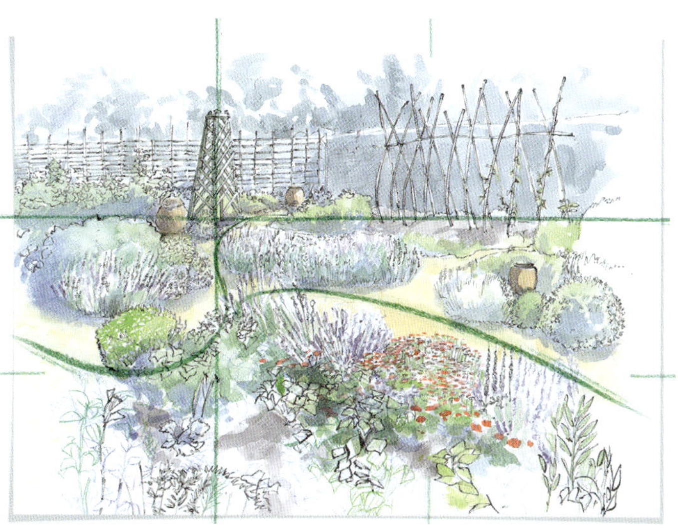

▲ Curving paths
The orange paths help to lead the eye through the composition, taking it on a walk through the garden.

Kitchen garden

Before sketching, I spent a moment contemplating what I wanted to use as the focal point. I liked the lattice crisscross of the oak trellis and felt that it was an interesting and entertaining part of the composition. I saw this as the main lead character, the one thing that will draw your attention, like a principal dancer dressed in a stand-out colour in a ballet performance. I purposely placed it a third in from the top of the paper.

1 *Sketch out the proportions and main shapes of the composition in a light blue to provide you with some scaffolding for the drawing before you dive in with the permanent dip pen and ink. Leaves and flowers come in a multitude of shapes and sizes, so vary the way you create marks with your dip pen to capture the different plant textures, from broad-leafed to the tiny spiked leaves of lavender.*

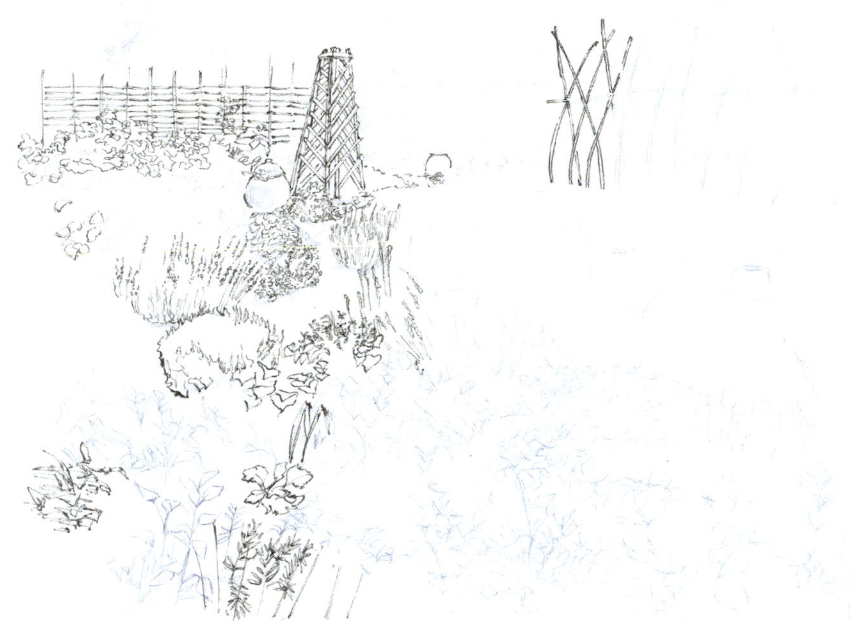

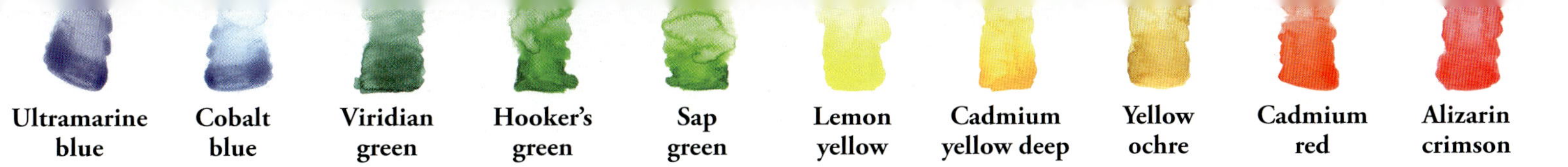

| Ultramarine blue | Cobalt blue | Viridian green | Hooker's green | Sap green | Lemon yellow | Cadmium yellow deep | Yellow ochre | Cadmium red | Alizarin crimson |

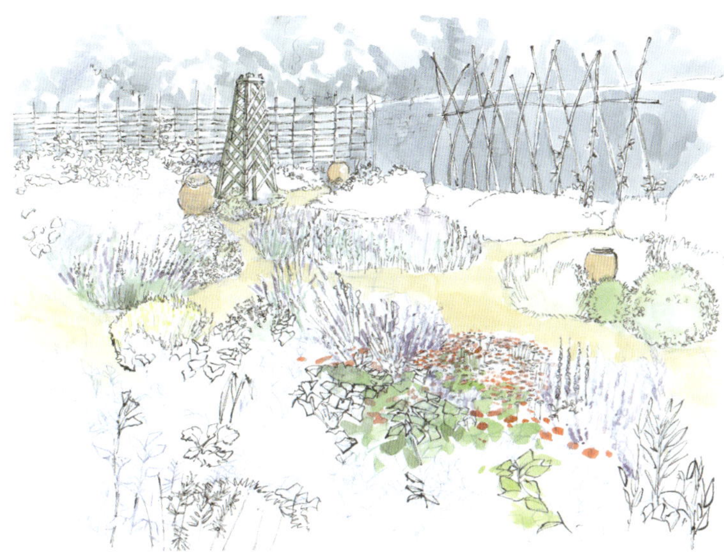

2 Next, lay down the base shades: the path was a mixture of yellow ochre with a touch of cadmium red. I switched between colouring pencils and watercolours depending on what pigments were instantly accessible, working from lightest and brightest to darkest and dullest. Watercolour has the benefit of quicker coverage.

3 Create highlights by leaving gaps of plain paper, and steadily build up the mid-tones. As the painting progresses, start adding shade, which will help create a feeling of luminosity. I added a bath of ultramarine blue to all the shadows.

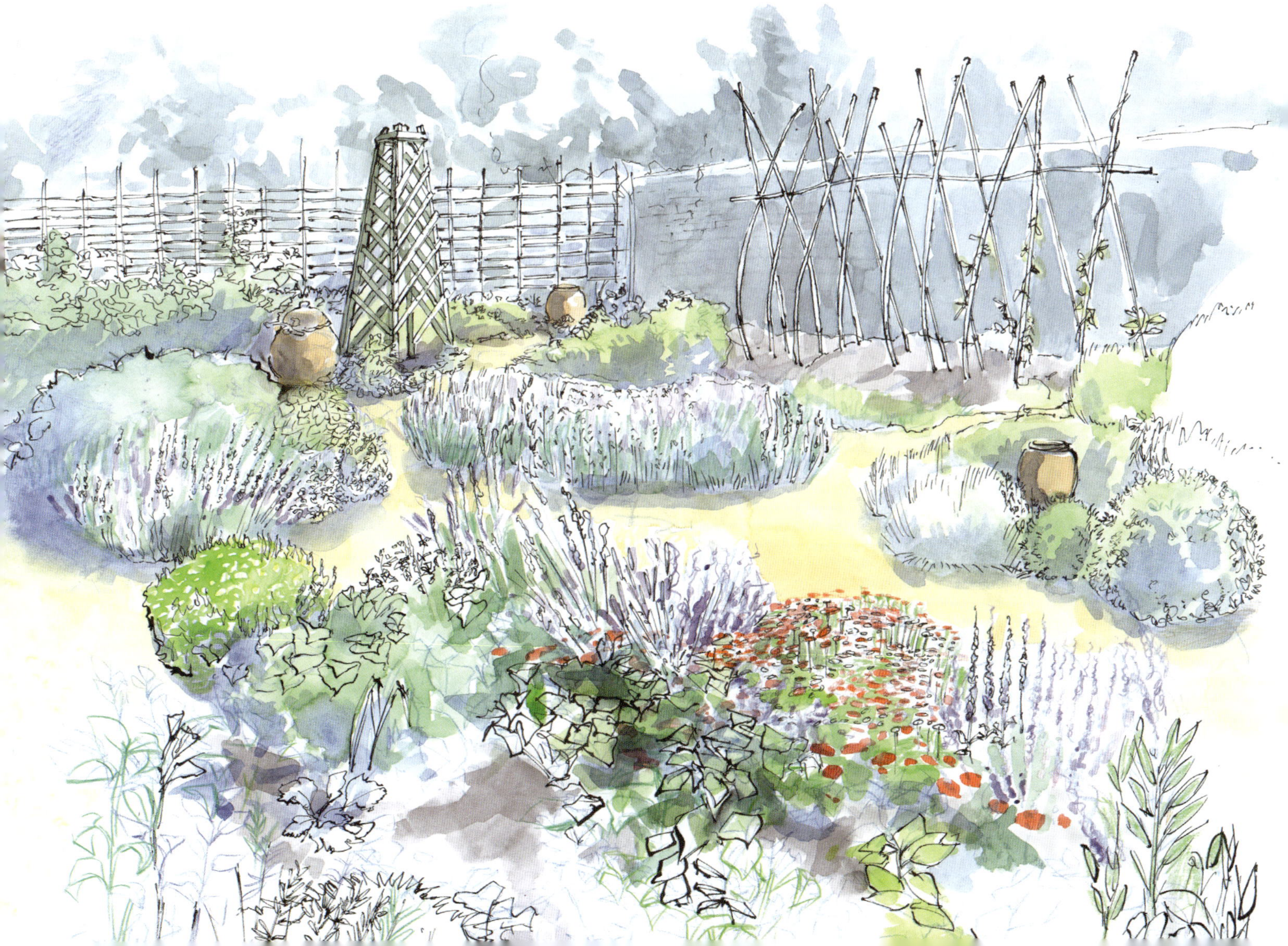

Ukiyo-e

White	Cool light grey	Payne's grey	Terre verte	Raw umber	Violet	Ultramarine blue

Meaning 'pictures of the floating world', ukiyo-e are Japanese woodblock prints that first appeared in the seventeenth century and became popular in the West in the nineteenth century. Ukiyo-e prints portray scenes that are relatively flat and without fine details, a style that can also be seen in nineteenth-century Impressionist paintings.

Japanese prints tend to have an asymmetrical composition that uses big empty spaces to counterbalance intensely detailed sections. Objects are often only partially visible with a simple background, and a single element tends to predominate, giving the image room to breathe and putting the full focus of attention on the motif. Frequently, a distant vista with a simple colour scheme can be seen juxtaposed against a striking, closely cropped object in the foreground.

Cherry blossoms

The challenge of drawing with oil pastels is mixing different colours directly on the paper by over-layering and smudging them. When colours that match the shades I see aren't directly available, I imagine what combinations will create the desired shade. Practise doing this; even when you are not sketching, you may find yourself thinking, what two or three colours would get me that exact hue?

Materials
- Blue-grey artist's quality colouring pencil
- Oil pastels (see swatches above right)
- Large cartridge (drawing) paper or sketchbook
- Sharpener
- Putty eraser

Japanese cherry blossom
(*Prunus serrulata*)

The Japanese cherry tree has a small trunk and a full crown of leaves. Their bounty of white blossoms signal the arrival of spring and signify happiness, health and life. The peak season for their shiny deep purple, almost black fruit is summer.

Focal point

A focal point is like an introduction, the area where the eye enters the composition. You can create one consciously or intuitively by using high contrast or bright colour. From here, the eye will track its own independent order of reading. You can decide on this focal point at the end of the drawing.

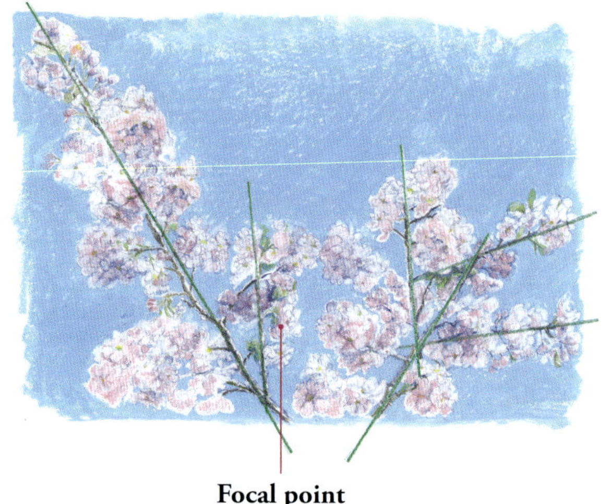

Focal point

1 *I created this composition from a photograph taken while looking up through the branches to the sky. Photography can be useful in capturing cropped images and unusual angles. Using two mount board offcuts (see page 135), zoom in on a printout to isolate a section that has enough variety but that is close enough to see each petal for intimacy. But rather than concentrate on biological accuracy, look for the transient effects of light and colour, like in a botanical illustration. This crop will allow you to work in a loose manner and liberate you from the burden of providing precise detail. As you sketch in a blue-grey oil-based pencil underdrawing, try to capture the negative and positive shapes (see pages 50–1) as accurately as possible.*

Cerulean blue	Sap green	Light pink	Dark pink	Scarlet

2 *Next, consider which of your oil pastel colours will be the best to get you close to the colours you can see by blending and mixing them on the surface of the paper. It is slightly more of an approximation or interpretative than a precise colour match. Prioritize these colours but keep the box nearby for odd subtleties and variations in colour and tone. Choose an area to start applying colour, working on a section at a time.*

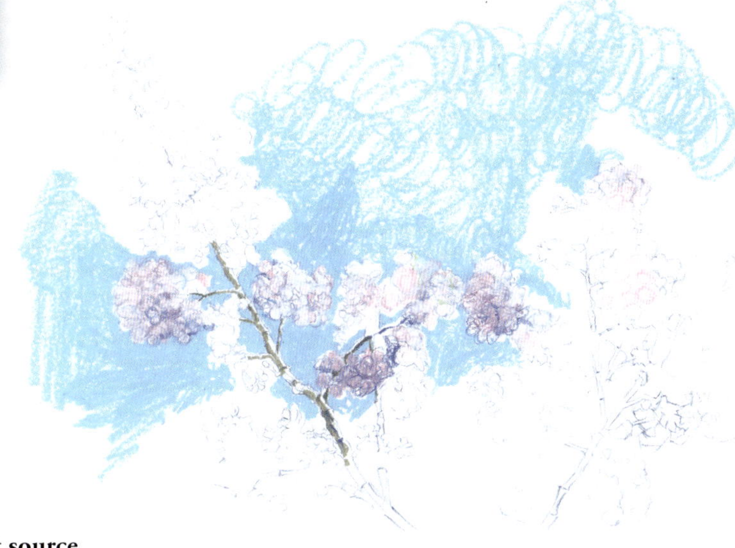

3 *The initial pencil line drawing will provide you with a scaffolding for the pastels, but redraw the scene, looking at the reference picture for clumps of light and dark areas, massing volumes before delineating the petals. In my photograph, the petals, some pinker and others dazzling white in the sunshine with the light delicate grey shadows, turned to a purple violet in the shade. I coaxed them from the paper by scribbling in a circular motion, using the scumbling method (see page 96).*

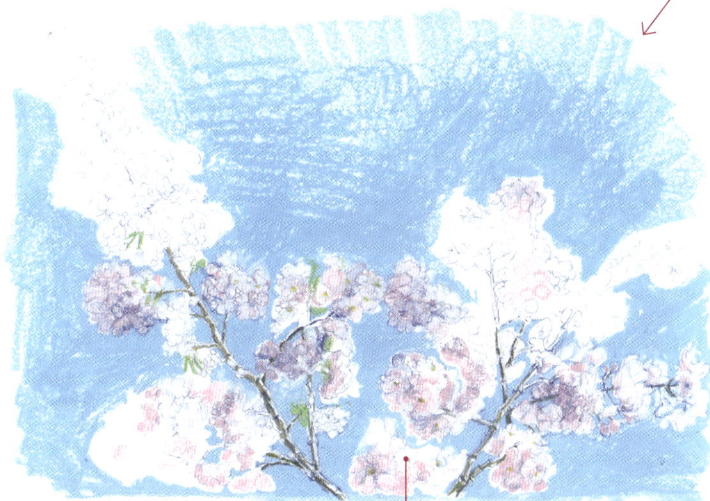

Leave the paper white to create a light corona, which will help capture the feeling of light emanating from the paper as it illuminates the petals' edges

Use the side of the oil pastel for maximum coverage

4 *Continue to fill in the blossoms from light to dark by layering scribbled colours, being careful not to muddy them by using too many colours. I continued to use the scumbling method as I overlaid with my limited palette and left the marks of the pastel showing to add life to the image.*

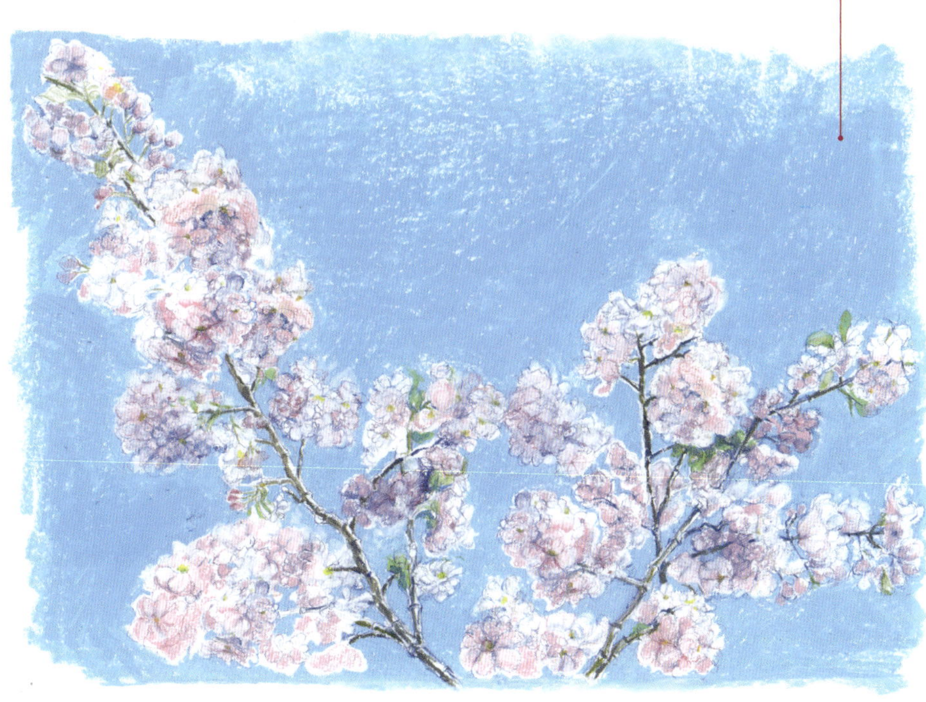

Index

First published 2023 by
Guild of Master Craftsman Publications Ltd
Castle Place, 166 High Street, Lewes,
East Sussex BN7 1XU

ISBN 978-1-78494-638-8

Publisher Jonathan Bailey
Production Director Jim Bulley
Senior Project Editor Tom Kitch
Managing Art Director Robin Shields
Editor Theresa Bebbington
Design Layout JC Lanaway

Colour origination by GMC Reprographics
Printed and bound in China

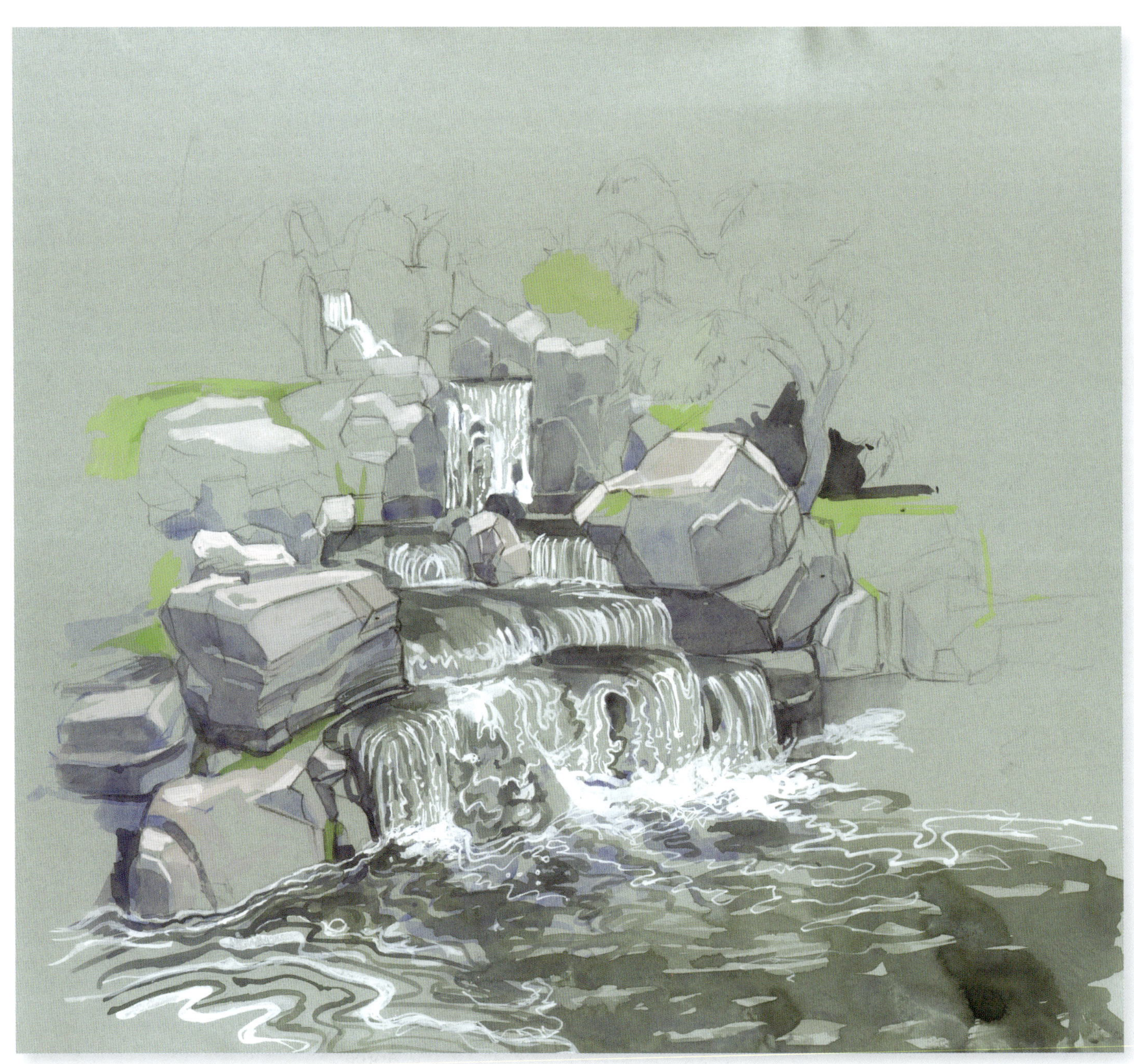

To place an order, contact:

GMC Publications Ltd
Castle Place, 166 High Street,
Lewes, East Sussex,
BN7 1XU
United Kingdom
Tel: +44 (0)1273 488005
www.gmcbooks.com